MODERN IRISH AND SCOTT

The comparative study of the literatures of Ireland and Scotland has emerged as a distinct and buoyant field in recent years. This collection of new essays offers the first sustained comparison of modern Irish and Scottish poetry, featuring close readings of texts within broad historical and political contextualisation. Playing on influences, cross-overs, connections, disconnections and differences, the 'affinities' and 'opposites' traced in this book cross both Irish and Scottish poetry in many directions. Contributors include major scholars of the new 'archipelagic' approach, as well as leading Irish and Scottish poets providing important insights into current creative practice. Poets discussed include W. B. Yeats, Hugh MacDiarmid, Sorley MacLean, Louis MacNeice, Edwin Morgan, Douglas Dunn, Seamus Heaney, Ian Hamilton Finlay, Michael Longley, Medbh McGuckian, Nuala ní Dhomhnaill, Don Paterson and Kathleen Jamie. This book is a major contribution to our understanding of poetry from these islands in the twentieth and twenty-first centuries.

PETER MACKAY has worked as a Research Fellow at the Seamus Heaney Centre for Poetry, and lectured on Scottish and Scottish Gaelic literature at Trinity College Dublin. He has written *Sorley MacLean* (2010), and is editing volumes of Gaelic poetry and critical essays.

EDNA LONGLEY is a Professor Emerita at Queen's University Belfast. Her publications include *Poetry and Posterity* (2000) and, as editor, *Edward Thomas: The Annotated Collected Poems* (2008).

FRAN BREARTON is Reader in English at Queen's University Belfast. She is the author of *The Great War in Irish Poetry* (2000) and *Reading Michael Longley* (2006).

MODERN IRISH AND SCOTTISH POETRY

EDITED BY
PETER MACKAY,
EDNA LONGLEY
AND
FRAN BREARTON

CAMBRIDGE UNIVERSITY PRESS
Cambridge, New York, Melbourne, Madrid, Cape Town,
Singapore, São Paulo, Delhi, Mexico City

Cambridge University Press
32 Avenue of the Americas, New York NY 10013-2473, USA

www.cambridge.org
Information on this title: www.cambridge.org/9781107660724

© Cambridge University Press 2011

This publication is in copyright. Subject to statutory exception
and to the provisions of relevant collective licensing agreements,
no reproduction of any part may take place without the written
permission of Cambridge University Press.

First published 2011
First paperback edition 2013

A catalogue record for this publication is available from the British Library

Library of Congress Cataloguing in Publication Data
Modern Irish and Scottish Poetry / edited by Peter Mackay, Edna Longley, Fran Brearton.
p. cm
ISBN 978-0-521-19602-4 (hardback)
1. English poetry – Irish authors – History and criticism.   2. English poetry – Scottish authors – History and criticism.   3. English poetry – 20th century – History and criticism.   4. Rhymers' Club (London, England)   I. Mackay, Peter, 1979– editor of compilation.   II. Crotty, Patrick, 1952– Swordsmen.
PR8771.M62   2011
821'.914099411–dc22
2010052383

ISBN 978-0-521-19602-4 Hardback
ISBN 978-1-107-66072-4 Paperback

Cambridge University Press has no responsibility for the persistence or
accuracy of URLs for external or third-party internet websites referred to in
this publication, and does not guarantee that any content on such websites is,
or will remain, accurate or appropriate.

This book is dedicated to the memory of George Watson (1942–2009).

Contents

List of contributors		*page* ix
Acknowledgements		x
	Introduction Edna Longley	1
1	Swordsmen: W. B. Yeats and Hugh MacDiarmid Patrick Crotty	20
2	Tradition and the individual editor: Professor Grierson, modernism and national poetics Cairns Craig	39
3	Louis MacNeice among the islands John Kerrigan	58
4	Townland, desert, cave: Irish and Scottish Second World War poetry Peter Mackay	87
5	Affinities in time and space: reading the Gaelic poetry of Ireland and Scotland Máire Ní Annracháin	102
6	Contemporary affinities Douglas Dunn	119
7	The Classics in modern Scottish and Irish poetry Robert Crawford	131
8	Translating *Beowulf*: Edwin Morgan and Seamus Heaney Hugh Magennis	147

Contents

9 Reading in the gutters 161
   Eric Falci

10 'What matters is the yeast': 'foreignising' Gaelic poetry 176
   Christopher Whyte

11 Outside English: Irish and Scottish poets in the East 191
   Justin Quinn

12 Names for nameless things: the poetics of place names 204
   Alan Gillis

13 Desire lines: mapping the city in contemporary Belfast
   and Glasgow poetry 222
   Aaron Kelly

14 'The ugly burds without wings'?: reactions to tradition
   since the 1960s 238
   Eleanor Bell

15 'And cannot say / and cannot say': Richard Price, Randolph
   Healy and the dialogue of the deaf 251
   David Wheatley

16 On 'The Friendship of Young Poets': Douglas Dunn, Michael
   Longley and Derek Mahon 265
   Fran Brearton

17 'No misprints in this work': the poetic 'translations' of Medbh
   McGuckian and Frank Kuppner 280
   Leontia Flynn

18 Phoenix or dead crow? Irish and Scottish poetry magazines,
   1945–2000 294
   Edna Longley

19 Outwith the Pale: Irish–Scottish studies as an act of translation 313
   Michael Brown

Guide to further reading 328
Index 331

Contributors

ELEANOR BELL, University of Strathclyde

FRAN BREARTON, Queen's University Belfast

MICHAEL BROWN, Research Institute of Irish and Scottish Studies, University of Aberdeen

CAIRNS CRAIG, Research Institute of Irish and Scottish Studies, University of Aberdeen

ROBERT CRAWFORD, University of St Andrews

PATRICK CROTTY, Research Institute of Irish and Scottish Studies, University of Aberdeen

DOUGLAS DUNN, University of St Andrews

ERIC FALCI, University of California, Berkeley

LEONTIA FLYNN, Queen's University Belfast

ALAN GILLIS, University of Edinburgh

AARON KELLY, University of Edinburgh

JOHN KERRIGAN, University of Cambridge

EDNA LONGLEY, Queen's University Belfast

PETER MACKAY, Queen's University Belfast

HUGH MAGENNIS, Queen's University Belfast

MÁIRE NÍ ANNRACHÁIN, University College Dublin

JUSTIN QUINN, Charles University, Prague

DAVID WHEATLEY, University of Hull

CHRISTOPHER WHYTE, Budapest

Acknowledgements

The editors' grateful thanks go to all contributors; to other academic participants in the Irish and Scottish poetry project: Tom Hubbard, Caoimhín Mac Giolla Léith, Liam McIlvanney, Fiona Stafford and Roderick Watson; and to the poets and musicians who also participated: Ciaran and Deirdre Carson, Christine and Martin Dowling, Len Graham, Kathleen Jamie, Liz Lochhead, Michael Longley, Peter McDonald, Andrew McNeillie, Alison McMorland, Sinéad Morrissey and Pádraigin Ní Uallacháin. Details and recordings of the symposia, poetry readings and music events can be accessed on the website: www.qub.ac.uk/schools/SeamusHeaneyCentreforPoetry/irishscottishpoetry.

Grateful thanks are also due to the Arts and Humanities Research Council, the Research Institute of Irish and Scottish Studies at the University of Aberdeen and the Seamus Heaney Centre for Poetry for financial, administrative and institutional support.

We would like to thank the following for permission to reproduce copyright material: Faber and Faber Ltd for permission to quote from Douglas Dunn, 'Realisms', Seamus Heaney, 'Would They Had Stay'd', and Paul Muldoon, 'Hard Drive'; quotations from Alan Gillis, *Hawks and Doves*, by kind permission of the author and The Gallery Press; quotations from Michael Hartnett's translation of Nuala Ní Dhomhnaill, 'Támaid damanta', by kind permission of the Estate of Michael Hartnett c/o Gallery Press; Salt Publishing Ltd for quotations from Randolph Healy, 'Arbor Vitae'; Tom Leonard for permission to quote from 'Right Inuff', © Tom Leonard, *Ghostie Men* (Etruscan Books/Wordpower, 2009); Derek Mahon for permission to quote from 'Going Home' in *The Snow Party* (OUP, 1975). Quotations from W. B. Yeats, 'A Last Confession' and 'Solomon and the Witch', are reprinted with the permission of A. P. Watt Ltd on behalf of Gráinne Yeats, and with the permission of Scribner, a division of Simon Schuster, Inc. Copyright © 1993 by the Macmillan Company. Copyright © renewed 1961 by Bertha Georgie Yeats.

Introduction
Edna Longley

CHANGING THE AXIS

To compare modern Irish and Scottish poetry is to change the critical axis. It is to unsettle categories like the 'English lyric' or 'Anglo-American modernism'. We might begin with two Irish-Scottish poetic encounters a century apart. The Rhymers' Club, which foregathered in 1890s London, laid crucial foundations for modern poetry in English, and established the prototype for later avant-garde coteries. The club's make-up was strikingly 'archipelagic': a term that will recur in this introduction. The Rhymers' Club marks a space where literary and cultural traditions from different parts of the British Isles came into play; where late nineteenth-century aestheticism met Celticism; and, more materially, where Irish, Scottish and Welsh poets competed for metropolitan attention – W. B. Yeats with particular success. In 'The Tragic Generation' (1922), his memoir of the 1890s, Yeats recalls how he once out-manoeuvred the Scottish poet John Davidson:

An infallible Church, with its Mass in Latin and its mediaeval philosophy, and our Protestant social prejudice, have kept [Ireland's] ablest men from levelling passions; but Davidson with a jealousy which may be Scottish, seeing that Carlyle had it, was quick to discover sour grapes. He saw in delicate, laborious, discriminating taste an effeminate pedantry, and would, when that mood was on him, delight in all that seemed healthy, popular, and bustling ... He, indeed, was accustomed ... to describe the Rhymers as lacking in 'blood and guts', and very nearly brought us to an end by attempting to supply the deficiency by the addition of four Scotsmen ... I can remember nothing except that they excelled in argument. He insisted upon their immediate election, and the Rhymers, through that complacency of good manners whereby educated Englishmen so often surprise me, obeyed, though secretly resolved never to meet again; and it cost me seven hours' work to get another meeting, and vote the Scotsmen out.[1]

In contrast, Seamus Heaney's poem 'Would They Had Stay'd' mourns the absence of four Scottish poets: Norman MacCaig, Iain Crichton Smith, Sorley MacLean and George Mackay Brown. Attaching a symbolic deer to each dead poet, and evoking images from their work, Heaney holds them in a collective elegiac embrace. The poem ends:

> What George Mackay Brown saw was a drinking deer
> That glittered by the water. The human soul
> In mosaic. Wet celandine and ivy.
> Allegory hard as a figured shield
> Smithied in Orkney for Christ's sake and Crusades,
> Polished until its undersurface surfaced
> Like peat smoke mulling through Byzantium.[2]

What do these encounters suggest about relations between modern Irish and Scottish poetry? On the one hand, we might read them as unique occasions. 'Would They Had Stay'd' primarily expresses personal sorrow; Davidson later conceded that Yeats possessed 'blood and guts'; and any opposition between macho Scottish and 'effeminate' Irish poetics must reckon with the Celticist literary transvestism of the Scot William Sharp, pen-named 'Fiona Macleod'. On the other hand, Ireland conditions the terms in which Yeats and Heaney respond to Scottish poet-contemporaries. Thus Yeats contrasts Scotland's 'levelling passions' (implicitly ascribed to non-conformism) with Irish traditionalism (explicitly ascribed to Catholicism and Anglo-Irish/Anglican hauteur). Davidson's poetry, as in 'Thirty Bob a Week', often has a socialist or social-realist cast. Voiced by an underpaid clerk, the poem may hit at Yeats: 'With your science and your books and your the'ries about spooks, / Did you ever hear of looking in your heart?'[3] As much a manifesto of the 1920s as a memoir of the 1890s, 'The Tragic Generation' sets symbolic 'intensity', pursued by Rhymers like Ernest Dowson, Arthur Symons and Yeats himself, against all 'popular' verse. Davidson personifies the latter since he extroverted his talent, never acquired 'conscious and deliberate craft', and so 'lacked pose and gesture'.[4] Yet Scotland is more deeply at issue. Not only had Yeats a broad anti-Scottish bias that extended to Presbyterian Ulster,[5] he always blamed Walter Scott, even Burns sometimes, for debasing the currency of poetry during the nineteenth century. As for the future: Davidson, whose London scenes and voices influenced T. S. Eliot, stands at the beginning of emergent poetic trends to which Yeats was opposed. Eliot recalls: 'I found inspiration in the content of ["Thirty Bob a Week"], and in the complete fitness of content and idiom: for I also had a good many dingy urban images to reveal . . . The personage that Davidson created in this poem has haunted me all my life.'[6]

John Davidson haunted Hugh MacDiarmid too. When Davidson (in 1909) did his bit for intensity by committing suicide, the 17-year-old

MacDiarmid 'felt as if the bottom had fallen out of [his] world'.[7] In his poem 'Of John Davidson' elegist and elegised converge:

> ... something in me has always stood
> Since then looking down the sandslope
> On your small black shape by the edge of the sea,
> – A bullet-hole through a great scene's beauty,
> God through the wrong end of a telescope.[8]

MacDiarmid criticises Davidson for not realising that Scots was the right language for his (distinctively Scottish) concerns, but praises his politics, 'anti-religion', grasp of modern thought and the modern city: 'What Davidson, alone of Scottish poets, did was to enlarge the subject matter of poetry, assimilate and utilise a great deal of new scientific and other contemporary material . . . and, above all, to write urban poetry.'[9] Robert Crawford refers to MacDiarmid's 'nurturings of [a] Davidsonian encyclopaedic Muse'. Edwin Morgan (at times) and the so-called 'Informationist' poets also belong to this Scottish line.[10] While Yeats and Davidson both admired Nietzsche, Davidson never subscribed to Yeats's Goethe-derived maxim that 'the poet needs all philosophy, but . . . must keep it out of his work'. He also held the un-Yeatsian creed, approvingly cited by MacDiarmid, that poets should reject Matthew Arnold's 'vaunted sweetness and light' and read the newspapers, because '[t]he poet is in the street, the hospital. He intends the world to know it is out of joint . . . Democracy is here; and we have to go through with it.'[11] Formally, Davidson veers between relatively tight ballad modes and the discursive blank verse of his bombastic 'Testament' poems. 'Conscious and deliberate craft' is hardly absent from modern Scottish poetry (witness early MacDiarmid), but discursive freewheeling seems more prevalent than in Irish poetry (witness later MacDiarmid). In 1931, introducing MacDiarmid's *First Hymn to Lenin*, AE (George Russell) reacts to him as Yeats to Davidson: 'instead of the attraction of affinities, I began to feel the attraction which opposites have for us . . . a sardonic rebel snarling at the orthodoxies with something like the old Carlyle's rasping cantankerous oracular utterance. It was no spiritual kinsman of mine who wrote *Crowdieknowe*.'[12]

Beyond stereotype, from which Yeats and AE are not free, the 'affinities' and 'opposites' traced in this book crisscross Irish and Scottish poetry in many directions. Meanwhile England, still (up to a point) a poetic meeting-place or clearing-house, certainly a publication hub, hovers on the horizon. Yeats not only celebrates an Irish victory over Scotland: he also sidelines the English as poetic standard-bearers. The title and other elements of Heaney's

'Would They Had Stay'd' derive from Shakespeare (if from his Scottish play), and the poem is initially set in an Oxford 'meadow', in 'fritillary land'. The speaker commands: 'Norman MacCaig, come forth from the deer of Magdalen' (68). Calling the deer 'Heather-sentries far from the heath', he continues: 'Be fawn / To the redcoat, gallowglass in the Globe' (68). This imperative affirms Irish–Scottish poetic solidarity together with its challenge to the political and literary order signified by Hanoverian redcoats and Shakespeare's Globe. Iain Crichton Smith adds linguistic solidarity: 'Englished Iain Mac Gabhainn / Goes into linked verse – / Goes where the spirit listeth – / On its perfectly sure feet' (68). 'Linked verse', a term for the collaboratively composed Japanese *renga*, 'links' Crichton Smith's Gaelic and English poems, his English translations of the former, and Irish bilingualism. As a (rather polemical) landscaping of archipelagic poetry, 'Would They Had Stay'd' opposes the English 'meadow' to Highland heaths and tilts the terrain northwards. The speaker mentions Crichton Smith's sequence 'Deer on the High Hills', and hails Sorley MacLean as 'A mirage. A stag on a ridge / In the western desert above the burnt-out tanks' (69). The felt incongruity between stag and tanks may have an Irish inflection: see Peter Mackay's chapter here on poetry of the Second World War.

Heaney's symbolism revises an old trope. Poetic encounters between Irish and Scottish poets tend to occur on Highland, Jacobite, Gaelic ground where differences can be collapsed even as national claims are staked. In *To Circumjack Cencrastus* (1930) MacDiarmid invokes an Irish author of Jacobite *aislingi* (dream vision poems): '*Aodhagán Ó Rathaille sang this sang / That I maun sing again; / For I've met the Brightness o' Brightness / Like him in a lanely glen*'.[13] For MacDiarmid, Irish poetry itself becomes a kind of *aisling*: '*The great poets o' Gaelic Ireland / Soared up frae the rags and tatters / O' the muckle grey mist o' Englishry*'.[14] Invocations of another country's poets are always, at some level, for internal consumption. Yeats damns Davidson as he does the 'popular' Young Ireland ballads. MacDiarmid recruits Ó Rathaille for his Scottish (and Scots) political muse. Heaney's elegy reinforces aspects of his own aesthetic, as when he attaches MacCaig's poetry to Sutherland rather than Edinburgh, or subverts Yeats by likening George Mackay Brown's Orkney poems to 'peat smoke mulling through Byzantium' (68).

A poem is not a critical article any more than Yeats's memoirs are reliable. Yet both Heaney's sense of affinity and Yeats's sense of distance point to the fact that connections or disconnections between modern Irish and Scottish poetry have been more assumed than analysed. Since 1922 literary-critical, as well as constitutional, relations have fallen between 'national' and 'international' stools: the power of the national paradigm in Irish and Scottish literary studies is elaborated below. On the international front, the Anglo-American London coteries that succeeded the Rhymers' Club would prove more effective than their archipelagic prototype in securing an academic afterlife. This book encompasses different views as to how, where or whether the terminology of 'international modernism' applies to Irish and Scottish poetry. Or perhaps, if less critically segregated, these national traditions might modify the terminology: not all problems are resolved by talking about 'Irish' or 'Scottish' modernism. Yeats, for instance, is often swept into aesthetic generalisations that overlook his quarrels with T. S. Eliot and Ezra Pound, let alone his archipelagic posterity. Patrick Crotty's chapter pulls the origins of modern poetry further back by stressing Yeats's and MacDiarmid's common Romantic matrix. And Cairns Craig shows that the edition of John Donne, which the Scottish scholar Herbert Grierson published in 1912, did not only affect Eliot's poetic structures or affect poetic structure only in the way that Eliot advertised.

Eliot, with his metropolitan eye on 'the main current',[15] helped to occlude Ireland and Scotland. In 1919 he reviewed G. Gregory Smith's *Scottish Literature: Character and Influence* and Yeats's *The Cutting of an Agate*, which includes the essay 'Poetry and Tradition' (1907). Both books influenced Eliot's 'Tradition and the Individual Talent', which simultaneously displaced their influence. Smith, to quote Cairns Craig, unwittingly supplied ammunition for Eliot to depict Scottish literature as exemplifying 'the *failure* of tradition'.[16] This review bears the title 'Was There a Scottish Literature?' Eliot's Yeats review is headed 'A Foreign Mind'. In all these writings Eliot assumes the role of spokesman for unified tradition, for '[a] powerful literature with a powerful capital', and inclines to the first-person plural: 'In English writing we seldom speak of tradition.'[17] Robert Crawford shrewdly notes that, as an American poet making his way in London, Eliot is conscious of other 'provincial' claims to cultural authority. Crawford tries to square the circle between Eliot and Smith by arguing a case for 'Modernism as Provincialism'.[18] But, to Eliot then, some provincialisms were clearly more provincial than others.

This book seeks to repair critical sins of omission. It is the outcome of a collaborative research project based in the Seamus Heaney Centre for Poetry at Queen's University Belfast, and attached to the AHRC Centre for Irish and Scottish Studies at the University of Aberdeen. Northern Ireland makes an apt vantage-point from which to pursue Irish–Scottish comparative studies; from which to conceive poetry in an archipelagic frame; from which to broach MacDiarmid's vision of a literature 'broad-basing itself on all the diverse cultural elements and the splendid variety of languages and dialects, in the British Isles' (now more diverse and various).[19] The project was developed through symposia that brought together critics, poets and poet-critics. These lively occasions ensured that perspectives on 'relations and comparisons', across the past century, would be informed by Irish and Scottish poetry of the present moment.[20]

NATION AND ARCHIPELAGO

Poetry is at once central and peripheral to Irish and Scottish literary studies: central because both fields derive from the cultural nationalism of Yeats and MacDiarmid, itself founded on poetry; peripheral because, as these poets discovered in different ways, poetry does not always march with the nation. Even so, excessive weight on 'Scottish' or 'Irish' before 'poetry' still obstructs more strictly literary readings.

Yet such weighting reflects the struggle to assert a distinctive Irish literature or depose 'English Ascendancy in British Literature':[21] a struggle that has had to be renewed. During the mid-twentieth century little was done in indigenous Irish and Scottish criticism either to theorise national canons or to contest Anglo-American ascendancy in modern literature. In my chapter on poetry magazines, I find that pleas for 'better criticism' were a shared Irish/Scottish theme (p. 305). Meanwhile, Eliot's influence helped to precipitate 'the collapse of a whole conception of English literature to which Scottish writers like Hume, Burns and Scott were central'.[22] Some Irish writers (Burke, Moore) were once equally integral to what might be termed a 'unionist' canon. Conflict between unionist and nationalist criticism remains an underrated shaping force behind (perhaps still within) the archipelagic literary academy. Yeats's most powerful literary-critical antagonist was the Irish unionist Edward Dowden, Professor of English at Trinity College Dublin; and, despite inspiring MacDiarmid to write in Scots, Gregory Smith was a unionist who rubbished the Irish Revival and feared that Scotland would follow suit: 'Had the northern partner busied herself with a "Renaissance", harped on the sorrowful Deirdres and eloquent Dempseys ... and out-tartaned Kiltartan, she might have had readier recognition of "nationality" in literature – or opera-bouffe.'[23] But, as in other spheres, the conscious, if often fraught, unionism of the nineteenth and early twentieth centuries gave way to an Anglocentrism that either ignored Scottish and Irish writers or subsumed them into Eliot's 'main current'. Thus, when Irish and Scottish literary studies began to take off during the 1970s, their broad tendency was nationalist. Critics were less inclined to think of the archipelago than to kick away the Irish or Scottish props sustaining English literature's illusion of its organic unity. This tendency was accentuated by the Northern Ireland Troubles (from 1969), and by the lost referendum on Scottish devolution (1979).

The two-volume *Cambridge History of Irish Literature* (2006) and three-volume *Edinburgh History of Scottish Literature* (2006–7) exemplify the critical mass attained by Irish and Scottish literary studies during the past four decades. These works might also seem to consolidate a kind of apartheid. Yet they are unconscious twins. The *Cambridge History* editors, who asked contributors to be 'sensitive to the existence of differing cultural, political and literary traditions', define Irishness 'on an inclusive island-wide basis'.[24] For the *Edinburgh History* editors, Scottish literature is 'a continuous and multi-channelled entity', 'best understood as an inclusive, not an exclusive, term'.[25] The historical migration of Scots to Ireland, of Irish people to Scotland, is actually a key reason for protocols that rephrase national questions (not that these have gone away) as identity politics: 'A fundamental theme of this *History* is the role of literature in the formation of Irish identities.'[26] 'New Identities' appears in the title of the *Edinburgh History*'s third volume. But editorial efforts to orchestrate a pluralistic history are shadowed by unresolved tension between nationalist and revisionist (or unionist or archipelagic) models: 'inclusiveness' is itself double-edged, and may reinstate the nation. The *Cambridge History* editors, who repeat the word 'authoritative', seem unduly anxious to control the Irish literary brand. Meanwhile, poetry, however revisionist in implication, still shoulders the national burden: 'Contemporary poets have played a prominent recent role in both public and political life. In doing so, they have helped to generate a much needed sense of optimism and aspiration about the future direction of Scottish identity.'[27]

At the same time, Yeats and MacDiarmid deserve extraordinary credit, not only in the archipelago, for the fact that poetry retains any communal dimension or purchase or visibility amid modern conditions. Yet, if their nationalism held poetry's ground, they constituted that ground by artistic means. Colin Graham writes: 'Early twenty-first century Irish criticism finds identity everywhere ... The resultant breadth of what constitutes Irish writing may be newly liberal ... or it may simply attest to the way in which thinking primarily through an uncritical identity politics has blunted the critical faculties which give a shape to Irish literature.'[28]

It would compound 'uncritical identity politics' if 'Irish–Scottish' literary studies were to update MacDiarmid's pan-Celtic *aisling* rather than engage in specific cross-readings. Yet the very fact and growth of such studies (although they existed *avant la lettre*) is significant. Perhaps Irish–Scottish studies took off most readily among historians, for whom archipelagic paradigms, if disputed, were already in place: the 'new British history', 'three kingdoms' or 'four nations' history, 'Atlantic' history. In the 1990s, a more particular focus on Ireland and Scotland was ideologically and materially boosted by UK devolution, and by the shift in British–Irish relations that enabled the Northern Ireland peace process. Given the symbolic status of language, this particularly affected Gaelic/Celtic studies and Ulster Scots studies.[29] It was also now becoming normative to configure Irish and Scottish literature where union and empire constituted a shared context.[30] But, as we enter the twentieth century, as literature becomes indexed to the Irish Revival, Irish independence, the Scottish Renaissance and Scottish Nationalism, boundaries harden. Pioneering cross-overs were Fiona Stafford's *Starting Lines in Scottish, Irish, and English Poetry: From Burns to Heaney* (2000) and Ray Ryan's *Ireland and Scotland: Literature and Culture, State and Nation 1966–2000* (2004). Yet Ryan and Liam McIlvanney warn, in their co-edited *Ireland and Scotland: Culture and Society, 1700–2000*: 'To advocate an Irish/Scottish context is to establish a political – and in some eyes, a polemical – framework for debate. Within Irish studies, the Irish/Scottish comparison is viewed by some as unionism's answer to postcolonial studies.'[31] This is so because it appears to reconnect the Irish Republic with the UK; to pivot on Ulster (not necessarily the case nor *ipso facto* a bad thing); and to position Northern Ireland, not inside all-island 'inclusiveness', but as a zone where Ireland and Scotland interpenetrate.

From the angle of Scottish literary studies, the politics look rather different – more like nationalism's answer to English ascendancy. The North, compromised by familiar sectarianism, has always been less attractive to Scottish Nationalists (a troubling unconscious, perhaps) than independent Ireland.[32] Lately, too, a pan-Celtic Tiger beckoned. As for academic attraction: thanks historically to Yeats and Joyce, Irish literary studies have the stronger international profile (see Patrick Crotty's chapter).[33] Nevertheless, as *à propos* 'modernism', both countries have more successfully exported individual talents than traditions or templates. That being so, the paradigms best adapted to – or from – either field, let alone both together, remain at issue. On the one hand, literary theory has brought Ireland and Scotland closer since the same theoretical sources tend to sponsor the same findings, as when 'gender' meets 'nation'; or when Joyce, MacDiarmid, linguistic variety, and versions of the postcolonial become 'Bakhtinian hybridity'.[34]

On the other hand, theoretical divergences may have unexamined roots (historical, religious, philosophical) in Irish–Scottish relations, as when Scottish critics flag up the Enlightenment or Irish critics favour postmodernist, neo-Romantic ideas. Hence the faintly reflexive titles of Declan Kiberd's *Inventing Ireland* (1995) and Cairns Craig's *Intending Scotland* (2009). In the last chapter here, 'Irish–Scottish studies as an act of translation', Michael Brown ponders the slippery ground on which this book itself is situated.

Comparison sharpens self-consciousness. Irish and Scottish literary studies have more work to do in conceptualising their own history, in historicising their own concepts; and it might advance matters if some of this were done in tandem or on an archipelagic basis. In *Archipelagic English* (2008), John Kerrigan argues that the Anglocentric bias of 'English' studies has often obscured the 'expansive, multilevelled, discontinuous, and polycentric' aspects of 'the literary and cultural field', and overlooked the archipelago's capacity to 'foster fusions and transformations'. His own chapter here, 'Louis MacNeice among the islands', explores a poetic instance of the latter. Kerrigan also stresses that relations vary between the 'interactive', the 'ubiquitous' and the 'fixed'; noting that 'the appropriate unit of enquiry might be the nation or a locality'.[35] Comparative study of modern Irish and Scottish poetry helps to identify 'the appropriate unit(s) of enquiry' in specific cases. Archipelagic literary studies complement rather than usurp nation-based studies. They can expose internal disconnections – like the partition of Irish poetry by the Second World War – and transnational connections. And they can replace *a priori* assumptions with readings that elicit what is truly distinctive in national or literary terms.

HISTORIES, LANGUAGES, AESTHETICS

Why Ireland and Scotland? Our focus does not rule out other archipelagic permutations or wider horizons: the chapters by Justin Quinn and Christopher Whyte make comparative use of the latter. But, besides the historical rationale outlined below, the canonical ring-fences around modern Irish and Scottish poetry cry out for critical probes: most studies continue to be organised on a national basis.[36] Irish–Scottish comparisons bring aesthetics as well as paradigms into the foreground. They rearrange the poetic field by outflanking, not only English myopia, but also the distortions that stem from Irish or Scottish political fixation on England (an extreme case is *Inventing Ireland* where England and Ireland figure as Self and Other and Scotland does not figure at all). It is time to unpack 'poetry from Britain and Ireland': the diplomatic formula current since Seamus Heaney addressed a corrective *Open Letter* to the editors of *The Penguin Book of Contemporary British Poetry* (1982).

Poetic contact between Ireland and Scotland begins with an island: Iona. The first datable Gaelic poem, 'Amra Choluim Chille' by the Irish poet Dalánn Forgaill, is a tribute to St Colm Cille/Columba who died in 597. After going into Scottish exile and starting his Christian mission, Colm Cille, perhaps a poet himself, briefly returned to secure the survival of Irish *filí* (the poetic class) by getting them to curb their numbers and power. Gaels from Ireland had started to 'colonise' Scotland during the fifth century. In *Divided Gaels* Wilson McLeod argues against the view that this created a unified cultural province, which spanned *Sruth na Maoile* (the Sea of Moyle) for a thousand years. McLeod paints a more fluctuating picture of 'ambiguous connection', subject to developments within each country. Even so, during the high bardic period (*c*. 1200–1600), literary connection was constant: a 'supra-national' learned class shared a common literary language and trained in the same schools. By the same token, the collapse of the Irish bardic order 'deeply splintered' the Gaelic world.[37] To quote from Máire ní Annracháin's chapter here: 'vernacular Irish and Scottish Gaelic became increasingly separate ... accelerated by the loss of a common written standard' (p. 105). The Reformation had already ensured the loss of a common religion. A further splinter was the clash between Scottish and Irish antiquarians over James Macpherson's *Ossian* (1760–5). This 'modern fantasia on fragments and themes from a much older [oral] tradition' laid a Scottish claim to legendary materials that circulated in Scotland, but had originated in Ireland, and for which the countries had different national uses.[38] If Colm Cille/Columba is the patron saint of Irish/Scottish poetry, Oisín/Ossian is the equally 'ambiguous' patron pagan. It's no coincidence that Yeats announced his poetic debut with 'The Wanderings of Oisin' (1889). This Celtic Twilight epic might be seen, in turn, as inaugurating the symbolic guises that the Irish/Scottish island would assume (as for MacNeice) during the next century.

Peter Mackay calls *An Guth* (*The Voice*) 'the first international poetry journal linking the Irish and Scottish Gaidhealtachdan'.[39] Launched in 2003, *An Guth* builds on the fact that: 'Communication between the realms of Irish and Scottish Gaelic poetry was re-engaged ... in the late sixties and early seventies following more than two centuries of almost total mutual indifference.'[40] Re-engagement began with the 'Bardic Circuit' whereby poets and musicians toured the other country in alternate years. Yet Mackay asks how deep reciprocity goes, since it is mainly *An Guth*'s editor, Rody

Gorman, a Dubliner living on Skye, who translates between Irish and Scottish Gaelic: 'a one-man walking contact zone'.[41] Ní Annracháin notes that 'few Irish or Scottish poets can read both forms of Gaelic with ease' (p. 103), and finds 'little articulated exploration of each other's distinctive ... literary traditions' (p. 103), despite echoes from a shared past that can make the Gaelic tradition appear 'uncannily unified' (p. 105). Certainly, survival – of the language and its poetry – presents an urgent unifying cause. 'Shall Gaelic Die?' asks a powerful sequence by Iain Crichton Smith. The chapters here on poetry in Irish and Scottish Gaelic do not always agree as to the ratio of 'traditional' and 'modern', 'native' and 'foreign' elements (Christopher Whyte uses the term 'foreignising'), on which survival might partly depend. But they all place translation at the heart of the matter, and perhaps of this book. For Eric Falci, collections where Gaelic poems appear alongside English translations do not mean surrender or suicide, but challenge our ways of reading: 'the facing pages ghost, rewrite and revivify each other, setting the other vibrating strangely' (p. 173).

Poetry in Scots also sets up strange vibrations. Rather than what Falci calls 'the double page', we often encounter a single page with a streel or substratum of English glosses. Seamus Heaney's version of Robert Henryson's *Testament of Cresseid and Seven Fables* (2009) is, however, double-paged. This indeed reads like a ghostly palimpsest, given the likeness and strangeness between fifteenth-century Scots and Heaney's modern English inflected by '"the hidden Scotland" at the back of my own ear', and spiced by Scots words which 'have always been part of my own Northern Irish vocabulary': '"*Se ye yone churll*", quod scho, "*beyond yone pleuch / Fast sawand hemp – lo se – and linget seid?*"' / '"Do you see", she said, "yon fellow with his plough / Sowing – look – hemp and lint, broadcasting seed?"' ('The Preaching of the Swallow').[42] Hugh Magennis, in his chapter on Heaney's and Edwin Morgan's translations of *Beowulf*, notices Heaney's need to connect *Beowulf* with 'his own language experience' (p. 155). It is as if Heaney designates Scotland a poetic buffer zone between himself and England (witness 'Would They Had Stay'd'): his *Open Letter* is written in Standard Habbie/the Burns stanza. Scotland may even enable him to assert his 'own' 'northern-ness' in implied tension with both Northern Ireland and the Irish Republic. Discussing 'The Language, Literature and Politics of Ulster Scots', Liam McIlvanney applauds Heaney's 'demonstration that Ulster's Scottish inheritance – in its Gaelic, [Scots] and English modes – is as available to the Catholic as to the Protestant writer'.[43]

Nevertheless, it was when Lowland Presbyterians arrived in Ulster at the start of the seventeenth century (not all officially 'planted') that Ireland and Scotland acquired their second overlapping linguistic domain, even while English encroached on both as Scots had encroached on Gaelic. Like religion and folk-culture, poetry travelled with the language: scholars no longer regard Burns and other Scottish poets as having been 'imported' into Ulster. Burns-influenced 'weaver' poets flourished there during the late eighteenth and early nineteenth centuries, most notably James Orr (1770–1816). Orr's celebrated 'Donegore Hill', a miniature epic in Scots, concerns the defeat of Presbyterian United Irishmen by Crown forces (1798).[44] Thomas Dermody, a Munster outlier, used Scots and Standard Habbie, and Burns's broader impact on archipelagic Romanticism permeated Ireland. Yet Burns's reception in Ulster involves an especially intricate set of political and cultural dynamics, which also distinguish it from his reception in Scotland.[45]

Scots has an ideological, cultural and aesthetic presence in modern poetry – not always all at once. To quote Roderick Watson: 'Hugh MacDiarmid's resistance to the hegemony of Standard English has been of immense importance to ... Scottish writing – even for those writers ... who would disagree with his political nationalism.'[46] In Ireland, contrastingly, Yeats's English-language Revival had to contend with the would-be hegemony of Irish. And whereas MacDiarmid's Renaissance could plausibly seek to unite Scots and Gaelic poetry against English, Irish politics divided the languages. Around 1900, when battle-lines were drawn over Home Rule, the ideal-typical 'Ulster Scot' was unionism's answer to the ideal-typical 'Irish Gael', Burns being 'promoted as a marker of northern cultural distinctiveness'.[47] In the 1940s, John Hewitt (b. 1907) built the weaver poets into a more genuinely cultural and literary ideology: Ulster 'regionalism'. He celebrated their Scots poetry as 'rooted', less 'colonial' than that of Anglo-Ulster.[48] Today 'the politics of Ulster Scots' confront Sinn Féin's politics of Irish. Both are equally remote from northern poets' creative relation to all available languages: a politics of poetry, perhaps.

In 1960s Scotland, some poets attacked Renaissance ideology with results that resembled the nineteenth-century Disruption of the Kirk. Although MacDiarmid himself was now writing in English, he saw his opponents as heretics not only because they wrote 'concrete' poetry but also because they denied the special position of Scots. Eleanor Bell's chapter explores some of these 'fierce debates' (p. 238) together with Irish 'reactions to tradition' (see chapter 18 in this volume too). In 1992 Douglas Dunn ratified a linguistic peace process: 'Scottish poetry ... is more and more the poetry in three languages of one nationality.'[49] Scots itself is still being poetically reinvented. At one end of the spectrum, whenever poets (like W. N. Herbert) write a poem wholly in Scots, they emulate MacDiarmid's 'synthetic Scots' taken from different regions and periods; also, perhaps, his mission to assert cultural difference. This mode of Scots 'begins with, rather than results in, literary expression'.[50] Yet, as in early MacDiarmid, synthetic diction is buoyed by Scots' survival within the idiom, syntax and sounds of Scottish speech. The poet and folksong collector Hamish Henderson, although an enthusiast for Scots (and Gaelic), queried any need for the synthetic 'while the reality of living Scots is there to be heard at every street corner and furrow end':[51] in part, an anticipation of Tom Leonard's 'Glaswegian' poems. As Heaney's example shows, Scots can have a similar cultural presence in poetry from Northern Ireland. That includes the rhythmic repercussions of a 'hidden Scotland' within the strongly stressed accents of northern Hiberno-English. Finally, poets sometimes deploy Scots with macaronic rather than ideological deliberateness: as a vivid colour in the verbal palette. Robert Crawford's chapter on 'The Classics in modern Irish and Scottish poetry', which complicates the equation by introducing two further languages, notices such effects in Michael Longley's translations.

Raised linguistic consciousness has been an inescapable – and mainly positive – force in modern Irish and Scottish poetry. It reaches an apotheosis in Edwin Morgan's and Ciaran Carson's shifting lexical guises; in Chinese boxes of 'translation' such as those that Leontia Flynn discovers here when she compares the poetry of Frank Kuppner and Medbh McGuckian. And it includes a sense of being 'Outside English', to quote Justin Quinn's chapter title, which is already poetic; which allows poets to reinvent that language too. Reading Irish and Scottish poetry together supports the (contested) idea that language – including its entries into the poetic foreground – is not wholly detachable from the history that works on it or through it. This is one instance (religion might be another) of Irish–Scottish comparisons highlighting contexts which are not fully factored into statements about poetic modernism or poetic modernity. Again, there are other models of the modern 'word-city' besides Eliot's London, even if haunted by John Davidson from Renfrewshire. Aaron Kelly's chapter focuses on distinctive ways in which the poetics of Glasgow and Belfast, cities with linked religious, economic and political histories, map urban consciousness. One link, which reflects denominational, cultural and literary-critical prejudices that go back to Matthew Arnold, is that both cities have been seen as unamenable to poetry. Philip Hobsbaum who ran a writers' 'Group', first in 1960s Belfast, then in Glasgow, helped to dispel literary inferiorism.[52]

REVIVALS

Networks have activated the fitful play of stimuli between Irish and Scottish poetry: the Rhymers' Club, Celtic soulmates, the Bardic Circuit, the poetry-reading circuit, friendship. Douglas Dunn's chapter explores his generational 'affinity' with certain Irish poets, locating it within the wider poetic field of the 1960s and '70s. Fran Brearton takes another approach to the same configuration. There are academic networks (like this one). The two books with most influence on Scottish literary studies, Gregory Smith's *Scottish Literature* and George Elder Davie's *The Democratic Intellect* (1961), were written when their authors taught at Queen's University Belfast, and were conditioned by that fact.[53] More briefly, in the late 1940s, Hamish Henderson ran the Workers Educational Association in Belfast. When he applied for the job, he stayed with John Hewitt, and they attended Yeats's burial at Drumcliff. For Henderson, the left-wing, 'Left-Bank' literary world of postwar Belfast was hardly foreign.[54] Such northern networks often slip beneath the radar of critical geographies centred on London or Dublin.

Above all, a kind of revival roundabout has kept the wheels turning. Stephen Gwynn notes that Yeats emerged as the white hope at a time when 'we were all painfully conscious that Ireland ... had little to show in the field of literature; we were in particular envious of Scotland's prestige'.[55] In 1845 the Ulster-born poet Samuel Ferguson (1810–86) had sought to make 'Dublin at least a better Edinburgh',[56] and wished for a national poet of Burns's stature: Yeats would later be annoyed by taunts that he was too esoteric to be Ireland's Burns. Ferguson is the most historically significant 'one-man walking contact zone' between Irish and Scottish poetry. In *Samuel Ferguson and the Culture of Nineteenth-Century Ireland* Eve Patten stresses the Scottish dimensions of Ferguson's life and thought from his childhood in 'the Scottish Presbyterian community of lowland Antrim' to an involvement with *Blackwood's Edinburgh Magazine* that derived from 'the sheer proximity of Ulster's intellectual community to the ... fall-out from the Scottish Enlightenment'.[57] The 'gloaming' and languorous cadences of Ferguson's 'The Fairy Thorn', subtitled 'An Ulster Ballad' (1834), in which 'a Highland reel' is danced, influenced the Celtic Twilight; his translations from Gaelic poetry were influential too; and, an antiquarian steeped in Ossianic matters, he wrote epic poems that suggested to Yeats the poetic and dramatic potential of Irish legend. He also wrote poems in Scots: among them 'A New Year's Epistle to Robert Gordon, M. D.' (1845). In these Standard Habbie stanzas Ferguson dedicates his Muse to Ireland, promising 'Some offerin's o' nae cauld haranguer / Put out for Erin', and praying: 'Let me but rive ae link asunder / O' Erin's fetter!' The poem continues:

> Let me but help to shape the sentence
> Will put the pith o' independence,
> O' self-respect in self-acquaintance,
>   And manly pride
> Intil auld Eber-Scot's descendants –
>   Take a' beside![58]

Eber-Scot was, supposedly, a Scythian king, great-grandson of Scota and a progenitor of the Irish race. Frank Ferguson calls these lines a 'nice hybridising of a Scots vernacular verse form and Celtic mythology, showing two of Ferguson's ancestral voices fusing together ... [W]hen he writes about Eber-Scot's descendants he may be talking about the Irish and also about the Scots.'[59]

While Ferguson retained trace-elements of northern radicalism, chain-riving and 'independence' do not necessarily imply a separatist agenda. Political nationalism had no monopoly of patriotism in nineteenth-century Ireland or Scotland. In 1884, when Ferguson had long been associated with Dublin's Tory and unionist circles, he quoted his epistle to Gordon ('So sang I . . . in our native Doric') in a letter to a friend who had given him 'continuing and strengthened confidence in the belief that a national literature is still possible for our country, and that I, even I, have had a hand in laying its foundation'.[60] Ferguson did indeed lay crucial foundations for the Irish Revival. But when, in 'To Ireland in the Coming Times', Yeats hopes to 'be counted one / With Davis, Mangan, Ferguson', he does not reckon with all the sources of Ferguson's dedication to 'Erin'. Similarly, Hugh MacDiarmid saw what he wanted to see in Yeats's own relation to Ireland. Rather as Yeats suppressed Ferguson's unionism, MacDiarmid exaggerated the extent to which Yeats had the Irish national ear; and, impressed by Yeats's foe Daniel Corkery, never grasped the tension between the Gaelic and literary revivals.[61] But these (on the whole) were creative misreadings. Twenty years later, John Hewitt, close to Henderson, Edwin Muir and other Scottish poets, overrated Scotland's literary confidence when he made the Renaissance one of his touchstones for a regionalism that might accommodate and maximise all Ulster's cultural elements.[62] Hewitt's regionalism helped to prepare the ground for later poetry from

Northern Ireland. The poetic 'revival' there since the 1960s is a complex phenomenon. Complex, too, are its archipelagic origins, horizons and influence. But it undoubtedly, if untidily, inherited a series of revivals in which Ireland and Scotland connected. Ferguson's 'Robert Gordon' lived in Bellaghy, Seamus Heaney's native place.

During this project, disconnections have also proved revealing, and they include distance between poetry and nationality. Alan Gillis, in his chapter on 'The Poetics of Place Names', argues that 'the purely aesthetic pleasure of embedded poetic sound persists, almost impervious to social-economic actuality' (p. 219). David Wheatley, discussing the formal practices of Randolph Healy and Richard Price, ironically wonders if there is 'such a thing as a non-Irish or -Scottish writer any more': that is, one whose work 'defiantly has nothing to do with those countries' (p. 251). Perhaps no poet gets away quite so easily. Nor is it only nation-based studies of modern poetry that reproduce long-entrenched ideas or prejudge what should be compared with what ('international' often seems synonymous with 'American'). Ideally, Irish–Scottish comparisons – which this book by no means exhausts – shake up the aesthetic kaleidoscope. They may also clarify where nationality has poetic meaning, and where it obscures other kinds of meaning.

NOTES

1. W. B. Yeats, *Autobiographies* (London: Macmillan, 1955), 317.
2. Seamus Heaney, *Electric Light* (London: Faber, 2001), 68–9.
3. This much-anthologised poem (though absent from Yeats's *Oxford Book of Modern Verse* [1936]) was first published in John Davidson, *Ballads and Songs* (London: John Lane, The Bodley Head, 1894). For Davidson, see Derek Stanford (ed.), *Three Poets of the Rhymers Club* (Manchester: Carcanet, 1974); John Sloan, *John Davidson, First of the Moderns: A Literary Biography* (Oxford: Clarendon, 1995).
4. Yeats, *Autobiographies*, 320, 318.
5. See Edna Longley, 'The Whereabouts of Literature', in Gerard Carruthers, David Goldie and Alastair Renfrew (eds.), *Beyond Scotland* (Amsterdam and New York: Rodopi, 2004), 151–65; Willy Maley, 'Away with the Faeries (or, it's Grimm up North): Yeats and Scotland', *Journal of Irish and Scottish Studies* 1:1 (2007), 161–77.
6. T. S. Eliot, 'Preface', in Maurice Lindsay (ed.), *John Davidson: A Selection of his Poems* (London: Hutchinson, 1961), unnumbered.
7. Hugh MacDiarmid, 'John Davidson: Influences and Influence', *Ibid.*, 47.
8. Hugh MacDiarmid, *Complete Poems*, Vol. 1 (Harmondsworth: Penguin, 1985), 362.
9. Lindsay (ed.), *John Davidson: A Selection of his Poems*, 51.
10. Robert Crawford, *Devolving English Literature* (Oxford: Clarendon, 1992), 248; in 1991, in the (Oxford) magazine *Interference*, Richard Price dubbed himself,

together with Crawford, David Kinloch and W. N. Herbert, the 'Informationist' school.
11. W. B. Yeats, 'Preface', in *Michael Robartes and the Dancer* (Dundrum: Cuala, 1920), unnumbered; Lindsay (ed.), *John Davidson: A Selection of his Poems*, 53.
12. AE, 'Introductory Essay', in Hugh MacDiarmid, *First Hymn to Lenin and Other Poems* (London: Unicorn, 1931), 2–3.
13. MacDiarmid, *Complete Poems*, Vol. 1, 224.
14. *Ibid.*, 210.
15. T. S. Eliot, 'Tradition and the Individual Talent', *Selected Prose of T. S. Eliot* (London: Faber, 1975), 39.
16. Cairns Craig, 'The Criticism of Scottish Literature: Tradition, Decline and Renovation', *Edinburgh History of Scottish Literature*, Vol. 3 (Edinburgh University Press, 2007), 46.
17. T. S. Eliot, 'Was There a Scottish Literature?', reprinted in Margery Palmer McCulloch (ed.), *Modernism and Nationalism: Literature and Society in Scotland, 1918–1939* (Glasgow: Association for Scottish Literary Studies, 2004), 10; Eliot, 'Tradition and the Individual Talent', 37. See A. Norman Jeffares (ed.), *W. B. Yeats: The Critical Heritage* (London: Routledge, 1977), 230–2; Edna Longley, '"Altering the Past": Northern Irish Poetry and Modern Canons', *Yearbook of English Studies* 35 (2005), 1–17.
18. See Crawford, *Devolving English Literature*, 216–70.
19. Hugh MacDiarmid, 'English Ascendancy in British Literature' (1931), reprinted in Alan Riach (ed.), *Hugh MacDiarmid: Selected Prose* (Manchester: Carcanet, 1992), 67.
20. For an audio record of the symposia, visit 'Irish-Scottish Poetry' on the Seamus Heaney Centre website www.qub.ac.uk/schools/SeamusHeaneyCentreforPoetry/irishscottishpoetry/.
21. See note 19.
22. Craig, 'The Criticism of Scottish Literature', 45.
23. G. Gregory Smith, *Scottish Literature: Character and Influence* (London: Macmillan, 1919), 278.
24. Margaret Kelleher and Philip O'Leary (eds.), 'Introduction', *The Cambridge History of Irish Literature*, Vol. 1 (Cambridge University Press, 2006), 4.
25. Ian Brown *et al.*, 'Preface', *Edinburgh History of Scottish Literature: Modern Transformations – New Identities*, Vol. 3 (Edinburgh University Press, 2006), viii.
26. Kelleher and O'Leary (eds.), 'Introduction', 6.
27. Eleanor Bell, 'Old Country, New Dreams: Scottish Poetry since the 1970s' in Brown *et al.* (eds.), *Edinburgh History of Scottish Literature*, Vol. 3, 196.
28. Colin Graham, 'Literary Historiography, 1890–2000', in Kelleher and O'Leary (eds.), *Cambridge History of Irish Literature*, Vol. 2, 591.
29. For example, the Columba Initiative/Iomairt Cholm Cille, which links Irish and Scottish Gaelic-speakers, funded (since 1997) by the Irish government and the Scottish and Northern Ireland Executives; the establishment of the Institute of Ulster Scots Studies at the University of Ulster; the annual 'Language and Politics' symposia organised (since 2000) at Queen's

University Belfast: for associated publications, by Cló Ollscoil na Banríona, see www.qub.ac.uk/cob.
30. For example, Katie Trumpener's influential *Bardic Nationalism: The Romantic Novel and the British Empire* (Princeton University Press, 1997) showed that, in the Romantic period, 'interconnected' Scottish and Irish cultural revivals 'partly offset a process of ... centralisation' (ix).
31. Liam McIlvanney and Ray Ryan (eds.), *Ireland and Scotland: Culture and Society, 1700–2000* (Dublin: Four Courts, 2005), 14.
32. See Graham Walker, *Intimate Strangers: Political and Cultural Interaction between Ulster and Scotland in Modern Times* (Edinburgh: John Donald, 1995).
33. And see Paul Barnaby and Tom Hubbard, 'The International Reception and Literary Impact of Scottish Literature of the Period since 1918', Brown *et al.* (eds.), *Edinburgh History of Scottish Literature*, Vol. 3, 31–41.
34. For a critique of the latter, see Cairns Craig, 'Postcolonial Hybridity in Scotland and Ireland', in Edna Longley, Eamonn Hughes and Des O'Rawe (eds.), *Ireland (Ulster) Scotland: Concepts, Contexts, Comparisons* (Belfast: Cló Ollscoil na Banríona, 2003), 231–43.
35. John Kerrigan, *Archipelagic English: Literature, History, and Politics, 1603–1707* (Oxford University Press, 2008), 82, 89, 84, 26.
36. For example, forthcoming *Oxford Companions* to modern Irish and Scottish poetry.
37. Wilson McLeod, *Divided Gaels: Gaelic Cultural Identities in Scotland and Ireland, c. 1200–c. 1650* (Oxford University Press, 2004), 222, 193, 1.
38. Trumpener, *Bardic Nationalism*, 77. And see Clare O'Halloran, *Golden Ages and Barbarous Nations: Antiquarian Debate and Cultural Politics in Ireland, c. 1750–1800* (Cork University Press, 2004).
39. Peter Mackay, 'An Guth and the Leabhar Mòr: Dialogues between Scottish Gaelic and Irish Poetry', *Journal of Irish and Scottish Studies* 1:2 (2008), 184–5.
40. *Ibid.*
41. *Ibid.*, 187.
42. Seamus Heaney, *Robert Henryson: Testament of Cresseid and Seven Fables* (London: Faber, 2009), xiii, xviii, 112–13.
43. Liam McIlvanney, 'Across the Narrow Sea: The Language, Literature and Politics of Ulster Scots', in McIlvanney and Ryan (eds.), *Ireland and Scotland*, 223.
44. The poem is included in Frank Ferguson (ed.), *Ulster-Scots Writing: An Anthology* (Dublin: Four Courts, 2008). See, too, Liam McIlvanney, *Burns the Radical: Poetry and Politics in Late Eighteenth-Century Scotland* (East Linton: Tuckwell, 2002), which includes a chapter on 'Burns and the Ulster-Scots Radical Poets'.
45. See Frank Ferguson and Andrew R. Holmes (eds.), *Revising Robert Burns and Ulster: Literature, Religion and Politics, c. 1770–1920* (Dublin: Four Courts, 2009).
46. Roderick Watson, 'Living with the Double Tongue: Modern Poetry in Scots', in Brown *et al.* (eds.), *Edinburgh History of Scottish Literature*, Vol. 3, 163.
47. Ferguson and Holmes, 'Introduction', *Revising Robert Burns and Ulster*, 13.

48. John Hewitt, 'The Course of Writing in Ulster', in Tom Clyde (ed.), *Ancestral Voices: The Selected Prose of John Hewitt* (Belfast: Blackstaff, 1987), 66.
49. Douglas Dunn (ed.), *The Faber Book of Twentieth-Century Scottish Poetry* (London: Faber, 1992), xxvii.
50. Wilson McLeod and Jeremy Smith, 'Resistance to Monolinguality: The Languages of Scotland since 1918', *Edinburgh History of Scottish Literature*, Vol. 3, 25.
51. See Timothy Neat, *Hamish Henderson: A Biography, Volume I: The Making of the Poet (1919–1953)* (Edinburgh: Polygon, 2007), 218.
52. 'Inferiorism' is a term coined by Craig Beveridge and Ronald Turnbull: see their *The Eclipse of Scottish Culture: Inferiorism and the Intellectuals* (Edinburgh: Polygon, 1989).
53. Smith's hostility to the Irish Revival reflects Ulster Unionist attitudes in the early 1900s; founded in 1845, and partly modelled on the Scottish universities, Queen's makes a suitable context for Davie's focus on their history in the nineteenth century.
54. Neat, *Hamish Henderson*, 225.
55. Stephen Gwynn (ed.), *Scattering Branches: Tributes to the Memory of W. B. Yeats* (London: Macmillan, 1940), 4.
56. See Peter Denman, *Samuel Ferguson: The Literary Achievement* (Gerrards Cross: Colin Smythe, 1990), 63.
57. Eve Patten, *Samuel Ferguson and the Culture of Nineteenth-Century Ireland* (Dublin: Four Courts, 2004), 16, 31.
58. Quoted in Lady Ferguson, *Sir Samuel Ferguson in the Ireland of His Day* (Edinburgh and London: William Blackwood and Sons, 1896), 125–6.
59. In a letter to me, after he spoke at a Ferguson bicentenary symposium (Linen Hall Library, Belfast, 10 March 2010).
60. Quoted in Lady Ferguson, *Sir Samuel Ferguson*, 128.
61. 'English Ascendancy in British Literature' (see note 19) lauds the pre-Renaissance, pre-Reformation emphasis of Corkery's nativist *The Hidden Ireland* (1925).
62. See John Hewitt, 'The Bitter Gourd: Some Problems of the Ulster Writer', in Clyde (ed.), *Ancestral Voices*, 108–9.

CHAPTER I

Swordsmen: W. B. Yeats and Hugh MacDiarmid

Patrick Crotty

From a long literary historical perspective, William Butler Yeats and Hugh MacDiarmid can look almost like twins. Each was a poet and the central figure in a patriotically inflected literary movement that had its context in a wider cultural repudiation of English hegemony in the United Kingdom and a political challenge to the inclusion of their countries in that polity. Seeing poetry and controversy as allied activities, both writers were vigorous self-mythologisers whose interventions in public life were condemned as hubristic by their opponents. Yeats and MacDiarmid not only projected themselves as avatars of a resurgent phase in the history of their ancient nations but shared a vision of leadership by aesthetic example – their distinctively national poetry (and, in the Irish poet's case, drama) would give their compatriots an enhanced sense of the riches of the past and the possibilities of the future, while their propagandistic endeavours would at once energise their art and create the conditions for its reception. They even shared a response to disappointment in the latter objective, exploiting it as an occasion of querulous lyric eloquence.

On closer inspection, however, the parallels become less persuasive. Even if the Scottish Literary Renaissance inaugurated by MacDiarmid was modelled to a degree on the Irish Literary Revival led by Yeats, these were in important respects disparate phenomena, which took place in divergent circumstances. The core personnel of the Irish Revival, particularly in its first two decades (1885–1905), was drawn from the ranks of a Protestant minority that had been progressively losing its privileges since the Act of Union of 1801: the movement's immediate political context was the ongoing shift in power from their Anglo-Irish ascendancy caste to the Roman Catholic majority community. Yeats in 1922 recollected the 'sudden certainty' that came upon him in 'a moment of supernatural insight' in the late 1880s that 'Ireland was to be like soft wax for years to come':[1] the implication was that he and his fellow Revivalists would set their seal on the wax, offering the inchoate Catholic masses cultural and intellectual guidance and thereby saving the newly reconfigured nation from the horrors of mercantile modernity, and their own class from oblivion. Predictably perhaps, history did not co-operate with these plans and the later decades of the Revival were played out against a background of rapid and in some respects revolutionary political change. In due course a strongly Catholic and emphatically mercantile independent Irish state was set up. It was a state to which Yeats, for all his misgivings about its character and direction, lent his practical and administrative talents, and one which in turn adopted the playhouse he had founded at the beginning of the century as its own publicly subsidised national theatre.

The Scottish Literary Renaissance was markedly less convulsive in its political context, and its *dramatis personae* emerged from ordinary and, in many cases, humble social backgrounds (even if in a radio interview broadcast a few months before his death the most eminent of them declared his allegiance to 'the native aristocracy of intellect').[2] The leading figures of the Renaissance were representative of the broad mass of their compatriots not only in their socio-economic but also their Presbyterian or Free Presbyterian religious origins. While the need to respond to a crisis of Scottish identity in the aftermath of the Great War functioned as a common motivating factor behind the work of the writers MacDiarmid, Edwin and Willa Muir, Lewis Grassic Gibbon, Nan Shepherd, Neil M. Gunn and Sorley MacLean, and of the composer F. G. Scott, only MacDiarmid's cultural nationalism was consistently underpinned by a separatist politics – and MacDiarmid is not often accused of consistency. Yeats lagged well behind popular opinion in the intensity of his commitment to breaking the Irish union with Britain, while MacDiarmid ran far ahead of his compatriots in his zeal to sunder the Scottish one with England. A year after Yeats's bones were interred in Drumcliff Churchyard in 1948, the southern Irish state severed its last links with the Empire by declaring itself a republic. A year after MacDiarmid was buried in Langholm Cemetery, Scottish voters opted for devolution by an insufficient majority to alter the constitutional relationship of their country to the rest of the United Kingdom. Yeats, we might say, lived through a national cataclysm that he tried with limited success to control, while MacDiarmid conducted the greater part of his career in a period of comparative torpor that he furiously tried to prod into the condition of cataclysm.

That torpor was by no means absolute. MacDiarmid witnessed and responded poetically to the General Strike of 1926 and the Great Depression of the following decade, and the more vituperative among his verses have much to say on Scottish, British and European political issues and personalities. It is not possible wholly to distinguish text from context in relation to the absorption of topical developments by literature. A good deal of our sense of the terror and exhilaration of the Easter Rising and the Irish War of Independence, after all, derives from the way these events and their implications have been made psychologically available to us through Yeats's poetry. 'The Ballad of the Crucified Rose', MacDiarmid's rueful commentary in *A Drunk Man Looks at the Thistle* on the collapse of the General Strike, reveals his poetry's ability to register the excitement and frustration of contemporary politics. Yet no one would claim that the 'Ballad', for all its virtues, represents his lyric art in Scots at its most resourceful. 'Easter 1916', conversely, operates at a higher pitch than anything Yeats had written up to that point. It is as if the poet was forced by the Rising and its aftermath to confront issues about the relationship of literature to politics and to come up with a defence of the 'living stream' of creativity and an associated critique of the petrifying effect on the inner life of the revolutionary dedication practised by the rebels, a defence and critique so magisterially formulated that they transcend their origin in a particular conflict. (MacDiarmid's 'Second Hymn to Lenin' takes up an analogous theme, offering an ingenious rearguard action on behalf of the autonomy of poetry against the demands of Marxist orthodoxy; the leisurely dialectical *modus operandi* of the 'Hymn', however, betrays the lack of urgency of its occasion.) The particularity of the Dublin conflict is nonetheless deeply inscribed in 'Easter 1916'. The scale of the destruction of the city brought about by the suppression of the rebellion lent an apocalyptic aspect to Yeats's immediate circumstances that had no counterpart in the Scotland of MacDiarmid's time, and the Irish poet's acquaintance with some of the insurrection's protagonists implicated him intimately (and in artistic terms enviably) in an episode of epoch-making national importance. Even the less seismic events surrounding the Irish Revival demonstrate how successful the writers and intellectuals of the time were in engaging the attention of a wide public. The controversy stirred up by the 'Contemporary Scottish Studies' articles MacDiarmid contributed to the *Scottish Educational Journal* from 1925 to 1927 under his birth-name C. M. Grieve was the closest the Renaissance got to the centre of national life but that entire affair amounted to little more than a sustained exchange of unpleasantries in the correspondence columns of a teachers' paper. The *Playboy* riots and the prolonged public stand-off over the Hugh Lane paintings, in both of which Yeats featured as the leading antagonist of popular opinion, seem spectacular by comparison.

The Revival was almost from its beginnings the subject of public debate in Ireland and of journalistic and critical attention in Britain, the United States and elsewhere. It not only produced the poetry of Yeats, the drama of Synge and much of the most enduring fiction of George Moore but provided an oppositional starting point for the work of Sean O'Casey, James Joyce, Patrick Kavanagh, Samuel Beckett and Flann O'Brien. Its reality has been taken for granted in the wider world from at least as early as the publication of Ernest Boyd's pioneering study *Ireland's Literary Renaissance* in 1916. The Scottish Renaissance, conversely, ran its much shorter course – two as opposed to five decades – in something of a public vacuum, and even in Scotland its reality was doubted as late as the 1970s. Furth of Scotland the Renaissance has been seen, when it has been seen at all, variously as a regional ripple, a pretension, or a figment of MacDiarmid's imagination. With the professionalisation and internationalisation of Scottish literary historiography in recent decades – and particularly in the past few years, which have treated us to a sudden outpouring of high quality monograph and multi-authored literary histories[3] – all that is changing, and the galvanisation of literary and other artistic energies that took place in the country in the 1920s and '30s is at last being recognised and investigated. Elsewhere, too, there is evidence of belated acknowledgement of the upsurge of cultural production in Scotland in the interwar years: the *Oxford Companion to English Literature* in its seventh (2009) edition for the first time carries an entry on the Scottish Renaissance to set beside its longstanding one on the Irish Literary Revival.

The disparity in attention accorded the Revival and the Renaissance has its counterpart in the disparity of impact between the literary achievement of Yeats and MacDiarmid. The Irish poet is the focus of a vigorous critical industry, and many scores of academics in Ireland, Britain, the United States, Japan and other countries have put the study of his poems and, to a lesser degree, his plays at the centre of their scholarly endeavours. An annual 2-week Summer school in Sligo draws students, lecturers and poets from all over the world. (It celebrated its fiftieth birthday in 2009.) Rival editions of Yeats's primary texts jostle for the attention of readers and instructors, while monographs, essay collections, book chapters and a designated *Yeats Annual* keep adding to an already unnavigably capacious secondary literature. Yeats's poetry, meanwhile, has cast a long shadow over the practice of his successors. In Ireland, negotiation of his legacy – in its formal, and even to some degree its thematic, aspects – can be identified as a key factor in the development of poets as different as Austin Clarke, Patrick Kavanagh, Louis MacNeice, Thomas Kinsella, Seamus Heaney, Michael Longley, Eavan Boland and Paul Muldoon. In Britain and the United States, the writing of such otherwise profoundly dissimilar poets as W. H. Auden, R. S. Thomas, Philip Larkin and Sylvia Plath reflects deep engagement with his achievement. Some midcentury poets – the American Theodore Roethke, for example – had to struggle very hard to free themselves from the commanding tonalities of their Irish master; others, such as the Welsh writer Vernon Watkins, never quite managed to escape them. In the early twenty-first century, however, the poetic, if not the critical, response to Yeats appears to have run out of steam. A combined tendency towards scepticism and egalitarianism in contemporary poetry has led to such distrust of the grandiloquence of his manner and the presumptive scope of his vision that it would be unwise to describe him as a living presence in the work of poets under 50 either in Ireland or elsewhere in the Anglophone world.

MacDiarmid's critical reputation is manifestly less secure than Yeats's and his influence on poets of subsequent generations in the wider English-speaking world is, to say the least, far from pervasive. Academic interest in his work was at its height in the decade or so after his death, when nearly a dozen monograph studies appeared. While the best of these are useful and illuminating, many are unsatisfactory as a result either of low critical ambition or an uncertain grasp of the chronology and complex bibliographical history of the poetry. (It is notable that the most reliable and informed studies are by Scottish critics.)[4] The energy and seriousness of the best-known commentaries on Yeats – those by internationally renowned scholars like T. R. Henn, Richard Ellmann, Denis Donoghue, Harold Bloom, Helen Vendler or Daniel Albright, to sample the most prominent names – suggest that MacDiarmid's work has by contrast never been subjected to the attentions of the international academy at the highest level. Nor has the poetry yet won a genuinely wide readership. It would be impossible to run a MacDiarmid Summer school, at least on the Yeatsian model. Where would the hundred or hundred and fifty students come from? And the twenty lecturers? In the last years of his life and for a time after his death MacDiarmid's reputation both at home and abroad seemed to be steeply in the ascendant but over the past decade or so it has slipped back to somewhere close to the doldrums in which it languished prior to the appearance of the first *Collected Poems* of 1962 – and this despite the fact that the same period has seen the full scope of his work in forms other than verse become visible for the first time through Alan Riach's ongoing *Collected Works* series with Carcanet Press.

The issue of MacDiarmid's impact on subsequent poets is less easily settled than the question of the current fortunes of his reputation. Within Scotland his poetry has been a good deal more influential – where all three of the country's literary languages are concerned – than is generally acknowledged. It is difficult to imagine that the very different varieties of Scots lyricism practised by William Soutar and Sydney Goodsir Smith would have got very far without his example (though the impishly learned colloquial satires of Robert Garioch would probably have been much the same had *Sangschaw* and *A Drunk Man* never been written). Sorley MacLean observed that the procedures of his unfinished poetic sequence of the late 1930s, *An Cuilithionn*, were modelled on those of *A Drunk Man*.[5] *An Cuilithionn* opens with an apostrophe to MacDiarmid, a Gaelic translation of one of whose English lyrics provides the climax of Part V, while the sequence's Christ–Lenin contrast clearly derives from the more politically explicit among the *Muckle Toon* writings of 1931–2. Indeed some of MacLean's most famous and successful shorter poems – 'Gaoir na h-Eòrpa', for example, or 'Calbharaigh' – suggest that he took not just inspiration but much of his understanding of the structure and iconography of lyric from the compatriot of whom he observed in 1978, 'it would be difficult to convince me that his poetic equal has existed in Europe this century'.[6] (Given the topic of the present chapter, it should be mentioned that Yeats features as the other major non-Gaelic source in MacLean's *oeuvre*.) Norman MacCaig's lifelong fascination with the contents of *Sangschaw* and *Penny Wheep* is reflected in the stellar imagery and sudden shifts of perspective that characterise some of the most vivid among his own later lyrics. It is possible also to detect a continuity, albeit one that can be explained as readily in terms of shared cultural inheritance as of direct literary influence, between MacDiarmid's work and that of his currently most widely admired Scottish successor, W. S. Graham: an obsession with language and the limits of communication and an associated fear of solipsism run through both.

Internationally, MacDiarmid's impact may not have been commensurate with an achievement seen by his advocates as one of the most significant in twentieth-century poetry but it is evident at least that his work was taken notice of and, to some degree, responded to by a number of his younger contemporaries. Louis MacNeice expresses admiration for short passages from *A Drunk Man* and *The Muckle Toon* in *Modern Poetry: A Personal Essay* (1938), recording his disapproval of MacDiarmid's use of Scots and evincing no awareness of the quoted segments' contexts in longer works.[7] The poet Cecil Day Lewis and the critic John Lehmann both acknowledged the precedence in relation to the English socialist verse of the 1930s of the earliest of the *Muckle Toon* pieces, 'First Hymn to Lenin',[8] though they did so in terms that fall short of asserting that the poem actually influenced the practice of Auden and his associates, those briefly engagé practitioners denounced by their putative forerunner in 1942 for their 'continual relapses into "boy scout communism", philistine "heartiness", and emotional obscurity'.⁹ An intriguing instance of MacDiarmid's presence (or possible presence) in subsequent poetry is provided by John Berryman's *Dream Songs*, the genesis of which may be related to the lines 'Wi' burnt-oot hert and poxy face / I sall illumine a' the place', which Berryman singled out for praise in a 1956 review for *Poetry* (Chicago) of *In Memoriam James Joyce* and the very slim 1954 *Selected Poems* edited by Oliver Brown.¹⁰ The American poet was at that stage just embarking on the Dream Songs project that would eventually see the light of day in *77 Dream Songs* (1963) and *His Toy, His Dream, His Rest: 308 Dream Songs* (1969).¹¹ It is instructive to view the Dream Songs sequence as a whole – a series of what Helen Vendler has described as Freudian cartoons¹² – as an extended gloss on the quoted lines from *A Drunk Man*, and to see Berryman's Henry as a partial re-embodiment of MacDiarmid's dishevelled alcoholic visionary. MacDiarmid's long poem of 1926 is a more unitary and philosophically ambitious work than the later sequence, if in some respects a more slapdash one, but it provides a striking precedent for Berryman's juggling of high and low cultural references, intermingling of tragic and comic perspectives and general air of ludic desperation.

Where immediately contemporary poetry is concerned, though, even in Scotland MacDiarmid seems to be less than an active influence. He has disappeared from the radar of younger poets for reasons not dissimilar to those that have led to the collapse of Yeats's paradigmatic status. The impossibilist yearning, allusive swagger and relentless chivvying on the issue of nationality inseparable from much even of his most innovative poetry are qualities unlikely to recommend themselves to practitioners of an art that at its best is characterised by chastened alertness and at less than its best by the cultivation of downbeat streetwise ironies. The unevenness of MacDiarmid's output and the unfortunate fact that the weaker among his poems are more linguistically accessible than the rest of his work make him a special case, perhaps, as of course does his use of Scots rather than English, but it is true also that he has fallen victim to a general retreat from the high ground of poetic modernism. That retreat, which has been in progress for decades, is partly to be understood in terms of a humane and egalitarian repudiation of the elitist view of culture informing the work of T. S. Eliot and Ezra Pound. The clamorously prescriptive and left-wing character of MacDiarmid's response to the sense of civilisational crisis shared by many writers in the interwar period does not wholly occlude the similarities between his cultural politics and those of Yeats and the two American poets (he competes robustly with all three in expressions of contempt for the masses). Yeats observes in his introduction to *The Oxford Book of*

Modern Verse, where he has much to say about Pound's status as an exemplar of the modern, that MacDiarmid has been omitted from the discussion because he 'might have confused the story'[13] of early twentieth-century poetry told there (he nevertheless includes four lyrics by the Scottish poet in the body of the book). The editor himself, it might be objected, is no easier to accommodate in a narrative of modern verse, at least if that narrative, like the one embraced by the academy for much of the mid- and later twentieth century, is founded on the claim that Pound and Eliot effected a revolution in poetic idiom and technique. Yeats and MacDiarmid are more or less equally tangential to the Eliot-Pound 'revolution' where the elemental poetic matter of versification is concerned; though rhythmically inventive, their work largely eschews *vers libre* and displays a persistent preference for stanzaic over looser forms. (I refer here to MacDiarmid's core achievement in Scots rather than his multiply problematic post-1933 writing in English.) 'Modernism' and 'modernist' are sometimes deployed as labels conferring aesthetic or even moral value rather than as terms of taxonomical convenience. That this is particularly true of commentaries on the national literatures associated with Yeats and MacDiarmid is probably an index of anxiety on the part of Irish and Scottish critics about the standing of their native cultures in a global literary-academic economy dominated by Anglo-American perspectives. Even taxonomically, however, modernism is a slippery concept when applied to poetry. Clearly there is an anti-traditionalist trend in twentieth-century poetics that at its most pronounced involves an explicitly 'experimental' approach to form and a rejection of received modes of versification. Much of the most distinctive poetry of Pound and Eliot exemplifies the trend, even if neither of them was as radically innovative as their compatriots William Carlos Williams and e. e. cummings, who dismantled and reassembled the thematic and structural machinery of lyric in the interest of an anti-hierarchical (and characteristically cheerful) outlook. The latter poets clearly inhabit the same universe as cubists, atonal composers and other early twentieth-century artists who fractured conventional unities to highlight disrupted cultural continuities and cock a snook at the solemnities of tradition. They are, in other words, unproblematically 'modernist' poets.

Eliot's article '*Ulysses*, Order, and Myth', contributed to the November 1923 issue of *The Dial*, is sometimes taken as definitive of his, very different, variety of modernism. Significantly, Eliot sees Yeats as foundational rather than marginal to the movement identified with Joyce, Pound and himself. The essay's major argument rests on a psychological criterion – one of content rather than form – though it is couched in terminology about literary procedure. It focuses on the resort by writers of the 1920s to what it calls a 'mythical method' in order to give 'a shape and a significance to the immense panorama of futility and anarchy which is contemporary history'.[14] Eliot traces the use of the *Odyssey* in *Ulysses*, and by implication his own recruitment of fertility myths in *The Waste Land*, to the example of the Irish poet who had from such early twentieth-century poems as 'No Second Troy' through to 'Easter 1916' and a range of subsequent pieces attempted to illuminate personal and political circumstances by way of a violent juxtaposition of two orders of time – the contemporary Dublin of his own experience and the Troy of Homeric legend: 'It is a method already adumbrated by Mr Yeats, and of the need of which I believe Mr Yeats to have been the first contemporary to be conscious.'[15] Yeats's exploitation of the disjunctive relationship between the present and the past, it might be countered, is powerfully self-dramatising, and thus deeply at odds with the impersonality so valued by Joyce and Eliot. Indeed, beyond his cultivation of a hard, dry idiom in the poems of his mid-career, there is little evidence of Yeats's aesthetic (as opposed to ideational) kinship with Eliot and Pound. Occasional flourishes of anti-realist exoticism and an intermittent resort to allusion-freighted diction might be cited along with acknowledgement of the body in the Crazy Jane poems and related bawdy lyrics to demonstrate the decisively post-Victorian character of the work, but to say this is to acknowledge its modernity rather than its modernism. The poetry is so traditional in technique by the standards of *The Waste Land* and the *Cantos* that most commentators have agreed with Yeats's own naming of Blake and Shelley as his crucial forebears and treated him as a late exponent of Romanticism. (There is a conspicuous lack of consensus about the extent of his debt to the proto-modernism of French symbolism.)

MacDiarmid, at least in his work up to 1933, is as traditional a poet as Yeats where versification is concerned. He never essays the 'mythical method'. His most persistent frame of reference is provided not by Greco-Roman myth and history but by the Bible, which pervades his poetry almost as comprehensively as it does Burns's and Wordsworth's. (It does so incidentally for the most part. In the *Muckle Toon* writings, however, the scriptural echoes are systematic, the ironic citations of Genesis underpinning the ruminations on origins and the repeated references to St John's Gospel acknowledging the ultimate derivation of the Water of Life figure.) In some respects at least, MacDiarmid's poetry is considerably more responsive than Yeats's to developments in *fin-de-siècle* and early twentieth-century thought and artistic practice. The rejoicing in their own textuality of the more linguistically rebarbative among the Scots lyrics is directly (by contrast with Yeats, very directly) continuous with symbolism, while the rifling of Jamieson's *Etymological Dictionary of the Scottish Language* and other lexicographical sources for the originating impulse of some of the most dazzling of the early poems demonstrates a thoroughly modern awareness of language's function as a determinant of consciousness and of the precedence of intrinsic verbal possibility to what used to be called 'inspiration'. Imagism and expressionism are absorbed and transformed – and at some points combined – in *Sangschaw* and *Penny Wheep*, as Roderick Watson has shown.[16] The materialist apprehension of the world underlying even such apparently traditional poems as 'Crowdieknowe' breaks cover in *A Drunk Man*, where it manifests itself most obviously in explorations of the delights and indignities of corporeality – the sequence is resolutely post-Darwinian and post-Freudian in its treatment of the body. In more superficial ways, too, MacDiarmid was very much a poet of his time. His growing preference for extended and 'open' forms links him to the Pound of the *Cantos* and to such 'experimental' practitioners of the long poem as David Jones and Charles Olsen. (Indeed *In Memoriam James Joyce* and the other book-length works in English are fragmentary and collage-like in a manner that may be identified with later modernist and postmodernist practice.)

In his Preface to *Sangschaw* John Buchan observed that the contents of the volume were simultaneously revolutionary and reactionary.[17] Though unfortunate overtones have accrued to the term 'reactionary' since 1925, Buchan's comment highlights something the poet himself saw fit to advertise in 1922 when he chose the conflicting epigraphs *Not traditions, precedents!* and *Back to Dunbar!* for *The Scottish Chapbook*, the periodical with which he launched the Renaissance, and that is that his vision mixes conservative and radical elements. Where his poems, if not his politics, are concerned, his traditionalism took a form that aligns him more closely to Yeats than to perhaps any other major modern poet. R. H. Westwater's famous 1958 portrait of MacDiarmid was disliked by its subject because of its Romantic élan but the painter can be said to have identified an aspect of his friend's work and personality that can easily be missed behind his persistent striking of avant-garde poses. In literary terms, that is to say, MacDiarmid's conservatism manifested itself as Romanticism. Indeed the poet followed Yeats's lead in using nationalism to supply the optimism necessary to a romantic poetic. James Joyce was no less Irish than Yeats, and John Davidson no less Scottish than MacDiarmid, but a rationalist cast of mind rendered these writers incapable of persuading themselves that their countries were unique crucibles of the human spirit. The subjects of this essay, however, managed to convince themselves that Ireland and Scotland, in spite (or indeed because) of their abjection, were fields of unbounded possibility (the former Yeats's 'soft wax', the latter the site of MacDiarmid's hoped for 'great upwelling of the incalculable').[18] And a romantic artist needs nothing so desperately as a field of possibility. The 'reactionary' aspects of the poems of *Sangschaw* and *Penny Wheep* are supplied by predominant ballad metres, rural settings and dependence upon 'folk' materials of one sort or another – songs ('Empty Vessel'), superstitions ('Reid E'en'), archaic customs ('In Mysie's Bed', 'Morning') and proverbs and sayings (*passim*) – the very stuff of romantic lyric. A profusion of echoes and citations of Wordsworth, Coleridge, Shelley, Keats, Tennyson and Arnold in *A Drunk Man*[19] and the poetry of the early 1930s suggests that MacDiarmid's neo-Romanticism was no less English in its lineage than Yeats's, and that his poetic mentality was to a significant degree shaped by his reading in nineteenth-century canonical English verse (the staple fare of his mentor George Ogilvie's classes at the Broughton Junior Student Centre).[20] There are, by contrast, relatively few allusions to his Scottish precursors in the poetry. Even Burns features almost exclusively in the context of attacks on the Burns cult – the scathing citation of 'The Cotter's Saturday Night' in Part II of 'Tarras' via the phrase 'scenes like these' provides, I think, the only piece of textual evidence that his work formed part of the furniture of MacDiarmid's mind.

One illustration of the Scottish poet's English literary ancestry may be sufficient to make the general point. The closing paragraph of 'Dover Beach' is described as one 'of the great sea-passages in English poetry' in *Lucky Poet*, where we are told that the author knew Arnold's work before he reached his teens.[21] Long after his teens, in the early Summer of 1933 and in the midst of the crisis that marked the end of his career both as a Scots and a lyric poet, he would record his own melancholy witness to the receding of the Sea of Faith and, under a title also ending with the word 'Beach', meditate on the eternal note of sadness by way of an imagery of ocean, strand and pebbles. 'On a Raised Beach' was published in *Stony Limits and Other Poems* in 1934 (a good year for Arnold: Wallace Stevens's 'The Idea of Order at Key West', a text modelled so strictly on 'Dover Beach' that it even introduces a surprise interlocutor in its closing verse paragraph, also appeared then). While MacDiarmid's poem rewrites Arnold's agnostic monologue in the light of twentieth-century atheistic materialism, it projects its ruminations onto a higher plane and creates an intertext with one of the key works of a greater writer than Arnold by casting itself as a romantic crisis ode. The hint in the ode-like title is corroborated by the way the verse paragraphs shadow the strophes and anti-strophes of the Irregular Pindaric

Ode. In its formal being as well as its subject matter, MacDiarmid's most ambitious and sustained English poem invites consideration side by side with Wordsworth's 'Ode: Intimations of Immortality from Recollections of Early Childhood', and much of its sombre power derives from its essentially comparative insistence that the messages that can be read from the stones of the Shetland storm beach carry intimations only of mortality. The anti-human sublime that makes 'On a Raised Beach' more terrifying than any other poem by MacDiarmid has no counterpart in Wordsworth and Arnold. It has much in common, though, with the superhuman celebrated in such late lyrics by Yeats as 'Byzantium' and 'The Gyres': The two poets were extenders rather than mere inheritors of Romanticism.

The informing power of that inheritance, nevertheless, is difficult to overstate. It is instructive to compare the description of central Dublin in Yeats's 'A General Introduction for my Work' (1937) with one of the fierce denunciations of Glaswegian squalor that recur in MacDiarmid's verse in the years after he had abandoned – or had been abandoned by – lyrical poetry:

When I stand upon O'Connell Bridge in the half-light and notice that discordant architecture, all those electric signs, where modern heterogeneity has taken physical form, a vague hatred comes up out of my own dark and I am certain that wherever in Europe there are minds strong enough to lead others the same vague hatred rises; in four or five or in less generations this hatred will have issued in violence and imposed some kind of rule of kindred.[22]

Elsewhere, and also in offshore rather than mainland Europe, there was another such strong mind, and in it the same hatred rose. 'Glasgow', composed possibly as late as 1943, includes the lines:

> Where have I seen a human being looking
> As Glasgow looks this gin-clear evening – with face and fingers
> A cadaverous blue, hand-clasp slimy and cold
> As that of a corpse, finger-nails grown immeasurably long
> As they do in a grave, little white eyes, and hardly
> Any face at all? Cold, lightning-like, unpleasant, light, and blue
> Like having one's cold spots intoxicated with mescal.
> Looking down a street the houses seem
> Long pointed teeth like a ferret's over the slit
> Of a crooked unspeakable smile, like the Thracian woman's
> When Thales fell in the well, a hag
> Whose soul-gelding ugliness would chill
> To eternal chastity a cantharidized satyr ...[23]

The recoil from the chaos of urban modernity enacted by these passages is predicated on ideas of unity that ultimately derive from Coleridge.

Imagination, these protests of outraged sensibility imply, can never be sufficiently esemplastic to confer order on the incoherence of twentieth-century cultural conditions. The conflicting politics of the rightward leaning Yeats (rarely so explicitly rightward leaning as in the aspiration for an anti-democratic 'rule of kindred' indulged here) and the noisily partisan communist MacDiarmid mask an intimate kinship of outlook: revulsion from mercantile modernity was as visceral and impassioned in the one as in the other, and what the Irish poet wrote of in 'The Statues' as 'this filthy modern tide'[24] his Scottish colleague was generally content to refer to as capitalism.

Yeats and MacDiarmid knew each other's work and appear to have had good personal relations. A letter from the former congratulating the latter on having done 'many lovely and passionate things' is quoted in *Lucky Poet*[25] and MacDiarmid was one of the few poets of continuing note from his generation to be represented in *The Oxford Book of Modern Verse*. There is evidence that he read his older contemporary's writing with particular attentiveness. His first book, published under his patronymic in 1923, includes among its prose explorations of heightened states of cerebral activity the following sentence:

He was now quite certain that the imagination had some way of dealing with the truth, which the reason had not, and that commandments delivered when the body is still and the reason silent are the most binding that the souls of men can ever know.[26]

If this third-person reflection sounds almost Shelleyan in its Romanticism that is because it bears more than a passing resemblance to a first-person observation by Yeats in 'The Philosophy of Shelley's Poetry' (1902):

Since then I have observed dreams and visions very carefully, and am now certain that the imagination has some way of lighting on the truth that the reason has not, and that its commandments, delivered when the body is still and the reason silent, are the most binding we can ever know.[27]

When working on *A Drunk Man* in the mid-1920s and looking for a way to reformulate in contemporary terms that sense of despondency at the long intervals separating moments of visionary excitement so characteristic of romantic poetry, MacDiarmid again found Yeats useful. In *Per Amica Silentia Lunae* (1917) the latter had written:

I think that we who are poets and artists, not being permitted to shoot beyond the tangible, must go from desire to weariness and so to desire again, and live but for the moment when vision comes to our weariness like terrible lightning, in the humility of the brutes.[28]

The Drunk Man would in due course complain:

> We wha are poets and artists
> Move frae inklin' to inklin',
> And live for oor antrin lichtnin's
> In the haingles atweenwhiles,
>
> Laich as the feck o' mankind ...²⁹

(The meaning of the source is transformed here, perhaps most revealingly in the substitution of the lowliness of the masses for the humility of animals.) Utility, however, did not necessarily signify approval, and the Romanticism MacDiarmid drew on for his own art could be an object of scorn when availed of by another. In the course of an article in *The New Age* in July 1926 on the French philosopher Denis Saurat's collection of metaphysical dialogues, 'The Three Conventions', he poured ridicule on Yeats's recently published *A Vision* (the italics are in the original):

Compare it [Saurat's book], for example, with Teat's [sic] 'A Vision' (Werner Laurie, 63s.), with its preliminary fantasy, its exposition of the difficult geometry of *Anima Mundi*, its use of such properties as the Great Year of the Ancients, and so on. How grotesque, how far-fetched, how insanely ingenious all these esoteric properties, these paraphernalia of *romanticism*, these endless Chinese puzzle-boxes are in comparison with Saurat's simple, short sentences, devoid of technical terminology of all kinds, his lucid *classicality* of utterance.³⁰

Yet within months of issuing this rebuke he had deployed ideas, images and even phrases from *A Vision* to construct 'The Great Wheel', the 460-line tour-de-force in tetrameter triplets that brings *A Drunk Man* to its tragicomic climax. Is it uncharitable to suggest that one thing Yeats and MacDiarmid incontrovertibly and exclusively shared was an ability to create poetry out of the spurious history and dubious speculations of *A Vision*?

MacDiarmid's reading in Yeats is reflected in larger ways as well. The Rosicrucian aspect of the thistle in *A Drunk Man* probably owes a good deal to the lyrics from the 1890s arranged under the title 'The Rose' in the Irish poet's *Collected Poems*. If so, it must be said that MacDiarmid's cross is a more vivid and compelling emblem – because more materially a site of crucifixion – than Yeats's rood. With its endlessly ramifying implications and ever-changing shape, the thistle elicits from the Drunk Man perhaps the most sustained display of figurative ingenuity in modern poetry. The richest play of metaphor and symbol in MacDiarmid's subsequent development is to be found in the poems written in 1931 and 1932 for *The Muckle Toon*, an ambitious work of intellectual self-portraiture which in turn was intended to constitute the first volume of a five-volume 'epic', *Clann Albann*. Even in its scattered, incomplete form *The Muckle Toon* elaborates a cogent personal myth of evolution, creating a figurative nexus linking Langholm's rivers to the Water of Life, Noah's Flood to the rising waters of Bolshevik revolution, the Scottish Borders to the frontiers of consciousness, and the author's boyhood to the infancy of mankind. The portrayal of Langholm (its woods, hills, rivers, bridges, monuments and neighbouring uplands, as well as its traditions) here and in related Scots prose sketches and stories makes south Dumfriesshire one of the most thoroughly imagined territories in literature since the Sligo-Leitrim of the Celtic phase of Yeats's poetry. The relationship of MacDiarmid's enterprise to the poems about violence, cultural authority and ancestral houses in *The Tower* is indicated near the climax of the piece designed to inaugurate *The Muckle Toon* when the poet opens a triumphant passage on the obscurity of his own origins by contrasting his situation to that of aristocrats (and would-be aristocrats) in their portrait-hung halls: 'Great hooses keep their centuried lines complete.'[31] The poems of *The Muckle Toon* were never arranged in careful sequence like the contents of *The Tower* and *The Winding Stair*, but they are comparable to them at least in the way they comment upon and qualify one another to create a complex, overarching symbolism. They resemble Yeats's mature work also in their interest in deploying unfamiliar stanza forms – a six-line stanza of MacDiarmid's own devising in most of the major poems from 1931, a dazzling array of verse shapes, including the elaborately rhymed 24-line unit repeated ten times in 'Depth and the Chthonian Image', in the material composed the following year. More broadly, it might be said that the work of both poets throughout their careers is characterised by a dialectic between the real and the actual Ireland/Scotland, a dialectic that receives a concise formulation in 'Lament for the Great Music', MacDiarmid's only poem to approximate the Olympian tonalities of Yeats, in the stately and desolating phrase: 'This Scotland is not Scotland.'[32] However, if the poets turn out after all to have been in some senses twins, they were twins of the polar variety. The spiritualism and interest in the afterlife and in supernatural otherworlds that remained constant throughout the career of one found no echo in the ever more resolutely materialist outlook of the other. MacDiarmid's only otherworld is a future imagined in political terms. Yeats's characteristic idealism is at the furthest possible remove from the celebration of the 'scunner' of love in one of the best-known lyrics from *Penny Wheep*[33] and from the visionary apprehension of the randomness of existence in terms of bodily emissions in *A Drunk Man* and 'Harry Semen'.

In a passage near the beginning of *To Circumjack Cencrastus* (1930), the longer and far less energetic Scots sequence with which MacDiarmid followed up *A Drunk Man*, he saluted his fellow poet as follows:

> I blink at Yeats as micht a man whom some
> Foul sorcery had changed into a pig,
> At Yeats, my kingly cousin, and mind hoo
> He prophesied that Eire 'ud hae nae Burns
> (Tho' it has tried to mair than aince) but haud
> Its genius heich and lanely – and think o' Burns,
> That Langfellow in a' but leid, and hoo
> Scots since has tint his maikless vir but hains
> His cheap emotions, puir ideas, and
> Imperfect sense o' beauty, till my race
> Lack even the foetus' luck o' Smith or Broon
> (A Hobson's choice to burst nae pigskin owre)
>   Bein' a' Jock Tamson's bairns . . .[34]

This is disconsolate in its desultory way, maybe all the more disconsolate for its desultory way. MacDiarmid implies that he shares Yeats's yearning for an austere and solitary poetry but that, unlike his Irish 'cousin', he has been born into a country that cannot fulfil his spiritual and artistic needs. The lines acknowledge a fear that he would never bring his gifts fully to fruition. The well-nigh tragic contrast in chronology between the two careers shows how well founded was that fear. Though MacDiarmid was the younger by 27 years, and did not publish his first Scots collection until Yeats was 60, his life as a lyric poet was over 5 years before Yeats wrote such famous poems as 'The Circus Animals' Desertion' and 'Under Ben Bulben'. Versions even of the two most serious and achieved of his later, emphatically anti-lyrical book-length poems, *The Kind of Poetry I Want* and *In Memoriam James Joyce*, are known to have been in existence before Yeats's death. (And therefore before Joyce's – in manuscript the Joyce poem was called *In Memoriam Teofilo Folengo*, after the sixteenth-century Italian macaronic poet; the title was changed to commemorate the author of the transcendently macaronic *Finnegans Wake* when the text was reassembled and complemented by a handful of 'found' passages prior to publication in 1955, almost two decades subsequent to its original composition.) It is well known that MacDiarmid was extraordinarily prolific and uneven but it is insufficiently appreciated that practically his entire production, from the brilliantly febrile English prose sketches of *Annals of the Five Senses* through the hugely various, rapidly evolving Scots verse to the later Anglophone 'poetry of fact', coincides roughly with the period of composition of a mere three of Yeats's thirteen major individual collections, *The Tower* (1928), *The Winding Stair and Other Poems* (1933) and *Parnell's Funeral and Other Poems* (1935).

The composer F. G. Scott, MacDiarmid's former schoolteacher and his main confidant on artistic matters, appears to have been the first to recognise that his protégé's gift was under threat. He wrote to him on 28 June 1932 to warn that the standard of the *Muckle Toon* poems was beginning to slip. Complimenting him on the comic earth-hymn 'Tarras' ('C'est magnifique – the very best thing you've ever done') he drew attention to a worrying trend towards the slipshod in other pieces sent to Scott in Glasgow from the Sussex cottage where the poet was living in penury with Valda Trevlyn:

> The rag-bag and waste-paper basket won't do. It's fundamentally a lack of self-respect like a man coming on the street after being in a public lavatory with his trousers hanging down. He invites a kick i' the arse and he generally gets a few.[35]

Yeats and MacDiarmid are arguably far closer in ultimate stature than criticism, at least criticism as practised beyond Scotland, has realised. Formally and stylistically, however, Yeats never appeared in the street with his trousers down or even his flies undone, while MacDiarmid was content at many stages in his career and with alarming regularity in its later stretches to emerge from the gents of composition onto the street of the page in a disgraceful state. Yeats's undone flies do feature, however, in an autobiographical narrative by MacDiarmid, who told me in Cork in 1973 that, as the two poets walked through Dublin together in 1928 after a lemonade-soaked soiree at AE's house, Yeats was 'called to nature' and stepped into an alleyway to relieve himself: 'If he did, I crossed swords wi' him – and I had the better flow!' The competitive implication in relation to poetic prowess was unmistakable. MacDiarmid was joking, of course, and we could extend the joke by describing the episode in terms of the troubling of the living stream by the Water of Life. If he was being gleefully infantile, however, he was also being true to his philosophical outlook in presenting a vignette of the twentieth-century Anglophone world's great idealist poet sharing a private moment with its great materialist poet in conditions illustrative of the unchallengeable imperium of the body.

NOTES

1. W. B. Yeats, *The Trembling of the Veil*, in *Autobiographies* (London: Macmillan, 1955), 199.
2. Hugh MacDiarmid, 'Hammer and Thistle: An Interview with Micheál Ó hUanacháin', Radio Teilifís Éireann, 'The Arts', 23 February 1978. Collected

in Hugh MacDiarmid, *The Raucle Tongue*, Vol. 3, ed. Angus Calder, Glen Murray and Alan Riach (Manchester: Carcanet, 1998), 592.
3. See Robert Crawford, *Scotland's Books: The Penguin History of Scottish Literature* (London: Penguin, 2007); Marco Fazzini (ed.), *Alba Literaria: A History of Scottish Literature* (Venice: Amos Edizioni, 2005); Roderick Watson, *The Literature of Scotland* (Basingstoke and New York: Palgrave Macmillan, 2007), 2 vols.; and *The Edinburgh History of Scottish Literature* (Edinburgh University Press, 2007 (Vol. 1, *From Columba to the Union*, Thomas Owen Clancy and Murray Pittock, general eds.; Vol. 2, *Enlightenment, Britain and Empire*, Ian Brown, general ed.; Vol. 3, *Modern Transformations: New Identities*, Ian Brown, general ed.).
4. Two works issued in the poet's lifetime, Kenneth Buthlay's *Hugh MacDiarmid* (Edinburgh: Oliver and Boyd, 1964; revised though not improved edition, Edinburgh: Scottish Academic Press, 1982) and Edwin Morgan's Writers and Their Work pamphlet, *Hugh MacDiarmid* (Harlow: Longman, 1976), are exemplary. Also indispensable are Roderick Watson's *MacDiarmid* (Milton Keynes and Philadelphia: Open University Press, 1985) and W. N. Herbert's *To Circumjack MacDiarmid* (Oxford: Clarendon, 1992). Nancy K. Gish's *Hugh MacDiarmid: The Man and His Work* (London and Basingstoke: Macmillan, 1984) and Harvey Oxenhorne's *Elemental Things: The Poetry of Hugh MacDiarmid* (Edinburgh University Press, 1984) are the most critically alert of the other studies.
5. Sorley MacLean, 'My Relationship with the Muse', in *Ris a' Bhruthaich: Criticism and Prose Writings*, ed. William Gillies (Stornoway: Acair, 1985), 11, 12.
6. Sorley MacLean, 'Lament for the Makar', in *Ris a' Bhruthaich*, 264.
7. Louis MacNeice, *Modern Poetry: A Personal Essay* (Oxford: Clarendon, 1968 [1938]), 151, 192.
8. See Hugh MacDiarmid, *Lucky Poet: A Self-Study in Literature and Political Ideas, being the Autobiography of Hugh MacDiarmid*, 2nd edn (London: Jonathan Cape, 1972), 158, 169–70.
9. Hugh MacDiarmid, 'John Singer', in *Selected Essays*, edited with an introduction by Duncan Glen (London: Jonathan Cape, 1969), 88.
10. John Berryman, 'The Long Way to MacDiarmid', *Poetry* 88 (April 1956), 52–61.
11. The two books were amalgamated as *The Dream Songs* (New York: Farrar, Straus, and Giroux, 1969). Forty-five out of a reported several hundred uncollected Dream Songs were posthumously published in *Henry's Fate and Other Poems, 1967–1972* (New York: Farrar, Straus, and Giroux, 1977).
12. Helen Vendler, 'John Berryman: Freudian Cartoons', in *The Given and the Made: Recent American Poets* (London: Faber, 1995), 29–57.
13. W. B. Yeats (ed.), *The Oxford Book of Modern Verse, 1892–1935* (London: Oxford University Press, 1936), xli.
14. T. S. Eliot, '*Ulysses*, Order, and Myth', in *Selected Prose*, edited with an introduction by Frank Kermode (London: Faber, 1975), 175–8.

15. Eliot, *Selected Prose*, 177.
16. Watson, *MacDiarmid*, 23, 26, 28–9, 31.
17. John Buchan, 'Preface', in Hugh MacDiarmid, *Sangschaw* (Edinburgh: Blackwood, 1925), x.
18. MacDiarmid, 'The Caledonian Antisyzygy and the Gaelic Idea', in *Selected Essays*, 73.
19. Many of these are identified in the commentary on the poem in Hugh MacDiarmid, *A Drunk Man Looks at the Thistle: Annotated Edition*, ed. Kenneth Buthlay (Edinburgh: Birlinn, 2008 [1987]).
20. As reported to me by Dr Ruth McQuillan, whose mother was a student of Ogilvie's.
21. MacDiarmid, *Lucky Poet*, 57.
22. W. B. Yeats, *Essays and Introductions* (London and Basingstoke: Macmillan, 1961), 526.
23. Hugh MacDiarmid, *The Complete Poems of Hugh MacDiarmid*, ed. Michael Grieve and W. R. Aitken, Vol. 2 (Manchester: Carcanet, 1994), 1049–50.
24. W. B. Yeats, 'The Statues', in *Collected Poems* (London and Basingstoke: Macmillan, 1950), 376.
25. MacDiarmid, *Lucky Poet*, 66.
26. Hugh MacDiarmid, 'A Limelight from a Solitary Wing', in Roderick Watson and Alan Riach (eds.), *Annals of the Five Senses and Other Stories, Sketches and Plays* (Manchester: Carcanet, 1999), 88.
27. Yeats, *Essays and Introductions*, 65.
28. W. B. Yeats, *Mythologies* (London and Basingstoke: Macmillan, 1959), 340.
29. Hugh MacDiarmid, *The Complete Poems of Hugh MacDiarmid*, ed. Michael Grieve and W. R. Aitken, Vol. 1 (Manchester: Carcanet, 1993), 100.
30. C. M. Grieve, 'The Three Conventions', *The New Age*, 15 July 1926, 120.
31. MacDiarmid, 'Kinsfolk', properly called 'From *Work in Progress*', in *Complete Poems*, Vol. 2, 1150.
32. MacDiarmid, 'Lament for the Great Music', in *Complete Poems*, Vol. 1, 472.
33. MacDiarmid, 'Scunner', in *Complete Poems*, Vol. 1, 64.
34. MacDiarmid, *To Circumjack Cencrastus*, in *Complete Poems*, Vol. 1, 185.
35. F. G. Scott–MacDiarmid correspondence, Edinburgh University Library.

CHAPTER 2

Tradition and the individual editor: Professor Grierson, modernism and national poetics

Cairns Craig

When T. S. Eliot sent a copy of his *Collected Poems* to Sir Herbert Grierson,[1] it was inscribed 'to whom all English men of letters are indebted'.[2] The largest debt was to Grierson's edition of the poems of John Donne, published in 1912 when Grierson was Professor of English Literature at the University of Aberdeen. That edition made available for the first time trustworthy versions of Donne's poems and, in its introduction and notes, radically revised the value of Donne's contribution to poetry in English, presenting his work as 'a poetry of an extraordinarily arresting and haunting quality, passionate, thoughtful, and with a deep melody of its own'.[3] Grierson not only transformed Donne's historical reputation (and, by his anthology of *Metaphysical Poetry* in 1921, the estimate of much seventeenth-century poetry) but effectively encouraged Donne to be taken as the model for a properly *modern* poetry. Grierson himself put this down later to a 'reaction against the smoothness of Tennyson like the reaction against Pope by Wordsworth and others. The moderns found inspiration in the "meta-physicals" and doubtless my edition had an influence.'[4]

The real reaction, however, was against nineteenth-century conceptions of 'beauty', and what Grierson emphasised was that Donne manages to produce *poetry* without depending on *beauty*. Donne's previous critics had denied that he was

a great poet because with rare exceptions, exceptions rather of occasional lines and phrases than of whole poems, his songs and elegies lack beauty. Can poetry be at once passionate and ingenious, sincere in feeling and witty, – packed with thought, and that subtle and abstract thought, Scholastic dialectic? Can love-poetry speak a language which is impassioned and expressive but lacks beauty, is quite different from the language of Dante and Petrarch, the loveliest language that lovers ever spoke ...?[5]

Grierson's answer is that Donne's is a 'dramatic' poetry – equalled only 'by Shakespeare's sonnets and some of Drayton's later sonnets' – which 'utters the very movement and moment of passion itself'.[6] Donne's poetry, more like a novel in its virtues than traditional verse, mimics passion in a 'vivid realism'[7] that challenges the conventions of love poetry, whether of the Petrarchan tradition or Victorian era. Beyond psychological realism, however, there is in Donne something of even greater significance for the modern era – 'a new philosophy of love'.[8] Donne's conception of love, unlike Dante's or Petrarch's, does not find in the beloved a route to a higher, religious spirituality, that must leave the body behind: rather, Donne uses the 'intellectual, argumentative evolution' of the medieval love poets 'to express a temper of mind and a conception of love which are at the opposite pole from their lofty idealism',[9] one which celebrates the body rather than denying it. For Grierson, 'it is only in the fragments of Sappho, the lyrics of Catullus, and the songs of Burns that one will find the sheer joy of loving and being loved expressed in the same direct and simple language',[10] a joy which attests to a 'consciousness of the eternal significance of love, not the love that aspires after the unattainable, but the love that unites contented hearts'.[11]

To a generation coping with the loss of any religious guarantee of a transcendental ideal, Grierson's account made Donne *the* truly *modern* poet, both in style and in content – the poet of subjectivism and relativism:

> The central theme of his poetry is ever his own intense personal moods, as a lover, a friend, an analyst of his own experiences worldly and religious. His philosophy cannot unify these experiences. It is used to record the reaction of his restless and acute mind on the intense experience of the moment, to supply a reading of it in the light now of one, now of another philosophical or theological dogma or thesis caught from his multifarious reading, developed with audacious paradox or more serious intention, an expression, an illumination of that mood to himself and to his reader.[12]

Donne's poetry, in effect, anticipates the stream of consciousness novel. As Grierson wrote in his entry on Donne in *The Cambridge History of English and American Literature*, 'Donne is the most shaping and determining influence that meets us in passing from the sixteenth to the seventeenth centuries. In certain aspects of mind and training the most medieval, in temper the most modern.'[13] By bringing out the modernity of that temper, Grierson made Donne so much a modern poet that Rosemond Tuve could enquire in 1943 whether 'any introduction to a scholarly edition of an early English poet ever had more marked influence upon contemporary criticism of contemporaries than Grierson's of Donne (1912) has had upon ours'.[14]

In an essay of 1915, entitled 'The Background of English Literature', Grierson insisted that 'all great poetry is in some measure metaphysical', and that the poet is as much engaged with scientific truth as the scientist or philosopher, except that 'the poet's imagination differs from the philosopher's only in its love for the concrete, and in that it works at the dictation of feeling'.[15] In that essay, Grierson had also set out a theory of 'tradition': the poet, Grierson argued,

> is connected with his audience by other links as well as that of a common language, – by a body of common knowledge and feeling to which he may make direct or indirect allusion, confident that he will be understood, and not only this, but more or less accurately aware of the effect the allusion will produce. He knows roughly what his audience knows, and what are their prejudices. A people is made one, less by community of blood than by a common tradition.[16]

That 'common tradition' was possible because although 'nature, life and experience' together with 'science and philosophy form perhaps the most important vista in the background of literature in every era, another, and that the most shaping and colouring, is formed by literature itself'.[17] It is from the common tradition of literature that it is possible for 'the poet's words [to] waken a succession of echoes in the ear of the scholar',[18] echoes which will go all the way back to ancient Rome and Greece. That common tradition had broken down in the nineteenth century and Grierson cited Yeats as an example of the kind of modern poet who had had to create a specialised tradition of his own 'out of revived Irish legends and literature', one of those whose poetry has 'grown curious of strange, new vistas, Celtic or Indian or Chinese' and whose 'poetry has become exotic in character'.[19] When Grierson wrote this in 1915, however, Yeats was already, under the influence of Grierson's editorial work, changing both the character of his poetry and its allusive context.

Famously, it was at Herbert Grierson's home in Aberdeen on Saturday 26 January 1907 that Yeats received two telegrams, the first announcing Synge's *The Playboy of the Western World* 'a great success', the second, arriving after 1 a.m. the following day, bearing the news that 'Audience broke up in disorder at the word shift.'[20] The meeting with Grierson that weekend and the confrontation with the Dublin audience that followed it, were to be mutually defining moments in Yeats's career. Looking back on his earlier work from the perspective of 1922, Yeats was to analyse its flaws as the separation of 'subtlety' from the 'common, wayward spirited man',[21] and to judge it by comparison with Donne:

> I have felt in certain early works of my own which I have long abandoned, and here and there in the work of others of my generation, a slight, sentimental sensuality which is disagreeable, and does not exist in the work of Donne, let us say, because he, being permitted to say what he pleased, was never tempted to linger, or rather to pretend that we can linger, between spirit and sense.[22]

This is the Donne whom Yeats had discovered in the copy of Grierson's edition which the editor had sent to him on its publication in 1912, the Donne who, 'with the same intensity of feeling, and in the same abstract, dialectical, erudite strain ... emphasises the interdependence of soul and body'; the Donne for whom 'the true escape from courtly or ascetic idealism was a poetry which should do justice to love as a passion in which body and soul alike have their part, and of which there is no reason to repent'.[23] Yeats wrote to Grierson that

> I ... find that at last I can understand Donne. Your notes tell me exactly what I want to know. Poems I could not understand or could but vaguely understand are now clear and I notice that the more precise and learned the thought the greater the beauty, the passion; the intricacy and subtleties of his imagination are the lengths and depths of the furrow made by his passion. His pedantry and his obscenity – the rock and loam of his Eden – but make us the more certain that one who is but a man like us has seen God.[24]

The Donne whom Grierson offered to Yeats was a Donne who fitted with Yeats's defence of Synge against his critics in Dublin: Synge, like Donne, was the writer who challenged a world which had 'broken from the past, from the self-evident truths, from "naked beauty displayed"';[25] the writer who brought 'the imagination and speech of the country, all that poetical tradition descended from the Middle Ages, to the people of the town'.[26] The modernity of Synge's art was its recovery of that lost unity which Grierson had shown Donne to have retained 'from the Middle Ages'.

This defence of Synge as a contemporary Donne was to define key ways in which Yeats's own poetry would develop: he would no longer be afraid of 'pedantry' – of invoking his own theories about the nature of the world – because 'the more precise and learned the thought the greater the beauty, the passion'; he would not be afraid of 'obscenity' because that is what it takes to acknowledge the body as well as the spirit; and he would not be afraid to adopt into his own poetry the language of a fallen world that deserves a poet's castigation. The Dublin audience's rejection of Synge confirmed that poet and audience – as Grierson had suggested – no longer inhabited the same world. Yeats would need to construct an aesthetic not of inclusion but of opposition, a poetry that sought a higher religion than that from which he was shut out by the majority in Ireland – just as Donne, as a Catholic, had been shut out from the majority religion in England. Grierson insisted that in Donne's case 'it was not of religion he doubted but of science',[27] a view which would have spoken to Yeats's own case, as a seeker after an alternative to the materialism of Tyndall's 'Belfast address', and in the immediately following passage Grierson quotes lines from 'The Second Anniversary':

> Thou look'st through spectacles; small things seem great
> Below; But up unto the watch-towre get,
> And see all things despoyl'd of fallacies[28]

From 1912, Yeats's poetry would be the poetry of the 'watch-towre'. It was Grierson, according to Yeats, who inspired him to visit Italy in 1907,[29] where he had the vision 'of a great culture which had been sustained with patronage':

One image came to him outside Urbino, when the sight of a medieval tower reared up against a stormy sunset summoned up the vision of Ariosto's life dedicated to artistic perfection: the notion of the poet in his tower, long ago suggested by Milton and painted by Samuel Palmer, now took on a vibrant reality.[30]

The tower – Donne's 'watch-towre' – symbolised a style at once traditional and contemporary; a style which made Yeats an Irish modernist rather than an Irish Revivalist, and made him so by defining his debate with contemporary Irish society through traditional values which Donne, like the Italian Renaissance, had retained and modern Ireland had forgotten.

From that time, Yeats's art becomes one that fulfils itself in spite of its audience and its context –

> What cared Duke Ercole, that bid
> His mummers to the market-place,
> What th'onion-sellers thought or did
> So that his Plautus set the pace
> For the Italian comedies?[31]

– one which flings defiance in the face of those who do not appreciate it:

> What need you, being come to sense,
> But fumble in a greasy till
> And add the halfpence to the pence
> And prayer to shivering prayer, until
> You have dried the marrow from the bone?[32]

The aggressive mode of address, the 'low' imagery, the disruptive intrusion of grammar into metre, the adoption of colloquialisms, are the tactics Yeats had learned from Donne, particularly from the 'Satires', which Grierson regarded as 'the most interesting, and, metrically, the most irregular of the late sixteenth-century work of this kind' and parts of which Yeats might have addressed to his own townsfolk:[33]

> Sir; though (I thanke God for it) I do hate
> Perfectly all this towne, yet there's one state
> In all things so excellently best,
> That hate, toward them, breeds pitty towards the rest.
> Though Poetry indeed be such a sinne
> As I thinke that brings dearths, and Spaniards in,
> Though like the Pestilence and old fashion'd love,
> Ridlingly it catch men; and doth remove
> Never, till it be sterv'd out; yet their state
> Is poore, disarm'd, like Papists, not worth hate.[34]

Whatever its innovations, this is not, for Grierson, a poetry which defies tradition, for no poetry 'is so classical, so penetrated with the sensual, realistic, scornful tone of the Latin lyric and elegiac poets'.[35] In the Shelley who had so influenced his own early poetry, Yeats came to recognise a visionary whose symbolism had no roots in tradition, for 'the poet of essences and pure ideas must seek in the half-lights that glimmer from symbol to symbol as if to the ends of the earth, all that the epic and dramatic poet finds of mystery and shadow in the accidental circumstances of life';[36] Donne, on the other hand, was a poet rooted in European tradition, his 'metaphysical' conceits deriving from 'the subtlety and erudition of a schoolman', his 'imagery drawn from an intimate knowledge of medieval theology', his poetic styles deriving from Dante and Petrarch and from the revival of the classics.[37]

The possibilities of this new, modernist mode of traditionalism were to dominate Yeats's development in the years between 1912 and the early 1920s. They are explored, initially, in other poems in 'Responsibilities', such as 'Fallen Majesty' and 'The Cold Heaven'. In the latter, Yeats's 'ghost', like Donne's lovers' ghosts in 'The Relique', becomes physical, and as Donne's lovers had hoped to enjoy again the fulfilment which death has denied them –

> Will he not let'us alone
> And thinke that there a loving couple lies,
> Who thought that this device might be some way
> To make their souls, at the last busie day,
> Meet at this grave, and make a little stay?[38]

– so Yeats's ghost will encounter again the despair of loss that is the defining experience of his love:

> Ah! When the ghost begins to quicken,
> Confusion of the death-bed over, is it sent
> Out naked on the roads, as the books say, and stricken
> By the injustice of the skies for punishment?[39]

In the 'quickening' of the ghost, however, is also a hope – 'Vague memories, nothing but memories / But in the grave all, all, shall be renewed'[40] – that Donne's 'new philosophy of love'[41] might indeed be fulfilled, however belatedly, in the flesh:

> For though love has a spider's eye
> To find out some appropriate pain –
> Aye, though all passion's in the glance –
> For every nerve, and tests a lover
> With cruelties of Choice and Chance;
> And when at last that murder's over
> Maybe the bride-bed brings despair,
> For each an imagined image brings
> And finds a real image there;
> Yet the world ends when these two things,
> Though several, are a single light,
> When oil and wick are burned in one;
> Therefore a blessed moon last night
> Gave Sheba to her Solomon.[42]

Here Yeats's 'metaphysical' style, his deployment of the conceit of the 'spider's eye', the rapid transition through dialectical debates, are conducted, as Grierson believed Donne's were, to reveal not only 'the interdependence of soul and body',[43] and to attest to love 'brought into harmony with his whole nature, spiritual as well as physical',[44] but to celebrate marriage (Yeats married eventually in 1917 at the age of 52): 'For Dante the poet, his wife did not exist. In love of his wife Donne found the meaning and the infinite value of love.'[45] Yeats's self-fashioning from Grierson's Donne was no short-term enthusiasm: 14 years after the publication of Grierson's edition, on 21 February 1926, Yeats wrote to Grierson about his poem 'Chosen', which is part of the sequence 'A Woman Young and Old': 'I have been reading your Donne again ... especially that intoxicating "St. Lucie's Day" ... I have used the arrangement of the rhymes in the stanzas for a poem of my own, just finished.'[46] Nor was this an isolated instance, for one of the most complex poems of the sequence, 'Her Vision in the Wood', echoes Donne's 'The Second Anniversarie',[47] and another, 'A Last Confession', exploits Donne-inspired imagery in a celebration of a spiritual body still sexual after death:

> I gave what other women gave
> That stepped out of their clothes,
> But when this soul, its body off,
> Naked to naked goes,
> He it has found shall find therein
> What none other knows[48]

The radical impact of Grierson's version of Donne on Yeats's understanding of the possibilities of poetry was also to change his conception of Scotland's national poet. Initially, Yeats had aspired to Burns's relationship with his national culture – 'I do not ask even a fiftieth part of the popularity Burns has for his own people, but I would like enough to help the imagination[s] that were most keen and subtle to think of Ireland as a sacred land'[49] – but perhaps because of his inability to use dialect, he had come to judge Burns as the proponent of a popular literature disconnected from ancient traditions:

Wherever I had known some old countryman, I had heard stories and sayings that arose out of an imagination that would have understood Homer better than *The Cotter's Saturday Night* or *Highland Mary*, because it was an ancient imagination, where the sediment had found time to settle . . .[50]

Burns's was a literature 'popular and picturesque' which could only 'create a province',[51] but since, for Grierson, 'Donne does not fall far short of Burns in intensity of feeling and directness of expression',[52] Burns becomes the measure of Donne's achievement, and Donne's achievement an indication of Burns's contribution to the poetry of 'the sheer joy of loving and being loved'.[53] For Grierson, Burns's work is the touchstone of a poetry of 'gusto' and of '*joie de vivre*', of passion 'most pure and delightful'.[54] This version of Burns was to lead Yeats to identify Burns with the Synge whom the Dublin press refused to recognise as the genius of modern Irish literature and to see Burns's strength, like Synge's, as his refusal of a repressive local culture: a Scotland which 'believed itself religious, moral and gloomy' was confronted by a poet prepared to speak 'of lust and drink and drunken gaiety',[55] just as Synge's work in Ireland was 'the rushing up of the buried fire, an explosion of all that had been denied or refused'.[56] Synge and Burns were united by their ability to 'say all the people did not want to have said'.[57] Synge 'was to do for Ireland . . . what Robert Burns did for Scotland',[58] because 'when Scotland thought herself gloomy and religious, Providence restored her imaginative spontaneity by raising up Robert Burns to commend drink and the Devil'; 'Burns himself', Yeats believed, 'could not have more shocked a gathering of Scots clergy than did [Synge] our players'[59] when he was introduced to the circle of Dublin artists.

If Grierson's work transformed Yeats's conception of Scotland's major poet, it was also reshaping the understanding of Scottish literature in Scotland. Grierson emphasised the tension in Donne's work between 'the strain of dialectic, subtle play of argument and wit, erudite and fantastic;

and the strain of vivid realism';[60] a similar opposition between 'vivid realism' and the 'fantastic' became, in G. Gregory Smith's *Scottish Literature: Character and Influence* (1919), the defining element of the tradition of Scottish literature. Scottish literature is shaped on the one hand by its 'grip of fact', its 'sense of detail', its 'realism',[61] and, on the other, by its enthusiasm for 'the horns of elfland and the voices of the mountains'.[62] The characteristic tenor of Scottish poetry is, for Smith, the combination of the 'mixing of contraries',[63] the 'easy passing in Scottish literature between the natural and the supernatural',[64] producing a 'zigzag of contradictions'[65] to which Smith gave the name 'the Caledonian antisyzygy'.[66] For Smith, 'the modern Scot is all for observation or given over to dream, a realist or a fantastic'.[67] It was a characterisation adopted by Christopher Murray Grieve, recently returned from service in the war and determined to create in Scotland the 'Renaissance' which Smith saw taking place in Ireland,[68] when he invented his Scots-writing poetic alter ego, 'Hugh MacDiarmid'. To MacDiarmid Grieve attributed the antisyzygetical energy – the desire to 'aye be whaur / Extremes meet'[69] – by which Smith defined Scottish culture in general.

This connection between Donne and a Scottish vernacular modernism was implicitly acknowledged by Grieve when he asked Grierson, in 1925, to write an introduction to his first collection of poems, *Sangschaw*, and when he dedicated one of the first poems in that collection to Grierson. In the event, Grierson declined to provide an introduction,[70] claiming not to be sufficiently knowledgeable about contemporary vernacular verse but perhaps made uncomfortable by Grieve's efforts to create a distinction between himself and MacDiarmid: 'MacDiarmid's poems only partially illustrate Grieve's esoteric propaganda with regard to the Vernacular', Grieve wrote to Grierson on 12 May 1925; 'MacDiarmid is by no means committed to Grieve's position.'[71] MacDiarmid, however, was clearly deeply indebted to Grierson's version of the Metaphysicals: if Grierson suggested modern poetry required a return to Donne, Grieve insisted it was 'back to Dunbar'; if Donne represented the continuity of a tradition linking medieval to modern, then, for Grieve, Dunbar offered the same, since Dunbar's 'unique intensity of feeling' derives from 'Braid Scots' as 'a great untapped repository of the pre-Renaissance or anti-Renaissance potentialities which English has progressively foregone';[72] if part of that continuity was Donne's underlying Catholicism, then Scotland, too, had to rediscover its Catholic heritage – 'the line of hope lies partially in re-Catholization',[73] MacDiarmid insisted in 1927, having already, in 1922, published a sonnet which he claimed to be 'illustrative of neo-Catholic tendencies in contemporary

Scottish literature'.[74] If 'Metaphysical poetry' was poetry 'inspired by a philosophical conception of the universe and the role assigned to the human spirit in the great drama of existence',[75] then Grieve, through the medium of MacDiarmid, set out to create a metaphysical poetry in Scots, one which would invoke not only the religious tenor of much metaphysical poetry – the poem dedicated to Grierson is 'I Heard Christ Sing', which begins 'I heard Christ sing quile roond him danced / The twal' disciples in a ring'[76] – but which would incorporate 'the clash between the older physics and metaphysics on the one hand and the new science . . . on the other'.[77] Thus a poem like 'Empty Vessel' would link a traditional ballad character –

> I met ayont the cairney
> A lass wi' tousie hair
> Singin' till a bairnie
> That was nae langer there.

– with both a 'metaphysical' conception of earth's place in the universe and the latest scientific understanding of the nature of light as revealed by the experiments to test its 'bending', carried out in 1919 as proof of Einstein's theory of relativity:

> Wunds wi' warlds to swing
> Dinna sing sae sweet,
> The licht that bends owre a' thing
> Is less ta'en up wi't.[78]

MacDiarmid's adoption of a Scots 'metaphysical' poetics produced a rush of creative energy that saw the publication of his two early volumes of lyrics in 1925 and 1926, followed by the epic achievement of *A Drunk Man Looks at the Thistle*, also in 1926. When working on *A Drunk Man*, Grieve wrote to his former school teacher and mentor, George Ogilvie, that he was trying to recast his material 'into a series of metaphysical pictures with a definite progression',[79] a 'metaphysical' intent which was to be underlined when, in 1962, the U.S. editor of his *Collected Poems* asked for 'titles' for the sections of *A Drunk Man* to make it easier for an American audience, and MacDiarmid entitled a key, culminating section – beginning 'I tae ha'e heard Eternity' (l. 2056) – 'Metaphysical Pictures of the Thistle'.

Another of Grierson's editorial works, his edition of *The Poems of Lord Byron*, published in 1923, was to prove equally significant to Grieve's effort to recapture the qualities of a Scottishness which had been distorted by anglicisation. In a lecture published in 1920, Grierson had placed Byron not only in the line of Donne but in the line of Burns: 'Byron was masculine and passionate, as Donne and Burns had been before him';⁸⁰ and after quoting passages from *Childe Harold*, Grierson asks,

Is there any love-poetry of the romantics which vibrates with so full a life of sense and soul as these verses? Compared with it, "I arise from dreams of thee" or "A slumber did my spirit seal" are the love strains of a disembodied spirit or a rapt mystic. There is nothing like it in English poetry except some of the songs of Burns and the complex, vibrant passion, sensual and spiritual, of Donne's songs and elegies.⁸¹

Grierson's Byron, who rescues poetry from a beauty 'of things somewhat remote from life'⁸² by giving us 'life and strength, passion and virility, wit and humour',⁸³ is, for MacDiarmid, the Scottish Byron, rejected by English literature because he challenged its moral boundaries:

The failure to claim Byron for Scottish literature – the deference paid to English standards of taste in that and other 'Scottish' anthologies – is a characteristic consequence of the Anglicisation of Scotland ... The type of people who are constrained to whitewash Burns are naturally anxious to disavow Byron – whom it would be impossible to 'puritanise'. And the reason for the general dislike, misprizing and neglect of Byron in England is mainly due to the fact that he stands outwith the English literary tradition altogether. He is alien to it and not to be assimilated.⁸⁴

The spirit of Byron is the spirit of Scottish literature, because 'unlike English literature Scottish literature remains amoral – full of illimitable potentialities, unexplored, let alone unexhausted, in the Spenglerian sense'.⁸⁵ Byron, rather than Burns, is the 'nationally typical' poet: 'he answers – not to the stock conceptions, the grotesque Anglo-Scottish Kailyard travesty, of Scottish psychology – but to all the realities of our dark, difficult, unequal, and inconsistent national temper'.⁸⁶ Grieve's 'MacDiarmid', as the type of the antisyzygetical Scottish poet, is modelled on the Byron who defies existing English tradition. Grierson had described the third canto of *Childe Harold* as having 'the turbid flow of a stream of lava, choked at times with the *débris* and scoriae of imperfect phrasing and tortured rhythms, again flowing clear and strong but dark, and yet again growing incandescent in felicitous and magnificent lines and stanzas'.⁸⁷ Grieve, writing to George Bruce on 1 July 1964, seems to recollect this image in his account of his own poetic persona: 'My job, as I see it, has never been to lay a tit's egg, but to erupt like a volcano, emitting not only flame, but a lot of rubbish.'⁸⁸

In the same years in which Grieve was creating MacDiarmid's 'metaphysical' poetry, Yeats's poetry, too, had come under the influence of Grierson's Byron and, in particular, Grierson's essay on Byron included in *The Background of English Literature*, of which Grierson sent Yeats a copy in

1925. 'I am particularly indebted to you', Yeats wrote, 'for your essay on Byron.'[89] Yeats himself figures in Grierson's essay, but in a fashion Yeats may not have appreciated, since he is treated as the product of 'the romantic and Hellenic revival' which produced 'exquisite poetry', a poetry contrasted with the 'scorn and mockery, the buoyant human and splendid satire' of Byron's work, a kind of work represented in the modern world by Kipling, 'le Byron de nos jours'.[90] Grierson's essay, however, had first been published in 1920 and it is from that time that Yeats began to adopt Byron's ottava rima in some of the poems which made *The Tower* of 1928 one of his most significant individual volumes. Indeed, Byron's rhyme scheme is used in what were to become some of his most important poems – in 'Sailing to Byzantium', in the first and fourth sections of 'Meditations in Time of Civil War', in the opening section of 'Nineteen Hundred and Nineteen', and in 'Among School Children'. What Burns had sought was, for Grierson, a stanza that allowed him 'to write poetry as he talked or as he wrote racy letters to his friends';[91] it was a public, oratorical style, that of 'a poet who was also a man among men and a man of the world'[92] and which fitted the expression of those 'feelings which belong to us as "political animals", whose source and sphere is national and civic life, the love of liberty, of justice, the passion of power, the hatred of oppression'.[93] Engaged as he was in the years between 1920 and 1928 in the public events of the establishment of the Irish state, of which he was nominated a senator in December 1922, the issues which Grierson identified as important to Byron were also urgent to Yeats, but for Yeats the imperative was to find a form which could be used to link his public, political life to his private, increasingly well-defined, 'mythology', as presented in *A Vision* in 1925; a form that would capture the immediacy of the voice of the ordinary man and yet would not reject the tradition to which Grierson had assigned Yeats, and which Grierson had described as 'the record of emotions begotten in the library, begotten of overmuch reading of Elizabethan plays and Greek tragedy and lyric'.[94]

The word 'begotten' in Grierson's essay is crucial: in 'Sailing To Byzantium', Yeats set out to challenge Grierson's account of his work by creating a poem that uses Byron's stanza form in order to capture the immediacy of the voice of the public speaker – 'That is no country for old men' – but, at the same time, to revel in the value of those 'emotions begotten in the library':

> Fish, flesh, or fowl, commend all summer long
> Whatever is begotten, born, and dies.
> Caught in that sensual music all neglect
> Monuments of unageing intellect.[95]

Where Grierson attributes 'begotten' to the arts of the library, Yeats inverts that implication and attributes it to the inevitable passage of the natural world. There is no 'begetting' in the place 'of unageing intellect'. There, instead, is 'such a form as Grecian goldsmiths make', the very image which Grierson had used in characterising the tradition of the 'Romantic Revival', of which Yeats's 'Irish Revival' was a late echo: 'Was it any wonder that these masters of cunning technique, goldsmiths who could carve and chase with the art of a Benvenuto Cellini cups and chalices of antique fashion . . . were startled and indignant when commanded to do reverence to the crudities of Byron's earliest verses . . .?'[96] Grierson's image for the *artificiality* of Romantic poetry – 'a beauty of things somewhat remote from life' whose 'exquisite art . . . seems touched with decadence'[97] – is reversed by Yeats in an acknowledgment that it is precisely such 'masters of cunning technique' to which his art remains devoted:

> O sages standing in God's holy fire
> As in the gold mosaic of a wall,
> Come from the holy fire, perne in a gyre,
> And be the singing-masters of my soul.

Yeats's *masters*, those poets like goldsmiths of 'cunning technique', are encountered within the verse form of the poet who, according to Grierson, is their absolute antithesis, so that 'Sailing to Byzantium' *performs* the reintegration of Byron and Shelley, of Byron and Morris, as the twin traditions of which W. B. Yeats is now the unique inheritor. The uncertainty about how seriously Yeats intends his image of 'Byzantium', about whether his mechanical bird on 'a golden bough' is apocalyptic or comic, is inscribed in this fusion of the casual Byronic stanza with the highly wrought art that the poem celebrates. But the key terms of Yeats's poem are gathered together from Grierson's essay in order to defy Grierson's implication that Yeats is incapable of the kind of public, passionate, virile poetry which connected Byron to Burns and Donne. So where Grierson invokes Byron's representation of 'the sublimity and indifference of nature',[98] Yeats answers with 'that sensual music' of 'Whatever is begotten, born, and dies'; where Grierson proclaims the poetry that appeals to us as 'political animals',[99] Yeats responds that we are no more than 'a dying animal'; where Grierson insists that the 'appeal that the south, the Mediterranean, made to Byron . . . was that of lands where passions are more intense and more unrestrained',[100] Yeats answers with a Byzantium that rejects such passions for the 'artifice of eternity'; where Grierson attributes Byron's success to 'this strain of passionate improvisation',[101] Yeats responds with a form of 'hammered gold and gold enamelling' that is entirely bound by tradition. If Byron fulfilled his life in 'heroic action and self-control in the cause of concrete liberty and humanity',[102] Yeats's response is to seek a place of hierarchy and order where art is intended to 'keep a drowsy emperor awake'. Yeats's poem is infused with the language of Grierson's essay and at its centre – 'And therefore I have sailed the seas and come / To the holy city of Byzantium' – is an echo of a passage quoted by Grierson from Canto 3 of *Don Juan*:

> Soft hour! which wakes the wish and melts the heart
> Of those who sail the seas, on the first day
> When they from their sweet friends are torn apart.[103]

What Byron offers as the pain of a literal setting sail, Yeats transforms into a mythological departure, and what Byron presents as the passing moment of that setting sail –

> As the far bell of Vesper makes him start,
> Seeming to weep the dying day's decay[104]

– Yeats transforms into the personal decay of 'a dying animal' that is 'sick with desire', a dying animal which contrasts painfully with Byron's lovers in *Don Juan*, who live,

> As if there were no life beneath the sky
> Save theirs, and that their life could never die.[105]

In Yeats's poem, by contrast, nature is death and only artifice can give access to eternity.

'Sailing to Byzantium' is both a homage to Grierson's explication of the virtues of Byron's style and a challenge to his belief that Yeats's tradition cannot accommodate those virtues. For Grierson, the issue is between two kinds of poetry, one dominated by 'technique', one by 'inspiration'; a choice between 'art and life'. 'Sailing to Byzantium' votes for art while, at the same time, adopting the style of 'inspiration'. The terms of Grierson's essay were to haunt Yeats's poetry in the following years: in rewriting 'Sailing to Byzantium' as 'Byzantium' in 1930, Yeats returned to Grierson's essay to pick up other possibilities. Byron's image of a world of calm in which 'all was stillness save the sea-bird's cry, / And dolphin's leap'[106] becomes 'That dolphin-torn, that gong-tormented sea',[107] which also recalls Byron's everlasting sea from *Childe Harold*:

> Dark-heaving, boundless, endless, and sublime
> The image of Eternity.[108]

Grierson quotes Professor Elton to the effect that Byron's verse narrative has 'pace and energy and flame', which Grierson qualifies, because 'for flame one would be tempted to substitute fire, the dark fire of which Donne speaks, which heats but does not illuminate':[109] this Yeats transforms into

> Flames that no faggot feeds, nor steel has lit,
> Nor storm disturbs, flames begotten of flame.[110]

In the end, Yeats may have accepted rather than rejected Grierson's account of his earlier poetic self, for the famous conclusion of 'Coole Park and Ballylee, 1931', another poem that adopts Byron's favoured verse form, announces,

> We were the last romantics – chose for theme
> Traditional sanctity and loveliness.[111]

The much-quoted phrase is Yeats's contraction of Grierson's account of late nineteenth-century poetry, in which 'a sense of echoing emptiness haunts the student who turns back on much of the exquisite, exotic, sensuous craftsmanship of these last of the romantics'.[112] If the phrase in fact turned out to be false to the real nature of Yeats's poetry between 1912 and 1939 – to Yeats as the first modernist rather than the last romantic – the credit was in part due to Grierson himself, and to the challenge which his choice of tradition – the tradition of Donne, Burns and Byron – posed to the Yeats who saw himself as the inheritor of the visionary possibilities of Blake and Shelley.

Grierson's rewriting of English literature stung Yeats into an Irish modernism and reinvented Christopher Murray Grieve as Hugh MacDiarmid, the first Scottish modernist. By the impact of Grierson's *Donne*, and his *Byron*, the dominant tradition of English literature was 'undone', allowing poets who were, each in their different ways, outsiders to that tradition, to create a new modernist poetics which was not committed to the urban cosmopolitanism with which modernism is so often identified but to the recovery of a national tradition – the Anglo-Irish tradition in the case of Yeats, and 'Braid Scots' in the case of MacDiarmid – with which the nation itself had dispensed. Grierson's recuperation of Donne was the model by which poetry could recover its relationship to the past by becoming again 'in certain aspects of mind and training the most medieval' ('My mediaeval knees lack health until they bend')[113] while being at the same time 'in temper the most modern'.[114]

NOTES

1. Herbert John Clifford Grierson (1866–1960), born in Lerwick, Shetland; educated at the universities of Aberdeen and Oxford; Professor of English

Literature, University of Aberdeen, 1894–1915, and at Edinburgh, 1915–35. Made a member of the British Academy in 1923, he was knighted in 1936.
2. Quoted in the transcript of a radio interview between Grierson and Henry W. Meikle, formerly Librarian of the National Library of Scotland; Aberdeen University Historical Collections, Herbert Grierson, Letters and Papers, MS 2478/8, 10.
3. Herbert J. C. Grierson (ed.), *The Poems of John Donne, Edited from the Old Editions and Numerous Manuscripts with Introduction and Commentary*, Vol. 2 (Oxford: Clarendon, 1912), iv.
4. Aberdeen University MS 2478/8, 11.
5. Grierson (ed.), *Donne*, Vol. 22, xxxi.
6. *Ibid.*, xxxiv.
7. *Ibid.*, xxxiv.
8. *Ibid.*, xxxv.
9. *Ibid.*, xxxv.
10. *Ibid.*, xlii–xliii.
11. *Ibid.*, xlv.
12. Herbert Grierson, *The Background of English Literature, and Other Collected Essays and Addresses* (London: Chatto and Windus, 1925), 132–3; originally published as the 'Introduction' to Herbert Grierson (ed.), *Metaphysical Lyrics and Poems of the Seventeenth Century: Donne to Butler* (Oxford: Clarendon, 1921).
13. Herbert Grierson, 'John Donne', in A. W. Ward and A. R. Waller (eds.), *The Cambridge History of English and American Literature: Prose and Poetry from Sir Thomas North to Michael Drayton*, Vol. 4 (Cambridge, 1909), Ch. IX, 198.
14. Rosemond Tuve, 'A Critical Survey of Scholarship in the Field of English Literature of the Renaissance', *Studies in Philology* 40:2 (April 1943), 204–55, 250.
15. Grierson, *Background of English Literature*, 6–7.
16. Grierson, *Background of English Literature*, 3. This is probably the source of T. S. Eliot's essay of 1919, 'Tradition and the Individual Talent'.
17. *Ibid.*, 12.
18. *Ibid.*, 13.
19. Grierson, *Background of English Literature*, 34.
20. W. B. Yeats, *Essays and Introductions* (London: Macmillan, 1961), 311.
21. *Ibid.*, 296.
22. W. B. Yeats, *Autobiographies* (London: Macmillan, 1955), 326.
23. Grierson (ed.), *Donne*, Vol. 2, xlvi–xlvii.
24. Allan Wade, *The Letters of W. B. Yeats* (London: Rupert Hart-Davis, 1954), 570.
25. Yeats, 'The Death of Synge', *Autobiographies*, 514.
26. Yeats, 'The Bounty of Sweden', *ibid.*, 570.
27. Grierson (ed.), *Donne*, Vol. 2, xxviii.
28. *Ibid.*, xxix.
29. R. F. Foster, *W. B. Yeats, A Life: The Apprentice Mage, 1865–1914*, Vol. 1 (Oxford University Press, 1998), 367.
30. *Ibid.*, 369.

31. W. B. Yeats, 'To a Wealthy Man who Promised a Second Subscription ...' in *Collected Poems* (London: Macmillan, 1965), 119.
32. Yeats, 'September 1913', *ibid.*, 120.
33. Professor Saintsbury (gen. ed.), *Periods of European Literature*, Vol. 7, Herbert J. C. Grierson, *The First Half of the Seventeenth Century* (Edinburgh, London: Blackwood, 1906), 155.
34. 'Satyre II', in Grierson (ed.), *Donne*, Vol. 1, 149.
35. *Ibid.*, Vol. 2, xxxix.
36. Yeats, 'The Philosophy of Shelley's Poetry', *Essays and Introductions*, 87.
37. Grierson, *First Half of the Seventeenth Century*, 156–7.
38. Grierson (ed.), *Donne*, Vol. 1, 62.
39. Yeats, 'The Cold Heaven', *Collected Poems*, 140.
40. Yeats, 'Broken Dreams', *ibid.*, 173.
41. Grierson (ed.), *Donne*, Vol. 2, xxxv.
42. Yeats, 'Solomon and the Witch', *Collected Poems*, 199.
43. Grierson (ed.), *Donne*, Vol. 2, xlvii.
44. *Ibid.*, xlvi.
45. *Ibid.*
46. Quoted in Helen Vendler, *Our Secret Discipline: Yeats and Lyric Form* (Oxford University Press, 2007), 410.
47. T. R. Henn, *The Lonely Tower: Studies in the Poetry of W. B. Yeats* (London: Methuen, 1965 [1950]), 315–16.
48. Yeats, 'A Last Confession', *Collected Poems*, 314.
49. W. B. Yeats, 'To John Quinn, 28 June 1903', in John Kelly and Ronald Schuchard (eds.), *The Collected Letters of W. B. Yeats*, Vol. 3 (Oxford: Clarendon, 1994), 389.
50. Yeats, 'Poetry and Tradition', *Essays and Introductions*, 250.
51. Yeats, 'J. M. Synge and the Ireland of his Times', *Ibid.*, 341.
52. Grierson (ed.), *Donne*, Vol. 2, xliii.
53. *Ibid.*, xlii–xliii.
54. Grierson, *First Half of the Seventeenth Century*, 146–7.
55. Yeats, 'The Death of Synge', *Autobiographies*, 520.
56. *Ibid.*
57. *Ibid.*
58. Yeats, 'The Bounty of Sweden', *Ibid.*, 567.
59. *Ibid.*, 567–8.
60. Grierson (ed.), *Donne*, Vol. 2, xxxiv.
61. G. Gregory Smith, *Scottish Literature: Character and Influence* (London: Macmillan, 1919), 5.
62. *Ibid.*, 19.
63. *Ibid.*, 34.
64. *Ibid.*, 36.
65. *Ibid.*, 4.
66. *Ibid.*, 4.
67. *Ibid.*, 279.

68. *Ibid.*, 278; this is perhaps the first use of the term 'Renaissance' in relation to Ireland and Scotland's shared national self-assertion in literature in the early part of the twentieth century.
69. Hugh MacDiarmid, *Complete Poems*, Vol. 1 (London: Martin Brian & O'Keeffe, 1978), 87, lines 141–2.
70. Alan Bold, *MacDiarmid: Christopher Murray Grieve: A Critical Biography* (London: John Murray, 1988), 160–1. John Buchan responded favourably.
71. Quoted in Bold, *MacDiarmid*, 160.
72. Alan Bold (ed.), *The Thistle Rises: An Anthology of Poetry and Prose* (London: Hamish Hamilton, 1984), 144; from *Albyn* (1927).
73. *Ibid.*, 146.
74. Hugh MacDiarmid, *The Scottish Chapbook*, Vol. 1, 3 (October 1922), 74.
75. Grierson (ed.), *Metaphysical Lyrics*, xiii.
76. Hugh MacDiarmid, *Complete Poems*, Vol. 1, 18.
77. Grierson (ed.), *Metaphysical Lyrics*, xiv.
78. MacDiarmid, *Complete Poems*, Vol. 1, 66.
79. Kenneth Buthlay (ed.), *Hugh MacDiarmid: A Drunk Man Looks at the Thistle* (Edinburgh: Scottish Academic Press, 1987), xii.
80. Grierson, 'Lord Byron: Arnold and Swinburne', *Background of English Literature*, 78.
81. *Ibid.*, 101.
82. *Ibid.*, 73.
83. *Ibid.*, 74.
84. Hugh MacDiarmid, 'The Neglect of Byron', in Angus Calder, Glen Murray and Alan Riach (eds.), *Hugh MacDiarmid: The Raucle Tongue: Hitherto Uncollected Prose*, Vol. 1 (Manchester: Carcanet, 1996), 76. Grieve is here commenting on an essay in *Edinburgh Review*, Vol. 234, No. 478 (October 1921), 331–46, on 'Byron in England' by Professor J. A. Strahan, which is a review of *Astarte*, by the late Earl of Lovelace, containing letters by Byron's sister Augusta, with which Lovelace tried to confirm the suspicions of Byron's relationship with his sister. Byron, however, was much discussed in this period because of the centenary of his death in 1824, and Grieve (under the pseudonym 'Isobel Guthrie') reviewed three books on Byron in May 1924, in which he wrote that 'Professor Grierson's essay is by a long way the best on Byron that his centenary has evoked' (Calder *et al.* (eds.), *Raucle Tongue*, Vol. 1, 206).
85. *Ibid.*, 77.
86. *Ibid.*
87. Grierson, 'Lord Byron: Arnold and Swinburne', *Background of English Literature*, 92.
88. Quoted in Bold (ed.), *The Thistle Rises*, xiii.
89. 4 February 1926; Kelly and Schuchard (eds.), *Letters of W. B. Yeats*, 710.
90. Grierson, 'Lord Byron: Arnold and Swinburne', *Background of English Literature*, 75–6. The relationship between Grierson and Yeats is discussed by Steven Matthews in 'Yeats's "Passionate Improvisations": Grierson, Eliot

and the Byronic Integration of Yeats's Later Poetry', *English* 49 (Summer 2000), 127–41.
91. Grierson, *Background of English Literature*, 86.
92. *Ibid.*, 85
93. *Ibid.*, 87.
94. *Ibid.*, 72.
95. Yeats, *Collected Poems*, 217.
96. Grierson, *Background of English Literature*, 72.
97. *Ibid.*, 73–4.
98. *Ibid.*, 75.
99. *Ibid.*, 87.
100. *Ibid.*, 81.
101. *Ibid.*, 84.
102. *Ibid.*, 94.
103. *Ibid.*, 97.
104. *Ibid.*
105. *Ibid.*, 100.
106. *Ibid.*, 99.
107. Yeats, *Collected Poems*, 280.
108. Grierson, 'Byron and English Society', *Background of English Literature*, 182.
109. Grierson, *Background of English Literature*, 83–4.
110. Yeats, *Collected Poems*, 281.
111. *Ibid.*, 276.
112. Grierson, *Background of English Literature*, 111.
113. Yeats, 'The Municipal Gallery Revisited', *Collected Poems*, 369.
114. Grierson, 'John Donne', *The Cambridge History of English and American Literature*, Vol. 4, 198.

CHAPTER 3

Louis MacNeice among the islands

John Kerrigan

On 1 January 1950, Louis MacNeice arrived in Athens as Director of the British Institute. It was one those 'new beginnings' that his creativity needed.[1] Behind him lay years of distraction at the BBC and months of silence as a poet. Ahead lay the challenge he had set himself in the dedication to *Collected Poems* (1949) of looking beyond the dazzle of life and finding the past buried in the present. At first, he threw himself into arranging cultural events. He set up a poetry reading that was memorable for 'his harsh, nasal rendering of "Bagpipe Music"' (his poem from 1937) and took part in a production of Synge's *Playboy of the Western World*.[2] Gradually, however, he put his British and Irish involvements into perspective by exploring Athens and the islands: Hydra, Ikaria, Crete. These places and their pasts went into the poetic sequence that was the major product of his stay in Greece. In *Ten Burnt Offerings* (1952) we read about the Areopagus and Odysseus' Ithaca, as well as Connemara and colonial Madras.

The most extraordinary poem in the sequence – lexically and metrically, at least – deals with the death of Byron during the Greek War of Independence. After visiting the dreary coast where Byron died, MacNeice wrote to a friend: 'There are some Victorian-Romantic (v. bad) canvasses in Missolonghi Town Hall featuring highly combustive battles with Ibrahim Pasha on a white horse rampant doing the King Billy act.'[3] Yet if Missolonghi reminded him of Ireland, the title of the poem points in another, related direction, because 'Cock o' the North' was a nickname associated with Byron's Scottish family, the Gordons, and the title of a pipe tune frequently played by Scottish regiments. Hence the vigorous, skirling start of the poem, in long-lined fours and threes like the 'Bagpipe Music' read in Athens, a travesty of the hexameter calculated to mock classical heroics: 'Bad Lord Byron went to the firing, helmet and dogs and all . . .'[4] And hence the Scottishness that comes to dominate the virtuosic farrago of Greek myth, satire and biography that makes up 'Cock o' the North'. Byron's 'tartan' may be 'faded', but the poem ends with a long monologue for him in braid Scots:

> Bards wha hae for Hellas bled –
> Oh Meleager, ah Meleager –
> Anemones flourin' frae your blude
> When twa white queens focht owre ye!
> Christ is wax, Adonis wax –
> Oh Cythereia, ah Cythereia!
> The dumb tongues o' the candle wicks
> Haud ne'er a hint o' harvest.
> A far cry here frae Aberdeen –
> Mither! Mither! Wae the Gordons! . . .

Even when we factor in what this essay will establish – MacNeice's longstanding interest in Scottish culture – this passage remains surprising. For although it is now common enough[5] to notice Byron's Aberdeen childhood and repeated use of Scottish subject matter, this sort of recognition was rare in 1950. What prompted MacNeice? Perhaps he was simply alerted by the lines from *Don Juan* that 'Cock o' the North' uses as an epigraph: 'But I am half a Scot by birth, and bred / A whole one, and my heart flies to my head . . .'[6] More likely he remembered T. S. Eliot's remarks on Byron as a Scottish poet in a 1937 lecture (a year to conjure with in this chapter).[7] That Byron is given Scots, however, makes it likeliest of all that the incitement came from Hugh MacDiarmid. He had been pushing Byron's Scottish credentials since the early 1920s,[8] and he restated the case, with an approving nod at Eliot, in his *Golden Treasury of Scottish Poetry*,[9] which MacNeice reviewed in 1941.[10]

This review shows MacNeice taking stock of the Scottish Renaissance and siding with MacDiarmid in his argument with Edwin Muir about Scots.[11] 'I would agree', he declares, 'that Scots is a better medium than English for Scottish poets.'[12] 'Cock o' the North' out-Hughs MacDiarmid by giving Byron, who, MacDiarmid acknowledges, became a Scottish poet of European significance while writing in English, Burnsian Scots. That it also takes from the ballad 'Edward' – one of the choices in the *Treasury* that MacNeice praised – the refrain, 'Mither! Mither!' supports the contention that 'Cock o' the North' has MacDiarmid behind it, but on MacNeice's own, maternally obsessed terms. (He lost his mother when he was young, and in some sense never recovered.) To grasp this is to see MacNeice in a new Irish–Scottish perspective, to understand more readily why he chose, in 1937, to make two trips to the Hebrides, writing about them in *I Crossed the Minch* (1938), and why those islands figure in more displaced and fabulated forms in his later work, through to the radio play *The Mad Islands* (1962).

MACNEICE AND THE SCOTTISH RENAISSANCE

For a long time read as a 'thirties poet', part of the Oxbridge network mocked by Roy Campbell as 'MacSpaunday', and more recently cast as an 'Ulster' precursor of Derek Mahon, Michael Longley and Paul Muldoon, MacNeice had a complex make-up which evidently included a Scottish aspect. Even as a child, the pull of Scotland was felt. He was brought up among what he called 'hybrid Ulster Scots'[13] and heard in the 'Scotch Quarter' of Carrickfergus something like the dialect he gave Byron. As his autobiography, *The Strings are False*, tells us, childhood holidays in Wales and the west of Ireland were matched by visits to Scotland. After the breakup of his first marriage, in 1935, he went to Edinburgh to interview a Scottish nanny for his son. 'I was seen off on my midnight train to Birmingham by a Scottish Nationalist young man who was holding in his hand a glass of brandy. We drank perdition to the British Empire and smashed the glass on the platform.'[14] It was a connection that MacNeice kept up, beyond 'Cock o' the North', moving in the same circles as MacDiarmid and Norman MacCaig, partly under the wing of his friend from the 1930s, the broadcaster and Gaelic translator Hector MacIver.[15]

His involvement with Scottish culture was not just the by-product of his upbringing but active and critical. This has been overlooked not least because the book in which it is made most explicit, *I Crossed the Minch*, was for decades out of print. Symptomatically, the first article that he published as an undergraduate at Oxford – his father had wanted him to go to Glasgow[16] – was a review of Hugh MacDiarmid's *A Drunk Man Looks at the Thistle*. This piece, which appeared in *Cherwell* in March 1927, was written at a time when MacDiarmid was almost unknown in England. It perceptively compares *A Drunk Man* with *Ulysses*, and praises, with a hint of reservation, its Lallans:

His artificial use of Scots dialect is nearly as powerful as Mr Eliot's 'elegant bombast used sincerely,' and can be very beautiful –

> But ilka evenin' fey and fremt
> (Is it a dream nae wauk'nin' proves?)
> As to a trystin'-place undreamt,
> A silken leddy darkly moves . . .[17]

That the phrase 'elegant bombast used sincerely' was lifted from Edwin Muir's critique of Eliot in his *Transition* (1926)[18] shows that, even as an undergraduate, MacNeice was reading the two most prominent Scottish advocates of modernism. His interest in both was kept up. In an early reviewing career that mixed such Scottish books as *Duncan Dewar's Accounts*[19] with pieces about Yeats and Synge,[20] his 1934 notice of Muir's *Variations on a Time Theme* stands out not just for its insight but its scrutiny of MacNeice's emerging preoccupation with 'worldliness' and the tragedy of 'time'.[21] MacNeice was still talking about Muir's thirties poetry – with more sympathy for his parabolic manner – in the Clark lectures of 1962.[22]

Muir and MacDiarmid, initially allies in the use of Scots, were by now parting company. In *Scott and Scotland* (1936), Muir argued that Scots was the dialect of childhood, a source of division and weakness where literary maturity requires 'a whole language'.[23] Given the minority status of Gaelic, Scottish writers should use English. MacDiarmid was already doing so for reasons of his own, but he was appalled by Muir's apostasy. In thrashing out the issues, both appealed to the precedent set by Yeats and the Irish Revival. For Muir, 'Ireland produced a national literature not by clinging to Irish dialect, but by adopting English and making it into a language fit for all its purposes. The poetry of Mr Yeats belongs to English literature, but no one would deny that it belongs to Irish literature pre-eminently and essentially' (179). MacDiarmid replied that Yeats's achievement was bound up with a cultural nationalism committed to indigenous language. No Yeats without the Gaelic League.[24]

This appeal to Ireland is typical of the Scottish Renaissance, especially for such participants as MacDiarmid and Compton Mackenzie who were active in nationalist politics. They saw in the Free State a template for Scottish independence, and in the role of poets in the Irish struggle an attractive model for themselves. Admiring James Connolly and John MacLean ('Scots steel tempered wi' Irish fire / Is the weapon that I desire'),[25] MacDiarmid hoped for the establishment of a string of Celtic Soviet republics from Scotland to Brittany.[26] Mackenzie, a nostalgic Jacobite, harked back to the old ways of Irish and Scottish Gaeldom, and discussed, unsatisfactorily, an alliance with De Valera.[27] In 1930 he and MacDiarmid attracted the attention of the Special Branch because of their involvement in Clan Albainn, a shadowy organisation inspired by Sinn Fein and the Irish Republican Brotherhood.[28]

It would be rewarding to explore the blocks and detours in MacNeice's response to MacDiarmid, from 'Poetry To-day' (1935), in which he calls his writing 'reactionary nationalist'[29] – a few months before the Communist Party expelled MacDiarmid for 'nationalist deviationism'[30] – through *Modern Poetry* (1938), in which he questions, however temporarily, the viability of his Scots.[31] I must fast forward, however, and establish the point that MacNeice was peculiarly qualified to test the claims and achievements of the Scottish Renaissance because, like Muir and MacDiarmid, though with on-the-ground experience, he knew about Yeats and the Revival. The hints of Irish cultural politics that show up around 'Cock o' the North' are commonly to be found when MacNeice reflects on Scotland. This was the product of a trajectory very different from that of Auden, Spender and even Day Lewis (who had his own claims to Anglo-Irishness). It led MacNeice to publish the first critical book on *The Poetry of W. B. Yeats* in the same year that he reviewed *The Golden Treasury*. MacDiarmid read William Soutar's copy, with surprised appreciation, later in 1941.[32]

So when MacDiarmid writes in the *Treasury* 'Mr Yeats returned to the Upanishads and commended these to the attention of our younger poets. That movement back to the ancient Gaelic classics and then North to Iceland and then East to Persia and India is the course the refluence of Gaelic genius must take',[33] MacNeice can decisively reply: 'Yes, Mr Yeats did return to the Upanishads and he got away with it, but we don't all have to go to Birmingham by way of *Shangri-La*.' Yet the impression is of knowledge deployed to discriminate, not destroy. And he is certainly not willing to dismiss the notion of 'Gaelic genius'. Finding common ground with MacDiarmid, he says: 'if people expect from the Scots what they insist on expecting from the Irish – a lot of loose blether and mist, they have only to read this book to be healthily disappointed'.[34]

The Hebrides were highly charged in all this. First, because, for Scottish Nationalists like MacDiarmid, they represented cultural purity, 'undefiled' by anglicisation and industry.[35] Second, they were insular exemplars of what separation from England could achieve. Yet their insularity was qualified, especially for those who had pro-Catholic and/or Gaelicising leanings, because they constituted a land-and-sea bridge in a Celtic zone that ran between the Highlands and Donegal, ran on, indeed, to Aran and the Blaskets, Irish equivalents of the Western Isles, as culturally and symbolically important to the Revival as the Hebrides were to the Scottish Renaissance. Finally, because of the above, the Scottish islands, and the Hebrides in particular, became a magnet for leaders of the Renaissance, places where they lived, which they wrote about with passion, and made the basis of their vision of Scotland.

What drew MacNeice to the islands, both physically in 1937 and imaginatively thereafter, had enough points of contact with all this for the differences to be productive. He is preoccupied in *I Crossed the Minch* with the question of how far the Hebrides had, and could, resist anglicisation and commercialisation, the two forces striking him as inextricable. He was fascinated by the insularity which made the islands exemplars (he agreed) of independence. And they were tied for him genealogically and experientially, as well as culturally and symbolically, to the islands off the west of Ireland. As he travelled towards them for the first time, he tells us in *Minch*, he remembered Omey off the coast of Co. Galway, where his father lived until the age of 9.[36] On Barra he recalled Achill (Co. Mayo), where he went with his first wife, his father and stepmother in 1929 (156). And again, at a dance on Lewis he thinks of Synge's Aran but adds 'There was nothing very *folk* or peasant' about it, 'none of Synge's hobnailed boots chasing girls' naked feet' (207). The observation is given point by MacNeice's awareness of the culturally given but also ideologically loaded association between these islands in the west. It was a conjunction which he could develop more inventively in his later, fabulating mode. By the time we get to *The Mad Islands*, the Irish and Scottish islands have fused at the level of parable.

That the Hebrides were inhabited and articulated in writing by leading participants in the Scottish Renaissance made them a potent, emblematic platform on which to stage an encounter with MacDiarmid, Eric Linklater and Compton Mackenzie. Even as MacNeice did this in *Minch*, however, he was showing more affinity than difference, for all these men were outsiders in the islands. Mackenzie was born in Co. Durham and educated at St Paul's and Oxford. During the mid-1930s he lived on Barra, but, as the model for D. H. Lawrence's 'man who loved islands', this was only the latest of his insular homes (Capri, Herm, Jethou, the Shiants), and he would soon return to London. MacDiarmid hailed from the Borders. After working in south Wales, Montrose, London and Liverpool he went to the Shetlands in 1933 and was based there for almost a decade. Though he came to think of the Hebrides as a more congenial locus,[37] he was only a visitor there, staying with Mackenzie on Barra – as Linklater also did several times – a few weeks after MacNeice passed through, while researching his own book on *The Islands of Scotland* (1939). He had just been to Skye, to visit Sorley MacLean, who was providing literal translations of Gaelic poetry that would end up, adapted by MacDiarmid, in *The Golden Treasury*.

As for MacNeice, he reached the Hebrides from St Pancras via Oban, not to mention via Marlborough and Oxford, and he brought along with him, in *Minch*, a couple of invented alter egos, Perceval and Crowder, who reek of literary London. 'Hoping to find that blood was thicker than ink', as he declares on the first page of the book, 'that the Celt in me would be drawn to the surface by the magnetism of his fellows', he often felt cut off, not least by his lack of Gaelic. Even as he admits, however, that his hope had been 'sentimental and futile', he insists on 'the Celt in me'.[38] One thinks of Alasdair Macdonald's 'Birlinn Chlann Raghnaill' ('The Manning of the

Birlinn'), which is quoted appreciatively in *Minch* from a nineteenth-century translation,[39] and made much of in the *Treasury*.[40] It describes a turbulent sea crossing between South Uist and – Carrickfergus. An epic adventure, but a short span. That MacNeice was in some sense closer to the Hebrides than were MacDiarmid or Mackenzie not just in his west of Ireland origins but his Carrickfergus boyhood helps makes his encounter with the Scottish Renaissance in *Minch* intimately critical.

I CROSSED THE MINCH

I Crossed the Minch is a loose assemblage of journals, poems, 'potted history', dialogues and parodies, plus a satirical letter. It includes drawings done by MacNeice's companion on his first, April trip – though she is nowhere mentioned in his text – Nancy Sharp. More of her later. MacNeice's motives for producing this 'potboiler' (125) were partly financial, but he thought it would be 'money for jam'[41] because he was heading into issues that he already knew something about, though he could not, as time would show, either resolve them or shake them off readily. What made the task look easier was the existence of a genre. I agree with Tom Herron, its recent editor, that *Minch* belongs to an interwar vogue for books about the islands.[42] Like Muir's *Scottish Journey* and MacDiarmid's *Islands of Scotland*, however, it breaks with the Celtic Twilight and deals with socio-economic realities.[43] Nor were the Hebrides, at this date, a tourist destination.[44] When MacNeice leaves St Pancras with a kit bag, he is not just 'pretending to be tough' (15), as Perceval unsympathetically puts it, but looking for the hard, stimulating discomfort he had found in Iceland with Auden. He did find plenty of that, monotonous food, bare lodgings, and so on – as well as irritating evidence of luxury – across the Minch. But his adventures triggered a deeper, more obscure unease as they turned into a search for who knows what; something to do with love. Those aspects of *Minch* would only become explicit when he revisited the scenario in *The Mad Islands*.

Every good quest needs shape within the randomness of among and between. In the case of *Minch* this was provided by a coincidence between history and geography. Following the advice of Hector MacIver, MacNeice first travelled north to south, starting up in Lewis before visiting Harris and North Uist. This took him from anglicised Stornoway, where Lord Leverhulme had tried to set up a canning factory[45] – an enterprise mocked by MacNeice in a sparkling, comic poem – through rural Gaelic communities, where the people lived in black houses full of peat smoke, on crofting, fishing and the dole, until, in South Uist and Barra, he got beyond not only modernity but the Reformation.⁴⁶ On Barra, they still believed in fairies, selchies (men and women turned into seals) and what a later visitor called 'the entire gamut of Celtic folklore and belief'.⁴⁷ This was the idealised heartland of Gaelicising nationalism, which MacDiarmid described as 'the island that gives me the most complete sense not only of passing into a spiritual climate of its own ... but is like being in a different world altogether'.⁴⁸

On his second tour, in July, MacNeice retraced his steps. After stopping off at Coll, he paused again in Barra, stifled by familiarity and even more counter-suggestible than on his first visit, before advancing through Vatersay, Harris and Scalpay and returning, through rural Lewis, to Stornoway. There *Minch* comes to a climax in the clash, and ultimately the confusion, between Gaelic culture and anglicising modernity. If Barra, on the April visit, was, as I believe, the place where MacNeice's general poem about the Hebrides, 'On those Islands', began to stir, it was Stornoway at the end of the second visit that whipped up 'Bagpipe Music', the great achievement of the book and one of the best things he ever wrote. Like most of the verse in *Minch*, both these poems are in Part II of the book. Part I moves rather purposefully towards MacNeice's encounter with the Renaissance on Barra.

Ahead of that, though written with hindsight, is an 'Introductory' chapter that grapples with nationalism. 'Many people in the Outer Islands are Scottish Nationalists', MacNeice observes,

I have always laughed at Scottish Nationalism as a precious affectation of bright young men with a distaste for real politics, but in the islands the concept has more meaning than it has in Edinburgh. Scotland as a whole will never regain a vital self-consciousness of her unity and individuality, but such a thing is still just possible for the Gaelic-speaking islands as a group in separation from the mainland. Their traditional language needs no artificial cultivation, their population is small enough to allow of a genuine community feeling, their social life is still homogeneous (though commercialisation may soon drive rifts through it), lastly the sea still separates them from their neighbours:

ἔστιν θάλασσα, τίς δέ νιν καταβέσει; ... (10)

The Greek is from Aeschylus' *Agamemnon*: 'There is the sea, and who shall drain it dry?' as MacNeice translated it in 1936.⁴⁹ But how far does the inexhaustibility of the sea help the nationalist cause? Nationalism might seem tenable on the islands but Scotland as a whole will not recover self-conscious unity. In practice, this is not far from the views of MacDiarmid and Mackenzie who had lost hope, by 1937, as Mackenzie later in the book tells MacNeice, of a revolutionary transformation in the status of Scotland, though both found encouragement in the Hebrides: MacDiarmid saw in the self-sufficiency of the Faroes a model for the rest of the islands,[50] and in the potential separatism of the islands a model for Scottish nationhood which was not based in unity at all.

MacNeice goes on in *I Crossed the Minch*:

> Nationalism of the Irish type is often regarded as reactionary. With the World Revolution and the Classless Society waiting for the midwife, why take a torch to the stable to assist at the birth of a puppy? Even if the puppy is pedigree. On this question I am unable to make up my mind. When I am in Ireland I find myself becoming Nationalist. If I lived in the Hebrides, I should certainly plump for the puppy. (10)

Just what is the puppy? It seems to slip from being the Hebrides to something more like Scotland. Encouraged, like Mackenzie and MacDiarmid, by the example of Ireland, by the experience of living there, MacNeice now seems to be saying that if he lived on the islands he would want Scottish independence. As to whether nationalism is reactionary, there is more uncertainty about that now than there was in 'Poetry To-day'. The emphasis placed in this introduction on the value of the individual and small communities, as against 'Collective Man' and 'the Highest Common Factor', is redolent of MacNeice's liberalism in the face of his contemporaries' agitprop. Yet the form his argument takes is not of the Left v. Right, or Liberal v. Communist sort that would slot into the debates in England.

On the one hand it develops along lines that are surprisingly compatible with those pursued by Compton Mackenzie in his celebrated address as Rector of Glasgow University, where he presents nationalism as benignly reactionary, a temporary ebb in the tide (reinforcing of individuality and community) that is carrying us towards a world state.[51] On the other, it chimes with MacDiarmid, thanks to MacNeice's invocation of Lenin as someone who 'saw clearly that differentiation is necessary' and his observation that 'The Soviet Union, I am told, encourages the maintenance of local traditions and culture though in subservience to the new order. Such is the proper programme for historical development.'[52] If this sounds like squaring the political circle, it probably did not seem so at the time. Mackenzie the Jacobite and Comrade MacDiarmid had enough in common to work together.[53]

No one could say that *Minch* is a systematic treatise. Perhaps it reveals more about MacNeice, though, for being immediate and sometimes flippant. We can gather, from how he makes jokes in the body of the book at the expense of what he had conceded to nationalism in his introduction, where his tolerances lay, and what he was willing to slight. Certainly when, towards the end of the first trip, he gets to Barra, he mocks Scottish Nationalist writers for their trivial-yet-dangerous secessionism and implies that they cash in on their politics. At this point his political scepticism was too easily seduced by a desire to lighten his prose. MacDiarmid was living in poverty; Mackenzie was deep in debt, as he worked on his British-and-Irish sequence of novels, *The Four Winds of Love*; only Linklater was doing nicely.[54]

Once MacNeice closes in on his targets, however, his paradoxes cannot be read as simply mocking the Renaissance because they are themselves structured by G. Gregory Smith's thesis of the Caledonian antisyzygy, made much of by Muir and MacDiarmid:[55]

> The three Scottish lions . . . are now couchant on their islands. Being good Scots they do not suffer from self-consistency. (The Scots as a race are a Hegelian marriage of opposites – aggressive and shy, ungracious and hospitable, prudish and bawdy, sentimental and practical.) Take Christopher Grieve (Hugh M'Diarmid) of the Shetlands, who writes poems in English while swearing that no good ever came out of England and gives a salaam to Lenin while crying Ourselves Alone for Scotland. But no one can say that Hugh M'Diarmid has not got verve –
>
> > 'Or a muckle bellows blawin'
> > Wi' the sparks a'whizzin' oot:
> > Or green tides sweeshin'
> > 'Neth heich-skeich stars,
> > Or centuries fleein' down a water-chute.'[56]

These lines will not seem less Scottish for coming from a section of *A Drunk Man* that describes the sound of the bagpipes.[57] They are less straightforwardly so, however, because of 'Ourselves Alone for Scotland'.

'Ourselves Alone' is of course an unidiomatic translation of 'Sinn Fein'. And part of the joke is that the Scottish Nationalists are far from going it alone; they are tagging along behind the Irish, whose self-involved nationalism MacNeice would treat unsympathetically a few months later in *Autumn Journal*:

> Ourselves alone! Let the round tower stand aloof
> >   In a world of bursting mortar!
> Let the school-children fumble their sums
> >   In a half-dead language;
> Let the censor be busy on the books; pull down the Georgian slums . . .[58]

In *Minch*, the phrase is more than a jibe, because, once offered *as* a jibe, it encourages us to question MacDiarmid's belief that the Sinn Fein revolution had been good for Irish culture. But it is a jibe not least because setting it against 'a salaam to Lenin' cues us to think of nationalism as reactionary after all.

This was familiar ground for MacNeice, and the routineness of his paradoxes, together with the appreciative quotation, give the passage an almost genial air. With Linklater, the philosophers A. E. Taylor and J. A. Smith, he is even more wryly perfunctory, as though saving himself for Compton Mackenzie. What bugged him about Mackenzie? That he was kept waiting for 2 days before getting the summons to visit him? A sense of the bogus (Mackenzie the invented Scot?) His self-regard[59] and monologuing? Or was this generational friction, between an Edwardian man of letters and an ambitious poet of 30, whose own career, we can see with hindsight, would have some of the same contours: public school and Oxford Greats, government work in Greece, officially sponsored visits to India, broadcasting and freelance writing? The satirical treatment of Mackenzie might owe something to class and occupational resemblances of which MacNeice was scarcely aware.

One impulse to hostility that MacNeice *was* at least half aware of sprang from his own liking for comfort. Lying sick in Lewis, 'I ... longed for my flat in Hampstead, my curtains in peach-coloured chintz with white Victorian bows and my borzoi sleeping on the sofa' (55). Later his Guardian Angel says, 'The case against you is black. On your own admission you are preoccupied with luxury values' (128). This is something he had crossed the Minch to purge, manage or punish. So his animus makes sense in the light of his first reaction to Mackenzie's well-appointed household: '"Comfort", I said, walking along the passage to the drawing-room, "where have I heard that word before?"' (71). The answer is that 'comfort' and 'comfortable' – words at best ambivalent in MacNeice's poetry of the thirties[60] – had been used earlier in *Minch* to describe the intrusive cosiness of one of Leverhulme's shooting lodges wedged into the countryside near Loch Morsgail (59).

Mackenzie, in other words, is not just an invented Scot but the sort of metropolitan Gael that troubled the compromised Celt in MacNeice:

He stood on a sumptuous white mat in front of his fire looking like Lionel Barrymore on the point of turning into a bird. Tiers of books rose around him to the ceiling in elegant maple (?) bookcases à la Heal ... His library and himself looked exceedingly comfortable. His Fair Isle pullover was almost too good a match for his green check suit. Socks of a darker green in lace-stitch pattern led the eye down to ginger-coloured monk suede shoes. Perhaps Catiline looked like this. (92)

With the practised hand of the novelist which at this date he was, MacNeice deftly captures Mackenzie's garrulity: how the dole and the west wind demoralise the people of the Hebrides; what it was like being a child prodigy; running the 100 yards in 10 seconds and playing lacrosse for the 'Varsity. 'Mr Mackenzie kept on talking ... Shropshire was a good county, he said, were it not for Mary Webb and Stanley Baldwin. The effect of cocoa drinking on women was everlastingly deleterious; look at their hockey costumes' (94–5).

Into this Evelyn Waugh-like comedy are dropped, however, some jagged bits of politics: Mackenzie's willingness to countenance a bloody uprising in Scotland, and his notion that 'It might be a good idea if the Hebrides attached themselves to the Irish Free State' (93).[61] 'Incidentally', he went on,

the time was ripe for a spot of trouble in Belfast. He would like, if he had the time, to go over and foment it. These things were all a matter of timing. He told me a sensational story about Carson and Greece, Lloyd George and Rumania. The Rumanian trouble cropped up first and Lloyd George cashed in on it. Otherwise Carson and himself between them – but perhaps this is confidential history, which I should not repeat ... (93)

This is all very intriguing. Why the Ulster Unionist Sir Edward Carson for a start? It would be interesting to reconstruct the monologue more fully, if not the other side of the conversation.

We can do both, to some extent. Mackenzie read *I Crossed the Minch* and gave his version of the meeting. Scholars have missed this, perhaps because *My Life and Times* put the encounter in 1936, a year too early. When they met, Mackenzie apparently spoke of the dispute of the poet's father, Bishop MacNeice, with the Belfast Orangemen around the time he was party to a decision to refuse the flying of a Union flag over Carson's tomb in St Anne's (Church of Ireland) Cathedral:[62]

So the first thing I said to Louis MacNeice when he arrived with a young woman whose name I have forgotten was to express my admiration for the courageous attitude of his episcopal father.

'Oh, I'm not interested in what my father is doing.' And as he said this he looked quickly at his young female companion as if for an approving nod. I suppose he was piqued because I did not express my interest in his poetry. As I had never read any of it this was unfortunately beyond me ...

In a book he wrote called *I Crossed the Minch*, which he seemed to think was a feat of condescension, he wrote with evident disapproval of my wearing a green jumper to match a green tweed suit and went on to talk about the rich white rug in the billiards-room as if it was an ostentatious display of luxury to find across the Minch; it was in fact a cheap Indian rug that cost eight guineas ...[63]

About the nameless Nancy Sharp, and MacNeice's relationship with his father, initially repudiating but later respectful,[64] I shall say more. Whether

Minch is 'a feat of condescension' we shall be in a better position to dispute once we have thought more about its critique of 'luxury'.

MACNEICE, MACDIARMID AND 'BAGPIPE MUSIC'

In *The Islands of Scotland*, MacDiarmid writes evocatively about the diversity of the islands, though the cock-eyed structure of his book, which cramps his account of the Hebrides, makes it hard for him to do justice to a point which was, for him, political. 'Scotland', he notes, 'is broken up into islands other than, and to a far greater extent than merely, geographically.' As against Muir and MacNeice, who assume that 'unity' is a prerequisite of independence, he argues, ahead of his time, that Scotland is inherently 'a numerous archipelago'.[65] MacNeice, though less ideological, is equally alert. As he goes from Lewis to Barra, Coll and Tiree, then back again, he produces sharply differentiated images: 'Stornoway . . . reminded me of little towns in the North of Ireland, the same streets of grey cemented houses, the same slummy smell' (41);[66] 'Benbecula was spattered with lakes, South Uist had brown mountains' (70); on Vatersay, he 'walked through fields of silky barley and clover, meadowsweet, ragged robin and poppies' (148).

Yet he does have an overview. Appropriately, given its relative consistency with the values of the Scottish Renaissance, the poem which most fully presents this began its life on Barra. While he waited to call on Mackenzie, he was 'very happy . . . generalising about the islands' (87). 'On those Islands' (245–8), printed as an epilogue or conclusion to *Minch*, even starts by making serious use of a thought about the west wind that had been satirised in Mackenzie's conversation:[67]

> On those islands
> The West-Wind drops its messages of indolence,
> No one hurries, the Gulf Stream warms the gnarled
> Rampart of gneiss, the feet of the peasant years
> Pad up and down their sentry-beat not challenging
> Any comer for the password – only Death
> Comes through unchallenged in his general's cape.

Why is Death so potent? An archetypal connection between death and westness had been hinted at earlier in *Minch* (18–19) and it would be developed in the postwar MacNeice. For now, the scene is darkened by emigration to America, an ageing population and ghosts of the past.

MacNeice gives us snapshots in the poem: a tethered cow grazing among orchids, crofters in blue calico, a 'black minister' preaching hellfire. Yet these images could have come from almost any moment in a past which is ubiquitously present. Among the black houses, 'stories circulate like smoke', rippling away 'till they hardly crease / The ebony heritage of the herded dead'. The air rings with echoes of 'MacCrimmon's pipes lost in the cave' – the ancient pibrochs taught by the MacCrimmons of Skye – and of old beliefs: 'seals cry with the voices of the drowned'. Yet, if the sounds of the dead mingle with those of the living, the impact of mortality is softened by communal mourning. Where death is almost detached from 'the tyrant time' – MacNeice's great obsession –

> There is still peace though not for me and not
> Perhaps for long – still peace on the bevel hills
> For those who still can live as their fathers lived
> On those islands.

The third-person, expository overview has always implied that MacNeice was not of the islands. At the end of the poem we are told why. Their peace is not for those who repudiate their fathers – those whose fathers lived, with their own fathers, on islands such as Omey.

When, in *The Islands of Scotland*, MacDiarmid praises MacNeice's poems about the Hebrides (18), he surely includes 'On those Islands'; it is so often close to his own, even finer 'Island Funeral'. There, too, in a poem that aims to capture the essentials of the Hebrides, death is a communal, dignified experience, free of the 'bitter pageantry / And the ramp of undertakers and insurance companies'.[68] And there, again, in a poem that was inspired by Barra (to judge from the Latin of the priest), but which probably and characteristically uses details from a description of Aran[69] – that is, of Irish islands important to the Revival – we are witnessing what is almost the funeral of 'the Gaelic way of life'. In the Hebrides, according to MacNeice, 'All is known before it comes to the lips – / Instinctive wisdom'. Strangely unqualified for him, this could be straight out of MacDiarmid, who says of an island home, 'That those who once inhabited it / Were sure of every thought they had'.[70]

This is a bare, unreflective sureness that MacDiarmid writes into his verse. Instead of the heightened detachment – which should not be mistaken for 'condescension' – of MacNeice's third person, MacDiarmid starts at ground level, confused by a cencrastian overlap of walls as grey as the sea, putting the reader there with him as 'we', until roused to claim authority by an assertion of first-person omniscience that MacNeice cannily avoids: 'I know all there is to know / About their traditional plenishing / And native arts and crafts.'[71] Cut off linguistically from the islands almost as completely as MacNeice, MacDiarmid does not just overcompensate with claims to knowledge. He achieves an ardent, declamatory plainness, in verse that is colourlessly lucid, like paraphrase, in English but not English, the work of an auditor as much as a writer – the auditor, in an astonishing turn, of jazz:

> this island note,
> This clear old Gaelic sound,
> In the chaos of the modern world,
> Is like a phrase from Beiderbecke's cornet,
> As beautiful as any phrase can be. (579)

Hugh MacDiarmid knew about music not least because he edited from 1929 to 1930 Compton Mackenzie's *Vox*, offshoot of *The Gramophone*. By the mid-thirties, however, his taste usually ran to the strictest mode of pibroch playing, associated with the MacCrimmons. What could Beiderbecke bring to this? Both Ceol Mor and jazz are, as MacDiarmid would see it, arts of the people which combine the impersonality of the received – like his plagiaristic verse technique – with high artistry within a structure of variation. Beiderbecke's playing also suspends time. Though it starts from a rhythmic base, it hypnotically repeats and elaborates a twelve- or sixteen-bar melody. In this it resembles not just the long, quantitative mode of the pibroch, as MacDiarmid contentiously understood it,[72] but the cumulative, recursive phrasing of 'Island Funeral' and 'Lament for the Great Music' and 'Bagpipe Music':

> Let me play to you tunes without measure or end,
> Tunes that are born to die without a herald,
> As a flight of storks rises from a marsh, circles,
> And alights on the spot from which it rose.[73]

MacNeice, in other words, was not the only poet of the thirties to emulate the music of the pipes. *His* 'Bagpipe Music', however, has a more conflicted relationship with jazz and 'the chaos of the modern world'. Out in rural Lewis, at the end of his second visit, he escaped into 'Celtic timelessness' (204). He went to a dance at Shawbost where shadows flickered on the walls and music was provided by a couple of pipers in Highland dress. Stirred by this, Hector MacIver and he 'talked about the complexities of civilisation till about four in the morning' (208). The next day, though, on a bus to Stornoway, he noticed that the driver's Gaelic was shot through with English hybrids: 'The fault of Stornoway, said Hector, with its ideas of progress; they mix English and Gaelic and lose all definite personality. He would like to see Stornoway destroyed.' Now the future of civilisation looks more apocalyptic than complex. 'Hector said that he foresaw within ten years the total collapse of our civilisation' (209).

What is meant by 'our'? The civilisation of the West, with its supposed apogee in Hampstead, or the 'Gaelic civilisation' that for MacDiarmid and others was the best hope for Europe?[74] *Minch* worries at this question in a very thirties way,[75] and confronts it in Stornoway. After attending a Gaelic concert larded with pompous speeches,[76] where 'The Lewis Pipe Band ... obsessed the stage like gaudy grotesque vegetation' – an event in which paid-for, musically coarse spectacle replaced the communal spontaneity of Shawbost – MacNeice and MacIver went to a Grand Dance in which a reel danced 'to the pipes ... gave way to the saxophone and they danced fox-trots – rather jerkily as might be expected' (217–18). The Gaels danced jerkily because they were unpractised in fashionable ways, but also because they were becoming objectified, alienated products of the music industry.

If that sounds rather too much like the voice of the Frankfurt school, it does help us make sense of the cross-currents of parody and dismay in 'Bagpipe Music' if we recall that, while MacNeice was visiting Lewis, Theodor Adorno, then an unlikely graduate student at the poet's Oxford college, Merton, was denouncing saxophone dance bands as agents of commodification.[77] MacNeice is less decisive than that, and less extreme than MacIver – he does not want Stornoway destroyed – but still surprisingly purist. It is as though his mistrust of comfort and its mass-market ally commodification drew him despite himself to the austerity of hard-leftists like MacDiarmid, who sought the stony limits and detested Lerwick.[78] 'One might deplore', MacNeice writes,

> that one was not a native of Shawbost but one could thank God that one was not a citizen of Stornoway. There is a natural culture which can subsist without comfort. And there is a sophisticated culture which depends upon comforts. But when the deserters from the former 'gatecrash' the industrial world and try to live by its bread or its cake alone – its grand pianos, its club chairs, its blue underclothes – then one is presented with European man at his worst. (219)

It was one thing for MacNeice to disparage the modish 'blue locknit underclothes' displayed in a women's shop in Stornoway.[79] But how could he declare, a few months after Guernica, that the wearing of blue knickers by Celts showed 'European man at his worst'? Self-rebuke, rather than what Compton Mackenzie called 'condescension', seems to have cost him his balance. A couple of years later he would describe himself as 'a peasant who has gate-crashed culture'[80] – which makes *him* 'European man at his worst'.

Evidently he did feel implicated in the energies that run through 'Bagpipe Music' (159–60):

> It's no go the merrygoround, it's no go the rickshaw,
> All we want is a limousine and a ticket for the peepshow.
> Their knickers are made of crepe-de-chine, their shoes are made of python,
> Their halls are lined with tiger rugs and their walls with heads of bison.

Readers who are swept along without registering the difference between the 'we' of lines 1–2 and the 'they' of 3–4 are not entirely wrong, because 'we', in traditional societies, have simple pastimes and vehicles but aspire to the sorts of pleasures and cars and no doubt blue, crepe-de-Chine knickers that are enjoyed by the greedily sophisticated. And who is MacNeice to blame them? His inner Celt had been stifled by an upbringing which had left him 'preoccupied with luxury values'.

The drone and chant of the writing reminds us that this poem is about the Hebrides. But the aboutness of that is global. The merry-go-round and the rickshaw could be in many places, from Blackpool to Shanghai, while the tiger rugs and heads of bison show 'luxury values' ransacking the globe. Even the central stanzas, with their Scottish proper names, are dislocated:

> John MacDonald found a corpse, put it under the sofa,
> Waited till it came to life, and hit it with a poker,
> Sold its eyes for souvenirs, sold its blood for whiskey,
> Kept its bones for dumb-bells to use when he was fifty.

This Eliotic farce is shiftingly Irish–Scottish. There are plenty of MacDonalds in Belfast as well as in the Highlands and Islands, rather as, elsewhere in *Minch*, MacNeice jokes that the Mac in his name is Scottish (56). And then, what about 'whiskey'? Although it is usually in this book an Ulster poet's mistake for 'whisky' without an 'e' (i.e., for Scotch) – a potent mistake, since, as MacDiarmid says, 'there *is* all the difference in the world / Between whisky and whiskey'[81] – it is not invariably so. On Tiree, MacNeice has 'a little Irish whiskey' (143). The 'e' would not be 'corrected' until 'Bagpipe Music' appeared in *Eighty-Five Poems* (1959),[82] and perhaps the change was not all right, given MacNeice's pattern of usage, not to mention the Yeatsian Irishness that gets into the poem's cosmopolitan London: 'It's no go the Yogi-Man, it's no go Blavatsky, / All we want is a bank balance and a bit of skirt in a taxi.'

Compared with early Eliot, 'Bagpipe Music' is tolerantly amused by sexual peccadilloes and the culturally ersatz. It does, though, develop a disturbing, even hysterical dynamic out of commodification and waste. New and old forms of community are alike swept up in rejection: 'It's no go the gossip column, it's no go the Ceilidh.' The poem pointedly highlights the systemic failures of capitalism.[83] Yet when Willie Murray uses the hide of an entire cow to bandage his thumb and his brother throws his herring catch back into the sea because it is easier to go 'upon the parish', the collapse of civilisation is spiritual as well as economic. How God-fearing is that parish? There are overtones of Carrickfergus rectory, of the black, preaching ministers of the islands, in the words attributed to the idle hands: 'It's no go the Herring Board, it's no go the Bible, / All we want is a packet of fags when our hands are idle.'

The same spiral of rejection runs deep into affluent England, with its cinemas, stadiums and elections, where the nostalgically authentic is debased into the marketable. The verse thrives as it proceeds by replicating that voracity, caught up in a dance-band travesty: 'It's no go the country cot with a pot of pink geraniums.' So now the poem rounds on us. 'It's no go' starts to mean not 'we don't want' but 'it's no use', while terms of endearment turn belittling and ominous: 'It's no go my honey love, it's no go my poppet; / Work your hands from day to day, the winds will blow the profit.' No point in graft. The fickleness of the market is stronger. Anyway disaster is coming (Hitler yells on the wireless), so why seek redemption through prudence. The falling glass is a barometer; it warns of an approaching storm. But we are also, including MacNeice, in a glass house where no one can afford to throw stones: 'The glass is falling hour by hour, the glass will fall for ever, / But if you break the bloody glass you won't hold up the weather.'

GOING BACK TO THE ISLANDS

When Compton Mackenzie and Hugh MacDiarmid in *Minch* and other works of the thirties compare the Hebrides to 'the Isles of Greece',[84] they are not just echoing Byron. They had lived in Athens, Salonika and Capri and had sailed among the islands. That came to MacNeice later, when he went to Greece in 1950. The poems that he wrote at the time, particularly 'The Island' and 'Day of Returning', about Odysseus' longing for Ithaca, connect variously with his account of the Hebrides. They also show, however, a growing mythical element. Even when writing matter-of-factly about emigration to America, he declares: 'Where was the land of the dead / Rise now the towers of life' ('The Island').[85] This helps us grasp why, in 'On those Islands', 'only Death / Comes through unchallenged'.[86] For in classical literature, if not archetypally,[87] westness, the home of the setting sun, is associated with death. In the best known of the *Ten Burnt Offerings*, 'Day of Renewal',[88] MacNeice describes how, as a child, all was black to the west of

Carrickfergus, and how beyond his imaginary birthplace, 'Further, more truly, west', in Connemara, lay a zone where 'The dead must lap fresh blood to recover sense / As Homer rightly thought.' 'Rightly' is droll enough, but it barely disguises what the syntactical awkwardness of the gloss betrays: a willed quality in MacNeice's determination to conflate different sites of insular westness. The impulse clearly sprang from his desire to reorientate his imagination in relation to myth at a time when he was seeking to write a less documentary sort of poetry. It reinforced at the level of fable his existing tendency to run together the Hebrides and the islands off the west of Ireland.

One symptom or byproduct of this shift is the prominence granted not just to the voyaging Odysseus, in such poems as 'Thalassa',[89] but his Irish equivalent: Brandan, the 'spindrift hermit' of 'Western Landscape' (1945), who, sailing west, discovered America and Tír na nOg, and who then sailed to Wales and Iona, in a mission that is discussed in the historical chapter of *Minch*. The ninth-century Irish *Voyage of St Brendan* describes the blessed, floating and other Irish–Scottish and Atlantic islands that he visits. These supernatural sites were already finding a place in *Minch*,[90] and when, during the fifties, MacNeice recalled his Hebridean adventures, he was encouraged by Brandan to fabulate. In 'Country Week-End', he remembers Tiree as 'a low-slung floating island, / Hardly afloat that day', then describes a cottage 'in an Irish island ... where one small ark / Was casting off to find Atlantis'.[91]

The journalism makes similar links. In 1954, he reviewed David Thomson's *The People of the Sea*, a book explicitly drawn on for *The Mad Islands*, about the seal lore shared by the Scottish islanders and the west of Ireland, and, in 1962, the year of that radio play, he reviewed memoirs by men brought up in South Uist and Donegal.[92] Though the latter article, especially, stresses the extent to which the romantic, nationalist view of the islands had fallen out of fashion, he is drawn to what remains distinctive in their songs and story-telling. Writing about the selkies who are as much Thomson's 'people of the sea' as are the people who believe in them, his review becomes a draft of his play: 'The initial inspiration of this book (which is really a Quest in which the hero must find an animal to talk to) lies back in Mr Thomson's childhood. On the coast of Nairn he was drawn to the great grey seal (or selchie) before he had ever seen one – and the first one he met was being killed in a bothy.'[93] It is a quest which takes the book through South Uist to Ballinskelligs Bay in Co. Kerry.

MacNeice had always been impressed by seals. Whenever he describes a sea coast, one is likely to haul into view. The opening of the early 'Valediction', for instance, represents Ireland as a country in which the brutal killing of the seals that bob about off its western shores morphs into the killing of people – all one history of violence. Yet he cannot disown the place: 'Cursèd be he that curses his mother', as he puts it in a loaded couplet: 'I cannot be / Anyone else than what this land engendered me.'[94] On Barra, where he chatted to Mackenzie about seals and their bathing requirements, he tells us that he once dreamed he was a seal and that 'there are few bodies which I would prefer for my next incarnation'.[95] It is a fascination that goes into *The Mad Islands*, where a seal-woman and the hero's mother battle it out for the soul of Muldoon.

The play is based on the medieval *Immram Maelduin*, and its protagonist is a Brandan or Odysseus, visiting strange islands and looking for home in the form of a resolved set of family relationships. MacNeice said in an introduction, '*The Mad Islands* I wrote because I have always been addicted to the legendary Ancient Irish voyages which suggested it.'[96] But aspects of these islands come out of 1937, not just locally, as in the 'password' required to access the Island of Progress,[97] but in their overall variety. When the seal-woman says 'there's not one island among them the same as the one before or after' (313) she might as well be describing the Hebrides of MacDiarmid and MacNeice as the Island of Foolish Laughter, the Happy Island, and so on in the play – inspired by the thirty-one islands visited in *Immram Maelduin*, though only a few of them are re-used directly. In short, these are islands more modern than medieval, concerned, *inter alia*, like *Minch*, with the encroachments of industrialisation (ultimately, with the atomic bomb), and keyed to MacNeice's growing appetite for the archetypal, as when the Miller of Hell, on an island drawn from the *Immram*, declares 'What I take I take and it flows away west. To the west, to death, to hell.'[98]

The seal-woman, Skerrie, who is MacNeice's addition to the *Immram*, helps mix these islands in the west. She comes from Orkney, where there is a Sule Skerry (i.e., 'sea rock'),[99] but swims into an Irish story. As a figure from folklore, she is, as Thomson's book shows,[100] Irish–Scottish. And at a turning-point of the drama, when Muldoon encounters his real father without knowing it, '*She croons something that suggests the Hebrides*' (338). There is, though, a deeper connection between these islands and those of *Minch*, in the correlation between Skerrie and Nancy Sharp. This might seem implausible for several reasons, only the first of them being that Nancy is never mentioned by MacNeice in *Minch*. But that, as a letter to MacIver makes clear, is because of the scandal – MacNeice feared 'blackmail' – of a married woman accompanying him as though she were his wife.[101] Her importance is in inverse proportion to her visibility.

And she *does* have visibility, in her drawings, attributed on the title-page, and in the poem 'Leaving Barra',[102] which is, one gathers from the biography and the lines about Nancy in *Autumn Journal*, about leaving or losing her too.[103] Her presence can be more subtly felt in the way *Minch* clones and splits MacNeice to produce the dialogue that she provided in reality, and that Skerrie provides in the play: Perceval and Crowder; Foot and Head; Myself and Guardian Angel; above all, Hetty to Maisie, in the closing satirical letter, which gets a version of their relationship, their failure to marry, as brittle comedy, into the book. By 1962, MacNeice was living happily with Mary Wimbush. If all was well, however, why such poems as 'Coda', in which the poet's life is reviewed as a series of failures to connect? New, testing relationships always drag up the memory of old ones, often with a clearer sense of how they went wrong. There was, as his second wife, Hedli Anderson, got MacNeice to agree in the fifties, a 'pattern which repeats itself' in his affairs,[104] one in which, he would be the first to agree, the early loss of his mother figured.

In both the *Immram* and *The Mad Islands*, the young protagonist, Muldoon, has been given up to step-parents. There is, however, a difference. In the medieval story, the natural mother is on hand and easily introduced to her son. It is the killers of his father that have to be sought for among the islands. In *The Mad Islands*, by contrast, the mother is far away in 'the blackest bogs of Ireland' (310). Elusive and demanding, she requires Muldoon to kill the Lord of the Eskers (i.e., the glacial morrains), 'now a sea-rover in the west' (312), who, she says, killed his father. What Muldoon learns on his journey is that he is the product of an affair between his mother and this lord who was incited by her to murder his apparent father. She now wants the lord disposed of because he has been unfaithful to her. Like Edward in the ballad, he has been persuaded ('Mither! Mither!') to stab his father.

That *The Mad Islands* is much more the mother's story than is *Immram Maelduin* goes back to MacNeice's psychology. One way in which the psychology is expressed, though, is in a return to the arguments about nationalism that characterised *I Crossed the Minch*. The mother becomes a version of the feminised Ireland who had been an inspiration not just to the men of 1916 but to MacDiarmid and other Scottish Nationalists,[105] apparently now past her sell-by date yet 'well preserved' enough (as events after 1969 would prove) to find bidders on the Island of the Auction (333). She belongs to a conflicted train of thought about Ireland that goes back to 'Valediction' ('Cursèd be he that curses his mother') and *Autumn Journal* XVI ('Kathaleen ni Houlihan! Why / Must a country, like a ship or a car, be always female, / Mother or sweetheart?') and the 'mother / Earth' of 'Western Landscape'.[106] Tenacious in the play, she refuses Muldoon's offer to free her from an auction in which she will be sold into death, preferring him to kill his father.

The knottiness of the family romance is caught up in the fact that Skerrie is (in the spelling used by MacNeice) virtually an anagram of Eskers. Is the selkie the opposite of the father not just in her name but in her fidelity, or will she betray Muldoon? Both, in a way. As in that other, self-revealing late play, *Persons from Porlock* (1963), an abandoning, absent mother frustrates a settled relationship with a woman. The selkie cares for Muldoon and keeps calling him to love, but he is too obsessed with his quest, needing to please or placate his mother. The *Immram* ends with a revenge plot resolved in forgiveness. At the end of *The Mad Islands*, Muldoon, ageing and unfulfilled, though no longer parricidal – something has been allayed – sees the ghost of his mother going off with the Lord of Eskers. Then the selkie leaves him also, eloping with a drowned man. 'Give me your lips, Muldoon', she says, 'Our first kiss and our last. I thought I could break the rules – I could have perhaps if you'd helped me' (349). Now 'alone' in a small boat, he can only restart the motor and sail off among the islands on a quest which, according to the selkie, never made sense, and which now has no objective.

Where, finally, does this leave Louis MacNeice? Psychologically as adrift as Muldoon, he must have thought in his darker moods. Culturally, in a more interestingly archipelagic, well-connected condition. By education, he had been drawn into what MacDiarmid called 'the English Ascendancy'.[107] But when MacDiarmid parcels him up with 'Auden, Spender, those bhoyos',[108] he is more sweeping than incisive. Spender exaggerates the other way when, in 'Louis MacNeice', he writes,

Now, reading his poem 'Bagpipe Music', I don't know how to pronounce

> C-e-i-l-i-d-h – nor what it means –
> He looks down from high heaven
> The mocking eyes search-lighting
> My ignorance again.[109]

It is hard to believe that Spender was actually quite so ignorant. But even if the passage is something of a put-up job – the better to do down MacNeice's aloofness – the impression that it gives of MacNeice being at a cultural as well as an intellectual remove is telling. The Irish–Scottish axis contributed to the unsettled, productive position he held in British and Irish poetry, never quite one thing among the islands.

NOTES

I am grateful to Jonathan Allison and Jon Stallworthy for letting me read their transcripts of letters by MacNeice.

1. See John Kerrigan, 'The Ticking Fear', *London Review of Books*, 7 February 2008, 15–18.
2. Jon Stallworthy, *Louis MacNeice* (London: Faber, 1995), 377–8.
3. To George McCann, 22 June 1950, quoted by Stallworthy, *Louis MacNeice*, 382.
4. With the exception of poems first published in *I Crossed the Minch* (1938), the verse is quoted from Louis MacNeice, *Collected Poems*, ed. Peter McDonald (London: Faber, 2007). 'Cock o' the North' can be found at 326–31.
5. See, for example, Hamish Monboddo [Peter Cochran], 'Byron and Scotland', *Newstead Abbey Byron Society Review* (2004), 96–100; Robert Crawford, *Scotland's Books* (London: Penguin, 2007), 392–5.
6. Byron, *Don Juan*, X.17. MacNeice had reviewed Peter Quennell's edition of *Don Juan* in an article headed 'Heart of Byron', *The Observer*, 3 April 1949, 3, though no reference is made to Byron's Scottishness.
7. T. S. Eliot, 'Byron', in Bonamy Dobrée (ed.), *From Anne to Victoria* (London: Cassell, 1937), 601–19. The Aberdonian context had been stressed by J. D. Symon, *Byron in Perspective* (London: Secker, 1925), who rounds up the poet's few Scotticisms.
8. See, for example, *The Scottish Nation*, 22 May 1923, noted by Alan Bold, *MacDiarmid: Christopher Murray Grieve: A Critical Biography* (London: John Murray, 1988), 144.
9. Hugh MacDiarmid (ed.), *The Golden Treasury of Scottish Poetry* (London: Macmillan, 1940), xxxv, qualified on p. 366.
10. Louis MacNeice, 'Scottish Poetry', *New Statesman and Nation*, 18 January 1941, 66.
11. MacDiarmid, *Golden Treasury*, xvi–xxxii.
12. For the encouragement that MacDiarmid drew from this see, for example, his letter to Sorley MacLean, 2 April 1941, in Hugh MacDiarmid, *New Selected Letters*, ed. Dorian Grieve, Owen Dudley Edwards and Alan Riach (Manchester: Carcanet, 2001), 189–91, 190, enclosing the *TLS* review of the *Treasury*, and his letter to *The Glasgow Herald*, 11 November 1946, against James Fergusson's attack on 'plastic Scots', in Hugh MacDiarmid, *The Letters of Hugh MacDiarmid*, ed. Alan Bold (London: Hamish Hamilton, 1984), 784–6, 785.
13. Louis MacNeice, *I Crossed the Minch* (London: Longmans, Green and Co., 1938), 26.
14. Louis MacNeice, *The Strings are False: An Unfinished Autobiography* (London: Faber, 2007 [1965]), 153.
15. Mary and Hector MacIver, *Pilgrim Souls* (Aberdeen University Press, 1991) 127–9, 130, 154–6. Cf. letter to Norman MacCaig, 8 December 1952, in MacDiarmid, *New Selected Letters*, 297–8.
16. MacNeice, *Strings are False*, 97.

17. Louis MacNeice, review of *A Drunk Man Looks at the Thistle*, *Cherwell* 19:6 (5 March 1927), 168.
18. Edwin Muir, 'T. S. Eliot', in *Transition: Essays on Contemporary Literature* (London: Hogarth, 1926), 131–44, 143.
19. Louis MacNeice, review of *Duncan Dewar's Accounts: A Student of St Andrews 100 Years Ago*, *Cherwell* 20:3 (21 May 1927), 88.
20. Louis MacNeice, 'Some Notes on Mr Yeats' Plays', *New Verse* 18 (December 1935), 7–9; Louis MacNeice, 'The Newest Yeats', *New Verse* 19 (February–March 1936), 16; Louis MacNeice, '*Dramatis Personae* by W. B. Yeats', *Criterion* 16:62 (October 1936), 120–2.
21. Louis MacNeice, 'Poems by Edwin Muir', *New Verse* 9 (June 1934), 18–20, 18.
22. Louis MacNeice, *Varieties of Parable* (Cambridge University Press, 1965), 125–6, on Muir's *Journeys and Places* (1937).
23. Edwin Muir, *Scott and Scotland: The Predicament of the Scottish Writer* (London: Routledge, 1936), esp. 18–22, 41–2 (on MacDiarmid), 70–2, quoting 22. Cf. Eric Linklater, *The Lion and the Unicorn: What England has Meant to Scotland* (London: Routledge, 1935), 114–20.
24. For example, Hugh MacDiarmid, *Lucky Poet: A Self-Study in Literature and Political Ideas* (1943), quoting the edition introduced by Alan Riach (Manchester: Carcanet, 1994), 200–2.
25. 'The Weapon' from *To Circumjack Cencrastus* (1930), in Hugh MacDiarmid, *The Complete Poems of Hugh MacDiarmid*, ed. Michael Grieve and W. R. Aitken, 2 vols. (Harmondsworth: Penguin, 1985), Vol. 1, 263. For his loyalty to this position see, for example, his letter to the *National Weekly*, 28 June 1952, in MacDiarmid, *Letters*, 796–7, 796.
26. See, for example, MacDiarmid, *Lucky Poet*, 26.
27. Compton Mackenzie, *My Life and Times, 1930–38*, Vol. 7 (London: Chatto and Windus, 1968), 82. The meeting was in 1932.
28. See, for example, Andro Linklater, *Compton Mackenzie: A Life* (London: Chatto and Windus, 1987), 234; 'Clan Albainn' (1930–1), in Hugh MacDiarmid, *Selected Prose*, ed. Alan Riach (Manchester: Carcanet, 1992), 54–60.
29. Louis MacNeice, 'Poetry To-day', *The Arts To-day*, ed. Geoffrey Grigson (6 September 1935), 25–67, reprinted in Louis MacNeice, *Selected Literary Criticism of Louis MacNeice*, ed. Alan Heuser (Oxford: Clarendon, 1987), 10–44, 41.
30. The Party wrote to him on 30 November 1936; he was subsequently reinstated (Bold, *MacDiarmid*, 343–4). On MacDiarmid's Leftism see C. Day Lewis, *A Hope for Poetry* (Oxford: Blackwell, 1934), and W. H. Auden and Louis MacNeice, 'Last Will and Testament', in *Letters from Iceland* (London: Faber, 1937), 244: 'To Hugh M'Diarmid a gallon of Red Biddy' (i.e., red wine with meths).
31. Louis MacNeice, *Modern Poetry: A Personal Essay* (Oxford University Press, 1938), 151. Contrast 69, 192 and the review of the *Golden Treasury*, where MacNeice praises MacDiarmid's 'animal vitality' in the 'Scots tradition of Dunbar and Burns' ('his Red Flag fails to flap; he remains incorrigibly tartan').

32. Letter to William Soutar, 8 December 1941, in MacDiarmid, *Letters*, 188–9, 188.
33. MacDiarmid, *Golden Treasury*, vii.
34. MacNeice, 'Scottish Poetry', 66.
35. '*I took him to the islands / Where the wells are undefiled / And folk sing as their fathers sang / Before Christ was a child . . .*' This section of *To Circumscribe Cencrastus* was first published, relevantly for what follows, in *The Irish Statesman*, under the title 'The Irish in Scotland . . .' (note in MacDiarmid, *Complete Poems*, Vol. 1, 207).
36. MacNeice, *Minch*, 29. David Fitzpatrick, '"I Will Acquire an Attitude Not Yours": Was Frederick MacNeice a Home Ruler, and Why Does this Matter?', *Field Day Review* 4 (2008), 141–55, 143 notes, among other, more significant changes to the record, that the family fled Omey when Frederick was 13.
37. See his letter to Bessie J. B. MacArthur, 5 November 1937, in MacDiarmid, *Letters*, 458–9, 459; cf. the letters to Neil Gunn, 21 October 1937, *ibid.*, 259–60, 259, and to his wife Valda Grieve, W. R. Aitken and Sorley MacLean, 15 September to 21 October 1937, in MacDiarmid, *New Selected Letters*, 143–8, and the poem generated by his tour, 'A Golden Wine in the Gaidhealtachd' (MacDiarmid, *Complete Poems*, Vol. 1, 721–2).
38. Cf. MacNeice, *Minch*, 29–30, 131–2.
39. MacNeice, *Minch*, 142, quoting the translation by Thomas Pattison, *The Gaelic Bards, and Original Poems*, ed. George MacNeill, 2nd edn (Glasgow: Archibald Sinclair, 1890), 9–28, 25.
40. Under the title 'The Birlinn of Clanranald'; cf. MacDiarmid, *Lucky Poet*, 53. MacDiarmid's version, based on MacLean's translation, first appeared in *The Modern Scot* 5:4 (January 1935), 230–47.
41. Letter to Mary MacNeice, 10 March 1937; cf. letter to T. S. Eliot, 28 March 1937; in Louis MacNeice, *Letters of Louis MacNeice*, ed. Jonathan Allison (London: Faber, 2010), 295, 297.
42. Louis MacNeice, *I Crossed the Minch*, ed. Tom Herron (Edinburgh: Polygon, 2007), xi.
43. Rejecting the Celtic Twilight was almost a convention in itself. See, for example, Compton Mackenzie, 'Catholic Barra', in John Lorne Campbell (ed.), *The Book of Barra* (London: George Routledge and Sons, 1936), 1–30, 21, and Hugh MacDiarmid, 'The Stone Called Saxagonus', *The Islands of Scotland* (London: Batsford, 1939), xiv–xv, also 15.
44. MacNeice calls *Minch* 'a tripper's book' (3), but on the absence of tourism see Hector MacIver, 'The Outer Isles', in George Scott Moncrieff (ed.), *Scottish Country: Fifteen Essays by Scottish Authors* (London: Wishart, 1935), 139–57, 153.
45. MacIver was antagonistic (MacNeice, *Minch*, 23). For an overview see Roger Hutchinson, *The Soap Man: Lewis, Harris and Lord Leverhulme* (Edinburgh: Birlinn, 1983).
46. MacNeice's Ulster background made him particularly attentive to differences between the Catholic and Protestant islands. On Barra and religion see, for example, Compton Mackenzie, 'Catholic Barra' and Donald Buchanan, *Reflections of the Isle of Barra* (London: Sands, 1942).

47. Alasdair Alpin MacGregor, *The Western Isles*, new edn (London: Robert Hale, 1952), 193.
48. MacDiarmid, *Islands*, 134.
49. *Agamemnon*, line 958; Louis MacNeice (trans.), *The Agamemnon of Aeschylus* (London: Faber, 1936), 45.
50. MacDiarmid, *Islands*, 2–4, 54.
51. Compton Mackenzie, *Address by Compton Mackenzie ... Delivered in the St Andrew's Hall on January 29th, 1932* (Glasgow: Jackson, Wylie, 1932).
52. MacNeice, *Minch*, 11, 12 – the latter in some tension with MacNeice's 'The Play and the Audience' (1938), reprinted in MacNeice, *Selected Literary Criticism*, 87–97, 93. For MacDiarmid on this see, for example, his letter to William Soutar, 13 December 1935, in MacDiarmid, *Letters*, 153–6, 156, MacDiarmid, *Lucky Poet*, 145, and MacDiarmid, *Golden Treasury*, xvii.
53. For Mackenzie's anti-Communism see, for example, MacNeice, *Minch*, 100; for MacDiarmid's resistance to Jacobitism see, for example, 'Bonnie Prince Charlie' in *To Circumjack Cencrastus* (MacDiarmid, *Complete Poems*, Vol. 1, 274).
54. MacNeice, *Minch*, 71. For a fuller list of writers, from Arran to the Shetlands, see MacDiarmid, *Islands*, 5–6.
55. For example, the extract from *Dìreadh I* in MacDiarmid, *Islands*, xix–xx, 'The Caledonian Antisyzygy and the Gaelic Idea' (1931–2), in Hugh MacDiarmid, *Selected Essays of Hugh MacDiarmid*, ed. Duncan Glen (London: Jonathan Cape, 1969), 56–74, and Hugh MacDiarmid, 'The Caledonian Antisyzygy', *Scottish Eccentrics* (1936), ed. Alan Riach (Manchester: Carcanet, 1993), 284–320; Muir, *Scott and Scotland*, 61–2 (citing MacDiarmid).
56. MacNeice, *Minch*, 86, quoting *A Drunk Man*.
57. Hugh MacDiarmid, *Collected Poems* (New York: Macmillan, 1962) adds the section heading, 'To the Music of the Pipes'; see Hugh MacDiarmid, *A Drunk Man Looks at the Thistle*, ed. Kenneth Buthlay (Edinburgh: Scottish Academic Press, 1987), 37.
58. *Autumn Journal* XVI, in MacNeice, *Collected Poems*, 139–40.
59. Cf. the poet's letters to Mrs E. R. Dodds, 2 May 1937, and Mary MacNeice, 7 May 1937, in MacNeice, *Letters*, 299–302.
60. For example, Epilogue to Auden and MacNeice, *Letters from Iceland*, and MacNeice, *Autumn Journal* V, VIII and XXI.
61. Compare MacNeice, *Minch*, 22; cf. MacKenzie, *My Life and Times*, Vol. 7, 228, and Compton Mackenzie, *The East Wind of Love* (London: Rich and Cowan, 1937), 280, 295.
62. Stallworthy, *Louis MacNeice*, 172–4, Fitzpatrick, '"I Will Acquire an Attitude Not Yours"', 146, 151–2.
63. Mackenzie, *My Life and Times*, Vol. 7, 221–2.
64. See Terence Brown, 'MacNeice: Father and Son', in Terence Brown and Alec Reid (eds.), *Time was Away: The World of Louis MacNeice* (Dublin: Dolmen, 1974), 21–34, 25–34, and Fitzpatrick, '"I Will Acquire an Attitude Not Yours"', 154–5. For stirrings of appreciation see 'Auden and MacNeice: Their Last Will

and Testament', *Letters from Iceland*, 230; resolution of a sort comes in the late poem 'The Truisms'.
65. MacDiarmid, *Islands*, 8.
66. The Irish-Scottish cross-referencing is typical, whether MacNeice is comparing indifference to clock time (9), Irish and Scottish dogs (44), whitewashed stones (62) or use of the Gaelic (170–1).
67. MacNeice, *Minch*, 44.
68. Quoting the text given in MacDiarmid, *Islands*, 29–36. Contrast MacGregor, *Western Isles*, 256–63, on the drinking and brawling that accompanied island funerals.
69. See Douglas Sealy, 'Hugh MacDiarmid and Gaelic Literature', in Duncan Glen (ed.), *Hugh MacDiarmid: A Critical Survey* (Edinburgh: Scottish Academic Press, 1972), 168–83, 179, and personal communication to me (6 June 2008).
70. Not that he was consistent; contrast MacDiarmid, *Lucky Poet*, 299, 370.
71. MacDiarmid, *Islands*, 33.
72. For example, MacDiarmid, 'English Ascendancy in British Literature' (1931), *Selected Prose*, 61–80, at 78n; MacDiarmid, 'Charles Doughty and the Need for Heroic Poetry' (1936), *Selected Prose*, 125–36, 126 (quoted in MacDiarmid, *Lucky Poet*, 290, cf. 375–8); MacDiarmid, *Islands*, viii, xii–xiii (quoting the Doughty essay, again).
73. MacDiarmid, *Complete Poems*, 462–82; *Lucky Poet*, 378. Cf. 'A New Scots Poet' (1952), *Complete Poems*, Vol. 2, 1366–7, in which MacDiarmid, or a version of him, is 'like the Pìob mhòr, or Great Highland Bagpipe'.
74. For example, MacDiarmid, 'English Ascendancy', on 'the Conservation of European Civilization', in *Selected Prose*, 80; MacDiarmid, *Islands*, vii, ix, xi, 49; MacDiarmid, *Lucky Poet*, 143–4; and the poem 'Our Gaelic Background' (MacDiarmid, *Complete Poems*, Vol. 1, 664).
75. See, for example, 'that wider civilisation ... that clique!' represented by the contributors to a copy of *The Listener*, bought in Stornoway, and known to MacNeice (4), and the exchange between Crowder and Perceval that ends Part I of the book, concluding: 'Civilisation! Requiescat in pace' (102, cf. 133). For contexts see Richard Overy, *The Morbid Age: Britain between the Wars* (London: Allen Lane, 2009).
76. On the 'vulgar and ridiculous' manner of Gaelic concerts in the cities, including pompous chairing, see MacGregor, *Western Isles*, 204–9.
77. See 'On Jazz' (1936), in Theodor W. Adorno, *Essays on Music*, ed. Richard Leppert (Berkeley: University of California Press, 2002).
78. MacDiarmid, *Lucky Poet*, 51.
79. MacNeice, *Minch*, 216. The *Oxford English Dictionary* dates 'locknit' from 1935: 'Knitted piece goods composed wholly or mainly of artificial silk'.
80. Letter to Eleanor Clark, 21 May 1940, in Stallworthy, *Louis MacNeice*, 273–7, 274. Contrast MacNeice, *Minch*, 131–2.
81. 'The World of Words', from *In Memoriam James Joyce* in MacDiarmid, *Complete Poems*, Vol. 2, 824.

82. As Peter McDonald puts it in his edition of MacNeice, *Collected Poems*, 802.
83. Cf. Kerrigan, 'Ticking Fear'.
84. For Mackenzie see MacNeice, *Minch*, 95, and his 1936 radio broadcast, 'Living Off the Map', in Mackenzie, *My Life and Times*, Vol. 7, 189–93, 192. Cf. MacDiarmid, *Islands*, 130, quoting his own 'Lament for the Great Music', xiii, and 136, quoting Daniel.
85. MacNeice, *Collected Poems*, 344–5.
86. MacNeice, *Minch*, 245.
87. See the crypto-Jungian account of westness, in 'Autobiographical Talk: Childhood Memories' (1963), in Louis MacNeice, *Selected Prose of Louis MacNeice*, ed. Alan Heuser (Oxford: Clarendon, 1990), 267–73, 268.
88. MacNeice, *Collected Poems*, 349–54.
89. On its likely origins in the period of *Springboard* (1944), see McDonald's note in MacNeice, *Collected Poems*, 818.
90. See esp. MacNeice, *Minch*, 34, 153–4, 158, 161.
91. Louis MacNeice, 'Country Week-End', *Collected Poems*, 546.
92. Louis MacNeice, review of David Thomson, *The People of the Sea*, *London Magazine* 1:9 (1954), 94–6, and 'C'est la Terre' (Angus MacLellan, *The Furrow Behind Me*, and Michael MacGowan, *The Hard Road to Klondike*, along with Kate O'Brien, *My Ireland*), *New Statesman*, 22 June 1962, in MacNeice, *Selected Literary Criticism*, 198–200, 243–5.
93. MacNeice, *Selected Literary Criticism*, 199.
94. MacNeice, 'Valediction', *Collected Poems*, 8.
95. MacNeice, *Minch*, 96–8.
96. Louis MacNeice, 'Author's Introduction to *The Mad Islands* and *The Administrator* (1964)', in *Selected Plays of Louis MacNeice*, ed. Alan Heuser and Peter McDonald (Oxford: Clarendon, 1993), 305–7, 306.
97. 'On those Islands' (quoted above), *The Mad Islands: A Radio Parable Play*, in MacNeice, *Selected Plays*, 309–49, 328–30.
98. MacNeice, *Mad Islands*, 322; cf. 'The Voyage of Maildun', in the source cited by MacNeice – P. W. Joyce (trans.), *Old Celtic Romances* (London: David Nutt, 1879), ch. xv.
99. MacNeice, *Mad Islands*, 313. Cf. the Scottish ballad 'The Great Silkie of Sule Skerry', though the selkie there is male.
100. *The People of the Sea* is acknowledged as a source in MacNeice's introduction, along with another pan-Celtic work reviewed by him, in 1961, Alwyn and Brinley Rees, *Celtic Heritage* (London: Thames and Hudson, 1961).
101. Quoted in MacIver, *Pilgrim Souls*, 99.
102. MacNeice, *Minch*, 157–8.
103. Stallworthy, *Louis MacNeice*, 202–14, 233–4; MacNeice, *Autumn Journal* IV and XIX. Tenacious feelings were involved; on 'the possibility of us fixing up somehow', see the letter to Nancy of 20 January 1940, Bodleian Library.
104. Letter to Hedli MacNeice, quoting this phrase from her, 21 October 1955, in Stallworthy, *MacNeice*, 417.

105. For example, MacDiarmid in 'The Gaelic Muse': 'our Sheila ní Gadhra, / Our Cathleen ní Houlihán ... And she leads us all over Scotland and the Isles / As the faery queen in Eire led Seán Clárach' (MacDiarmid, *Complete Poems*, Vol. 1, 660).
106. MacNeice, *Collected Poems*, 8, 138, 267.
107. MacDiarmid, *Lucky Poet*, 167–9. Even when MacNeice is being complimented on his Hebridean poems (MacDiarmid, *Islands*, 18), he is 'English'.
108. MacDiarmid, 'Third Hymn to Lenin' (1934), *Complete Poems*, Vol. 2, 900. Cf. MacDiarmid, *Lucky Poet*, 156, 167–9, and 'British Leftish Poetry, 1930–40' (*Complete Poems*, Vol. 2, 1060).
109. Stephen Spender, *Collected Poems, 1928–1985* (London: Faber, 1985), 177–8.

CHAPTER 4

Townland, desert, cave: Irish and Scottish Second World War poetry

Peter Mackay

When C. Day Lewis asked 'Where are the War Poets?' he not only opened a debate surrounding the role and perceived absence of poetry of the Second World War but also revealed a concern with location – and in particular the relationship between place and politics, or between geography and history – which would characterise much Second World War poetry. The status and role of 'war poetry' are problematic for Day Lewis: in an act of moral abnegation he suggests that the obligation he and other poets felt to defend 'the bad against the worse' was 'No subject for immortal verse'.[1] Day Lewis's moral dilemma is what role, if any, poets and poetry should play in the war; his own answer is that poetry should have no role in a war so ideologically dubious.

This dilemma comes into sharp focus when distinctions within national contexts – Irish neutrality, the absence of conscription in Northern Ireland, Scottish Nationalist conscientious objection[2] – are taken into account; when, instead of defending 'the bad against the worse', there was the possibility of letting the bad and worse decide their fates among themselves. The emphasis on location (and subsequently on perspective) in Day Lewis's dilemma is important because there are quite different roles for poetry from three different locations for war poetry (and these are only three possible locations for this poetry): the African desert, where many poets (including many Scottish poets) served with the 51st Highland Division; 'Plato's cave', to borrow F. S. L. Lyons's dismissive metaphor for the Republic;[3] or the townland described by John Hewitt in 'Townland of Peace', and the disrupted townlands of many other poets of the period. This chapter explores the two sides of Day Lewis's question, examining tensions between status, role and location in Second World War poetry from Scotland, Northern Ireland and the Republic. It does so from three directions: the particular problems of defining war poetry in the Second World War; the way in which Second World War poetry troubles exclusive national definitions of poetry; and location/dislocation as a defining feature of the war poetry.

Day Lewis's difficulty was partly that he and many of his fellow poets did not fit into the idea of the war poet that had endured from the First World War. Keith Douglas wrote in 'Poets in This War' that 'hell cannot be let loose twice: it was let loose in the Great War and it is the same old hell now... Almost all that a modern poet on active service is inspired to write, would be tautological';[4] Robert Graves went further, claiming that 'war poet' and 'war poetry' were 'terms first used in World War I and perhaps peculiar to it' – they could only with difficulty be applied to the Second World War.[5] The First World War conception of the war poet as a distinct category lies behind what Fran Brearton describes as a

'one size fits all' approach to war poetry ... (war poetry is soldier poetry; war poetry is always anti-war poetry; war poetry is experiential; war poetry, if it is to be any good, speaks from disillusionment, not patriotism; war poetry is meant to shock the complacent public; the war poets have some kind of shared agenda).[6]

Though such a definition would broadly fit the Scottish poets who fought in the desert,[7] Day Lewis, for example, would immediately be excluded since he was not an active soldier. For the same reason it would be difficult to identify any Irish, or indeed any women's, Second World War war poetry from these islands. More suitable is the alternative label of 'wartime poetry',[8] which is defined historically and includes poetry written by those not actively involved in combat. As General Sir John Hackett suggests, wartime poetry 'need not be concerned only with experience of battle' but should

be such as would be unlikely to be written except in wartime. It is the product of the pressures and tensions, the pangs and passions, the fears and frenzy, the loneliness, excitement, boredom and despair, the disgust, the compassion and the weariness, and all the other stimuli to self-expression which, though they are not uniquely found in wartime, react then upon the human condition with special force.[9]

There are problems with both of these as definitions for poetry, as both 'war poetry' and 'wartime poetry' serve to exclude large amounts of poetry. Sorley MacLean's 'Coilltean Ratharsair' ('The Woods of Raasay'), for example, is rarely if ever read as a wartime poem despite having been completed in (and conspicuously dated) 1940. Although the wartime context can only obliquely be read into the poem's narrative of tumultuous organic growth from childhood to maturity (and any direct thematic or emotional influence would be extremely difficult to trace), this very obliqueness, and the refusal of an explicit war-based theme, are in themselves important wartime responses.[10]

Also, both war and wartime poetry so defined necessarily respond to or reflect the emotional conditions of the war during which they are written and are therefore more dependent on being true to 'lived experience' than is normally allowed or desired of poetry. Different criteria are generally applied to the reading of war or wartime poetry. Seamus Heaney's tentativeness at using 'the artistic consideration' to criticise Wilfred Owen's poetry is a good example of this: he feels his concern 'with what is artistically good as well as what is generally true' to be 'nit-picking criticism' when compared to 'the heavy price, in terms of emotional and physical suffering, the poet paid in order to bring it into being'.[11] Here, as often in the evaluation of war and wartime poetry, aesthetics are deemed less important than experience. As Hackett suggests, in the *Oasis* anthologies they were looking for work 'unlikely to be written except in wartime', a search deliberately drawn to include non-established and occasional poets (perhaps at the expense of established poets).[12] There is the temptation to see such work as, to some extent, the product of the war itself, and not solely of an individual artist; indeed, in the search for emotional response – 'the loneliness, excitement, boredom and despair, the disgust, the compassion and the weariness' of war – or for poetry that 'witnesses' the war, work that is too polished or artistic may be seen as suspicious or untruthful.

In the best of this wartime verse, however, the emotional response to the war is matched with artistic skill. A useful comparison can be made between the poems of Rosamund Praeger and Ruth Tomalin, for example, as they both tell of the intrusion of war into otherwise peaceful routines – both social and natural – with more or less propagandistic intent. Both, in effect, disrupt a landscape constructed in John Hewitt's 'Townland of Peace'. Hewitt emphasised distance and shelter from the conflict: he described the change that 'was strange and far / where a daft world gone shabby choked with war / . . . from Warsaw to the Yangtze' and proposed in the face of this 'change' a regional rather than a national identity, a 'small-compacted space / where every voice declares its native place, / townland, townquarter, county at the most'.[13] Rejecting the national scale of the conflict while also distancing himself from it (the war is imagined as happening east of Warsaw), Hewitt attempts to celebrate and cherish a townland extracted from the war (and a locality not associated with any national perspective). The work of Praeger (from Co. Down, sister of the famous naturalist Robert Lloyd Praeger) disallows such a succouring rural setting, as the war intrudes even into such a 'small-compacted space'. Her

1940 'War' describes how 'Lovely delicate things ... pushing upwards through the warming earth' at Easter time meet 'the war-planes crashing from the clouds, / And mangled men upon a thousand roads':[14] Praeger's imagery in the poem is, however, clichéd and vague: what precisely are the 'Lovely delicate things'? What, elsewhere in the poem, is 'the hidden Power, / That fosters in us life, and love and mirth'? A similar intrusion takes place in Tomalin's poems; here, though, the disruption of everyday life, and of a 'natural' setting, is figured as a surprising and unsettling clash of modes or registers. 'Embroidery, 1940', for example, uses an image that hovers between the redemptive and the ironic, as air raids are pushed from the mind by the act of embroidering butterflies:

> The day the shattered Germans lay in shreds
> among the placid nettles at the gate,
> I took a skein of sunset-coloured threads
> to make my brave Red Admiral a mate.[15]

Similarly, 'Invasion Spring' has a disjunctive meeting of the pastoral and the deathly, with airmen being described as shepherds who 'know and call their lambs by name – / Susannah, Charmer, Cheyenne Belle, / Calamity and Texas Dame'.[16] (This ambiguous use of contrasting registers is reminiscent of the meeting of texts in MacNeice's 'Whit Monday': '*The Lord's my shepherd* – familiar words of myth / Stand up better to bombs than a granite monolith.')[17]

Tomalin was born in Kilkenny and educated in England before serving in the Women's Land Army and as a staff reporter on various newspapers; her Irish origins have, however, little relevance to the Blitz poetry she was writing, even if they may have been important to her experience of the war. Are these Irish, English or British poems? Does it make sense to ask? Does the national context have any role whatsoever? Similar questions arise from examination of the experience of two other female poets. In 'A Curse' Wilma Cawdor appropriates an old curse from the family of her husband, the Earl of Cawdor, to threaten those who would not support the free-French forces;[18] Stephanie Batstone, meanwhile, stationed as a signaller in the WRNS in Oban (and later Northern Ireland) during the war, wrote love poems to an American sailor with whom she first communicated by Aldis lamp.[19] Both Cawdor and Batstone were born in England, and were writing in Scotland either as a result of marriage or military posting. Should their work be considered 'Scottish' war poetry or – at least – as a necessary context to Scottish war poetry? Equally, what status have anonymous songs such as 'Oh! Fucking Halkirk' or 'The Twats in the Ops Room'[20] (which raucously dismiss Scotland as a military base) as 'Scottish' war songs? Does the adjective 'Scottish' – or Irish, English or British – cease to have any relevance whatsoever in the face of the large-scale displacement of peoples and the resultant meeting of different nationalities? Or is it of particular importance given the context of war between nations?

Although the war on many levels solidified notions of nationality, the mass movements of people during the war problematised international boundaries; as such, the war created new patterns of intellectual and cultural commerce between nations and cultures (just as it was disallowing and troubling others). Maggie Ferguson's biography of George Mackay Brown, recounts the disorientating social and cultural effects of the mass movement of troops into Scapa Flow on Orkney during the war (as well as the effect of German raids on Orkney); Seamus Heaney's 'Anahorish 1944', meanwhile, describes the presence of large numbers of American troops in Northern Ireland during the war.[21] Similarly, the encounter between different languages and nationalities (and the subsequent dissolution of national stereotypes) is repeated many times in Scottish Second World War soldier poetry; the extent to which this is a refocusing of the prewar internationalism of Hugh MacDiarmid and Edwin Muir suggests that the poetry of Hamish Henderson, Sorley MacLean, George Campbell Hay and others is in effect a continuation of the tropes and images of the Scottish Renaissance at war.

This dissolution of nationalities was to such an extent, however, that even a fervent Scottish Nationalist like Hamish Henderson could consider (after being educated in England and then serving in the Army) that 'his long exile has seriously disqualified [him] as a Scottish poet; though [he] may be better as a European poet'.[22] It would certainly be misleading to define a narrowly Scottish context for Henderson's wartime songs and his *Elegies for the Dead in Cyrenaica*. Henderson himself emphasised that the Eighth Army with which he served in Africa and Italy was 'a literate army, its soldiers the beneficiaries of the 1918 Education Act';[23] it was also a heterogeneous army, made up of different nationalities, languages and classes. Despite Henderson's emotional (and at times official) attachment to the 51st Highland Division, the immediate context in which he wrote was international, and English as much as Scottish: fighting in Africa were also English poets of the calibre of Keith Douglas, Vernon Scannell and Sidney Keyes.[24] Scannell served in the 51st Highland, as did John Jarmain (whose poetry features heavily in anthologies of the time) and Denholm Young, commander of the Signal Regiment in the 51st and author of 'Dead German Youth', one of the many poems from the conflict to echo Wilfred Owen's 'Strange Meeting'.[25] Meanwhile, a battalion of the

Cameron Highlanders, which served as part of the 51st in France, was under the command of the Earl of Cawdor (whose wife was in Cawdor castle writing pro-French verse).[26] Although Henderson himself was 'out of sympathy with the English, with their tepid self-control, mild dislikes, liberal hesitations, and their passion for compromise',[27] for other Scottish Nationalist poets the importance of encounters with English soldiers as comrades cannot be overstated. One of the most unusual moments in Sorley MacLean's war poetry, for example, is the surprised realisation that an English 'Fear beag truagh le gruaidhean pluiceach' ('poor little chap with chubby cheeks') could act as bravely as the heroic subjects of traditional Gaelic clan-and-chief panegyrics.[28]

The work of the polyglots Henderson and George Campbell Hay offers the fullest exploration of other nationalities and cultures. Hay had always been a reluctant soldier, and was serving in the army despite pacifist – and socialist and Scottish Nationalist – convictions which initially led him to oppose conscription as a conscientious objector; only after a period evading arrest in the hills of his native Argyll and a short spell in prison did Hay join the Army.[29] Hay's best poems from this period focus not so much on life in the Army, or his own experiences of conflict, as on the inhabitants of North Africa; he quickly learnt Arabic[30] and his friendships with locals influenced the poems 'Mochtár is Dúghall' ('Mokhtâr and Dougall'),[31] 'Atman',[32] 'Bisearta' ('Bizerta')[33] and 'Meftah Bâbkum es-Sabar'.[34] The impetus in each of these poems is to show the similarities and fraternity (Hay's odd and exclusively masculine worldview was well suited to the experience of war in the desert) between the Arabs and the Gaels, and the adversity and suffering they share. In 'Atman' the affirmation of friendship – ''S b'e 'n toibheum, Atmain, àicheadh / Gur bràthair dhomh thu fhéin' ('And it would be blasphemy, Atman, to deny / That you are a brother of mine')[35] – comes despite Atman's conviction as a thief; meanwhile, in 'Mochtár is Dúghall' the eponymous Scottish and Arab characters die together under mortar fire, their friendship and shared humanity annulled by the war.[36]

Henderson's multilingualism and position as an interrogator put him in constant touch with both locals and captured enemies; his *Elegies for the Dead in Cyrenaica* recreate on a textual level repeated encounters between Scottish and other cultures. These encounters, and the polyglossia of the texts, are to some extent the *point* of the poems. Cavafy's descriptions of Alexandria[37] are incorporated into the text along with references to ancient Egyptian religion (38–9), and fragments of untranslated Italian and German appear alongside Scots and English. The dedications and epigraphs make this encounter somewhat programmatic: there are dedications to Luigi

Castigliano, Gregorio Prieto and John Lorne Campbell,[38] the epigraphs are untranslated passages from Goethe (15) and Hölderlin (25), balanced by the Gaelic of Sorley MacLean (31). The presence of German texts here is, of course, crucial: in Henderson's work Germans are not figured propagandistically or negatively, but are instead treated with sympathy and humanism. In his 1948 Foreword Henderson writes: 'It was the remark of a captured German officer which first suggested to me the theme of these poems. He had said: "Africa changes everything. In reality we are allies, and the desert is our common enemy."'[39]

This fellow feeling across the front line is nuanced by a 'curious "doppelgaenger" effect' (58) caused by the fact that the British and German armies lived off supplies and machinery salvaged from each other, and so were, to some degree, dependent on each other; to this extent, for Henderson the conflict is not between the two armies but between '"the dead, the innocent" – that eternally wronged proletariat of levelling death in which all the fallen are comrades – and ourselves, the living' (59). The *unheimlich* nature of this doppelgänger relationship becomes apparent in the 'strange' meeting with dead German soldiers. Henderson's seventh elegy is subtitled 'Seven Good Germans' and ends with the nullifying:

> Seven poor bastards
> dead in African deadland
> (tawny tousled hair under the issue blanket)
> *wie einst Lili*
> dead in African deadland
> *einst Lili Marlene.* (37)

The repetitions of 'dead' suggest that the agency of the soldiers themselves is disallowed, that the 'deadland' is responsible for their deaths, and that in their death they have become part of that deadland (and so are in some way doubly dead).

Henderson focuses on the desert (Keith Douglas's 'nightmare ground')[40] as an enemy: as 'brutish' (59), 'malevolent' (20), 'impartial' (20), 'hostile' (20), and a place of 'moron monotony' (25). For Sorley MacLean, however, the desert is more important as an alien and alienating space. Writing in his introduction to Henderson's elegies, MacLean suggests that the desert is a no-place, with 'little of human achievement' to mark it out or give it meaning, and that the soldiers fighting in the North African desert during the Second World War were 'as if abstracted from a real world to fight on a remote moon-like terrain'.[41] For MacLean, the desert is an environment which alternates between being benign, hostile and impartial, seemingly at random. In 'Latha Foghair' ('Autumn Day'), for example, the poet is trapped in a shell-hole with six dead men

> Ris a' ghréin 's i cho coma,
> cho geal cràiteach;
> air a' ghanmhich 's i cho tìorail
> socair bàidheil;
> agus fo reultan Africa,
> 's iad leugach àlainn.

[In the sun, which was so indifferent, / so white and painful; / on the sand which was so comfortable, / easy and kindly; / and under the stars of Africa, / jewelled and beautiful.][42]

The precise rhythms of life and death in the conflict are viewed *sub specie aeternitatis*, and the line separating life and death – the fate or 'Taghadh' ('Election', with Presbyterian overtones) that chose the poet's comrades but not him – is discovered to be 'cho diabhlaidh coma' ('as devilishly indifferent') as the shells.[43]

These experiences of the desert as a site of death and dislocation, in which national identities pale alongside human suffering on both sides of the conflict, are in marked contrast to other Scottish Nationalist experiences of the war. While Sorley MacLean – like Henderson and Hay a committed nationalist and socialist – tried to sign up on the first day of the war,[44] Douglas Young, who oversaw the preparation of MacLean's *Dàin do Eimhir* (*Poems for Eimhir*) while his friend was recovering from the injuries he received at the second battle of El Alamein, opposed the war effort in a (failed) legal action based on his own interpretation of the 1707 Treaty of Union.[45] His subsequent imprisonment meant that his experience of the war had more in common with that of Irish Nationalists interned in the Curragh for the duration of the conflict – including Máirtín Ó Cadhain and the young Brendan Behan[46] – than with that of his friends MacLean and Garioch (though Garioch was in a German prisoner-of-war camp).[47] The poems of Sydney Goodsir Smith, meanwhile, offer an undiluted emphasis on Scotland and Scottishness in marked contrast to the internationalism of Henderson and Hay. In 'El Alamein', Smith – who did not take part in the war, being New Zealand-born and therefore not subject to conscription – twice strikes a particularly nationalist note, suggesting 'That this was for Alba / Maun we mak siccar!' and concluding 'O, the gleds foregaither / Roun Alba's deid.'[48] There is irony here, as there is in 'The Mither's Lament', in which Smith exclaims 'Doutless he deed for Scotland's life; / Doutless the statesmen dinna lee; / But och tis sair begrutten pride / An wersh the wine o vitorie!'; there is also, however, assertion of a nationalist 'fighting for Scotland' line (a type of Scottish Redmondism), which has remained unaffected by the multinational and multicultural reality of the military experience.[49]

The Scottish Nationalist dilemma during the war was almost precisely mirrored in the Republic, where there was concern about the ramifications – and correctness – of the Republic's neutral stance in poetry just as in more general cultural and political debates. The neutrality of the Republic and the lack of conscription in Northern Ireland meant that the vast majority of Irish poetry written during the war was that of non-combatants; this is reflected in the lack of Second World War soldier-poetry in Gerald Dawe's *Earth Voices Whispering: An Anthology of Irish-War Poetry, 1914–45*. Instead of experiential war poetry there tends to be a concern with the political and geographical location of the country in respect of the war: its superiority to, or absence and isolation from, the conflict. Clair Wills suggests that there were diametrically opposed narratives of the Republic's neutral stance, drawn along national lines, and both understanding the stance in terms of 'a battle of darkness against light':

In Britain the Irish were portrayed as dwelling in a cave, lost in the dark, fumbling around in a state of ignorance induced by the harshness of the censorship, but also by their own lack of interest in a world from which they had deliberately withdrawn. In Ireland the right to an independent foreign policy, and to protect the Irish state, was also argued in moral terms. Political and religious imperatives seemed to overlap as neutrality was associated with pacifism, and with an ability to feel compassion for all suffering, regardless of which side the victims were on. According to this account, neutrality was a source of enlightenment. Irish society might be called on to 'dispel the darkness' of the 'seething European cauldron', as Aiken put it – to calm the warmongering on both sides.[50]

Máirtín Ó Direáin rather bluntly makes the case for neutrality as enlightenment in 'Cuireadh do Mhuire' ('Invitation to the Virgin'). The poem ignores politics and instead promotes a moral position created and fortified by geographical isolation:

> Deonaigh glacadh
> Le cuireadh uaimse
> Go hoileán mara
> San Iarthar cianda:
> Beidh coinnle geala
> I ngach fuinneog lasta
> Is tine mhóna
> Ar theallach adhainte.
> *Nollaig 1942.*

[Deign to accept / My invitation / To a sea-bound island / In the remote West: / Shining candles will be / Lit in each window / And a fire of turf / On each hearthstone kindled. / *Christmas 1942*.]⁵¹

Elided here is the political neutrality that actually keeps the Republic out of the war. Instead it is geographical circumstance, Ireland's location 'San Iarthar cianda' ('In the remote West'), which is pictured as setting the island outside the history of continental Europe, and which allows Ó Direáin to offer the island as a moral haven.

Louis MacNeice's 'Neutrality', on the other hand, insists on recognition of the fact that it is political rather than geographical isolation. Though sensitive to the moral side of the Republic's stance against the 'archetypal sin' of the war, MacNeice firmly denies the geographical separation Ó Direáin emphasises in his English translation of his own poem. Ó Direáin's 'oileán mara' ('sea-bound island', literally 'sea-island') is figured in MacNeice's poem as a 'neutral island in the heart of man';⁵² rather than 'sea-bound', Ireland is 'close' to the continent and so inculpated in the war taking place there:

> But then look eastward from your heart, there bulks
> A continent, close, dark, as archetypal sin,
> While to the west off your own shores the mackerel
> Are fat – on the flesh of your kin.⁵³

From his 1939 'Coming of the War' MacNeice had considered Ireland as both outside and inside the war. Ireland is both nightmare and dream, 'the crossbones of Galway ... the rubbish and sewage' and a weir on the Corrib with 'a hundred swans / Dreaming on the harbour'. Despite the attempt to set Ireland apart, it is not exempt from the pressures of the war: the poem's refrain states that 'The war came down on us there.'⁵⁴

This simultaneous experience of, and distance from, the Second World War is most famously captured in Patrick Kavanagh's 'Epic', which figures the war in miniature: a 'local row' about land between the Duffys and old McCabe set alongside and given precedence over the 'Munich bother'.⁵⁵ The ambiguities relating to this celebration of the parochial are exploded in *The Great Hunger*, however, in which the Republic's neutrality offers a backdrop to the sexual frustration and emasculation of Patrick Maguire. In connecting neutrality to 'neuterality' – Maguire's emasculation and entrapment – Kavanagh condemns the Republic as a state, in Wills's words, 'peopled by the old and poor, a country with no future'.⁵⁶ Maguire has only a 'lowly position' in the pub conversations in which a pseudo-superiority to the participants in the war is played out, as 'the generals / On both sides were shown to be stupid as hell. / If he'd taken *that* road, they remarked of a Marshal, / He'd have ... O they know their geography well.'[57] The conflation of history and geography is once more important: in this case the conflict is reduced to a matter of geography, with the implicit understanding that since the Irish do not 'share' the geography of the war they should have no part in it. The Republic of *The Great Hunger* – the Republic which, in Kavanagh's 'Lough Derg' 'froze for want of Europe'[58] – is thus in line with the version of 'Ireland's wartime story' that Wills associates with 'absence – the absence of conflict, of supplies, of social dynamism, of contact with "the outside world"', with the understanding that participation in the war would have led to the 'presence' of each of these things (as well as centrality instead of isolation, artistic wealth instead of cultural impoverishment).[59]

This notion of the Republic as an 'absence' sits uncomfortably alongside the Scottish soldier poets' experience of the desert as an absence. They are both dislocated spaces at once within and outwith the war; however, only one is an impartial no-place in which there are no traces of life and civilisation. Perhaps the only redeeming feature of the desert was that, despite their sympathy for their enemies, the very fact of their dislocation gave the poets a sense of purpose and a clarity about their roles, as soldiers if not as poets. In 'Dol an Iar' ('Going Westwards'), Sorley MacLean claims ''s ged nach fuath liom armailt Roimeil, / tha sùil na h-eanchainn gun claonadh' ('though I do not hate Rommel's army, / the brain's eye is not squinting').[60] This is, however, only made possible by the adoption of a traditional role for the soldier-poet derived from within the Gaelic tradition, as MacLean draws upon genealogical and clan history in a manner that was not possible for English- or Scots-language poets of the war:

> Agus biodh na bha mar a bha e,
> tha mi de dh'fhir mhór' a' Bhràighe,
> de Chloinn Mhic Ghille Chaluim threubhaich,
> de Mhathanaich Loch Aills nan geurlann,
> agus fir m' ainme – có bu tréine
> nuair dh'fhadadh uabhar an léirchreach?

[And be what was as it was, / I am of the big men of the Braes, / of the heroic Raasay MacLeods, / of the sharp-sword Mathesons of Lochalsh; / and the men of my name – who were braver / when their ruinous pride was kindled?][61]

MacLean would in later years, however, also sympathise with the position of the Republic, suggesting that he 'would never have expected Ireland ... to be anything other than neutral' despite his support for the war as an anti-Fascist 'crusade'.⁶² Alongside the clarity of his role in the desert, that is, there came an understanding that there was no single, correct response to the war, and that there was no single location or standpoint for poetry of the war: though his 'brain's eye' was unsquinting, it certainly did not have the only possible outlook.

NOTES

1. See Gerald Dawe (ed.), *Earth Voices Whispering: An Anthology of Irish-War Poetry, 1914–45* (Belfast: Blackstaff, 2008), 135.
2. To avoid ambiguity I will anachronistically use 'the Republic' throughout this chapter: the name 'Irish Free State' was dropped with the adoption of the 1937 constitution, with 'Ireland' being used until the passage of the Republic of Ireland Act in 1948.
3. F. S. L. Lyons, *Ireland since the Famine* (London: Fontana, 1973), 557–8.
4. Keith Douglas, 'Poets in This War', *A Prose Miscellany* (Manchester: Carcanet, 1985), 119–20.
5. Robert Graves, 'The Poets of World War II' (1942), *The Common Asphodel: Collected Essays on Poetry* (London: Hamish Hamilton, 1949), 307, quoted in Hugh Haughton (ed.), *Second World War Poems* (London: Faber, 2004), xviii.
6. Fran Brearton, 'A War of Friendship: Robert Graves and Siegfried Sassoon', in Tim Kendall (ed.), *The Oxford Handbook of British and Irish War Poetry* (Oxford University Press, 2007), 209.
7. These include G. S. Fraser, Hamish Henderson, Robert Garioch, Edwin Morgan, George Campbell Hay and Sorley MacLean. See Roderick Watson, '"Death's Proletariat": Scottish Poets of the Second World War', in Kendall (ed.), *Oxford Handbook*, 318.
8. See Hugh Haughton, 'Anthologising War', in Kendall (ed.), *Oxford Handbook*, 440.
9. John Hackett, 'A Preliminary Note', in Victor Selwyn (ed.), *Poems of the Second World War: The Oasis Selection* (London and Melbourne: Dent, 1985), viii. Hackett was Australian, his father being a Wicklow-born barrister who had emigrated in 1875 and became a newspaper proprietor.
10. In MacLean's case it may be that his oblique 'wartime' poems are passed over in favour of the poems he wrote while serving in the Western Desert which obviously and directly comment on the conflict; for these poems see Sorley MacLean, *O Choille gu Bearradh/From Wood to Ridge* (Manchester/Edinburgh: Carcanet/Birlinn, 1999), 204–15.
11. Seamus Heaney, 'Nero, Chekhov's Cognac and a Knocker', *The Government of the Tongue* (London: Faber, 1988), xv–xvi.
12. Victor Selwyn, editor of the *Oasis* anthologies, claimed that their concern in the anthologies had been 'to seek the writings of those who *became* poets as a result of going to war. Naturally we select from the established poets, too. But to get the feel of war we deliberately sought unpublished manuscripts, the verses written by unknowns from the airfields of Britain to the POW camps of

South-East Asia.' Quoted in Hamish Henderson, *Alias MacAlias: Writings on Songs, Folk and Literature* (Edinburgh: Polygon, 2004), 319.

13. John Hewitt, 'Townland of Peace' (in 'Freehold'), *Selected Poems* (Belfast: Blackstaff, 2007), 131–2.
14. See Anne Powell (ed.), *Shadows of War: British Women's Poetry of the Second World War* (Gloucestershire: Sutton, 1997), 34, 330.
15. *Ibid.*, 68.
16. *Ibid.*, 262.
17. Louis MacNeice, *Collected Poems* (London: Faber, 2007), 222.
18. See Powell (ed.), *Shadows of War*, 52.
19. Selwyn (ed.), *Poems of the Second World War*, 353.
20. Kenneth Baker (ed.), *The Faber Book of War Poetry* (London: Faber, 1996), 110–12. The chorus of 'The Twats in the Ops Room', which was written in what has been termed 'British Army demotic', ends 'Ain't the Air Force fucking awful? We made a fucking landfall in the Firth of Fucking Forth'.
21. Maggie Ferguson, *George Mackay Brown: The Life* (London: John Murray, 2007), 43–66 (p. 45 gives two stanzas of the song 'Bloody Orkney', a variation on 'Oh! Fucking Halkirk'). Mackay Brown's 1970 novel, *Greenvoe*, offers an apocalyptic rewriting of this military 'occupation'. See Seamus Heaney, *District and Circle* (London: Faber, 2006), 7.
22. Timothy Neat, *Hamish Henderson: A Biography* (Edinburgh: Birlinn, 2007), Vol. 1, 163.
23. Hamish Henderson, 'The Poetry of War in the Middle East, 1939–45', in Henderson, *Alias MacAlias*, 319. The extent of the army's literacy (and literariness) is evident from journals such as *Citadel*, *Personal Landscapes*, *Orientations* and *Oasis*. For the importance of Henderson's songs to the soldiers in the Army, especially the 51st Highland Division, see Neat, *Hamish Henderson*, 67–104.
24. Watson, 'Death's Proletariat', 318.
25. Denholm Young, 'Dead German Youth', in Selwyn (ed.), *Poems of the Second World War*, 69. Keith Douglas's 'Vergissmeinnicht' is the most famous, but far from the only, Second World War poem to reconfigure the meeting with a dead enemy that is central to Owen's poem.
26. Henderson did not serve with the 51st in France but remained in Italy to help organise the Italian resistance against the Germans.
27. G. S. Fraser, *A Stranger and Afraid – The Autobiography of an Intellectual* (Manchester: Carcanet, 1983), quoted in Neat, *Hamish Henderson*, 78.
28. 'Curaidhean' ('Heroes') in MacLean, *O Choille gu Bearradh*, 208–9.
29. George Campbell Hay, *The Collected Poems and Songs of George Campbell Hay*, ed. Michel Byrne (Edinburgh University Press, 2002), Vol. 1, 27–30.
30. During his life Hay was also able to translate from Irish, Welsh, French, Spanish, Italian, Icelandic, Norwegian, Greek and Arabic. See Caoimhin Mac Giolla Leith, 'At one with Mokhtar', www.timesonline.co.uk, 10 August 2001.

31. Hay, *Collected Poems*, Vol. 2, 105–61.
32. *Ibid.*, 162–4.
33. *Ibid.*, 176–7.
34. *Ibid.*, 193–6.
35. *Ibid.*, 164. The importance of 'blasphemy' as a marker of cultural difference (and soldierly identity) during the war can be picked up from a letter Hamish Henderson wrote from Italy in the Winter of 1944: 'These hills are a great breeding ground of blasphemy. The partisans swear by Madonna the pig and Jesus the assassin, and in spite of Monty's old Orders of the Day his veterans in the Apennines are now much given to taking in vain the name of the God of battles' – Hamish Henderson, *The Armstrong Nose: Selected Letters of Hamish Henderson* (Edinburgh: Polygon, 1996), 7.
36. Hay, *Collected Poems*, Vol. 2, 159–61.
37. Hamish Henderson, *Elegies for the Dead in Cyrenaica* (Edinburgh: Polygon, 1990), 22.
38. Castigliano was a close associate of Henderson's during the war, having deserted from Mussolini's army – see Neat, *Hamish Henderson*, 124–5. John Lorne Campbell (1906–96) was a renowned Gaelic scholar and folk-collector.
39. Henderson, *Elegies for the Dead*, 59.
40. Keith Douglas, 'Vergissmeinnicht', *The Complete Poems* (London: Faber, 2000), 118.
41. Sorley MacLean, 'Introduction', in Henderson, *Elegies for the Dead*, 12.
42. 'Latha Foghair' ('Autumn Day'), in MacLean, *O Choille gu Bearradh*, 214–15.
43. *Ibid.*
44. Sorley MacLean, *Dàin do Eimhir*, ed. Christopher Whyte (Glasgow: Association for Scottish Literary Studies, 2002), 173.
45. Other high profile Scottish poets not directly involved in the conflict include Norman MacCaig and George Bruce, who were accepted as conscientious objectors; Hugh MacDiarmid was employed in a munitions factory during the war – see Watson, 'Death's Proletariat', 330.
46. Clair Wills, *That Neutral Island* (London: Faber, 2007), 13.
47. See Robert Garioch, *Two Men and a Blanket* (Edinburgh: Southside, 1975) for Garioch's own account of his period of captivity.
48. Sidney Goodsir Smith, 'El Alamein', in H. Haughton (ed.), *Second World War Poems*, 269. *Alba* is the Scottish Gaelic for Scotland; the Scots words are *siccar*, sure; *gleds*, kites.
49. Smith, 'The Mither's Lament', in Haughton (ed.), *Second World War Poems*, 270; *lee*, lie; *begrutten*, lamented; *wersh*, sour. The 'fighting for Scotland' line was by no means Smith's alone: for the possibility of the 51st Highland Division metamorphosing at the end of the war into a prototype Scottish national army, see Neat, *Hamish Henderson*, 111–12.
50. Wills, *That Neutral Island*, 423.
51. Máirtín Ó Direáin, *Selected Poems: Tacar Dánta*, trans. Tomás Mac Síomóin and Douglas Sealy (Newbridge: Goldsmith, 1984), 8–9. Ó Direáin's first (self-published) pamphlet, the 1942 *Coinnle Geala* (*White Candles*) shares the same suggestion of enlightenment as 'Cuireadh do Mhuire'.

52. MacNeice, *Collected Poems*, 224.
53. *Ibid.*
54. *Ibid.*, 684. Samuel Beckett's response was more vehement than MacNeice's, as seen by his (in Clair Wills's terms) 'absolute rejection of neutral Ireland for Paris and later Roussillon – his stated preference for France at war to Ireland at peace'; Wills, *That Neutral Island*, 12.
55. Patrick Kavanagh, *Selected Poems* (London: Penguin, 1996), 101–2.
56. Wills, *That Neutral Island*, 257.
57. Kavanagh, *Selected Poems*, 33.
58. *Ibid.*, 59.
59. Wills, *That Neutral Island*, 10.
60. MacLean, *O Choille gu Bearradh*, 206–7.
61. *Ibid.*
62. Sorley MacLean, Hamish Henderson and Seán Mac Réamoinn, *An Turas Seo*, public conversation, 1996. Private recording.

CHAPTER 5

Affinities in time and space: reading the Gaelic poetry of Ireland and Scotland

Máire Ní Annracháin

In the early years of the twentieth century, Patrick Pearse engaged in heated debate in the pages of the newspaper *An Claidheamh Soluis* about the future direction of literature in Irish. The Irish cultural revival was in full swing. Douglas Hyde, who later became the first president of Ireland, had written of the need to de-anglicise Ireland, and modernisers and conservatives were at daggers drawn. Pearse's position was nuanced and wise. 'We want no Gothic revival'[1] was one of his more famous statements, one which seemed to place him firmly at a distance from those who would eschew the modern world and modern forms of the language in favour of older native models and an outdated, if highly codified, form of language. But Pearse also called for balance, and advocated that 'if Irish literature is to flourish it must get in touch on the one hand with its own past and on the other with the mind of contemporary Europe'.[2] As literary criticism *re* Irish developed through the following century, it engaged in vigorous debate, much soul searching and a good deal of experimentation, subtle and brash, on these issues until it arrived at a state, towards the end of the twentieth century, where the most creative and persuasive markers of its modernity were – I will argue – precisely achieved through the reconfiguration of many of its most deeply rooted and traditional components, whether conceptual, formal or tropic.

Engagement with thorny issues of tradition placed Irish-language literature within one of the liveliest strands of Western literary reflection throughout the twentieth century. More is at stake than literary history. Theoretical reflections on various forms of intertextuality abound internationally, concerning themselves with issues of quotation, imitation, influence, irony, the rewriting of myth. Some of the texts on these topics are among the most iconic in literary studies: T. S. Eliot's seminal reflection on tradition and the individual talent,[3] Roland Barthes's on the death of the author,[4] and Harold Bloom's on the misprision of strong poets,[5] to mention just a few. If romantic concern with authorial originality has ceded ground to an understanding that no text is an island, the Gaelic versions of the debate, which have taken place primarily in Ireland, have focused the integration of a modern poetic sensibility with a tradition that had endured a century, or, as some would argue, two and a half centuries of decline, but had nevertheless not died out. The concept of 'integration' places this paper at quite a distance from Eric Hobsbawm's assertion that '[t]he object and characteristic of "traditions", including invented ones, is invariance'[6] although in general terms scholarly analysis of the constructed nature of many modern concepts of traditions is helpful and enlightening.[7]

Literary history is nonetheless a core concern. As Joep Leerssen[8] has pointed out, the idea of a self-conscious national literary history is relatively recent. Even in European societies that did not come under the type of pressure that Gaelic suffered, no overview of national traditions was available before the nineteenth century; and since development was incremental over the centuries there could have been little awareness on the part of even an educated readership of the full span of national traditions in their respective countries. Within Gaelic, literary history had been well served during the early and later medieval periods: in the monasteries in the case of the former era and in bardic schools in the latter. In the case of Irish, this history was conserved and transmitted orally and in manuscript form but not in print, with the result that only a handful of literary texts, and therefore no literary history, was available in printed form to early revivalists at the start of the twentieth century. Scottish Gaelic literature had fared better, with a considerable number of collections of later song and poetry published in the original language,[9] but this did not extend to the earlier bardic material that formed the backbone of the shared Gaelic literary tradition of Ireland and Scotland.

The question of fidelity to an earlier tradition is made more complex by the relationship between Irish and Scottish Gaelic. The extent and nature of the literary connections between Ireland and Scotland has been the subject of a good deal of discussion, and various conceptual frameworks have been put forward: mother country/daughter country, cultural continuum, culture province, coloniser/colonised.[10] Irrespective of one's preferred model, by the start of the twentieth century the two poetic traditions had diverged. Today, notwithstanding the effects of the regular fêting of Irish and Scottish Gaelic poets and musicians during reciprocal visits across the Sea of Moyle in creating a sustained tradition of concerts and sessions of enchantment, few Irish or Scottish poets can read both forms of Gaelic with ease, and there has been little articulated exploration of each other's distinctive Gaelic literary traditions. There have been occasional performances of songs from the other's repertoire; infrequent direct translations; and – from time to time – some allusion or acknowledgement, as in, for instance, Colm Breathnach's dedication to Sorley MacLean in his collection *Scáthach*,[11] the title of which also evokes the tradition that Cú Chulainn learned the arts of war in Scotland. Despite a growing number of speakers of both forms of Gaelic, such allusions evoke little more than a superficial response. Few Irish people, for example, would know of the association of Scáthach with a particular castle on Skye. Few would recognise the allusion to one of the most canonical of Scottish Gaelic poems, Alasdair Mac Mhaighstir Alasdair's eighteenth-century 'Allt an t-Siùcair', in the short and beautiful poem by Aonghas Pàdraig Caimbeul that was shortlisted in the 2009 Strokestown Poetry Festival's Gaelic (Irish and Scottish) competition:

'Eapaic'

Thig an tè
a chruthaicheas
an ath eapaic
Ghàidhlig

o bhonn na mara.

Cha bhuin i dhan talamh.

Bidh a h-adhradh
sligeach, croimheal.

Bidh Mac Mhaighstir Alasdair
mar chreig dhi, marbh, balbh.

Thig i le a h-òrain fhèin
a' sèideadh bholgain-ciùil,
ann an ainm Cholm Chille
no ann an ainm Tiara Xzing

agus bidh a' cànan
mar allt an t-siùcair, air madainn

chùbhraidh chèit.

['Epic': The one /who will create / the next Gaelic epic / will emerge from / the bottom of the sea. She will not belong to earth. / Her worship will glitter / like the shell of a coral. / Mac Mhaighstir Alasdair / will be like a rock to her, dead, dumb. / She will ascend with her own song / blowing bubbles of music / in the name of Columba / or in the name of Tiara Xzing / and her language / will be like the babbling brook, on a bright / May morning.][12]

A mutual sense of recognition exists but is nebulous, deriving on the whole from a shared older tradition that underwent significant modifications and developments since the eighteenth, and to some extent the seventeenth, centuries and that created an increasing sense of distance between the Irish and Scottish Gaelic communities. I refer here to developments in a broad range of areas that impinge on poetic production. In the linguistic domain, vernacular Irish and Scottish Gaelic became increasingly separate from each other, accelerated by the loss of a common written standard. Political forces were at work too, with widespread cultural oppression, famine and emigration marking the eighteenth and nineteenth centuries in both countries although the reasons for these did not entirely overlap. Later on, in the twentieth century, the political context for cultural revival was quite distinct in Ireland and Scotland, with Irish enjoying the status of a national language while Scottish Gaelic remained exclusively the preserve of local and regional communities. There were numerous other forces at play as well, religious, educational and intellectual.

Nonetheless, although George Steiner's argument that '[w]hen using a word we wake into resonance, as it were, its entire previous history'[13] is probably overstated in a general sense, it proves disconcertingly close to the mark for those readers of modern Gaelic literature who do make the effort to engage with each other's literature and who are constantly surprised to encounter unsuspected echoes from their older literature emerging in a modern guise in the contemporary literature of each other's countries. The centuries of cultural and linguistic divergence have left their mark, and an early common tradition, or at least a tradition that had much in common on both sides of the Sea of Moyle, can on occasion seem hopelessly divided, but at other times uncannily unified, as Christopher Whyte suggests:

> If one were to attempt an outline survey of Gaelic language poetry and songs written in Scotland over the past four centuries there are real grounds for arguing that the significant intertext, rather than writing elsewhere in Scotland, would be writing in the Irish language of the same period.[14]

A good example is the resilience of images that imply a female personification of the Scottish landscape that would do Ireland proud, even though Gaelic in Scotland was theoretically devoid of sovereignty goddesses. William Ross's eighteenth-century 'Feasgar Luain' ('Monday Evening')[15] tells of the sudden appearance of a beautiful maiden in terms scarcely distinguishable from Irish *aisling* poetry:

> Dhiùchd mar aingeal, ma mo choinneamh
> 'N ainnir òg, ba ghrinne shnuadh;

'Seang shlios fallain air bhlà canaich,
No mar an eal' air a chuan . . .

[There suddenly appeared, like an angel, in front of me a beautiful maiden with the loveliest countenance, her slender flawless body like the flower of the bog cotton, or a swan on the ocean . . .]

On a daily basis, however, the ramifications of centuries of separation can be frustrating when the simplest of greetings elicit blank faces and phonetic differences induce a mild form of something akin to panic. However shallow the historical foundations of such obstacles, it does erect a formidable barrier to human communication. It can, to some extent, be turned to good advantage if approached in a ludic spirit and many entertaining hours have been, and are still, spent trawling wide-eyed through each other's dictionaries.

Entertainment aside, the impulse to seek connections between the Gaelic sections of these islands can be as motivated by a political agenda as by historical or aesthetic concerns. In this respect, it is of course no different from the highlighting of any other connections, literary or other, between any two groups. The Northern Ireland peace process, solidarity with other lesser-used languages within Europe and resistance to the levelling effect on smaller cultures of prevalent globalising forces all provide a rationale for strengthening links between Gaelic Ireland and Gaelic Scotland over and above the facts of history. On a broader scale, it is a commonplace that the search for, and celebration of, literary tradition in Europe has often been shackled to questions of national identity. Within this context, the concept of authenticity can degenerate into the futile search for uncontaminated origins and a vanquishing attitude to outside cultural influences. There are countless examples, of which the following, from Seán Ó Riada, is representative: 'By traditional I mean the untouched, un-Westernized, orally-transmitted music ... Ireland has had a long and violent history during which she remained individual, retaining all her individual characteristics. Such foreign influences as were felt were quickly absorbed and Gaelicised.'[16]

That is not to argue against using the prism of tradition when reading contemporary literature. Rather, it is to warn that antennae ought to be sharpened, faint bells allowed to ring, and in general the possibility of a constantly evolving tradition treated with seriousness, not as an anachronism and not in the expectation of an unchanging monument, but as foundation stones. Individual critics or even the best part of a generation may sail with the wind of tradition or alternatively against it; the cultural politics that manifest themselves are as much the critics' as the texts'. I should perhaps state my own at this juncture, to explain why I have chosen here and elsewhere to emphasise the influence of tradition, and to explore some of its ramifications for a Scottish-Irish perspective. First, tradition is sometimes only subtly present. To pass over it is to do an injustice to the texts that enshrine it, and to risk blindness. I do not share the accusatory tone adopted by Christopher Whyte when he says, in reference to Kurt Wittig's 1958 study *The Scottish Tradition in Literature*, 'He makes no attempt to disguise the extent to which a preoccupation with that tradition, and with the "Scottishness" it embodies, dictates the nature of his study.'[17] Second, I have no fear that the presence of, or the investigation of, traditional roots is anti-Enlightenment: a charge levelled by Douglas Sealy against Nuala Ní Dhomhnaill,[18] and by Christopher Whyte against Angus MacNeacail.[19] Whyte has criticised MacNeacail for failing to modernise, in particular for writing poetry that might have difficulty coping with topics such as, say, the night of the general election. I have argued elsewhere to the contrary, suggesting that it is MacNeacail's engagement with the tradition that is one of his most modern features, and this form of modernisation is by no means confined to MacNeacail.[20] On the whole, modernity in Gaelic is not expressed over against the tradition, but through it, even to the extent, as Cairns Craig has put it, of rejecting it: 'one can engage with a tradition by rejecting it, and it is manifestly the case in Gaelic, both Irish and Scottish, that the revival of a cultural tradition has no necessary connection with antiquarianism'.[21] Third, there is, for certain writers and readers who may still mourn the loss of a hermetically sealed formalism, a welcome sense that one is dealing with a properly aesthetic question, albeit one with inevitable political side-effects.

Foregrounding tradition has not always had currency within Irish-language studies, which suffered from a well-meaning though happily short-lived move, with which I have no desire to associate this paper, to reject almost everything that pertained to the modern world as unworthy of inclusion in Irish literature. A more fruitful approach has been advocated by Breandán Ó Doibhlin.[22] From the vantage point of the present day, it seems naïve and ahistorical to imagine that one could neatly compartmentalise literature into native–traditional on the one hand, and externally inspired–modern on the other, as though these were a binary pair, any more than one could seriously argue that Gaelic was at any time since the introduction of Christianity a primarily oral culture. Better to see a literary tradition as constructed, dynamic and dialogic. We now know how cultures grow by engaging with other cultures, and some argue that cultural growth takes place in the space between different cultures in dialogue.[23] We also know that, regardless of outside influences, traditions are neither stable nor unchanging in themselves, and that they can indeed experience reversals of so complete and ironic a nature that one can almost lose sight of the line of continuity, as has been shown, for instance, by René Girard in the case of the development of the Bible from earlier religious beliefs.[24] Furthermore we now know that nostalgia for a pure origin is vain and doomed from the outset. More positively, modern Irish and Scottish Gaelic poetry is an amalgam of echoes and developments from its own past, and from the past and present of the other cultures with which it has come into contact, with the added spice in the mixture of the very specific neither-self-nor-other relationship between the two strands of the Gaelic tradition, Irish and Scottish. This is not an appeal for balance; it is more a testament to the surges of vitality that have marked Gaelic literature since its inception, and its capacity to bear soundings.

My approach does, however, cut slightly across the grain of a strand of literary history that overly privileges external and non-traditional influences as a marker of modernity. However hungry for identity minority language groups may be, they also hanker after the modern, and too often the modern has been reduced to an openness to external influence, usually from continental Europe. This is in part responsible for the particular gloss that has on occasion been placed on past interactions between various minority traditions and other cultures. Certain of these have attracted more than their fair share of attention, though in general academic rigour can be relied on to redress the balance in due course. For instance, for some time French literary influences were particularly welcome in Irish-language literary studies. Seán Ó Tuama, who dominated the field for a good deal of the second half of the twentieth century, and whose sensitive responses to major Irish texts remain unsurpassed, argued for the debt owed to medieval French genres by the body of Irish love songs.[25] The route to Ireland was believed to be from the troubadours in Provence, via the Normans. Gradually the focus shifted away from French sources, however. Mícheál Mac Craith undermined the Ó Tuama thesis, arguing that the particular Irish version of *amour courtois* that Ó Tuama had analysed arrived later than previously imagined, and came through English, not French.[26]

This illustrates the ongoing drive in Irish-language circles, certainly within the intelligentsia, to highlight echoes and influences from outside the language. The reasons for doing so are diverse, and many are laudable: resistance to the premodern and folkloric literature in Irish before the revival; resistance to the constraining effect of cultural nationalism, with its propensity to censor, close and limit; fidelity to Irish literary history with its waves of interaction with other cultures from as early as the introduction of Christianity; taking at face value the language revival's cornerstone belief that Irish was or could be an unapologetically modern language in modern Europe and, conversely, a niggling concern that a new literature in tune with such a belief would need to be forged by renouncing swathes of its history in favour of more obviously modern models from other languages.

I would like now to offer a small number of readings to illustrate the engagement with the older literary tradition practised by recent or contemporary Irish and Scottish poets. First, however, two caveats need to be lodged. The first concerns translation. Blanket dismissals of literary translation are rare; the rewards of translation in practice outweigh the unpalatable implications of *traddutore tradditore*, even for text-specific genres; and anyway various theories of translation have arisen that respond creatively to the problem of *tradditore*. The uncomfortable fact remains, nonetheless, that a sensitivity to the seismic rumbles of tradition beneath the surface of a poem is too easily blunted by translation, whether by facilitating ownership of a body of work by those who are unfamiliar with the tradition from which it sprang, or by eliding crucial features of the text that are absent, or resonate differently, in the target language. One obvious example in the case of Gaelic texts translated into English is the loss of gendered pronouns, and the immediate effect this has on the all-pervasive female personification of the land, where 'she' becomes 'it' in translation. Echoes and ironies are frail creatures, and need careful tending. The second caveat relates to the scope of the analysis. I have concentrated largely on images and concepts, at the expense of certain formal features, in particular rhythm and stanza form. Very little work has been done on these, and the question is especially complex within a Scottish-Irish context because of the wide disparity between the two countries. Irish poetic form underwent something akin to a root-and-branch rupture when the work of Ó Direáin and Ó Ríordáin appeared in the early 1940s; the development was less acute in Scotland, and the growth of untraditional forms and the introduction of modern topics took place more gradually over the course of the first half of the twentieth century. It may be part of Scottish literary folklore that everyone remembers where they were when they first read Sorley Maclean's *Dàin do Eimhir*, but that was probably more for its extraordinary emotional intensity than for any radical formal experimentation.

The relationship with the land is one of the core concerns throughout the entire Gaelic tradition. This may be considered under three themes: the female personification of the land, the idea of the land as paradise, and the responsiveness of the land to human activities, flourishing when the rightful leader is in place, withering when he dies or proves delinquent. This immediately suggests a context for what is possibly the single most iconic Irish language poem of the twentieth century, Seán Ó Ríordáin's 'Adhlacadh mo mháthar' ('My Mother's Burial'). The collection in which it appeared, *Eireaball Spideoige* (*A Robin's Tail*),[27] was fêted for introducing a modern sensibility into that poetry, by which was generally meant a spirit of religious doubt, and the couching of that doubt in vaguely philosophical terms, albeit distilled into simple, accessible imagery. The subject is poignant, the death of a mother, and many readers will identify with the poem's anguish. It is a poem that would respond, say, to a reading in a psychoanalytical light, focusing on the death of the mother or indeed more generally on the topic of dead female bodies in literature.[28]

Fruitful as these and other lines of enquiry might be, I have argued elsewhere[29] that the explanation for this poem's pre-eminent position in the Irish poetic constellation may well have to do with the identification of the woman with the land both darkly and literally (the mother is now dead and literally a part of the land). This represents an ironic reversal of the long tradition of the female personification of the land as abundant and sustaining for the legitimate sovereign. Both the irony and the usurpation of the figurative by the literal are recognisably, though not exclusively, modern aspects of Irish poetic technique. Christianity, too, has lost its redemptive aspect and is reduced to suffering. I am not referring here to the slighting of the worldliness of the priest who officiates at the burial, but to the fact that the memories within the poem derive from an identification between the dead mother and Holy Communion – the whiteness of her hand is compared to the whiteness of the communion host and the whiteness of what seems to be the dress the poet's mother wore on the day of her first communion. While mildly anti-clerical, this is not so much an anti-Christian poem as a poem that speaks of the loss of the mother in terms that echo both Christian and Gaelic narratives of redemption. In Gaelic terms, the mother's identification with the land is bleak: a Winter burial, a literal identification. In Christian terms, the loss of the mother represents the loss of the risen Christ as present in Holy Communion, and what remains is an echo of Christ crucified. This is presented through a self-aggrandising identification of the speaker himself with Christ, which becomes visible in a cluster of images that includes a robin, a piercing thorn and the clear water of tears that is forced from the speaker's breast. This clearly evokes the common belief in Irish and other European folklore that the robin acquired its red breast by attempting to remove the nails from Christ's body on the cross. The other main echo of traditional concepts is the land's responsiveness to the plight of the sovereign. Here the speaker's memory of the day of his mother's burial, represented as a quasi-magical transformation of the land from orchard to grave, is another dark subversion of a cornerstone of Irish literature. This is central to an understanding of the poem: 'Thit an Meitheamh siar isteach sa gheimhreadh / Den úllghort deineadh reilig bhán cois abhann'[30] [June fell back into winter / The orchard was turned into a white riverside cemetery'].

We find something similar in the work of many other poets, and the effect can still often be one of shock. For the Scottish poet Donald MacAulay, the island home he left outlives people and their history, and does not wither when they do:

> Air mo làimh chlì
> tha tobhta;
> air mo làimh dheis muir a' gluasad.
> ... am fianais na tobhta
> 's na mara
> tha saoghal 's a bhial fodha –
> ... eachdraidh a' dol am fuar-mheas'

[On my left hand / a ruin; / on my right the sea in motion / ... in sight of the ruin / and the sea / a world is reflected, face down – / ... a history being cold-shouldered.][31]

A recognition of the irony and the force of the despair in poems like this depends on an extensive knowledge of just how traditionally pervasive were the ideas they subvert. Less darkly, Sorley MacLean's 'Hallaig', whose iconic status is even higher than Ó Ríordáin's 'Adhlacadh mo Mháthar', creates a small miracle with its salvific reversal of the norm, its vision of the people of the Isle of Raasay who had been cleared from their land and were now long dead. They are seen alive in the very trees that supplanted them:

> 's tha mo ghaol aig Allt Hallaig
> 'na craoibh bheithe, 's bha i riamh ...
> tha i 'na beithe, 'na calltuinn,
> 'na caorunn dhìreach sheang ùir ...
> Chunnacas na mairbh beò.

[and my love is at the Burn of Hallaig, / a birch tree, and she has always been / ... she is a birch, a hazel, / a straight slender young rowan / ... the dead have been seen alive.][32]

The figure of the sovereignty goddess presides over and pervades Biddy Jenkinson's poetry.[33] She frequently echoes the female personification of the land, nowhere more than in poems that give voice to the natural world. The message is new, however, and overturns traditional dominance by the male leader, replacing it with a new heaven and a new earth founded on equality and mutual respect. In 'Lá Feabhra' ('The 1st February')[34] Jenkinson's semi-apostrophic address to an unnamed 'you', whom she variously suggests might be called God, Saint Brigid (1 February is her feast day), the Morrigan (Gaelic goddess of war) or one of the secret names for Ireland, and who is compared to a bird and described as a muse, explicitly refrains from naming or indentifying the other, and is marked by a loving patience to wait and allow the other to name herself. Both Nuala Ní Dhomhnaill and Biddy Jenkinson experiment with the freedom a female voice offers to create forms of identification between the land and the male body. Some of these poems are humorous, such as Jenkinson's 'Toisí do Ghloine' ('The Dimensions of Your Glass'),[35] in which a woman beseeches her beloved to cut down on his drinking on the mock-scientific grounds that he is accelerating the loss of bodily material by pressuring his kidneys to pump faster:

> Is a mhuirnín níl tú ach ag fualbhrostú,
> gach pionta leanna thall ag cosaint dhá phionta abhus ort
> is an nócha naoi faoi gcéad sin díot nach bhfuil ann ach uisce ag éalú
> sa taoide chomónta san . . .

['Darling, you're just pisspumping / each pint up here costing you two pints down there / and the ninety-nine percent of you that is just water escaping in that common tide . . .']

Others are poignant, such as Ní Dhomhnaill's well-known 'Oileán'[36] ('Island'), where a formerly otherworldly personification (goddess and land) becomes, as the otherworld frequently does, metaphor. Although most Gaelic readers would recognise that a long tradition is echoed and reversed (this time, the man is the land), it is the penultimate word, the adjective 'iathghlas' (green-land), that adds historical depth and creates special echoes of the otherworld. 'Iathghlas' was a common description of Ireland in poetry up to the seventeenth century, and during this period the female personification of the land was still largely that of a goddess. It was not until the eighteenth century that the goddess began to appear in the more quotidian guise of an ordinary woman. Michael Davitt ironises the idea of nature as a bounteous paradise in his 'Urnaí Maidine' ('Morning Prayer') which reduces the world to suburban proportions where nature appears as three bottles of milk on a doorstep, and creates faint echoes of personification in the kitchen blind that swallows its tongue and a kettle whose coming to the boil is described in sexual terms:

> Slogann dallóg na cistine a teanga de sceit
> Caochann an mhaidin liathshúil

> Seacht nóiméad déag chun a seacht
> Gan éan ar chraobh . . .
> Tagann an citeal le blubfhriotal miotalach
> Trí bhuidéal bainne ón gcéim . . .

[The kitchen blind suddenly swallows its (i.e., 'her') tongue / Morning opens a grey eye / Seventeen minutes to seven / No bird on a tree . . . / The kettle comes with a metallic bubbling expression / Three bottles of milk from the step . . .][37]

The hero, another traditional Gaelic staple, has reinvented himself in a variety of ways in keeping with the democratic impulses of modernity, the sense of betrayal that flows from the failure of Gaelic political leadership in both countries in the early modern period and, more recently, with the women's movement. Poetry has been versatile in rethinking this major building block of the tradition. It has done so with a range of techniques, including parodic humour and gender reversals. Heroic status has been transferred to the sacrifices and efforts of nameless foot soldiers or children or entire clans (rather than named heroes), and a heroic code that had traditionally been unambiguously synecdochal has frequently found itself recast in metaphoric form. The main interest, for me, lies in ironic reconfigurations of elements of the heroic code. Thus, for example, when Nuala Ní Dhomhnaill praises her seemingly cantankerous and arrogant aunt in heroic terms in 'In Memoriam: Elly Ní Dhomhnaill (1884–1963)'[38] the irony lies not so much in praising unheroic qualities like refusing to give money to the church, or refusing to marry, but in the unravelling of the categories of insider and outsider. Praise for generosity was a traditional cornerstone of Irish poetry, but Ní Dhomhnaill admires her aunt for refusing to give money publicly to the church on the grounds that it bolstered up a system that accepted money from the poor whose children went hungry; and while her aunt failed in the traditional duty to marry well, she did so as a free choice. Furthermore, praise of academic learning was a staple of Irish heroic poetry, but it is ironically undercut by her aunt's having been one of the first women to open up the bastion of the universities to women. Naming, and celebrating the names, of valorous heroes was another cornerstone of the heroic poetic tradition and this too finds itself reimagined in modern poetry, primarily by Sorley MacLean. In various poems he turns the act of naming into a counter-cultural gesture, by praising the valour of entire clans rather than individuals, or of unnamed junior soldiers. See, for example, 'Làrach Eaglais' ('Ruined Church'):

> Ach dè mu na ciadan eile
> is ficheadan dhiubh ceart cho àrd

> anns an spiorad ri'n ceann-cinnidh
> is ri bràthair a' bhàird?

[But what of the hundreds of others / of whom scores were quite as high / in spirit as their chief / or as the brother of the bard?][39]

    Donald MacAulay chimes with this ironic-heroic stance. In a poem that would lend itself as well to a discussion of the land as of the hero, he presents us with a military hero who, to his shame, is eventually vanquished by the forces of nature and dies by freezing. Not only is he opposed rather than supported by nature, he is at the mercy of the environment. This may have Darwinian overtones concerning the influence of the environment, and it is right that such overtones be recognised, but the ironic reversal of Gaelic heroic literature is at least as visible:

> Chaidh e air chall san fhaoilleach
> 's tha a lorg air a bàthadh
> fon t-sìor chathadh air a gilead
> (bha fhuil gun a leigeil
> ragadh gu bàs e –
> mullach na tàmailt)
> choisinn am fiar-chath ùmhlachd.

[He got lost in the dead of winter / and his footprint is drowned / by the incessant snow falling on its whiteness / (his blood was not let / his death was by freezing – / the greatest shame) / he succumbed in a devious fight.][40]

    For readers today, the most conspicuous aspect of continuity from the tradition is arguably the transformation of the otherworld into metaphor. The most celebrated and sustained example is probably Nuala Ní Dhomhnaill's sequence of poems about mermaids,[41] and in general terms the capacity of Ní Dhomhnaill's poems to generate fruitful psychological readings,[42] based on a metaphoric interpretation of their otherworldly elements – mermaids and other sources – is by now well recognised.

    In my view, the Irish-language poetic tradition (I do not necessarily include Scottish Gaelic here) is dramatically tilted in favour of metonymy, rather than metaphor. It is arguable that much of what is expressible through metaphor was traditionally represented by the otherworld. The disenchantment of the world that came about in Enlightenment Europe did not take place to any real extent in Irish. As a result, it was not until the twentieth century that the otherworld started to lose its status as literally true, and otherworldly creatures began to be interpreted metaphorically. However, they still carry some of the weight of authority that derives from their having been regarded with respect until so recently. This creates a liminal, resonant atmosphere that does not fit effortlessly into, say, Todorov's taxonomy of the fantastic, the marvellous and the uncanny.[43] It is closest to the fantastic, meaning texts about which an element of undecidability exists as to whether one should interpret something as natural or supernatural. But that is not quite what I refer to here. Rather, the natural and supernatural coincide and illuminate each other; it is not a reductive metaphor, where the supernatural is the vehicle for a natural tenor. When a young child falls to her knees and marvels at the beauty of what is referred to as the miracle of a whitethorn bush in Nuala Ní Dhomhnaill's 'An Sceach Gheal' ('The Whitethorn')[44] it is impossible to choose whether the 'miracle' is a reductive metaphor for 'wonderful beauty', or whether the traditional magic of the whitethorn is somehow still present, informing the child's reaction and the poet's description. In a similar vein, in Biddy Jenkinson's 'Lá Bealtaine i nGleann Dá Loch' ('May Day in Glendalough'),[45] the legend of the young woman who drowned in the lake in Glendalough, having been spurned by St Kevin, is juxtaposed with a contemporary account of a funeral in the same place, after which an old woman remains behind berating God, until 'gur tháinig fionnaire de dhroim an locha / is fionnachrith ar shruth séimh na mblian' ('a coolness came from the lake / and a shudder from the stream of years'). There are clear metaphoric similarities between the grief of the two women in the same place, and of course in one sense the 'stream of years' is a straightforward metaphor, but the deep resonance of the poem comes from the echoes of the sovereignty goddess-hag and the authority that she brings to the story. Within the Irish tradition I do not believe the freshness from the lake, the shiver on the stream of years or the juxtaposition of the two women can be read reductively as simple coincidence. The overlay from the otherworld is too strong and too recent for that, and the poem does not demand it. In this respect it differs from, say, Seán Ó Curraoin's 'Loch Inse', which narrates the exploits of some children on a lake that the old people in their area feared as magical and malevolent following a drowning. Far from expressing what some would consider conventional childhood joy in the presence of magic, these children rejoiced in walking on the frozen lake precisely because, for them, this stripped the lake of its magical power:

> Ach ag breathnú amach air ón mbruach
> Mhothaíomar inár bpáistí aríst
> Go suáilceach, gealgháireach
> Mar bhí an draíocht bainte den loch againn.

[Looking out on it {the lake} from the bank / we felt like children again / happy and smiling/ for we had taken away the magic of the lake.][46]

The conflation of metaphor and magic in contemporary Irish poetry adds the electric charge of history to what might otherwise appear only innocent metaphors. In doing so, it can carry an ethical and emotional weight. In Louis de Paor's 'Iarlais' ('Changeling'),[47] for instance, the poet's daughter, raising her arms to take off her jumper before bathing suddenly appears to him as a changeling for Kim Phúc, the young girl from the infamous 1972 Vietnam photograph of children running from their burnt village. Using the term 'changeling' expresses a palpable or superficial similarity between the two girls, and in one sense is a metaphor for a metaphor; more importantly, it makes the horror of changelings available as a way of indicating empathy with the people of Vietnam; and, further, makes an ethical connection between the poet and the suffering girl by eliminating the physical distance between them: a changeling is found within one's own family, on one's own hearth. The changeling introduces an element of darkness deriving from the sinister side of the otherworld; it – or she – also introduces a depth of ethical concern through its foregrounding of issues of identity, of self and other. To read the changeling as an innocent metaphor for the similarity between the two girls would be to miss the entwining of the two dimensions, the dark and the ethical. This poem may even go some way towards rehabilitating the figure of the changeling, whom we see here in an unusually ethical role, promoting solidarity with the child in Vietnam.

The examples presented here demonstrate more than anachronistic refusal to embrace modernity, or nostalgia for lost origins, or a simple source of local colour for new generations of Gaelic poets. The older Gaelic tradition is a primary source from which complex modern concerns can be illuminated with resonance, depth and wisdom. I confidently await an impressive poem on the general election with roots firmly planted in the last millennium.

NOTES

1. Patrick Pearse, *An Claidheamh Soluis* (26 May 1906), 7.
2. *Ibid.*, 6.
3. T. S. Eliot, 'Tradition and the Individual Talent', *The Egoist*, September and December 1919.
4. Roland Barthes, 'The Death of the Author', *Aspen* 5–6 (1967).
5. Harold Bloom, *The Anxiety of Influence: A Theory of Poetry* (Oxford University Press, 1973).
6. Eric Hobsbawm (ed.), *The Invention of Tradition* (Cambridge University Press, 1983), 2.
7. See, for example, Benedict Anderson, *Imagined Communities: Reflections on the Origins and Spread of Nationalism* (London: Verso, 1983).

8. Joep Leerssen, 'Literary Historicism: Romanticism, Philologists, and the Presence of the Past', *MLQ: Modern Language Quarterly* 65:2, 2004, 221–43.
9. See Niall Ó Ciosáin, 'Print and Irish, 1570–1900: An Exception among the Celtic Languages?', *Radharc: A Journal of Irish and Irish-American Studies* 5–7 (2004–6), 73–106. See also Ó Ciosáin, 'The Angus Matheson Lecture, 2009' (forthcoming).
10. Wilson McLeod, *Divided Gaels: Gaelic Cultural Identities in Scotland and Ireland, c. 1200–c. 1650* (Oxford University Press, 2004), 3.
11. Colm Breathnach, Frontispiece to *Scáthach* (Baile Átha Cliath: Coiscéim, 1994).
12. www.strokestownpoetry.org/Shortlist%202009,%20Irish.htm.
13. George Steiner, *After Babel*, 2nd edn (Oxford University Press, 1998), 24.
14. Christopher Whyte, *Modern Scottish Poetry* (Edinburgh University Press, 2004), 20.
15. John MacKenzie, *Sar-Obair nam Bard Gaidhealach/The Beauties of Gaelic Poetry and Lives of the Highland Bards* (Edinburgh: John Grant, 1907), 310; my translation.
16. Seán Ó Riada, *Our Musical Heritage* (Port Laoise: Dolmen, 1982), 19.
17. Whyte, *Modern Scottish Poetry*, 11.
18. Douglas Sealy, 'A New Voice for the Seanachie', *The Irish Times*, 8 February 1990, 9.
19. Christopher Whyte, Review of A. MacNeacail, *Oideachadh Ceart agus Dàin Eile/A Proper Schooling and Other Poems*, in *Lines Review* 141, June 1997, 45–6.
20. Máire Ní Annracháin, 'The Force of Tradition in the Poetry of Aonghas MacNeacail', in C. Ó Baoil and N. McGuire (eds.), *Rannsachadh na Gàidhlig 2000* (Department of Celtic, University of Aberdeen), 117–27.
21. Cairns Craig, *The Modern Scottish Novel: Narrative and the National Imagination* (Edinburgh University Press, 1999), 23.
22. Breandán Ó Doibhlin, 'Nóisean an Traidisiúin', *Aistí Critice agus Cultúir II* (Béal Feirste: Lagan, 1997), 1–11.
23. See, for example, Homi Bhabha, *The Location of Culture* (London: Routledge, 1994).
24. See René Girard, *Violence and the Sacred* (London: Athlone, 1988).
25. Seán Ó Tuama, *An Grá in Amhráin na nDaoine* (Baile Átha Cliath: An Clóchomhar, 1960).
26. Mícheál Mac Craith, *Lorg na hIasachta ar na Dánta Grá* (Baile Átha Cliath: An Clóchomhar, 1989).
27. Seán Ó Ríordáin, *Eireaball Spideoige* (Baile Átha Cliath: Sáirséal & Dill, 1952).
28. See, for example, Elisabeth Bronfen, *Over Her Dead Body: Death, Femininity and the Aesthetic* (Manchester University Press, 1992), or consider a possible analysis within a Kristevan theory of the abject.
29. Máire Ní Annracháin, 'Seán Ó Ríordáin agus Fréamhacha an Dúchais', in Liam Mac Amhlaigh and Caoimhín Mac Giolla Léith (eds.), *Fill Arís: Oidhreacht Sheáin Uí Ríordáin* (Indreabhán, Conamara: Cló Iar-Chonnachta, forthcoming).
30. Ó Ríordáin, *Eireaball Spideoige*, 2nd edn (Baile Átha Cliath: Sáirséal & Dill, 1970), 100.

31. Domhnall MacAmhlaigh/Donald MacAulay, 'Air Tràigh Bhostaidh/On Bosta Beach', *Seobhrach as a' Chlaich/Primrose from the Stone* (Glaschu: Gairm, 1967), 77 and 106.
32. Sorley MacLean, 'Hallaig', *O Choille gu Bearradh/From Wood to Ridge* (Manchester: Carcanet, 1999), 226–31.
33. See Máire Ní Annracháin, 'Biddy agus an Bandia', in P. Riggs, B. Ó Conchúir and S. Ó Coileáin (eds.), *Saoi na hÉigse: Aistí in Ómós do Sheán Ó Tuama* (Baile Átha Cliath: An Clóchomhar, 2000), 339–58.
34. Biddy Jenkinson, 'Lá Feabhra', *Dán na hUidhre* (Baile Átha Cliath: Coiscéim, 1991), 61–2.
35. Jenkinson, *Dán na hUidhre*, 80–1; my translation.
36. Nuala Ní Dhomhnaill, 'Oileán', *Pharaoh's Daughter* (Oldcastle: Gallery, 1990), 40.
37. Michael Davitt, 'Úrnaí Maidine', *Bligeard Sráide* (Baile Átha Cliath: Coiscéim, 1983), 14; my translation.
38. Nuala Ní Dhomhnaill, *An Dealg Droighin* (Baile Átha Cliath: Cló Mercier, 1981), 69–70.
39. MacLean, *O Choille gu Bearradh*, 234–5.
40. Domhnall MacAmhlaigh/Donald MacAulay, *Deilbh is Faileasan: Dàin le Domhnall MacAmhlaigh/Images and Reflections: Poems by Donald MacAulay* (Stornoway: Acair, 2008), 48–9.
41. Nuala Ní Dhomhnaill, *The Fifty Minute Mermaid* (with translations by Paul Muldoon) (Oldcastle: Gallery, 2006).
42. See, for example, B. Nic Dhiarmada's analysis of Ní Dhomhnaill's *Feis* in 'Immram sa tSícé: Filíocht Nuala Ní Dhomhnaill agus Próiseas an Indibhidithe', *Oghma* 5 (1993), 78–94.
43. Tzvetan Todorov, *The Fantastic: A Structural Approach to a Literary Genre*, trans. R. Howard (Cleveland: Case Western Reserve University Press, 1973).
44. Nuala Ní Dhomhnaill, *Feis* (Maynooth: An Sagart, 1991), 33.
45. Biddy Jenkinson, *Uiscí Beatha* (Baile Átha Cliath: Coiscéim, 1988), 42; my translation.
46. www.strokestownpoetry.org/Shortlist%202009,%20Irish.htm
47. Louis De Paor, *Seo. Siúd. Agus Uile* (Baile Átha Cliath: Coiscéim, 1996), 32.

CHAPTER 6

Contemporary affinities
Douglas Dunn

In the Summer of 1963 or '64 I hitchhiked through much of Ireland with my fiancée, developing a fondness for the place and discovering the metabolic mysteries of Guinness. We already knew Dublin. The night ferry from Glasgow's Broomielaw had for years been a well-known rendezvous of the west of Scotland's lovers in search of a night's amorous privacy. It is not the manner in which Irish–Scots connections are discussed these days, but it will do.

In a Dublin bookshop I bought a copy of a magazine, *Arena*, edited by James Liddy. It contained a poem by Derek Mahon, an uncharacteristic one to be sure, but I found it interesting. At the age of 21 or 22 I was in the process of identifying writers, poets especially, with whose work I could find an affinity. As a young librarian I had access to books, but the Andersonian Library of the Royal College of Science and Technology, subsequently University of Strathclyde, was not exactly stocked with volumes of modern or contemporary verse, never mind little magazines. While I knew a few who wrote poems, or tried, and knew of others, and was becoming familiar with the work of my immediate elders, mainly Scots such as MacDiarmid, Edwin Muir, W. S. Graham and Norman MacCaig, in the early 1960s Iain Crichton Smith was just beginning to establish a reputation, as was George Mackay Brown. Edwin Morgan was little more than a name to me. His position in Scottish poetry was not to be established definitively until the publication of *The Second Life* in 1968. It is difficult to be clear or sure about this, but it was certainly the case for me that books by the likes of MacDiarmid were difficult to come by outside of library copies, and that was the case with others too. In the end it does not matter where you find the books you want or need to read, just so long as they come into your hands one way or another. To an extent it might have depended on the kind of family into which you were born. My parents were far from literary, but they were generous enough to allow me the weekly delivery of the *Times Literary Supplement* and *Listener*. My father disliked the former, and read

The Listener, but then he was always a man for his wireless. We had had a television set in time for the Coronation – the first in the village – and he grew to hate its presence, the way it transformed our living-room into a space crowded with people he came to look on as sorners instead of neighbours, my mother baking for them, my brother and I forced to watch the evil box through people's legs.

My aspirations in poetry, whatever they were to begin with, were altered in 1962 with the publication of two Penguin anthologies. Alvarez's *The New Poetry* alerted me to work I had never or seldom come across before, except perhaps in magazines. Scotland in the early 1960s was not a provincial backwater so much as – or so it seemed to me – a municipal paddling pool in which the tirelessly complacent stood in lukewarm liquid, careful not to let it rise too far above their ankles. Or, as friends of mine were, and as I sometimes pretended to be, laid-back Beatniks, café existentialists misquoting Sartre, Camus and many others with confident arrogance and youthful abandon while at the same time passing around dog-eared copies of *Evergreen Review* and books published by San Francisco's City Lights Bookshop.

What cured me of that – if I needed a cure – was not Alvarez's anthology (although I admit its significance) but Donald Hall's *Contemporary American Poetry*. Immediately prior to that I had been immersed in Dylan Thomas's poetry – not a bad thing, in my opinion, and I am still an admirer of Thomas, especially his short stories. But to be introduced to Robert Lowell, and the poetry of James Wright, X. J. Kennedy, Donald Justice, W. D. Snodgrass and Richard Wilbur, was exhilarating enough for me to then look for books by their predecessors such as Edwin Arlington Robinson and Robert Frost. Not having gone to university immediately after school but trained as a librarian instead, I was in process of educating myself. All poets are, or should be, autodidacts. Their educations are eccentric and unpredictable. Or such is my conviction.

At the same time as reading the poets I have mentioned, I was also reading Eliot, Pound, Yeats, Stevens, and especially W. H. Auden and Louis MacNeice. In fact, I had been reading Auden since the late 1950s when he had been upheld to me at school as *the* modern poet. On a topic such as this, that of 'contemporary affinities', there is almost always a teacher lurking in the background, pointing a way which might not be in the right direction but is at least a destination to be considered, if only to be rejected once visited. In my case his name was Thomas McCrossan, the head teacher of English at Camphill Senior Secondary School in Paisley. He was a man of the 1930s and very much interested in Auden's poetry. He was also a

Burnsian, and a defender of the reputation of Robert Tannahill, the 'poet of Paisley'. And I enjoyed the advice and teaching of others. The late John Redmond taught English in the Scottish School of Librarianship in Glasgow and I learned a lot from him when I was a student there. I would be hard put to say what exactly, but I could paraphrase it as 'Do what you want to do. Teach yourself and don't be led by others.'

On that visit to Ireland I mentioned earlier, I bought a copy of *The Kilkenny Review*, in Kilkenny. Printed there was the first poem by Seamus Heaney I ever read. It was 'Mid-Term Break', Heaney's poem on the accidental death of his young brother. While finding the poem extremely moving, I did the young poet's trick of latching on to it as a poem. By that, I mean that while the subject of the poem was overwhelmingly in the foreground what impressed me was the triumph of its voice and artistry, its achievement of tenderly asserted feeling. It was immediate, it was actual, it was distressingly necessary.

In this gathering of reading any poet seeks to discover his or her present tense. You wonder who else around your own age is out there. It is the same as saying that in an early career of reading and writing a poet attempts to define a poetic identity, a vague sense of purpose, and from that suggestions of a way forward, an appropriate or inevitable way in which to write – at least, it will come to seem inevitable, even if in later life it feels that is not all that you might have done. It could be a mistake to establish a poetic identity too soon. Unsurprisingly, there are bound to be enthusiasms that turn out to be no more than short-lived fads or dead ends. In such disappointments exist the fun and the chastisement of the tyro. At the same time as reading poetry – the most important reading for a poet, and as much of it as possible – it is essential to read criticism and biography and determine an individual judiciousness. Serendipity determined that Ian Hamilton's magazine *The Review* was on sale in John Wylie's bookshop in Glasgow's Sauchiehall Street, and in Porteous's shop off Exchange Square you could buy *London Magazine*. Together with *Listener* and *Times Literary Supplement*, these were my escapes from the prevailing mood of a local Glaswegian absence of critical engagement in favour of rampant spontaneity – although there were exceptions of which I was unaware at the time – or of the tones and principles of F. R. Leavis and T. S. Eliot.

Release from what can be perceived as the entrapments of a provincial mentality can always be discovered. It would be mistaken and insulting to suggest that poets who remained chiefly in Scotland for almost all of their lives were caught in the nets of a local complacency from which they could not fly. Hugh MacDiarmid's choice of where he lived and worked – Montrose in the Mearns of Angus on the east coast of Scotland, the island of Whalsay in the Shetland Islands, or Biggar in southern Lanarkshire – are provincial only if you deem them to be, and they were far from that to MacDiarmid. They were remote, salutary and cheap; but the range of his poetry and thought, his sometimes tedious and bludgeoning erudition, show that they were far from intellectually inhibiting. Although he served in the Royal Army Medical Corps in the Balkans and in southern France during the Great War, and made occasional subsequent sallies to Ireland, London and Europe, MacDiarmid was, by the standards of most contemporary poets amenable to invitations from the British Council, relatively under-travelled. Like Keats, he 'travelled in the realms of gold'. Or, as Peter Porter writes,

> Oft have I travelled in the realms of gold,
> For which I thank the Westminster and Paddington Public Libraries,
> And I have never said 'Sir' to anyone since I was sixteen years old . . .[1]

The travels of poets important to me, such as Norman MacCaig, Iain Crichton Smith, Sorley MacLean and Edwin Morgan, could be understated. Indeed, Morgan is perhaps the most internationalist of poets, as well as the most secular, while the others took advantage of invitations to give readings abroad, and a poet like Robert Garioch exercised an intimacy with Renaissance Scottish Latinity as well as the Roman dialect of Giuseppe Belli. George Mackay Brown, on the other hand, preferred to be nowhere other than his native Orkney Islands. He lived for a time in Edinburgh, as a mature student, and mounted an exhilarating visit to Ireland, but it is clear from his biography that his life support system was grounded in his home in Stromness. Indeed, in Mackay Brown's life and work there can be sensed a virtually heroic, if also perhaps misguided, dedication to a single and singular place. Like his Orcadian early mentor, Edwin Muir, he did not consider himself a Scot so much as Norse, or a Scandinavian Scot. Interestingly enough, both these Orcadians were inspired by a religious impulse which, as Graham Greene once suggested, perhaps underlies all great art.

By late November 1964 I was married and in Akron, Ohio. It would be easy to mythologise this and claim it was a flight from the provincialism of Scotland as it then was, or as I thought it to have been, or a surrender to the pull of the American poetry I admired. Anyone who knows Akron, or who knew it in the mid-1960s, knows it was not a centre of major cultural delights, although it was good for rhythm 'n' blues, and later for rock music. In truth, the reason was 'professional'. It was considered a good thing for a young librarian to have experience of more developed American public libraries. Akron was at the top of the alphabetical list, and I had been given a contact there. If that had not worked out I might have fetched up in Albuquerque. Another reason, a more personal one, was that my wife disliked the prospect of becoming a young married woman in a predictable, bourgeois district of Glasgow. She was more venturesome than I was. The journey from Prestwick – a KLM flight to New York, with a connection to Cleveland and then a bus to Akron – was a bit like the night boat from the Broomielaw to Dublin. It was an extension of the same erotic adventure. For a reason I might have known then but have since lost it was an adventure that had to happen anywhere except Glasgow or even Scotland as a whole.

There was a literary life in Akron and it was a lot less provincial than the one I had known in Glasgow, at least from my point of view. Above all, it did not depend on class, or who you knew. There was nothing like the experience I had undergone in the interval bar at the Citizens' Theatre in Glasgow when my fiancée introduced me to a so-called family friend of hers. 'You're not Douglas Young,' he said, having misheard my name. 'I know him. He's much taller and older than you are and wears a bigger beard!' All I can say is 'Ach!' and wince at the memory of a man's willingness to be meanspirited. 'Dunn, you fool. Dunn.'

A year in America at that time was a good and a bad idea. On the plus side was exposure to more American poetry, as well as friends who not only read widely and talked about books, but considered it less than eccentric or risible to want to write. But as 1965 wore on the United States became a society to which the war in Vietnam introduced tensions and divisions, griefs and hand-wringing, rhetoric and lamentation. By the middle of the year young men were flitting across the border to lie low in Canada, including one I knew who was a poet and studied at Kenyon College. Library 'pages' – shelvers of books, deliverers of internal mail – sometimes turned up in their Reserve Officers' Training Corps uniforms, but were otherwise determined to earn good grades at Akron U and avoid the possibility of being drafted, or put it off for as long as possible.

In 1966 I matriculated at the University of Hull. Philip Larkin's poetry was known to me first of all through Alvarez's anthology, and I could quite possibly have been the first person in Glasgow to have bought *The Whitsun Weddings* in 1964. (I ordered it weeks before publication.) Early that Summer the late Jon Silkin, accompanied by the also regrettably late Ken Smith, accosted me on a bench in Glasgow's George Square during my lunch break. They were hawking copies of *Stand* and did not believe me when I told them I already had that issue, having bought it from the bookstall at Glasgow Central. They were not keen on Larkin's work, which surprised me. In my innocence I thought everyone must be. That was where I first read the poems of one 'T. W. Harrison', now well known as Tony Harrison.

Larkin's presence in Hull was not the reason I went there. No Scottish university would have me as I had flunked maths and failed the compulsory arithmetic paper, twice. Like Jean Brodie's girls, I count on my fingers, with more or less reliable results. But Hull was a good choice. Cox and Dyson, with their journal *Critical Quarterly*, had just left, but the English department was a good one. Professor Ray Brett took a shine to me, as did Margaret Espinasse, a teacher of Old and Mediaeval English but who had turned herself into a historian of science, and a historian of labour, having first, under her maiden name of Wattie, edited the eighteenth-century Scottish poet Alexander Ross for the Scottish Text Society. If Ray Brett was in appearance a dead ringer for Edwin Muir, whose work he admired, then Mrs Espinasse (which is what one always called her) looked a bit like a smaller version of Margaret Rutherford and rode a large bicycle accordingly, with a big handlebar basket invariably stuffed with books and papers. In my second year she insisted I study Henryson, Dunbar and Gawain (as she called him) Douglas, would not take no for an answer and devised a personal syllabus. I took no papers in modern literature but a mediaeval option which involved papers in iconography, Aquinas, Duns Scotus and Petrus Lombardus in the Theology department (at times it felt as if studying for the priesthood). It did not do me any harm.

During my first Easter vacation I worked as a secretary to a philosopher. He taught me a lot about writing, all of it in the department of How Not To Go About It. He was writing a book on the subject of Liberty. He would dictate a sentence, I would write it down, then type it out. My next duty was to count the number of words. If it was longer than twenty-six, it had to be revised. No sentence of his could be longer than twenty-six words. I was supposed to be paid 10 shillings a session for this nonsense. Instead, he invited my wife and me to dinner. Even that was a penance. His wife wrote poetry. It could seem like a pointlessly digressive paragraph, but I feel that the experience that teaches you 'Don't' is as important as the one that insists on 'Do'. Even so, I liked the man. Despite his stylistic eccentricity, he possessed a mind.

During the first Summer vacation I worked in the university library. My task was to catalogue a collection of playbills of Hull theatres of the nineteenth century. Larkin did not frequent the cataloguing room all that often – he once said to me that it looked so much like industry that it depressed him – but on an occasion when he did he stopped by my desk and looked at what I was doing. '"The officers of the garrison have the pleasure of inviting..." Didn't know there was a garrison. Suppose there must have been. Do you enjoy this?' To which the answer was an outright lie – 'Yes.'

There was quite a bit of poetry on campus. An old friend and mentor of Larkin's, Vernon Watkins, gave a reading not long after I arrived in 1966. Douglas Houston was in the first-year English class and we soon got to know each other. He had attended the same school in Scotland as my wife and been taught art there by her uncle. He has since published collections with Bloodaxe and Poetry Wales. There were others, too, and a couple of student poetry magazines. Having begun to publish poems occasionally in *London Magazine, Listener, Times Literary Supplement, Stand* and then *New Statesman*, I treated the locals to a snooty miss, or – well, I was a bit older than them – a condescending smile. Like most of the people I got to know in Hull at that time, I knew I did not 'belong' there; but I grew to *like* it. I was also learning that whatever 'affinity' meant to me in poetry, it had little to do with nationality.

In 1968 I entered for the Gregory Awards and was interviewed. Larkin was on the committee. I hardly knew him then. He once stopped me on campus and asked, 'Was that you in the *Listener*?' I think the implication might have been 'Nothing good will come of it.' At the interview I brought the house down when someone asked, 'What sort of poet would you like to be?' and I answered, 'Well, great.' Four hundred pounds was the result.

In 1968 I met Ian Hamilton for the first time, in his apartment in Westbourne Terrace. It was to become an enduring friendship. Many admire Ian's criticism, his essays and biographies. I do, too, but I also cherish his poems. It was not long after that when I found myself in 'Ian's circle', with poets such as Colin Falck, John Fuller, Hugo Williams and David Harsent. Although I appeared in *The Review*, and in the *TLS* when Ian was its poetry and fiction editor, I was never a fully paid-up enlistee in its unit. I lived too far away from London for that. What Hamilton and myself had in common were poetry, criticism, football, long-suffering wives, booze and Scottish parents, mothers especially.

Recent literary history has sometimes had it in for *The Review*, and then *The New Review*, as examples of cliquishness, of a cabal, or cenacle. But this is how modern poetry has worked, or has seemed to work, in its own times if not retrospectively. One thinks of Ezra Pound, that 'talented Mr Ripley', of the Imagistes, of MacSpaunday, of the Apocalypse poets, of the Movement, of the Agrarians of the Southern States, of Lowell, Berryman, Schwartz and

Jarrell, of The New York School, of the Beats, and of more recent attempts, all of them silly, to establish 'schools' or 'movements'. Poetry's vulnerability over the past hundred-and-odd years has made it practically inevitable that like-minded poets and their supporters should stick together within poetry's relatively small demography. But if it is 'small', then it is so for the simple and obvious reason that it fails to appeal to a larger audience in a culture which finds itself far more enlivened by other forms of creativity, many of them as attractive or legitimate as poetry. That does not bother me. Whenever I hear a poet or anyone else proselytise on behalf of poetry, I cringe. Its readership may not be as wide as one would like, but poetry has always been there, and always will be. Perhaps poetry has cultivated itself a bit too much as a walled garden, and it could just possibly be the case that too many poets (and academics too, for that matter) like it like that more than they should. It could also be true that poetic groups, or movements, or the choices and loyalties of publishers, have been directed towards that inwardness as much as the encouragement of public taste which, ostensibly, they've sought, or continue to seek. Instead, the result seems to be the making of marketable reputations. There seems to be a competitive, nest-feathering climate among poets younger than myself. It is in danger of becoming a poe-biz grounded on 'gigs', prizes and appointments where he or she does as little for as much money as can be got.

Poets' friendships, their affinities, but perhaps especially their differences from each other, constitute another matter entirely. 'Generation' is an awkward term. Inevitably, within any generation of poets in this recent and contemporary phase there will be factions, oppositions, enmities even (although I think these are usually overstated with the convictions associated with minorities, and, in poetry, everyone is in a minority, no matter his or her stance). I prefer the thought and feeling of these lines of Derek Mahon's, from 'Beyond Howth Head':

> Centripetal, the hot world draws
> its children in with loving paws
> from rock and heather, rain and sleet
> with only Calor Gas for heat
> and spins them at the centre where
> they have no time to know despair
>
> but, without final purpose, must
> 'accept the universe' on trust
> and offer to a phantom future
> blood and bones in forfeiture –
> each one, his poor loaf on the sea,

> monstrous before posterity,
> our afterlives a coming true
> of perfect worlds we never knew.²

Is that not a much better acknowledgement of poetic or any other endeavour than carping competitiveness?

After reading Seamus Heaney's *Death of a Naturalist*, Stewart Conn's *Stoats in the Sunlight*, Michael Longley's *No Continuing City*, Derek Mahon's *Night-Crossing*, Tony Harrison's *Loiners*, and poems by Ian Hamilton, Hugo Williams, John Fuller, David Harsent and Fleur Adcock, as well as poems by a number of others, I began to suspect that a generational 'project' might conceivably be involved. While this must have grown from the poetry of immediate predecessors, but with amendments, it is when considered as a process of continuity *and* divergence that it could be of interest. If I am right, and I admit to feeling a bit jumpy about it, then it is a moral as well as an aesthetic project.

In 1972 I was invited to read at Queen's. Seamus Heaney picked me up at the airport. Some events you never forget. And I will always remember that drive to Belfast and being stopped at several roadblocks. Did the Troubles galvanise North Irish poetry and poets? I would hesitate to say so, but it gave them an atmosphere in common, a shared sorrow from which there was no escape, and which was exclusive to them, although it made serious and bloody incursions on the mainland of the UK. An hour or so later I met Michael and Edna Longley for the first time, and stayed the night in Edna's mother's house. I was introduced also, by Seamus, to Paul Muldoon, still a student at the time. 'The coming man', Seamus said. 'Oh. My prophetic soul!' does not sound adequate. Paul Muldoon's influence on poets of around his age and younger has been strong.

The best way I know of evoking this project is by quoting Browning's 'How It Strikes a Contemporary'. He is writing about a Spanish poet, possibly of the sixteenth or seventeenth century:

> He walked and tapped the pavement with his cane,
> Scenting the world, looking it full in face . . .³

What is that, if not an image of the observational and civil courage of the characteristic poet of the past half century or so?

> He took such cognizance of men and things,
> If any beat a horse, you felt he saw;
> If any cursed a woman, he took note;
> Yet stared at nobody, – you stared at him,
> And found, less to your pleasure than surprise,

> He seemed to know you and expect as much.
> So, next time that a neighbour's tongue was loosed,
> It marked the shameful and notorious fact,
> We had among us, not so much a spy,
> As a recording chief-inquisitor,
> The town's true master if the town but knew![4]

Dated? Absolutely not. Contemporary poetry, as I understand it, has been, and is, concerned with the topicalities, the immediacies, of life as it can be lived and observed, and, perhaps more significantly, of the thoughts and feelings of life which are less immediately perceptible until revealed in poetry.

Browning's meaning comes close to Shelley's 'unacknowledged legislators'. It is a vulnerable idea. Poetry, thought, contemplation, are easily by-passed in favour of ease. As Browning's speaker says:

> Well, I could never write a verse, – could you?
> Let's to the Prado and make the most of time.[5]

What I liked about Seamus Heaney's *Death of a Naturalist* in 1966, and his work ever since, was its sheer rootedness, its cleaving to a back-of-the-mind concept of loyalty to country craft and community and to family. In Michael Longley's *No Continuing City*, I warmed to his metrical dexterity, his humour and humanity, an admirable fastidiousness that is anything but prissy. In Derek Mahon's *Night-crossing* (1968) there were already poems indicating him as a provincial cosmopolitan, or cosmopolitan provincial, Irish but European, European but Irish, poems of panache, elegance and of the singing line. All three poets have written of the personal life, and poems drawn from topical happenings, the awful murders and assassinations in Ireland. Ian Hamilton's poems are almost consistently drawn from autobiographical emergency, usually erotic, or marital, while Hugo Williams's, too, customarily express the immediacy of his own life and mind. To be honest, I did not much care for David Harsent's early poems, but he has now become a poet of undoubted significance and stature. John Fuller was, and is, a virtuoso metricist, whose skills have tended to lead readers to undervalue his work's sentience.

While being engrossed by the poems of writers around one's own age, it is also likely that a poet will actually *enjoy* being in the shadow of his or her immediate and admired elders, especially if they get to know them. In poetry, as in everything else, I doubt if it is entirely wise to be outrageously rebellious, unless circumstances demand it. An affinity with Larkin's poetry does not mean an affinity with his personality, but with the best moments (and there are many) of his poetry. I found it possible to admire Ted Hughes, Sylvia Plath and Thom Gunn as well as Larkin, Porter, Mackay Brown, MacCaig, Graham, MacLean, Garioch, Crichton Smith and Morgan.

Despite his involvement in The Poetry Book Society, and committees that struggled to retain modern manuscripts in the UK, the more Larkin aged, the more he grew dismissive of the poetry being published by those younger than him. At the same time, it seemed to please him that Hull became a focus for poetry, but he wanted no active part in it. He could give the impression of a poet in hiding within the perimeters of his own renown. The only readings I knew him to attend willingly were given by D. J. Enright and Gavin Ewart. On these two occasions his hearing aids seemed to work perfectly. During readings by Ted Hughes and Robert Lowell they whistled painfully. Draw your own conclusions.

It bemused him that I was willing to teach Workers' Educational Association classes in writing and that I enjoyed the company and work of Sean O'Brien, Peter Didsbury, Tony Flynn, Douglas Houston and several others. While they admired Larkin's poetry, I think they wondered how my wife and I could be on such friendly terms with someone so grumpily on the Right (and in the wrong). But I enjoyed these WEA workshops. Three of my predecessors who worked for the Hull WEA were Jacob Bronowski, Richard Hoggart and Malcolm Bradbury. That tickled me. It still does.

One of the first poets whose work I commented on was Tom Paulin. Tom was a year behind me in the English class at Hull and would visit my flat in Marlborough Avenue. Once a week I worked late in the library, until 10.00 at night. Tom popped in one evening around 7.00 p.m. to deliver a few copies of *The Honest Ulsterman*. I had never seen the magazine before and was keen to set eyes on it. This would be late 1969 or early 1970. Larkin worked late quite frequently. Not that it matters, but he was more a 'ten-to-seven man who had seen poetry', than 'a nine-to-five salary-slave'. He called in that evening too. Tom's accent elicited memories of Queen's. When he saw copies of *The Honest Ulsterman*, in those days subtitled *A Handbook for Revolution*, Larkin exclaimed, 'Good God, do we subscribe to this?' We did not. But I did soon after that. Hull was a very Left university, and the library subscribed to many Marxist journals and purchased many books of a Leftish slant. I know. It was my job to acquire them. Professor John Saville approached me saying he had the offer of a large collection of Red Scare (or Reds-Under-the-Bed) posters from the 1920s. Would the library buy them? Saville (co-editor with E. P. Thompson of *Socialist Register*, etc., and a fine social and economic historian) brought them over. As the suggested cost was higher than the expenditure I could authorise, I took Saville and the posters – garish, but fascinating – to Larkin's office. A bit cheaper, and I could have slipped them in unnoticed. Once he had perused them, to my surprise Larkin agreed. Later that day, I was called back. Larkin had spread several of the posters on his table. 'We'll have them framed, and hang them all over the library,' he said gleefully. 'Philip, I don't think that's exactly what Professor Saville has in mind. Basement? Closed access?' In case you are wondering, the point of this paragraph is that you can co-exist with others' politics, just so long as you do not believe them.

Beginnings of some sentences are beyond me. Among them are 'In my young days . . .' and 'When I started out . . .' I have heard them from the lips of many an oldster and, when I do, my skin wrinkles and through my mind passes the thought that the universe is totally insane, and that it's nuttiness is brought about by self-centred so-called 'wisdom'. Be that as it may, in the 1960s there were few 'poetry workshops'. In all likelihood, I would not have attended if one was on offer. There was an occasion where I was more or less obliged to do so. Cecil Day Lewis had been appointed Compton Lecturer in Poetry in 1968 and not many undergraduates were showing him their verses. Larkin passed an agreeable hour in the new Poetry Room of the university library. He was kind and generous and offered some pertinent remarks, most of which I took on board. It was a memorable experience and it taught me a lot about the courtesy and humility with which one discusses another's poems in their presence.

NOTES

1. Peter Porter, 'Sanatised Sonnets', in *The Last of England* (Oxford University Press, 1970), 41.
2. Derek Mahon, *Collected Poems* (Oldcastle: Gallery, 1999), 56.
3. James F. Loucks (ed.), *Robert Browning's Poetry* (London and New York: Norton, 1979), 149.
4. *Ibid.*, 149–50.
5. *Ibid.*, 151.

CHAPTER 7

The Classics in modern Scottish and Irish poetry

Robert Crawford

Latin is the most ancient literary language of Ireland, Scotland and England, but usually it has been extirpated by general anthologists of Scottish, English or Irish poetry. Exceptionally, Hugh MacDiarmid included a few English prose versions of Scottish Latin poems in his 1940 *Golden Treasury of Scottish Poetry*, but almost six decades would pass before Thomas Owen Clancy's more specialised landmark medieval anthology *The Triumph Tree* (1998) reminded modern Scots through translation that they, too, inherited a multilingual trove of ancient poetry linking them to Europe, not just to ancient Scotland or the British Isles. For all that they printed work only in modern English translation and omitted the original poems, the wish of Clancy to call attention to a fully multilingual past was salutary.

Yet there were also signs among anthologists in Ireland and Scotland of nationalist anxiety about origins. In Ireland the 1991 *Field Day* anthology may be structured historically, but its first section, entitled 'Early and Middle Irish Literature' (*c*. 600–*c*. 1600), occupies a chronological space that begins not before but *after* the period covered by the second section, 'Latin Writing in Ireland' (*c*. 400–*c*. 1200). The historical course of the anthology seems skewed so as to position native Irish – *The Táin* – ahead of the more cosmopolitan Latin – the confession of St Patrick – as the foundational language of Irish writing. It is very hard to date these early texts, but we know St Patrick died around 492, and Ciaran Carson's 2007 translation of *The Táin* presents its material as dating from around the eighth century, even if its fragmentary origins may lie earlier. One could interpret this initial skewing in the *Field Day* anthology as a gesture of native confidence, or as a manoeuvre of nationalist anxiety. Most likely it has something of both. There is a displacement of the literary primacy of the 'dead language' – Latin – in order to foreground a still continuing 'live' native tradition, that of writing in Irish. Discernible, too, are other arguments, centuries old in Scotland and Ireland, about the sometimes awkward relationship between oral and textual traditions.

My involvement in several recent anthologies makes me a partial but also, I hope, alert observer. Like the laboriously titled *Penguin Book of Poetry from Britain and Ireland since 1945* (1998), which Simon Armitage and I edited, both *The New Penguin Book of Scottish Verse*, which I edited with Mick Imlah in 2000, and the anthology of *Scottish Religious Poetry*, which Meg Bateman, James McGonigal and I edited the same year, aim to be resolutely and richly polylingual. Each of the Scottish anthologies begins with Edwin Morgan's translation of the 'Altus Prosator', a Latin poem attributed to St Columba. This was a work which James McGonigal and I had invited Morgan to translate around 1995 for our proposed anthology of Scottish religious poetry, but that book was not published until 2000, so that before then 'The Maker on High', Morgan's version of the 'Altus Prosator', had already appeared in his *Collected Translations* in 1996. A slightly different version of the poem was published in a 1997 pamphlet, soon distributed to the members of the newly founded Scottish Parliament. In his pamphlet Morgan calls the 'Altus Prosator' 'the earliest extant Scottish poem' and 'a concentrated, relentless blast of fearful praise' – descriptions which suggest why I was particularly keen to have this poem at the start of the religious poetry anthology and why it also seemed the right way to open what is now *The Penguin Book of Scottish Verse*.[1]

Morgan's version of the 'Altus Prosator' is among the most remarkable of twentieth-century Scottish translations. Though in Latin the text is sometimes set out in short lines with end-rhymes (as in the *Oxford Book of Latin Verse*), Morgan uses a version which sets the verse in long lines with an internal rhyme. His own English captures this impressively, and the structures of his sentences, almost all running for the full length of each stanza, mirror the Latin sentences, so that Morgan catches not just rhyme but syntax. Michael Longley also relished verse syntax when he studied Latin at Trinity College Dublin, and he has commented on his schoolboy engagement with Latin verse:

From reading the Latin poets I was alerted to the possibilities of syntax, which is the muscle of poetry. I get bored by so much poetry which is written in short jerky sentences. I love stretching out over a stanza, a sentence, and playing the pauses of meaning against the line endings and trying to make the sentence, the grammatical unit, coincide with the stanzaic unit.[2]

This is a pleasure Classically trained poets may particularly relish. The positioning of the 'Altus Prosator' as 'the earliest extant Scottish poem' and its splendid modern translation by Morgan emblematically open the development of what we now call Scottish verse with a striking clarion call.

It also links the work of the Irishman Columba – viewed as Scotland's first recorded poet – to the international, cosmopolitan culture of Latin Christendom. Made accessible to new audiences by Scotland's greatest modern verse translator, an internationalist celebrated also for his support of Scottish independence, the poem becomes for twenty-first-century readers at once ancient and modern. It signals Scotland's links with other cultures, such as those of Ireland and of continental Europe, and stands impressively at the threshold of what will become a polylingual inheritance of Scottish poetry in Latin, Gaelic, Old Norse, Old French, Old English, Old Welsh, Scots and modern English. All of these are international languages. Some, like Scots and Gaelic, are used by restricted communities outside Scotland – Gaelic in Canada is fast eroding; others among these languages, most notably Latin and English, have each functioned as a transnational lingua franca.

The Irish–Latin tradition, at least as presented in the *Field Day* anthology, seems to have faltered earlier, and lacked the sustaining impact of a major poet such as George Buchanan. Patrick Crotty's *Penguin Book of Irish Poetry* (2010) – which follows *The Penguin Book of Scottish Verse* in its full-throated polyvocality – helps to clarify what happened. In Scotland, however, Latin was a significant poetic language until the start of the nineteenth century. Among Scotland's literary languages, only Gaelic – because it is still spoken – has been used over a longer period. From Columba through to Thomas Muir and the Latin translation of Ossian – surely the strangest convergence of Gaelic, English and Latin – the Classical tongue in Scotland was both active and inventive. Its strength and longevity gave it cultural vigour. Also, many Scottish poets over several centuries had grown up learning English, Scots and Latin, whereas very few poets in English or Scots had also grown up with Gaelic. This surely explains why when modern Scottish poets in Scots and English have translated earlier work from another Scottish language they have turned to Latin more often than to Gaelic. In Ireland the reverse is true. Many modern English-language Irish poets have studied at least some Irish language at school, whereas there is not such a strong tradition of Irish–Latin verse. Both Scottish and Irish poets have translated ancient texts – from Aristophanes to Catullus. Yet Scots may also have recourse to the Latin of earlier Scottish poets – as in Morgan's 'Altus Prosator' or Robert Garioch's Scots versions of Buchanan. This impulse is neither narrowly inward-looking, nor a betrayal of the native for the cosmopolitan. It complements translation of ancient and modern work by non-Scottish writers, at the same time as complicating and enriching notions of what Scottish poetry has been, is, and may be in the future.

Several essays treat aspects of modern Scottish and Irish poets' engagement with Latin and Greek culture.[3] What I want to provide here, however briefly, is the first overview of the use of the Classics in modern Irish and Scottish non-dramatic verse. Albeit sometimes refracted and multiply reflected, Classical culture pervades twentieth-century and early twenty-first-century Irish and Scottish poetry – from Yeats's 'Leda and the Swan' or 'The Scholars' to Don Paterson's *Orpheus* or 'Letter to the Twins'. Several poets, including MacNeice, MacCaig and Longley, studied Classics at university, while a plethora of others studied at least Latin at school. In surprising ways this importance of Classics to so many poets tends not to be recognised: there are no entries for 'Classics', 'Latin' or 'Greek' in the index to Jon Stallworthy's biography of Louis MacNeice, even though that book is filled with evidence of how much the Classics meant to a poet who progressed from reading Homer, Horace and Vergil in the 'Classical Fifth' at Marlborough public school to studying *literae humaniores* at Oxford. With a first in Greats and a first in Mods in Classics, MacNeice went on to work as Assistant Lecturer in Classics under his great mentor, Professor E. R. Dodds, at Birmingham University. Whatever else is true of *Autumn Journal*, it is unusual in being one of the few English-language poems that manages to incorporate a sense of the routines of intellectual work. From one (and only one) angle it is a campus poem, whose speaker, an 'impressario of the Ancient Greeks', recalls 'Coming across the sea to unknown England',[4] and writes from a standpoint that incorporates 'Teaching the classics to Midland students' and hearing 'the prison-like lecture room resound / To Homer in a Dudley accent'. If these words exhibit a hint of resigned snobbery, the poem in its close detailing of Birmingham life – 'the chocolate factory and the B.S.A.' (117) – also shows an alert, even affectionate engagement with the place, anticipating Roy Fisher's later 'Birmingham's what I think with'.[5]

Surveying the era from the vantage point of one whose 'work' means 'lecturing, coaching' (120), MacNeice invests his freewheeling, rather Audenesque documentary poem with a discernible Classical accent. His world is not just that of 'the M.A. gown, / Alphas and Betas, central heating, floor-polish' (122), but also a space where the inhabitants of modern England and ancient Greece are seen by this Irishman as living in each other's social space. So the words 'The Glory that was Greece' (title of a once famous Classics textbook by John Clarke Stobart) give rise to another version and vision of ancient Greek life as both fused with, yet removed from, the day-to-day grind of modern England. 'These dead are dead', the poem asserts, though its speaker is aware that when he 'should remember the paragons of Hellas' he recalls instead 'the crooks, the adventurers, the opportunists, / The careless athletes and the fancy boys', not to mention 'the demagogues and the quacks' (121–2). If MacNeice's 1938 poem asserts that the Classical world 'was all so unimaginably different / And all so long ago' (122), then the very diction of this same passage, with its 'demagogues ... quacks' and 'dummies', suggests it was not. There may be something a little arch here, but if Auden's early masterpiece *The Orators* has tended to outshine *Autumn Journal*, MacNeice's poem, with its inclusion of university education and Classics as distinct from Auden's focus on schoolboy education and English studies, achieves in some senses a wider, if more diffuse, resonance.

The very routine dailiness – the journal quality of *Autumn Journal* – makes it a more companionable poem than Auden's, and one to which today's information-bound workers may readily relate. Certainly MacNeice's Classically informed day-to-day work is not nearly as far from us as we might assume. His fusion of Classical and contemporary material would not be matched until the generation of Tony Harrison and Seamus Heaney, though MacNeice also uses his ability to inhabit a Classical perspective to give him a standpoint from which to mount a critique of Ireland, not just 'tight and narrow' England (144). His love–hate relationship with his country of birth as well as with his host nation is Classically inflected: '*Odi atque amo*' (140) he writes of Ireland (echoing Catullus). The dead languages of the Classicist counterpoint the 'half-dead language' (139) of Irish.

Autumn Journal is a poem aware of its author's Irishness, not least the Irishness of 'the North, veneered with the grime of Glasgow' (140), but it is more preoccupied with England. What Auden called his 'English Study', *The Orators*, is quickened by being written in a 1930s Scotland where Auden was well aware of Scottish Nationalism; part of *The Orators* was published in *The Modern Scot* while that journal's editor, J. H. Whyte, was formulating the most influential (and non-essentialist) modern theoretical underpinning for Scottish Nationalism. Similarly, MacNeice's sense of 'This England' is all the stronger for its complicated point of origin. *Autumn Journal*, like other work by MacNeice, comes from a sensibility shaped not only by an Irish upbringing but also by a rich reservoir of Classical knowledge and imagery which is ancient and European, rather than confined to modern England. The outsider's view and the insider's view are multiplied. MacNeice's is an impressively compound eye.

That sense of compound, or at least generously stereoscopic, vision is one of the most important gifts of the Classics to modern poetry, not least to verse by recent Scottish and Irish poets. For them upbringing already provides stereoscopic sensibility. They – we – grow up conscious of Scottish or Irish filiations, but also of wider bonds that come through language, linking us to America (as the most powerful English-language culture) and, in many cases, to England, the dominant English-language culture in what, following Les Murray and others, we have learned to call the Anglo-Celtic archipelago. A training in or inclination towards Classics further complicates this complex pattern of national filiations, supplementing them with a sense of the riches of ancient European culture which still – in Homer, for example – form a template for contemporary perception, supplying something necessarily distant to poets who find themselves enmeshed in the close-up pressures of contemporary national(ist) politics.

Yes, MacDiarmid in the 1930s writes such poems as 'Why I Became a Scots Nationalist' and pens his hymns to Lenin, but he also authors the poem called 'Like Achilles and Priam', which contends that the people of modern societies split by killings, ideological conflict and class divisions

> have a long way to go
> Before the supremest test, when, like Achilles and Priam, –
> Priam kissing the hands that slew so many of his sons –
> They must all manifest too the fact that the things
> That unite men are stronger than those that divide.[6]

When he wrote these lines, or composed his poem 'Another Epitaph on an Army of Mercenaries', or when he glanced towards the *Greek Anthology*, MacDiarmid may have been seen in the 1930s as writing 'In reply to A. E. Housman's' work.[7] Today, though, we are more likely to hear him as anticipating the poetry of Michael Longley, whose 'Ceasefire' makes more moving and more memorably resonant use of the meeting between Achilles and Priam. Longley, too, does so as a way of achieving a stereoscopic vision which sees simultaneously modern nationalist conflict and the near-yet-distant Classical equivalent. This stereoscopy is not the least of the pressures which produce those powerful concluding lines, so convincing because, for all their debt to Greek, they are thoroughly Anglophone in their use of full rhyme,

> 'I get down on my knees and do what must be done
> And kiss Achilles' hand, the killer of my son.'[8]

Their politics may be dissimilar, but what both MacDiarmid and Longley are doing here is turning to the same episode in the last book of the *Iliad* to provide an overarching, emotionally strong context. Their Homeric affinities take account of political division but also provide a much wider sense of unity – enacted in Longley's poem through rhyme, in MacDiarmid's by ringing plain statement. This unity is sanctioned by the aesthetic authority, the recognised wisdom, of ancient poetry. For either the Scottish or the Irish poet to have turned towards English literature (towards Shakespeare, say) at this moment would have been less effective. Inevitably it would have introduced political assumptions about English cultural power and unionism which would have been detrimental to the poems. Again, a turn towards the literature of another modern language such as French or Spanish could have seemed wilfully odd, if perhaps less politically loaded. Only the Classical text here can have the requisite balance of acknowledged authority, familiarity and sufficient distance from the immediate concern of the milieu in which the modern poets's poem is written. The Classical reference carries a power which English could not carry alone. It deepens the resonance of a poem without negating or imposing a Unionist solution on the conflicts with which the Scottish or the Irish poet is dealing. The Classical reference is deployed by MacDiarmid and by Longley to offer at least a glimpse of a kind of engaged, healing neutrality.

Unlike MacDiarmid but like MacNeice, Longley was a university student of Classics. He has written recently about what that meant and still means to him as what he calls a 'lapsed Classicist'.[9] Among Longley's finest poems are a significant number that are directly or indirectly Classical. I have written elsewhere recently about his elegant and eloquent use of Sappho in 'The Evening Star', a poem all the more distinctive for its intimate Ulster Scots infusion.[10] A melding of Classicism and dialect also powers 'Phemios & Medon', where 'Phemios the poet / . . . bannies and bams wi this highfalutin blether' in a poem at once dark and funny.[11] To my mind, the finest use in recent poetry of the Homeric parting between Hector and Andromache occurs in the French poet Michel Deguy's poem 'Passim', but Longley's poem, too, carries deep emotional conviction. His vernacular version in 'The Helmet', which expands on a famous passage in Book 6 of the *Iliad*, is at once measured and confident as the 'mammy laughed' and the 'daddy . . . kissed the babbie and dandled him in his arms' before going off to fight and be killed.[12]

A clutch of war-related poems in Longley's 1995 collection *The Ghost Orchid* are understandably among his best known Classical pieces. Often they are free translations, and there is much to be learned from pondering on the balance between translation, re-creation and vernacular flow, which the poems not so much exhibit as pivot around. There is also something exemplary in the way Longley deftly embeds Classical fragments into his own verse. A Classicist from the start, when his first (1969) collection,

No Continuing City, included such poems as 'Odyssey', 'Nausicaa', 'Circe', 'Narcissus', 'The Centaurs' and 'Persephone', Longley even then excelled as a miniaturist. The last line of 'Nausicaa' – 'The ocean gathers where your shoulder turns'[13] – is strong not so much for its encoding of narrative potential (though it does contain that) as for its music and its Henry-Moore-like sculptural juxtaposition of body curve and expansive vista.

Repeatedly in his writing career Longley has taken passages of extended Classical works – most clearly the Homeric epics – and mined them for extracts, fragmented them in ways that allow the extracted core – the 'gist' as Ezra Pound might have put it – to resonate in a remarkably expansive way. As his work has matured, Longley has turned more and more to incorporating actual Classical fragments, rather than extracts he has selected. It is as if the making of extracts has led him to appreciate all the more the force of the fragment itself, an elusive power heightened at times by its own breakage, its condition of being fragmented by history, broken by events, peculiarly bitty.

So, for instance, in 'Praxilla' Longley takes a short Greek fragment of a hymn to Adonis which ancient and modern Classicists have often seen as absurd, and which translates literally as, 'The most beautiful thing that I leave behind is the light of the sun; secondly, the shining stars and the face of the moon; also ripe cucumbers and apples and pears.'[14] Longley's poem 'Praxilla' defends this ancient woman poet from the mockery levelled against her. Acknowledging her apparent absurdity, the poem also sides with Praxilla, identifying poetry's own need to align itself with perceptions and materials that may seem eccentric. Not least because his Praxilla poem is followed by 'Corinna', I suspect Longley encountered Praxilla's lines in the fourth volume of the Loeb *Greek Lyrics* series, which is subtitled *Bacchylides, Corinna, and Others*. There, Praxilla's peculiar fragment is prefaced by a quotation from the *Proverbs* of Zenobius which explains that 'Sillier than Praxilla's Adonis' is a phrase 'used of stupid people' and that 'In her hymn … Praxilla represents Adonis as being asked by those in the underworld what was the most beautiful thing he left behind when he came, and giving as his answer [the Greek fragment quoted above].'[15]

This is what gives rise to Longley's poem and its defence of Praxilla as '*not* "feeble-minded"'. Instead, the modern poet Longley, also a treasurer of small daily details, follows his embedding of Praxilla's fragment in his own poem with the startling, yet engaging, remark,

> She is helping me unpack these plastic bags.
> I subsist on fragments and improvisations.

> Lysippus made a bronze statue of Praxilla
> Who 'said nothing worthwhile in her poetry'
> And set her groceries alongside the sun and moon.[16]

Setting groceries beside the sun and moon is how some of the most effective modern poetry works. *The Waste Land* juxtaposes 'food in tins' and 'drying combinations' with 'the sun's last rays'.[17] Beguilingly, Longley manages to be much less ironic, or, if there is irony, it is sympathetically self-directed, and turned towards the celebration of the power of lyric poetry. While Longley's use of Homer in his war poetry has been greeted, rightly, as superb, it is only just to salute, too, his deft use of the fragments of Sappho and Praxilla where, arguably, a certain feminine character is just as consonant with Longley's sly lyric grace as the masculine Homeric grumbling, and pathos is appropriate to some of his rather better-known Classical poems which can be related to the Irish Troubles. If the power of the Greek fragment in modern poetry has been explored most thoroughly by Anne Carson in *If Not, Winter: Fragments of Sappho* and in her prose study *Economy of the Unlost*, then Longley, too, is one of the Classical fragment's finest contemporary exponents in verse.

Probably Longley's use of Sappho and Praxilla is more poetically alluring than his use of other fragments. In his teasing poem 'The Group', for example, a certain unavoidable self-consciousness about the remarkable 'Ulster Renaissance' outlined by Heather Clark (who was working on her monograph of that title around the time Longley composed his poem) leads to what, depending on your point of view, is either one of the glories or one of the recurring annoyances of modern Irish – particularly Northern Irish – poetry. This feature is a familiar tribal nodding and winking, as poets invoke each other's poems in a way academic critics all too cosily welcome as 'intertextuality', yet which can also smack of the sort of cultural incest which is an inevitable problem for small nations and communities whether in Ireland, Scotland, Wales or elsewhere. At their best, much broader perspectives are afforded by the Classics which are (or were) familiar through the native education system and traditions of verse or prose composition, yet also unfamiliarly non-native because ancient and ultimately Mediterranean in inflection. The perspectives afforded to Longley and other poets by such Classicism have led to a way round the challenge of incest to small cultures. In Longley's work generally, and not least when he allies himself with Sappho or Praxilla, it is easy to detect, in Seamus Heaney's phrase, an admirable mixture of 'strictness and susceptibility'.[18]

Yet that is not a phrase which Heaney used of his friend Longley. Instead, it is one he applied to a Scottish poet of an earlier generation, another trained Classicist, Norman MacCaig. Towards the end of his life MacCaig attempted to explain why he had become a Classicist in his studies and, after an early intense engagement with surrealism, in his poetry too. He argued:

> Celtic art is very classical. In old Celtic art, all of their arts, songs, poems, sculpture ... are very formal and I think I have always loved form unconsciously. This is hindsight. But probably that's the reason I chose to take Classics at the university. And my native preference was, of course, reinforced by the study of Classics.[19]

Yet MacCaig was also a poet deeply suspicious of modernism. While not an English 'Movement' poet, he had reinvented himself in the 1950s, the era of the Movement:

> I disapprove terribly strongly of people who make references – say to classical or Greek literature or Chinese or anything else. When I write about classical figures, they are always very well-known ones like Hercules, Ulysses. And funnily enough, generally I take the Mickey out of them ... I don't know why I do that, but nearly every time I write about them – not always, but a lot of times – I use what's known as the reductive idiom, you know, I reduce them, I don't know why.[20]

In MacCaig's posthumous 2005 *Poems* – the fullest available edition – there are over a dozen pieces with obviously Classical titles. This may not seem many, but from 'Socrates' of 1952 to 'Nausicaa' in 1989 MacCaig's ostensible fascination with the Classics was a readily detectable and continuing thread in his work, most noticeable after the mid-1970s. If MacNeice in *Autumn Journal* had sounded both impressed and a little annoyed that 'The mind of Socrates still clicks like scissors', then for MacCaig who came to maturity in the period of the Cold War, a Socrates who walks 'in his own clarity' through 'the Greek air / So clear it seemed not there' is an image of the poet's ideal: a doubting, yet truthful and even celebratory, intelligence aware of being under threat and sceptical of such grand abstractions as 'The Good and Beautiful, his executioners'.[21] Clear and dry, this Classical ideal seems to hold for MacCaig something Heaney, too, has located in a Classical milieu: '*Claritas*. The dry-eyed Latin word'.[22] In MacCaig's Socrates, as in MacCaig's later remarks on the Classics, there is a clear love of form, but also an adherence to the way that 'Greek air', which represents the atmosphere, the *habitus* of the Classics, offers a remarkable intimacy with the remote, a clear and clarifying ability to bring 'close to him what was lives away'.[23]

For all that the public schoolboy MacNeice was aware of a sometimes uneasy relationship between Classics and class, and a danger that such 'humane studies' as 'Lit. Hum.' could lead simply to 'cushy jobs' for 'spiritually bankrupt / Intellectual snobs',[24] Classics for modern poets has tended to align itself with critiques of authority, as if all too aware of its own past as a subject bound up with British imperial education. For an English republican poet like Tony Harrison, class offers a subject matter that upsets knee-jerk reactions to what 'Classics' might mean. Always, to some extent at least, outsiders in the English class system and alert to linguistic, religious or geographical nuances in their own countries which often have different meanings, little meaning or no meaning in England, Scottish and Irish poets may come to the Classics with attitudes that are less bound up with native assumed imperial superiority – or one would like to think so, at any rate.

In MacCaig's work Socrates returns in a poem of 1980, 'Clio', where the Greek philosopher represents a kind of penetrating irony which 'The Muse of history, yawning with boredom',[25] regards as more important than the views of those who condemned him. Clio 'judges the judges and finds them guilty' (387). This use of Classical imagery to produce a sharply ironic, yet apparently apolitical critique, of modern society may owe something to the use of Classical figures and episodes in the work of Zbigniew Herbert and Miroslav Holub. MacCaig ends his poem about the Muse of History with the words,

> Sighing, she licks her finger
> and wearily
> turns over another page.   (387)

Beautifully lineated, all the stronger for being plain and clear, these lines sound close to the ironically inflected anti-authoritarian Czech Classicism of Holub, some of whose best work (such as 'The corporal who killed Archimedes')[26] works so well in translation because it combines stinging clarity with irony and confident reference to a common European zone of Classical allusion. Like Holub's, MacCaig's poem could be read in the context of his nation's politics, but (as with work by Longley or Heaney) its Classicism is also a way of moving beyond contemporary national politics. If critics call attention to Heaney's statement about MacCaig that 'He means poetry to me', they may not realise that among the concerns both poets shared was not only a lovingly sharp eye for their own terrain and its peculiarities but also a tendency to look back to the Classics and abroad to Eastern Europe, where Holub, Herbert and others had reinvented the Classics as a form of ironically tinged political critique. MacCaig's 'Clio' might be aligned with poems like Holub's 'The corporal who killed Archimedes' or 'Caligula' from Zbigniew Herbert's 'Mr Cogito' sequence first published in 1974, then translated into English by John and Bogdana Carpenter for Herbert's 1977 *Selected Poems* and subsequent collections.

Still, the strength of MacCaig's direct dealings with the Classics lies less in political critique than in a sure intimacy with Classical material. This lets him write of Vergil's 'pius Aeneas' that, conversing with blood-drinking shades in Hades,

> He was not only pious, he was clever
> and knew how to change their bat-squeaks
> to brave baritones.[27]

MacCaig's Aeneas seems un-Vergilian in having 'had enough of empires', but he has been so assimilated as to become very like MacCaig himself. Like Edwin Muir, MacCaig has a keen, close sense of the Classics, of a Trojan war 'that has been won and lost / and still goes on in the green field of my mind', as he puts it in 'Reading *The Iliad*'.[28] The Classics can be made to sound intimate, but can also provide a distancing or masking. Perhaps this happens when MacCaig meditates not only on loss but on infidelity in such a late poem as 'Nausicaa' where that abandoned lover, staring out to sea, realises with sharp clarity, 'I'll never see him again.'[29]

If it is less intimate, Heaney's sometimes schoolmasterly engagement with the Classical world does seem more full-blooded, more exuberant than that of MacCaig. From the early 'Antaeus' who 'cannot be weaned / Off the earth's long contour' to the twenty-first-century 'Sonnets from Hellas' and version of Vergil's ninth Eclogue Heaney, too, has turned towards the Classics for an enhancement of stereoscopic vision. Just such a necessary going-beyond may be felt by any poet conscious that he or she practises a universal and ancient art-form. Yet it may be felt especially acutely by poets from small cultures whose local political struggles can consume, even engulf, imaginative energies. Turning to the Classics adds ballast and perhaps offers release – not 'escapism' but a sense of being released into a world of wider resonances. This, surely, is what Heaney is after when he deploys a passage from the *Aeneid* as one of the two great doorposts which frame his most visionary book, *Seeing Things*. To put it another way, that 'Greek air / So clear it seemed not there' which confirms in MacCaig his love of melded slyness and clarity is akin to the expansive, resonant Greece where Heaney beholds 'electric light'. The Classics provide not the escape of exoticism but a deepening, at once a paralleling and an opening out that is subtly different from the vistas afforded by English literature. However loved, the literature of England for Scottish and Irish poets gets bound up often with the pressures of English dominance in British Unionism. If that dominance encourages the provincialisation of the non-English parts of the British Isles, then a direct relationship with the Classics promises imaginative independence as well as interdependence. The Yeats whose interests led him in 'No Second Troy' and elsewhere to align Ireland with Classical Greece was alert to this in his era. More recently, Heaney's translations of Robert Henryson's Aesopian fables and of Henryson's *Testament of Cresseid* – a Scottish work rooted both in the Classics and in Chaucer – further complicate a treasuring of poetry's subtle and multiple affiliations, something which poets, not least in Ireland or Scotland, must repeatedly assert and cherish.

Arguably the most exciting use that can be made of the long perspective of the Classics is to enhance an awareness of dynamism, of everything being open to change: even national identity may be refashioned. This is how MacDiarmid seems to have viewed the *Greek Anthology*, for instance, presenting (as if in imitation of it) his own tiny verses 'From the Scots Anthology' in *To Circumjack Cencrastus*. MacDiarmid's re-imagining of this Classical gathering, like his re-imaginings in other poems such as 'Ulysses' Bow' and 'Prometheus', are at one with his metamorphic re-imagining of Scotland.[30] Heaney's increasing Classicism, too, may be viewed in the light of re-imagining. It has been accompanied both by an impressively wide-angled view of poetry (sought by MacDiarmid, Pound, Eliot and, ultimately, by all good poets) and by a sense that, as Heaney puts it, 'whatever is given / Can always be re-imagined'.[31] In Scotland Ian Hamilton Finlay's work is the most striking example of a metamorphic re-imagining that draws on the Classics. Finlay is rightly celebrated for having stones laid on the landscape bearing the message, 'THE PRESENT ORDER IS THE DISORDER OF THE FUTURE', a wording relished by nationalist critics such as Cairns Craig. In Finlay's work, Theocritean pastoral undergoes its most radical modern reinvention. Much of that reinvention takes place in forms that draw on poetry but head beyond into conceptual and visual art. Undeniably, though, in Finlay's art the Classical component is vital to a dialogue involving simultaneous surprise and recognition. Finlay's obsessive returning to themes of interlinked authority and violence, whether in his 'Apollon Terroriste', his garden temple 'To Apollo, his Music, his Missiles, his Muses', or his use of Classical tags elsewhere – all these show how, as his caption to a warship puts it, 'for the temples of the Greeks our homesickness lasts forever'.[32] To detect such homesickness is to recognise a continuing relationship between authority, empire, violence and beauty which conditions our relationships to, and our need for, interaction with the articulate energies of the Classics.

In the work of Finlay and others such interactions can be playful. The Scots language of W. N. Herbert's *Big Bumper Book of Troy* has pop culture from the *Beano* and the topless towers of Ilium topple into one another. But, particularly for younger writers, there is also a darker side to engaging with Classical culture. It's not simply the perennial reservoir of violence which may attract, say, Tom Paulin or Robin Robertson to figures such as Marsyas, the Minotaur or Actaeon. Beyond such individual tropes, there is the larger issue of linguistic death. In Iain Crichton Smith's 'Shall Gaelic Die?' mentions of 'a Roman' and of 'Plato' represent not just cultural greatness but also language death. Having studied so-called 'dead languages' at school, I still remember the shock of walking into a bookshop in my early thirties and realising that a book I spotted called *Language Death* was about a language of my own country. Scotland and Ireland have lived for centuries now with questions of language death as culturally central – whether the language in question is Irish, Scots, Gaelic or Latin. In England, unusually, this just isn't an issue. Until recently England was the only country in the world where the cultural dominance of English seemed unproblematic. But in Scotland and Ireland, as in most other nations, there is a keen literary awareness of plural linguistic inheritances. In Scotland, as recent anthologies and literary histories demonstrate, this has led to an awareness that not just Gaelic but also Latin has been one of our ancient literary languages. To many people Latin's status is similar to that of Gaelic: it is unknown, yet oddly familiar. It is dead, whereas Gaelic (which, unlike Latin, is a language with significant television output) is simply on a life-support system. The notion of Latin as, in part, an indigenous literary language is frightening: it shows that native languages can die. To write about, to make versions of, Classical poetry in today's Scotland or Ireland is to listen to the closing of a door. There is no longer a Classics department at any Northern Irish university, though there are at least five Classics departments in the Irish Republic. Among Scotland's fourteen universities there are only three Classics departments – at St Andrews, Glasgow and Edinburgh. In schools Latin and Greek are less and less taught. While Classical Studies is strikingly popular, direct access to Classical literature at school is reverting to a nineteenth-century situation where the only way to get it is to buy it through private education.

This cultural shrinkage, like the position of Scottish Gaelic, raises issues of linguistic biodiversity. To engage imaginatively with language in modern Scotland or Ireland is to feel this acutely, to sense ecosystems so imperilled that to reflect on them may offer metaphors for our wider plight on the planet. Use of Classical materials in modern Scottish and Irish poetry seems more and more like an act of resistance, a championing of access to cultural, linguistic and imaginative wealth which emblematises a vital stereoscopic vision. Perhaps the most successful recent resistance has taken place in drama, including dramatic verse. One thinks of the political critique of Heaney's Philoctetes or the recent terrifying mothers in several Scottish versions of *Medea*, that greatest of all plays about domestic violence. Yet in poetry, too, the presence of the Classics, against all the odds, remains strong. One could be too gloomy about this Classical presence as sounding only a note of extinction, though it often does sound that. Whether we think of ancient poetry, or of Scotland's greatest literary diaspora – that of her Renaissance Latin poets – the Classical presence also bears witness to the deep-rootedness and longevity of the poetic impulse: to what poetry demands and, at its best, also rewards. As Don Paterson puts it, in words which go back to German and ultimately to Greek poetry, 'Only Orpheus / Could stir you to the deepest listening.'[33]

To listen to the Classics in modern Scottish and Irish poetry is to listen to the dead, which is always vital in literature. But it is also to listen to the remarkably persistent love of varieties of native language and of wider-than-native perspectives in the poetry of two small nations. It is to do what poetry must do repeatedly, to listen to a native foreignness.

NOTES

1. Edwin Morgan, prefatory note to *The Maker on High* (Glasgow: Mariscat, 1997), i.
2. Michael Longley, quoted in Heather Clark, *The Ulster Renaissance* (Oxford University Press, 2006), 18.
3. These include John Kerrigan, 'Ulster Ovids', in Neil Corcoran (ed.), *The Chosen Ground: Essays on the Contemporary Poetry of Northern Ireland* (Bridgend: Seren, 1992), 237–69; Helen Vendler, 'Seamus Heaney and the *Oresteia:* "Mycenae Lookout" and the Usefulness of Tradition', *Proceedings of the American Philosophical Society* 143:1 (1999), 116–29; Graham Tulloch, 'Robert Garioch's Translations of George Buchanan's Latin Tragedies', in Bill Findlay (ed.), *Frae Ither Tongues: Essays on Modern Translations into Scots* (Clevedon: Multilingual Matters, 2004), 171–87; Lorna Hardwick, 'Classical Theatre in Modern Scotland – A Democratic Stage?', in *The Reception of the Texts and Images of Ancient Greece in Late Twentieth-Century Drama and Poetry in English*, Open University Seminar Series 2002, archived at www2.open.ac.uk/ClassicalStudies/GreekPlays/Seminar02/LHFinal.htm
4. Louis MacNeice, 'Autumn Journal', in *Collected Poems* (London: Faber, 2007), 122.
5. Roy Fisher, *The Long and the Short of It: Poems 1955–2005* (Newcastle: Bloodaxe, 2005), 285.

6. Hugh MacDiarmid, *Complete Poems*, Vol. 1 (London: Martin Brian and O'Keeffe, 1978), 551.
7. *Ibid.*, 551.
8. Michael Longley, *Collected Poems* (London: Cape, 2006), 225.
9. Michael Longley, 'Lapsed Classicist', in Stephen Harrison (ed.), *Living Classics: Greece and Rome in Contemporary Poetry in English* (Oxford University Press, 2009), 97–113.
10. Longley, *Collected Poems*, 263; see Robert Crawford, 'Maes Howe Sappho', *Yale Review* 93:1 (2007), 60–5.
11. Longley, *Collected Poems*, 229.
12. *Ibid.*, 226.
13. *Ibid.*, 15.
14. Praxilla, 'Fragmenta', in David A. Campbell (ed.), *Greek Lyric, IV: Bacchylides, Corinna, and Others* (Cambridge, Mass., and London: Harvard University Press, 1992), 374–5.
15. Campbell (ed.), *Greek Lyric, IV*, 375.
16. Longley, *Collected Poems*, 320.
17. T. S. Eliot, *Collected Poems* (London: Faber, 1974), 71.
18. Seamus Heaney, comment on rear jacket of Norman MacCaig, *The Poems of Norman MacCaig*, ed. Ewen McCaig (Edinburgh: Polygon, 2005).
19. MacCaig, *The Poems*, xli.
20. *Ibid.*
21. MacNeice, *Collected Poems*, 151; MacCaig, 'Socrates', *The Poems*, 33.
22. Seamus Heaney, 'Seeing Things, II', *Seeing Things* (London: Faber, 1991), 17.
23. MacCaig, *The Poems*, 33.
24. MacNeice, *Collected Poems*, 129–30.
25. MacCaig, *The Poems*, 387.
26. Miroslav Holub, *Poems Before and After: Collected English Translations*, trans. Ian and Jarmila Milner, Ewald Osers and George Theiner (Newcastle: Bloodaxe, 1990), 35.
27. MacCaig, 'In Hades', *The Poems*, 409.
28. MacCaig, *The Poems*, 480.
29. *Ibid.*, 495.
30. MacDiarmid, *Complete Poems*, 195, 172, 173.
31. Heaney, 'The Settle Bed', *Seeing Things*, 29.
32. These works are reproduced in Yves Abrioux, *Ian Hamilton Finlay: A Visual Primer*, 2nd edn (London: Reaktion, 1992), 65, 193.
33. Don Paterson, *Orpheus* (London: Faber, 2006), 58.

CHAPTER 8

Translating Beowulf: *Edwin Morgan and Seamus Heaney*

Hugh Magennis

Edwin Morgan started on his translation of *Beowulf* soon after he got his degree in 1947, his undergraduate studies having been interrupted by the war, and he published it in 1952.[1] He was working in Glasgow at this time in a literary context in which questions of identity and language politics were being hotly debated.[2] In his *Beowulf*, however, as in most of his other work, Morgan looks out beyond this immediate context, writing for a wider audience and not striving for a self-consciously Scottish inflection in the language of his poetry. As discussed below, in 1953 he produced a translation of a passage from *Beowulf* into Scots,[3] but in the translation of the complete poem into English (and published in England) he is placing himself in the wider context of poetry in English. Morgan was fully aware then, as later, of issues of English cultural supremacy that weighed heavily on Scottish writers: 'the Scots have, and have long had, to worry about their relation and attitude to England', he would write;[4] and in translating *Beowulf* he knew he was appropriating a great monument from the edifice of English literary history. He was appropriating it, however, on behalf of modern English poetry rather than for a more local constituency, though in doing so he was making a statement to that constituency. His polemical introduction to the translation of *Beowulf* is all about relating his translation to living modern poetry in English; in the introduction he is famously scathing about previous versions of *Beowulf* in English verse: 'Not one [of the existing translations of *Beowulf*]', he writes, 'has succeeded in establishing itself as a notable presentation, even for its own period, of a great original. [. . .] Nothing has been found [. . .] in these *Beowulf* translations to interest either the practising poet or the cultivated reader of poetry.'[5] Morgan is particularly scathing about translations produced after the end of the First World War, since they came from a time of great vitality for English poetry but showed not the slightest sign of doing so. 'The most notable fact about the post-1918 versions', declares Morgan, 'is that they fail to establish a contact with the poetry of their time, and therefore fail to communicate.'[6] He means they fail to communicate as poetry.

Morgan always resisted pigeonholing. As Ian Gregson writes, 'What sets him apart is his apparent refusal to forge a settled poetic identity and this despite the fact that he has material at his disposal which could have been used in this way.'[7] He had engaged in the debate going on, when he returned from the war, about whether Scottish poets should write in Scots or in English, and had advocated a permissive attitude rather than the kind of dogmatic approach insisted upon by Hugh MacDiarmid and others. Contributing to a heated discussion on the subject in the correspondence columns of *The Glasgow Herald* in 1946, Morgan stressed that the choice of language should be made with attention to the preferred audience that the poet has in mind and that poets should be free to write either in 'a Scots mixture' or in 'a northern variant of the standard language', enriching and rejuvenating it from their own experience.[8] His own choice in the *Beowulf* translation was for the latter, not only because of his preferred audience but also because he wished to place himself in the wider tradition of poetry in English, which for his purposes was more enabling than Scots. And, as illustrated by the opening lines of Morgan's *Beowulf*, this sense of a specifically 'northern variant' of English is not at all pronounced in the translation:

> How that glory remains in remembrance,
> Of the Danes and their kings in days gone,
> The acts and valour of princes of their blood!
>   Scyld Scefing: how often he thrust from their feast-halls
> The troops of his enemies, tribe after tribe,
> Terrifying their warriors: he who had been found
> Long since as a waif and awaited his desert
> While he grew up and throve in honour among men
> Till all the nations neighbouring about him
> Sent as his subjects over the whale-fields
> Their gifts of tribute: king worth the name!   (lines 1–11)

This passage, eloquently reflecting the original in its blend of exclamation and reflectiveness, sets the writing firmly in a Standard English mode.[9] The passage also illustrates the relative formality of Morgan's register, here evincing syntactical elaboration but also decorous restraint in expression and in rhythmical effects. The four-stress metre (based ultimately on that of Old English) is handled with sensitivity, and alliteration, though integral to the verse, is light. There is nothing of the *rum, raff, ruff* (as referred to by Chaucer) that alliterative poetry can lapse into.

Morgan's Scots translation of a passage from *Beowulf* (lines 2444–62a), 'The Auld Man's Coronach',[10] describing the grief of an old man whose son has died on the gallows, is an intimate and deeply lyrical piece of work, capturing the sense of numbed desolation of the Old English elegiac mood, to produce a compelling free-standing short poem. 'The Auld Man's Coronach' is very much a reworking of the corresponding Old English lines, and it does not seek to transport the reader to ancient Germania but to present emotion with dignity (as suggested by the Scottish-Gaelic word *coronach* itself, meaning 'lamentation') and also with idiomatic immediacy. The translation is down-to-earth in its language, significant elements of which are everyday words deriving directly from Old English, though not in use in the standard language: examples are *dowie* (sorrowful), *thole* (suffer), *maun* (must), *minds* (remembers), *daws* (dawns). Among words from Old Norse are *toom* (empty) and *whidders* (gusts). And the poem is subdued in its rhythmical effects; it comes across as unforced and idiomatic, though it is also highly poetic in expression. Its rhetorical features – most notably repetition, omission of the verb 'to be', inverted word order and looseness of syntax – serve to emphasise the emotion and to lend dignity to the expression of that emotion, as in the opening lines:

> Waesome, waesome the hert that is his,
> Faither wha sees his only laudie
> Waive i the widdie on gallows tree.

Flowery language is avoided and, though free in his treatment of the original, Morgan is restrained in his additions. Most striking perhaps is his filling out of the Old English image of the father remembering every morning the *ellor-sið* (journey elsewhere; line 2451) of his son:

> He minds him on ilka morn that daws
> But his son has stravaig'd to the morn-come-never.

As in *Beowulf*, the verse is underlain throughout by a steady four-stress metrical structure, based on Old English metre, with pronounced caesura and an alliteration that is unobtrusive but highlights key images and thoughts. There is little sense of forward movement in the dirge-like poetry, as reflects the all-encompassing emotion. The closing lines work to a climax with reference to the old man's desires, which turns out, however, to be only the bleakness of 'Naethin ava'.

Published in *The Glasgow Herald*, 'The Auld Man's Coronach' is aimed at a Scottish readership and draws upon the rich associations of vernacular literary language to produce a powerful and moving poem, in which the Old English has been (in terms of translation theory) imaginatively 'domesticated'.[11] It is a mood piece rather than a developed narrative work, however, and Morgan did not seek to extend the use of Scots with reference to more complex or intractable material in Old English (or other languages). Chris Jones is surely correct when he writes, with reference to 'The Auld Man's Coronach', 'For Morgan, Scots is a medium associated with domestic emotion and folk and oral culture[;] it therefore provides the appropriate tenor here, but not for most of *Beowulf*, with its higher register, more closely associated with "official" cultural authority.'[12] One should not underestimate the subtlety and solemnity of 'The Auld Man's Coronach', however.

Unlike in 'The Auld Man's Coronach', for his *Beowulf* Morgan uses Standard English, and a Standard English not conspicuously 'northern' in character; there are some, but not many, obvious signs of a specific regional idiom. In line with Scottish vernacular practice, for example, is Morgan's consistent preference of the conjunction *till* (never *until*) in the translation (line 9, etc.), as is the use of *hid* as a past participle (line 161), not Standard English 'hidden', and of *throve* (line 8) and *pled* (line 1994) as the past tenses of 'thrive' and 'plead' respectively, though *throve* is perhaps also formal, with suggestions of the archaic; also consistent with Scottish usage is the use of the verbs *gally* (frighten; line 1429) and *sheen* (shine, polish; line 2257) and the noun *street* (road; line 320); Morgan's use of the (originally Norwegian) word *kraken* (sea-monster; line 422, etc.) may also reflect Scottish linguistic influence. But it should be emphasised that such instances are relatively few and far between and make little impression on the overall register.

Morgan's translation of *Beowulf* is remarkable, however, not only for the quality of its language, northern or not, but also for the vigour and range of its rhythmical effects, based on a four-stress metrical structure that derives ultimately from that of Old English itself, and it has been suggested that this metrical structure may provide a link with Morgan's Scottish background. This structure, with its in-built alliteration, had been inherited and developed by, among others, Scots poets of the later Middle Ages, most notably William Dunbar, whose alliterative verse is strongly percussive. Morgan's poetic output resembles that of Dunbar in other ways, most notably in its sheer 'restless variety' (in Kevin McCarra's phrase)[13] and its formal experimentation – Dunbar was also a poet who resisted pigeonholing – but in particular the influence of Dunbar and other medieval Scottish poets is likely to have reinforced the appeal of stress-rhythm for Morgan and to have given him an increased sense of its rhythmical possibilities. Morgan insists that experimentation with stress-metre is a feature of modern poetry anyway, but it is a feature that he finds particularly natural in his own Scottish context. In the 'Introduction' to his *Beowulf* he speaks of 'a generally renewed interest in Old and Middle English non-syllabic poetry',[14] but this interest was also specific to himself.

Six months before his *Beowulf* came out Morgan published his essay entitled 'Dunbar and the Language of Poetry'.[15] In that essay he writes that the practice of Dunbar and other medieval Scots poets 'proves that the older tradition was very pervasive and very congenial to the Scottish spirit and [Dunbar and other Scottish poets] pay it that debt of exemplification which is often more revealing than their addresses to Chaucer'.[16] He declares that 'the effects in Dunbar belong to something permanent in the spirit of the language'.[17] It is perhaps in Morgan's 'exemplification' of aspects of medieval Scots poetry (itself influenced by the Old English tradition with which Morgan is engaging) that we may observe Scottish literary influence in his *Beowulf*. Even here, however, we should note that alongside Morgan's appreciation of the Scottish Dunbar is his admiration for the alliterative poetry of later medieval England, notably in *Sir Gawain and the Green Knight*, *Pearl* and *Piers Plowman*.[18]

Terry Eagleton declares, characteristically, that *Beowulf* 'ultimately retains its pride of place in English studies mainly due to its function, from the Victorian period forward, as the cultural tool of a troubling nationalist romance with an archetypal and mythological past'.[19] There is certainly validity to Eagleton's perception of the eager appropriation of *Beowulf* for political and institutional purposes, which has gone on throughout its modern history. Tom Shippey, too, highlights the political role of *Beowulf* when he writes, surveying the 'critical heritage' of the poem, particularly in the period of what he refers to as 'nation-forging', 'one has to say that the poem itself at all times appeared as a source of potential authority and power'.[20]

For some modern commentators *Beowulf* has been tainted by association with originary myths and racial imaginings, as it has with its association with dry philological scholarship. As Kingsley Amis wrote dismissively of *Beowulf* not long after Morgan's translation,

> Someone has told us this man was a hero.
> Must we then reproduce his paradigms,
> Trace out his rambling regress to his forbears
> (An instance of Old English harking-back)?[21]

That was not how Morgan saw *Beowulf*. Morgan got beyond the philology and the racial myth to a deep appreciation of the literature. He was evidently not troubled by oppressive issues of authority and power or of language ownership and identity, and he was able to undertake the translation of *Beowulf* without the kind of soul-searching that Seamus Heaney would later go in for.

As a Scot, Morgan could relate to the Old English language as an older form of his own language, in a way that Heaney would profess that he could not. After all, what linguists call Old English had been spoken in Scotland as well as in England, long before the construction of notions of national identity in either area. English place names go back a long way in Scotland and indeed one of the great monuments of 'Anglo-Saxon' culture, the Ruthwell Cross, comes from southern Scotland, which was then (the cross dates from probably the early eighth century) part of the Northumbrian kingdom. And on the surface of this high cross is carved in runes the text of a poem of the cross in Old Northumbrian, the ancestor of Scots; these are lines that also form part of a longer poem that was copied into a manuscript, in West Saxon, some two and a half centuries later, *The Dream of the Rood*. This circumstance has led to the suggestion from some critics that *The Dream of the Rood* may be one of the oldest 'Scottish' poems.[22] Whatever our view of such a claim (as another kind of nationalistic appropriation perhaps?), the existence of the Ruthwell poem of the cross is one striking illustration of the slippage involved in the venerable tradition of equating Old English with Englishness.

Morgan himself did not make such an equation and seems untroubled by the issues of English cultural supremacy I mentioned earlier or indeed by potential supremacist connotations of the very language labels in use then, as now. It is only very recently that the use of the term 'Old English' has come to be questioned, in relation to a Scottish perspective on the language. At a recent conference the lexicographer Margaret Scott asked whether there was a case for linguists not calling Old English 'Old *English*'. Should we think of something else to call it, something that didn't have the marked word 'English' in it? – especially given the fact that for a considerable part of the Anglo-Saxon period (and certainly when the Ruthwell Cross was put up) there was no real *or* imagined entity called England, and that 'Old English' is the ancestor of modern Scots just as much as modern English.[23]

In postwar Scotland, and Ireland, such academic concerns were not to the fore in the way that they are now, due to the influence of more recent postcolonial thinking, though, as we have seen, issues of language politics were being urgently contested at the time. In writing in English Morgan sought to avoid the shackles of a position that would limit him artistically. For the translation of *Beowulf* the capacity of the English literary language makes it a natural choice for him and by using it, and indeed by translating

Beowulf, he places himself in relation to a wider literary tradition in a way that he does not see as compromising his Scottishness. Morgan encountered *Beowulf* in the world of traditional English studies, where it did occupy a canonical and originary position, but it was its poetry rather than its status that drew him; he was not investing in Englishness. And he produced an intelligent and exciting translation, though it has to be said that ultimately he did not succeed in changing the reputation of *Beowulf* by translating it out of its philological corner, nor did he succeed in bringing it to the fore for the wider readership of modern poetry, as his translation seems not to have been particularly popular with its intended audience.

Unlike Morgan, Seamus Heaney does express anxieties about translating *Beowulf* that have something in common with Eagleton's observation (as quoted above), though Heaney expresses those anxieties in terms very different from those of Eagleton. Like Morgan, Heaney was introduced to *Beowulf* through the philological approach but sought to bring the poem to a new readership. In terms of sheer sales, and also of the interest in the poem that he stimulated, he succeeded in this aim in a way that Morgan did not.

Heaney's translation of *Beowulf* was published in 1999 to a reception that was mostly very enthusiastic indeed.[24] Attracting a level of interest unprecedented in recent times for a verse publication, the translation caught the imagination of modern readers, even having lengthy stints at the top of the best-seller lists in Britain and Ireland and in the United States. It was praised by poetry critics for its freshness and vigour and by Anglo-Saxonists, who hailed it as a sensitive and generally accurate rendering of the great Old English poem.[25] Sympathetically reviewing the translation in *The Observer*, Michael Alexander, himself a gifted translator of the Old English poem, referred to Seamus Heaney as 'a generous poet [who] has brought back our own, in his own words'.[26] Alexander's praise is itself generous, though it also raises the issue of the place and significance of *Beowulf* in the modern world, and indeed of 'ownership' of the poem.

For Heaney, writing as an Irish poet, translating *Beowulf* was not a matter of 'bringing back our own' in any simple sense. Heaney's engagement with the poem is a more complex matter, raising questions of language and identity and cultural connections, and the starting-point for an understanding of his approach to his translation must be an awareness of the complexity of his relationship to, and interaction with, the Old English poem. 'Our own' for Heaney would have to refer to his own cultural situatedness and also to the readership of the 'global village' to whom he declares that he is making *Beowulf* available, transforming it in the process.

In addressing his audience of the global village, Heaney hones a kind of writing that is in one sense the antithesis of global. His translation is written in Standard English but a Standard English consistently inflected by the usage of the local speech area in which the poet grew up in the rural Ulster of the mid-twentieth century. In contrast to Morgan's, the language of Heaney's translation is a function of where he is coming from, so to speak, and of how he sees himself as relating to the original poem and the world from which *it* comes. The *Beowulf* that modern readers get in Heaney's version is self-consciously different from the *Beowulf* constructed by traditional scholarship, and Heaney's stance in approaching the poem is distinctively different from that of other translators.

This distinctiveness is apparent from the very opening lines, which begin with the famous '*So*' and proceed with a narrative that is dignified but also has its feet very much on the ground. The four-stress metre with structural alliteration provides rhythmical flexibility but also an underlying steadiness, and the opening passage is composed almost entirely of monosyllabic and disyllabic words. These features convey an impression of 'foursquareness' that Heaney associates with the verse of *Beowulf* itself (though foursquareness is by no means the whole story with the original, or with the translation).[27] Heaney's language is notably 'ordinary', with even *whale-road*, the first striking poetic expression that the reader comes upon in the translation (an imitation of an Old English kenning), being made up of familiar elements. The opening passage ends with the direct vernacular exclamation, 'That was one good king!'

Heaney has constructed something of a mythology of his relationship to *Beowulf*, a mythology that provides a desired justification of his approach to the translation. In my view, he was drawn to the idea of translating *Beowulf* anyway (as Morgan was) and his instinct was to translate the poem as he did, and indeed this is the only way he could have translated it while remaining true to his own poetic idiom. But since he was profoundly changing the register of the venerable poem he needed some kind of rational licence for doing so. Thus, he writes of the 'little epiphany'[28] of finding that the humble Ulster word *thole* is an inheritance from Old English. In a sense this recognition is a red herring, since it is perfectly possible to translate from languages with which one has no such personal identification (as Heaney himself has), and anyway *thole* appears in other varieties of English as well. But for Heaney *thole* and the like represent, in his romantic phrase, 'illumination by philology'.[29] They provide a rationale for his poetic approach, and politically they provide a way of breaking down what may be perceived as an Irish–English dichotomy. Such a perceived dichotomy is reflected in Heaney's statement, in a newspaper article published just before the translation of *Beowulf* came out, 'Before I set out to translate *Beowulf*, I had to persuade myself that I was born into its language and that its language was born into me.'[30] No other English-language translator of *Beowulf*, including Morgan, has had such a problem with the idea of translating *Beowulf*.

Being struck by correspondences between Old English and his native vernacular form of English, Heaney came to connect *Beowulf* with his own language experience in a way that he had not expected, but seems to have needed. He came to see that the language of *Beowulf* was in some immediate sense *his* language rather than being only an earlier form of the more prestigious language he was encountering in the wider world and in literature. This perception of connectedness was his 'little epiphany', and he explains that it was this that led him to fashion the distinctive stylistic register of his translation, 'the note and pitch for the overall music of the work'.[31]

Heaney's translation reconceives *Beowulf*. His approach takes the poem out of its perceived traditional context in the institution of English studies and relates it to a different kind of experience. It is an interesting fact, therefore, that the translation was commissioned by that bastion of the institution of English literature *The Norton Anthology of English Literature*. In its latest (seventh) edition, Heaney's translation comes right at the beginning of the *Anthology* and, with its distinctive register, has the immediate effect of unsettling easy notions about the canon of English literature. I do not know whether the publishers bargained for such a radical and self-consciously political take on *Beowulf* but Heaney's translation presents a challenging opening to the *Anthology*, making an impression on the reader much different from that of Talbot Donaldson's worthy prose version, which had appeared in earlier editions of the *Norton*.

Among the features that commentators have found most distinctive about Heaney's translation of *Beowulf* is his deployment of dialect words that belong to the vocabulary of his native Hiberno-English variety of English. The *key* choice that Heaney made was not at the level of individual words, however, but was that of the register in which the work is cast. Heaney has written famously about the language of the 'big-voiced Scullions' of his boyhood locality that gave him not just the distinctive lexical items but also that 'note and pitch for the overall music of the work'.[32] Heaney's adopted register is based on the real language of ordinary people, or rather, more particularly, the real language of ordinary people that he remembers from his youth. It is a language that is colloquial but at the same time measured, with its own decorum and formality. The vocabulary of this 'real language', reflective of a traditional way of life, is expressive but limited, with much use of stock phrases, which can be banal as well as apt. It does not go in for curiosities. Far from avoiding ready-made language, Heaney can be seen to favour it in many of his expressions, thereby calculatedly incorporating the prosaic into his poetry. The succession of colloquial everyday phrases is constant, including such stock items as the following (which occur both in the narrative and in speeches): *troubles they'd come through* (line 15), *hold the line* (line 24), *laid down the law* (line 29), *in full view* (line 77), *the killer instinct* (line 54), *a weather-eye* (line 143), *numb with grief* (line 234), *she flew like a bird* (line 218, used of a ship, and with colloquial use of feminine gender for the ship) and so on.

Such phrases are in general currency in English, of course, but Heaney knows them from the ordinary speech of his home area, where they provide the texture of a vernacular in which traditional forms of speech reflect a traditional outlook on life. It is their integral place in that vernacular that gives Heaney the confidence to make such widespread use of them in the translation of an epic poem, paying homage to the English of his home area of his formative years by doing so. Through the use of such language Heaney suggests communal experience, constructing a community that the *Beowulf*ian first-person narrator can appropriately relate to, though it is a community different from the early Germanic community constructed in the original poem. Morgan's version, reflecting the expected absence of a communal voice in modern poetry, excises the first-person-plural pronoun at the beginning of the poem and mostly dispenses with the formulaic use of the first-person-singular pronoun which is widespread in the original, but Heaney keeps the communal *we* of the opening sentence and first-person-singular formulations appear throughout his translation.

This chosen register provides Heaney with 'the note and pitch for the overall music of the work'. But to stick to it too literally would be to place significant limitations on what he could achieve in his translation: like the Scots of Morgan's 'The Auld Man's Coronach' discussed earlier, this register, while it might have its strengths, necessarily lacks the ornateness, variation and verbal brilliance that the original Old English poem sustains. In fact, of course, Heaney's translation is not written in the language of ordinary speech, any more than *Beowulf* is, but presents a *version* of that language 'raised to the power of verse', as Heaney puts it.[33] It is raised to the power of verse not only by the metrical structure that Heaney elaborates, loosely modelled on that of the Old English, and the accompanying rhythmical play in and across the lines of verse, but also by the (unscullionlike) inventiveness of Heaney's expression, the richness of his vocabulary and the precision and alertness of his diction and imagery, which constantly surprise and delight – features, of course, well recognised in his poetry more generally.

Heaney's translation raises the question, whose *Beowulf* is it anyway, in a way that Morgan's does not. Rather than 'giving us back our own', Heaney is presenting *Beowulf* from a new angle, bringing out new possibilities in how the poem might be understood. In my view the translations by Morgan and Heaney are the two most significant verse translations of *Beowulf* which have been published. They represent serious poetic engagements with the Old English poem, in each case making it into a living, modern poem that is poetically convincing and yet 'true' to the original in essential respects. Like all significant translations, they are translations of their time, and place. It is interesting that these two major translations came not from metropolitan literary circles, in which *Beowulf* continued to be of marginal interest throughout the twentieth century, but from Celtic contexts. Morgan is not hung up on issues of margin and centre, while Heaney demolishes the centre–margin binarism altogether, repositioning – and reconceiving – *Beowulf* in the process.

NOTES

1. Edwin Morgan (trans.), *Beowulf: A Verse Translation into Modern English* (Manchester: Carcanet, 2002 [1952]); Morgan describes working on the translation in Chris Jones, 'Edwin Morgan in Conversation', *P.N.Review* 31:2 (2004), 47–51, 48.
2. See Colin Nicholson, *Edwin Morgan: Inventions of Modernity* (Manchester University Press, 2002), 14–30.
3. Edwin Morgan, 'The Auld Man's Coronach', *The Glasgow Herald*, 8 August 1953, 3; the text of this poem is reproduced in Chris Jones, *Strange Likeness: The Use of Old English in Twentieth-Century Poetry* (Oxford University Press, 2006), 169–70.
4. Edwin Morgan, 'The Beatnik in the Kailyard', *New Saltire* 3 (1962), 65, quoted by Nicholson, *Edwin Morgan*, 15.
5. Morgan, *Beowulf*, vii.
6. *Ibid.*, viii.
7. Ian Gregson, 'Edwin Morgan's Metamorphoses', *English* 39 (1990), 149–64, 149.
8. *The Glasgow Herald*, 26 November 1946. See further Nicholson, *Edwin Morgan*, 21.
9. It may be helpful to quote the corresponding lines from the Old English original and to supply a literal translation:

> Hwæt we Gar-Dena in gear dagum,
> þeod-cyninga þrym gefrunon,

> hu ða æþelingas ellen fremedon!
> Oft Scyld Scefing sceaþena þreatum,
> monegum mægþum meodu setla ofteah,
> egsode eorlas, syððan ærest wearð
> feasceaft funden; he þæs frofre gebad,
> weox under wolcnum, weorð myndum þah,
> oð þæt him æghwylc ymb-sittendra
> ofer hron-rade hyran scolde,
> gomban gyldan; þæt wæs god cyning!

Fr. Klaeber (ed.), *Beowulf and the Fight at Finnsburg*, 3rd edn (Boston: D. C. Heath, 1950), lines 1–10; this is the edition on which Morgan says (*Beowulf*, xxxiv) that he based his translation. 'Listen [*Hwæt*, literally 'what', is a conventional call to attention, invoking an oral reception context], we have heard of the glory in days of yore of the kings of the people [*þeod cyninga*] of the Spear-Danes [*Gar-Dena*], how the noblemen accomplished [deeds of] valour [*ellen*]. Often Scyld Scefing deprived troops of enemies, many tribes, of their mead-benches [*meodu setla*], terrified/inspired awe in warriors. He experienced comfort [*frofre*] for that: he prospered [*weox*, literally 'waxed'] under the clouds [i.e., in the world], thrived in worldly honours [*weorð myndum*], until each one of the neighbouring tribes [*ymb sittendra*, 'those situated, or sitting, around'], over the whale's road, had to obey him, give him tribute; that was a good king!'

10. See above, n. 3.
11. For influential treatment of the issue of 'domesticating' versus 'foreignising' translations, see Lawrence Venuti, *The Translator's Invisibility: A History of Translation* (London and New York: Routledge, 1995) and *The Scandals of Translation: Towards an Ethics of Difference* (London and New York: Routledge, 1998); the debate can be traced back at least as far as Friedrich Schleiermacher, 'On the Different Methods of Translating' ['Ueber die verschiedenen Methoden des Uebersetzens', 1813], trans. Susan Bernofsky, in *The Translation Studies Reader*, ed. Lawrence Venuti, 2nd edn (New York and London: Routledge, 2001), 43–63. With reference to translations from Old English into Scots, see John Corbett, '*The Seafarer*: Visibility and the Translation of a West Saxon Elegy into English and Scots', *Translation and Literature* 10 (2001), 157–73.
12. Jones, *Strange Likeness*, 170.
13. Kevin McCarra, 'Edwin Morgan: Lives and Work', in Robert Crawford and Hamish Whyte (eds.), *About Edwin Morgan* (Edinburgh University Press, 1990), 1–9, 4.
14. Morgan, *Beowulf*, xix.
15. Edwin Morgan, 'Dunbar and the Language of Poetry', *Essays in Criticism* 2:2 (1952), 138–57; reprinted in Edwin Morgan, *Essays* (Cheadle Hulme: Carcanet, 1974), 81–99.
16. Morgan, 'Dunbar and the Language of Poetry', 139; quoted by Nicholson, *Edwin Morgan*, 46.

17. Morgan, 'Dunbar and the Language of Poetry', 157.
18. As expressed in 'Nothing is Not Giving Messages' (interview with Robert Crawford), in Edwin Morgan, *Nothing Not Giving Messages: Reflections on Work and Life*, ed. Hamish Whyte (Edinburgh: Polygon, 1990), 118–43, 122, and in Jones, 'Edwin Morgan in Conversation', 50.
19. Terry Eagleton, 'Hasped and Hooped and Hirpling: Heaney Conquers *Beowulf*', *London Review of Books*, 11 November 1999, 16.
20. T. A. Shippey, 'Introduction', in T. A. Shippey and Andreas Haarder (eds.), *Beowulf: The Critical Heritage* (London and New York: Routledge, 1998), 1–74, 74.
21. Kingsley Amis, *Collected Poems, 1944–1979* (London: Hutchinson, 1979), 18.
22. See, for example, Mick Imlah and Robert Crawford (eds.), *The Penguin Book of Scottish Verse* (Harmondsworth: Penguin, 2006), in which *The Dream of the Rood* is translated by Crawford (4–23).
23. Margaret Scott, 'Scottish Place-Names and Anglo-Saxon England', Conference of the International Society of Anglo-Saxonists, London 2007 (Session 9, 2 August).
24. Seamus Heaney (trans.), *Beowulf* (London: Faber, 1999); also published as Seamus Heaney (trans.), *Beowulf: A New Verse Translation*, bilingual edn (New York: W. W. Norton, 2000), and in M. H. Abrams and Stephen Greenblatt (eds.), *The Norton Anthology of English Literature*, Vol. 1, 7th edn (New York: W. W. Norton, 2000), 32–99 (as well as in other Norton volumes). References below are to the Faber edition.
25. Among dissenting voices has been Tom Shippey, who disapproves of what he refers to as Heaney's 'fashionable gestures towards post-colonialism and other anachronisms': Tom Shippey, '*Beowulf: A Verse Translation*, Revised Edition by Michael Swanton', in Herbert Grabes and Wolfgang Viereck (eds.), *The Wider Scope of English: Papers in English Language and Literature from the Bamburg Conference of the International Association of University Professors of English*, Bamberger Beiträge zur Englischen Sprachwissenschaft 51 (Frankfurt am Main: Peter Lang, 2006), 87–91, 91; see also Shippey's review of Heaney, '*Beowulf* for the Big-Voiced Scullions', *Times Literary Supplement* (1 October 1999), 9–10. See also Nicholas Howe, 'Scullionspeak', *The New Republic* 222:9 (2000), 32–7. Two other notable discussions of Heaney's translation by Old English scholars are Hans Sauer and Inge B. Milfull, 'Seamus Heaney: Ulster, Old English, and *Beowulf*', in Lucia Kornexl and Ursula Lenke (eds.), *Bookmarks from the Past: Studies in Early English Language and Literature in Honour of Helmut Gneuss*, Münster Universitätsschriften, Texte und Untersuchungen zur Englischen Philologie 30 (Frankfurt: Peter Lang, 2003), 81–114, and Hans Sauer, 'Heaneywulf, Liuzzawulf: Two Recent Translations of *Beowulf*', in Uwe Böker (ed.), in collaboration with Dieter A. Berger and Noel Harold Kaylor, Jr, *Of Remembraunce the Keye: Medieval Literature and its Impact through the Ages: Festschrift for Karl Heinze Göller on the Occasion of his 80th Birthday* (Frankfurt: Peter Lang, 2004), 331–47. See also the following reviews: E. G. Stanley, 'Seamus Heaney (trans.), *Beowulf*', *Notes & Queries* 245

(2000), 346–8; Graham Caie, 'Beowulf – Dinosaur, Monster or Visionary Poem?', *The European English Messenger* 10:2 (2001), 68–70.
26. For Alexander's translation, see Michael Alexander (trans.), *Beowulf: A Verse Translation*, revised edn (Harmondsworth: Penguin, 2001). For a more extensive critical account of Heaney's poem, see Helen Phillips, 'Seamus Heaney's *Beowulf*', in Tony Curtis (ed.), *The Art of Seamus Heaney* (Dublin: Wolfhound, 2001), 265–85.
27. Heaney, *Beowulf*, xxvi.
28. *Ibid.*
29. *Ibid.*: on Heaney's 'illumination by philology' in the wider context of Anglo-Saxon studies, see Seth Lerer, *Error and the Academic Self: The Scholarly Imagination, Medieval to Modern* (New York: Columbia University Press, 2002), 94–101.
30. Seamus Heaney, *The Sunday Times*, 26 July 1998, Section 8, *Books*, 6.
31. Heaney, *Beowulf*, xxvi.
32. *Ibid.*, xxv, and Heaney, *Field Work* (London: Faber, 1979), 17; Heaney, *Beowulf*, xxvi.
33. Heaney, *Beowulf*, xxii.

CHAPTER 9

Reading in the gutters

Eric Falci

Contemporary poetry in Irish and Scottish Gaelic emerges out of a tangle of material conditions. Closely related minority languages, Irish and Scottish Gaelic have continually outlived their supposed deaths, surviving traditionally in regions in northwest Scotland and the west and southwest of the island of Ireland. Severely weakened in the eighteenth and nineteenth centuries, both have undergone periods of revitalisation since the late nineteenth century, and though the number of native speakers of both languages continues to decline, the second half of the twentieth century featured renewed efforts to incorporate Gaelic more substantially into educational programmes and bolster institutional support for Gaelic cultural activities within and without the *Gaeltacht* and *Gàidhealtachd*. While neither has yet achieved Welsh's sustained renaissance, both are healthier than the many languages around the world in immediate danger of extinction. Additionally, Irish and Scottish cultural activities and products have thrived in the Anglo-American marketplace, and Ireland and Scotland are cultural and genealogical touchstones for large numbers of people globally. Gaelic has long been imagined to be the repository of origins in Irish cultural debates, and while the situation is surely different in Scotland, where English, Scots and Scottish Gaelic exist in a nuanced tension, both languages carry notions of authenticity even as their actual day-to-day use has declined over the past two centuries. The relevance and portability of Irishness and Scottishness in a postmodern and hyper-capitalist global fabric has both furthered and forestalled their obsolescence.

The status of contemporary literature in Irish and Scottish Gaelic, then, is somewhat contradictory. Implicit in this set of contradictions are crucial and constant acts of translation. This is perhaps most immediately visible in the dual-language street signs throughout most of Ireland and in the northwestern parts of Scotland (particularly in the Hebrides). The Gaelic place name sits (usually) above the English name, which both translates it and undercuts it. For tourists (mostly English-speaking and, in most cases, not

Gaelic-speaking), the Gaelic place name becomes a kind of present absence, visible and unavailable at the same time. The Gaelic place name – a locus of cultural and historical richness in both Ireland and Scotland – is not, however, an empty signifier. Nor is the English translation posited as a sufficient substitution. The English translation is not there simply to help out the tourists, nor is the Gaelic original there as a necessary signal to locals. They act as a kind of translating tandem, chiasmically feeding back into one another while modelling both an excess and absence of cultural signification. Without implying that this scenario obtains in all multilingual cultural spaces, or that it characterises the circumstances of all minority languages, I want to think through such interactions of Scottish Gaelic and English and Irish and English as they occur in contemporary poetry.

For a series of reasons, contemporary poetry in Irish and Scottish Gaelic offers the clearest articulation of the set of contradictions that I have been outlining, and that exist *in proto* in the dual-language street signs. Poetry has occupied a central place in both the Irish and Scottish Gaelic literary traditions, and Irish and Scottish poets have long been privileged (and intensely complicated) figures within both cultures. Contemporary poets writing in Irish or Scottish Gaelic work within a series of material paradoxes. Publishing poetry (itself a precarious economic activity) in a language spoken by a minority of speakers within an Anglophone culture is not necessarily feasible. Publishing in Irish or Scottish Gaelic has been restricted throughout the twentieth century, and has generally existed with governmental or institutional subsidies. Literary activity in Irish and Scottish Gaelic has historically developed as part of an oral culture that had neither the impetus nor the means to establish regular modes of publication. So, the publication of contemporary poetry in Irish and Scottish Gaelic is deeply fraught, and will always be relatively limited. However, the scope and form of most Irish and Scottish poetry has allowed a method of publication that has bolstered its marketability and prominence: the dual-language book. Although the dual-language book – usually with Irish or Scottish Gaelic poems on one side of the double page and English translations on the other – is far from ideal and inevitably distorting, it does seem to be the most viable mode of publication and distribution of this literature. Poetry's compression gives it a distinct advantage in such a dual-language format, and has – for good and bad – assured its hegemony over prose writing in modern Irish and Scottish Gaelic literature.

I do not mean to suggest that this scenario applies to dual-language books in general, nor am I making an argument about translation as such. There has been heavy interest in translation practices in the past quarter-century, much of it focused on the politics of translation. Such scholarship has drawn a distinction between translations that are adequate (to the source language) and those that are acceptable (to the target language), and has worked to articulate the ideological underpinnings of translation practices throughout literary history.[1] In order to counter what Lawrence Venuti has described as the 'translator's invisibility,' literary translators often attempt to mediate between acceptability and adequacy in order to produce a translation that does not reify the original and at the same time can operate within the target language and culture.[2] The ways of staging this gap – a gap inherent to the necessarily distorting mechanisms of translation – are widely variable, and depend greatly on the shape and size of a text. Because of their size, novels and prose texts generally have to embed their theoretical premises within the translation itself, often by undercutting its fluency or defamiliarising its own processes. For the great majority of prose literature, the foreign-ness of the original would have to be evoked within the translation in which that original disappears. Poetry translations also foreground their own status as translations in such ways, by 're-lining' the poem, turning it into a series of prose paragraphs, deliberately leaving seams sticking out, or highlighting distortions or impossible moves.

However, the dual-language book offers another method of staging this pocket of linguistic difference, one that simultaneously preserves and displaces the source text. There have been numerous polemics about the dangers of such a mode of publication, but much less work on its effects on practices of reading and writing.[3] It is clear that the processes of production, transmission and reception of Irish and Scottish Gaelic poetry in an Anglo-American literary system conducted almost entirely in English mutes the textures and densities of the original work so as to ready it for export. But it is also clear that Irish and Scottish Gaelic poets have to consider these various material scenarios that will condition the reception of their work, and readers of that work must consider the multiply-mediated forms in which they receive it. The dual-language text is surely problematic, but it prohibits the processes of translation from going invisible. Rather than driving them into the underground of the text, contemporary dual-language volumes accentuate them. Original text and translated text occupy (usually) the same surface, while the fairly common practice of noting the translator at the beginning or end of the translation underlines their involvement. The matter is one of excessive visibility.

This, then, is not an argument about authorship, or even translation, but rather one about reading. The dual-language text encodes a particular kind of double-reading that can't be suppressed or explained away. It ensures that both iterations of a poem are present to the reader, even if one is unavailable for reading. Considering the particular history of Irish and Scottish Gaelic, ignoring either side of the double page is insufficient. 'Forgetting' the side in Gaelic and treating the English version as though it *were* the poem utterly misrepresents the complex workings of the literary act and is an example of monolinguistic blindness. At the same time, pretending that the Gaelic poem is in every way and without a doubt the only actual text, the English translation simply an unfortunate capitulation to economic realities, wilfully suppresses the material and historical conditions from which the work emerges and into which it is pitched.

Rather, a mode of chiasmic reading is necessary to describe the various ways in which the two sides of the text impinge upon each other, unsettling our usual notions of originality, authority and translation. Reading across the gutters of the double pages, tracking the ways in which each side remakes the other and is remade within particular spaces of reception, allows for a mode of engagement with contemporary Irish and Scottish Gaelic poetry that accounts for the various and idiosyncratic manoeuvres that the format allows its readers. If this is a species of 'bad reading' that upsets the aesthetic integrity of discrete texts, then it is a critical badness, a wrong reading that unearths the syncopated motions that characterise the ways these complex poems are often read.

While a historical, comparative look at dual-language texts would be extremely useful, I am hesitant to gesture towards any sort of universal applicability of my sense of Irish and Scottish Gaelic poetry, both because of the huge variety of dual-language texts produced throughout literary history, and because even a thumbnail history of dual-language texts in the English language literary tradition is beyond this essay's scope. Dual-language editions of poetry in Irish are a product of the past 30 or so years, and the major Irish poet of the twentieth century, Seán Ó Ríordáin, published Irish-only volumes throughout his career. The central Scottish Gaelic poet of the century, Sorley MacLean, did include English-language translations for many of the poems in his 1943 volume, *Dàin do Eimhir agus Dàin Eile*, as well as those for his 1977 selected volume, *Reothairt is Contraigh*, but he had written these poems in Gaelic over a 40-year period, forcing the English translations into clear subsidiary positions, as 'after-effects'.[4] This accords with Walter Benjamin's influential and vexed description of translation as having to do with the 'afterlife' rather than the 'life' of the text. In 'The Task of the Translator', Benjamin writes that 'a translation comes later than the original, and since the important works of world literature never find their chosen translators at the time of their origin, their translation marks their stage of continued life'.⁵ The kind of transformation an original text undergoes in being translated, Benjamin suggests, has a particular temporality. Even if, as Benjamin concedes, 'all translation is only a somewhat provisional way of coming to terms with the foreignness of languages,' such foreignness is subtended by a certain historicity.⁶ And it is based upon an underlying temporal scheme in which translation succeeds original. Such a scheme is disturbed in some presentations of recent Irish and Scottish Gaelic poetry. Though original and translation are not simultaneous events, they do occupy a temporality, and spatiality, significantly more condensed than Benjamin's model.

As dual-language editions have gained traction, recent poets in Irish and Scottish Gaelic have had to take this format into more immediate account. Some, most famously the Irish poet Biddy Jenkinson, have refused to allow their poems to be published with English translations, while others, such as Louis de Paor, have attempted to limit how and in what markets such translations could appear. Many have published dual-language editions only after several volumes of Scottish Gaelic- or Irish-only volumes, taking either an active or passive role in the production of translations. Nuala Ní Dhomhnaill's international renown is not entirely unrelated to her five (so far) dual-language volumes, with their impressive roster of translators. While Ní Dhomhnaill is something of a singular figure, her dual-language volumes are indicative of the array of strategies and effects – both writerly and readerly – that surround the production and reception of these complicated volumes. Starting with the assumption that exposing and describing such strategies is itself a necessary form of critique, I propose to discuss several of the more interesting texts in recent Scottish Gaelic and Irish poetry, beginning with two Scottish Gaelic poets, Meg Bateman and Rody Gorman, whose texts upset the original/translation doublet in radically different ways. Then I will turn to two Irish poets, Gearóid Mac Lochlainn and Ní Dhomhnaill, whose poems – as they appear in dual-language format – model other kinds of interference. Throughout, I will pay particular attention to what kinds of readings such texts allow, encourage or disavow. Or, at least what kinds of readings are allowed to this particular reader – a mutt from upstate New York who teaches in California and whose peculiar transits across the double page are enabled by dictionaries, grammars, guesswork and, in the very near distance, translations. So if I am overly interested in the benefits of wrong readings, it is because I occupy the position of the wrong reader of such texts.

Meg Bateman, who lectures at Sabhal Mòr Ostaig on Skye, one of the centres of Scottish Gaelic literature and language, has published one volume of Gaelic poetry, *Òrain Ghaoil/Amhráin Ghrá* (1989), and two dual-language volumes, *Aotromachd agus Dàin Eile/Lightness* (1997) and *Soirbheas/Fair Wind* (2007). This last volume does not list or acknowledge any translators, so the assumption is that the translations are Bateman's. For the most part, the English translations aim for fidelity to the sense and form of the original. Poem length and stanza shape stay consistent from the Scottish Gaelic verso to the facing English recto, and in general her traditional thematic material is consistently rendered in the English translations. To put it more simply, the translations resemble, both visually and semantically, the original Scottish Gaelic poems. This is the case even when Bateman articulates a dissatisfaction with the ways that Gaelic culture is too easily absorbed into Anglo-American commodity culture, as in her poem 'Consairt' (translated as 'Gaelic Concert'). The final poem in the volume, titled 'Envoi' and closely related to both the final poem, 'Dimitto', in MacLean's *Dàin do Eimhir* and to Ní Dhomhnaill's signature poem 'Ceist na Teangan', first worries that one of her Gaelic poems appears 'naked and incongruous' in its English translation (*borb*, 'barbaric or uncivilised', in the original).[7] She then quickly activates the generic imperatives implicit in the poem's title: 'Bitheadh an tàcharan ag imeachd' ('But let the changeling make its way'; 174–5). This manoeuvre both authorises the translation and marks it off as separate from the original. Bateman allows for readerly agency even as she keeps one 'particular revelation' ('an taisbeanadh cinnteach àraid') within the purview of the author: 'nach ionann firinn na beath is firinn na bàrdachd' ('reality and poetic truth are not the same'; or more directly, 'the truth of life and the truth of poetry are not the same'; 174–5).[8] The import of the final lines is undercut by the translation's fidelity to the original, and Bateman's poems often trouble their own processes in such understated ways. Key fissures between the two sides of the facing page occur through the volume.

One such fissure occurs in her poem 'Cànain', which she translates straightforwardly as 'Language'. The poem articulates the same emotional arc as 'Envoi', with a first stanza worrying about the disappearance of Gaelic mouths (*beòil*), which are compared to flowers withering at the end of Summer. The second stanza finds immediate recompense in the other mouths that will come with 'lips of the same crimson' ('bilean den aon chorcarachd'), and that will be nourished by the same 'goodness in the soil' ('maitheas san talamh'; 22–3). Both Scottish Gaelic original and English translation end with a seemingly rhetorical question that the English translation renders: 'and as there is goodness in the soil, / why doubt their sweetness?' (22–3). However, this translation is on somewhat shaky ground, and it forces a rereading of the relationship between both sides of the page. The final phrase of the Scottish Gaelic poem, 'boltrach staoin', which maps onto the final word of the translation ('sweetness'), means something more like 'bitter scent'. 'Boltrach' can cover a fairly wide semantic spectrum, from the relatively positive 'perfume' through the relatively neutral 'scent' or 'odour' to the relatively negative 'stink'. *Staoin* generally refers to tin or pewter, and seems to designate a bitterness rather than a sweetness (*caorainn staoine* are juniper berries). It can also refer to laziness, silliness or worthlessness, which again grates against the 'sweetness' of the translation. So the sweetness of English translation is something more like a tin-stink. This corresponds to a similar fissure at the end of the first stanza in which the line 'is a shearg iad dhan ùir' is translated as 'and they crumpled into dust'. The verb *searg* does have the force of 'decay', 'fade' or 'wither', which gesturally accords with 'crumpled'. But the final phrase 'dhan ùir,' can also mean something more like 'into the earth' or 'into the soil', and *ùir* can refer fairly widely to mould, dust or soil. The regenerations outlined in the second stanza are telegraphed by the original Gaelic, but foreclosed by the wording of the translation. Crumpling into the earth implies possible rebirth or regrowth, but crumpling 'into dust' rings with an ominous finality. A loss of the generative ambiguity touched off by the word *ùir* occurs in the transfer across the pages. It is not simply that the translation positively spins the original, or that the optimism of the original is muted in the translation. Rather, at two different – and crucial – moments in the poem, the tonal relationship between original and translation is inverted. Here is an instance of chiasmic reading (and translating). At the end of the first stanza, a potentially healthy Gaelic soil or earth or mould (*ùir*) is transposed into an arid English 'dust'; and in the second stanza the quasi-bitterness of the final phrase 'boltrach staoin' is rescored into the more straightforward 'sweetness'. Processes of semantic decay and growth occur over the gutters of the double page, but they do not move in the same direction. The original and translation exist in a feedback loop (soil: dust: bitter: sweet) that destabilises the integrity of both, and sutures them over the aporia of the volume's gutters.

Bateman's subterranean incursions find their inverse in Rody Gorman's work. The improbabilities of translation are extravagantly foregrounded in Gorman's dual-language volumes, and Gorman, who writes in English, Scottish Gaelic and Irish, has made the traductions and transgressions that occur over the binding a constitutive aspect of his style. His 2000 dual-language volume *Air a' Charbad fo Thalamh/On the Underground* is a sprawling collection that includes translations of Gorman's poems into

English (and sometimes Scots) by ten different translators, Gorman's English translations of several Gaelic poems, his English and Gaelic translations of Korean and Japanese Zen poems, several poems in English and a few Gaelic concrete poems. Gorman's short lyrics clutter the pages and make for a reading experience quite different from reading Bateman's. He often approaches the vicissitudes of translation conceptually, exploding the possibility of translation rather than unrigging it from within. The poem 'Leadan' consists almost entirely of a catalogue of place names divided into seven-line stanzas, each of which features a different kind of landmark (*bealach, beinn, cnoc, coire, loch, sgùrr*). A parodic comment on the *dinnseanchas* tradition, the poem (whose title translates as 'litany') is left largely untranslated, so the litany of place names in Gaelic is countered by a blank page where a translation would have appeared. The short colophon that ends the poem is a prayer that is translated into English but placed into parentheses. This quasi-concrete poem both privileges the Scottish Gaelic place names by resisting the impulse to anglicise them, and also registers the historical processes of anglicisation (in Ireland and Scotland) by correlating the Gaelic place names with blank space on the facing page. Such witty formalisations of the limits of translation appear in numerous guises, and Gorman, more than any other poet in Irish or Scottish Gaelic, blatantly experiments with the interactions of the facing pages of dual-language books. In addition to such formalisations, the 'foreignness' of Gaelic (and Irish, and Scots, and English) is consistently thematised, most forcefully in the book's final poem, 'Bás' ('Language Death'), where the final lines of the putative Gaelic side of the double page are largely in English:

> Aidh. Shin agad e.
> That's it –
> End of story.
> Gaylick's fucked, so it is. Fucked forever.⁹

The ostensible English side, in turn, includes a good bit of Gaelic:

> Aye. Shin agad e.
> That's it –
> cnag na cùise.
> The Gaylick's fucked, tha –
> fucked gu sìorraidh.   (169)

While such displays of macaronic writing appear occasionally throughout, it is significant that the most flagrant and extended example occurs in a concluding poem that figures the death of the language as a domineering sexual violation. The interplay of the two sides of the page suggests a different sort of encounter, though, and by poem's end each side is 'fucking' the other.

Such frontal modes of interference are characteristic of the volume, and they are analogous to those of Belfast poet Gearóid Mac Lochlainn in his first dual-language volume, *Sruth Teangacha/Stream of Tongues* (2002). In the Author's Notes to the volume, Mac Lochlainn concedes that while 'English translations are a reality,' 'each Irish language writer must approach them cautiously for they often gain an autonomy of their own and eclipse the Irish'.[10] Mac Lochlainn's approach is to treat the English translation as a version of, or improvisation on, the poem in Irish, 'inspired by the originals but not independent of them' (190). This often results in macaronic texts that slip the tracks between original and translation. By foregrounding and playing on such slips, Mac Lochlainn more vigorously cultivates the peculiar dynamics of the dual-language text – actively deconstructing the directionality of the double page. Often, the slips between the left and right side of the page are fleeting and playful (in one poem a pair of Nikes in the Irish text becomes a pair of Reeboks in the English). Occasional phrases in Irish remain untranslated in the English versions, allusions crop up in the English version which have no counterpart in the Irish version, many of the Irish poems are studded with English words and phrases, and often there are such minor, seemingly irrelevant changes from the Irish to the English version that one wonders if they are intentional or accidental (in one poem a British soldier's words are changed from 'OK, sur, could you move over to the wall' to 'OK, sur, can you move over to the wall'; 40–1). So, even when they are slight or seemingly superficial, transactions between the gutters of the page become transmutations across it. This results in texts at once more immediately bracing and more deeply vexing. His attempts to resist or upend the processes of translation sometimes thematise such resistance rather than enact it critically. Mac Lochlainn's poems forcefully read against the grain of Irish- and English-language literary culture, but rarely do they read against the grain of their own forms.

To give a quick sense of this, I want to turn to his poem 'Teanga Eile' which he, working with Séamus Mac Annaidh, translates as 'Second Tongue'. This improvisational catalogue suggests one of the predominant styles of the book, and Mac Lochlainn's poetry is indebted to performance poetry, jazz, 'dub' poetry (especially Linton Kwesi Johnson), and – of course – Irish storytelling and 'craic'. Mac Lochlainn immediately muddies the waters of linguistic priority by calling his poem 'Teanga Eile' (does the 'eile' point to the poem on the other side of the page, therefore making English the second language? or the other way round?). In the translation, 'other' mutates to 'second' and the text operates via this trigger of distortion. 'Teanga Eile' – constructed, like Amairgin's originary poem in *Lebor Gabála Érenn*, as a metamorphic self-definition – puts this mode of translation-transmutation on display. However, such a free-wheeling strategy has side-effects, and in this case the poem becomes symptomatic of the linguistic 'otherness' it explores.

The translation is often quite straight, and the simple syntactic mechanism allows for local variations that do not derail the movement and tenor of the whole. But odd mutations do occur, and they occur at odd moments. In this poem about the 'subsidiary' status of the second language – presumably Irish – which has been pushed to the margins of society, first the *teanga* is kidnapped, then tortured, then buried. It then returns to haunt the metropolitan centres from which it has been banished. In the fourth stanza, it becomes a shadowy aggressor – avoided on roads, in pubs, waiting on dark corners, stalking like a rejected lover. And in the last stanza, it is silenced, and yet still a source of power – a charm in the 'odd poet's back pocket' who lives on charity (56–7). The poem's motor is metamorphosis. But perhaps the oddest mutations that occur are not from line to line in the original, but the several that occur across the spine. Essentially, culturally specific references in the Irish are translated into references that centre on African, Caribbean and African-American cultural experience. 'Ceolta sí, Micí Mí-ádh' in the Irish becomes 'Johnny Dark, Creole' in the English. 'Croi dubh' becomes 'hoodoo'. In the final stanza, the charm (*ortha*) becomes 'mumbo-jumbo, juju, / a mojo of words' (56–7). A Gaelic formation of 'otherness' – the *sí* – is translated into another set of cultural terms. The introduction of racial difference into the process of linguistic silencing brings up a cache of troubling issues. Mutations made, perhaps, for sonic reasons spark semantic shifts that enforce simplistic cultural parallels. So, while Mac Lochlainn's translation plays more insistently over the gutter of the page, in doing so it sets a further range of issues ramifying. An Irish poem critical of linguistic appropriation, one that seemingly approves of 'minorness' and the appealing exoticism of socio-cultural margins, itself troublingly appropriates non-Irish cultural material as it transfers its metaphorical content across the double page. 'Teanga Eile,' like most of the poems in *Sruth Teangacha*, forcefully stages a mode of textual co-dependence, but the two sides of the page just as forcefully repel each other's projects, leaving poems overly knowing about, and oddly blind to, their implications.

Mac Lochlainn was enthusiastically endorsed by Nuala Ní Dhomhnaill, who titled her introduction to his volume 'An Stuif Ceart' ('The Right

Stuff,' or, as the introduction's translation has it, 'The Real McCoy'), and it is with her body of work that I'd like to conclude. Ní Dhomhnaill's poetry is both the archetype for the mode of double-reading that I am arguing for and its most complicated case. Her poetry emerges from the heart of Gaelic culture and is steeped in Irish folklore, myth and traditional stories (*béaloideas*). She learned Irish upon moving to Ventry in west Kerry as a child and was a key figure in the Irish poetry renaissance centred at University College Cork in the early 1970s. She has spoken forcefully about the continuing importance of writing literature in Irish and about the devastating effects of linguistic colonisation.[11] She is doubtless the most celebrated Irish-language writer in the world; even more interestingly, however, she has become one of the best-known Irish poets (in English or Irish) on an international scene that does not exactly suffer from a shortage of famous Irish poets. Again, this recognition is partly connected to her five dual-language volumes that have appeared since the late 1980s.[12] Unlike Bateman, Gorman and Mac Lochlainn, Ní Dhomhnaill takes no part in translating her work, and has relied on a cache of translators that includes nearly every well-known poet in Ireland. Michael Hartnett translated the bulk of the poems in her first dual-language volume, *Selected Poems: Rogha Dánta*; thirteen poets wrote translations for her 1990 volume, *Pharaoh's Daughter*; Medbh McGuckian and Eiléan Ní Chuilleanáin split translating duties in *The Water Horse* (2000); and Paul Muldoon, who has become Ní Dhomhnaill's main translator, wrote the English versions for two volumes, *The Astrakhan Cloak* (1992) and *The Fifty Minute Mermaid* (2007). Ní Dhomhnaill has repeatedly claimed that she is 'not a poet in English,' but there exists a sizeable body of English-language poetry that – however uneasily – belongs to her.[13] And many of her readers will find her in dual-language editions that are widely available on both sides of the Atlantic. As I have been arguing throughout, one must take into account the transactive dynamic necessarily central to the reception of her work.

In Ní Dhomhnaill's case, this dynamic is complicated by her distance from the process of translation and by the distinction of many of her translators. Though Paul Muldoon is by now her translator of choice – and, in the estimation of many, her most successful – I will turn to a non-Muldoon translation, though one that clearly evokes what Michael Cronin has identified as a problem of 'fluency' in the translations.[14] In *Translating Ireland*, Cronin notes that each of Ní Dhomhnaill's translators 'has his/her unmistakable form of fluency, so that it is the original poet rather than the translator who becomes invisible'.[15] Here Cronin highlights a distinctive facet of Ní Dhomhnaill's dual-language books. Many of the translations in these volumes are relatively faithful to the sense and form of their originals, but one cannot help reading through the prism of the translator's own style. We expect (and often get) a wry and witty playfulness in Muldoon's translations, and much of the success of his versions of Ní Dhomhnaill's poems is due to the subtle theorisations embedded in his dexterous versions. On the other hand, we might expect (and often get) an extreme and subjective looseness in Medbh McGuckian's translations, so that while Muldoon's translations feel like magic tricks, McGuckian's feel like transmogrifications. Readerly expectations, then, come into play when negotiating Ní Dhomhnaill's double pages in a way that we have not seen thus far.

Ní Dhomhnaill's 'Mo Mhíle Stór' is included in *Pharaoh's Daughter*, and is translated by an Irish poet whose name on the page would certainly set off stylistic expectations. Unlike most of the other translators in the volume, Seamus Heaney leaves the title's idiomatic phrase ('My dearest love') untranslated in his version. For the most part he hews closely to the sense of the original, in which a lover sets out over four stanzas four different instants in a romance: first the beginning of love, then the beloved's departure by sea and the lover's loneliness, then the beloved's passionate return to the bed of the lover, and then a brief concluding turn that returns to the youthful appearance of the beloved that still lives in the lover's memory. Even though the beloved returns with hair that has 'gone grey and straight' ('fachta liath is díreach'), in the memory of the lover blond curls continue to grow.[16] Ní Dhomhnaill's poem is inscribed within a traditional lyric topos that Heaney's version transmits in a straightforward manner.

Except in the final lines. It is here that we are forced to pay specific attention to the translation's transformation of the original. The final stanza of the original is entirely given over to describing the beloved's hair as it exists in the memory of the beloved:

> Fós i mo chuimhní
> tánn tú bacahallach,
> tá dhá chocán déag i do chúl buí
> cas.   (48)

Michael Hartnett provides a faithful rendering in his earlier translation of the poem:

> But still in my memory
> you are ringleted:
> you have twelve knots

> in your curly yellow
> locks.[17]

This version gives the basic sense while maintaining the shape of the final lines. Heaney combines the third and fourth stanzas of the original into one stanza, and gives this as his version of the final lines:

> but in my memory the curls grew on,
> twelve coils in the ripening
> crop on your head.   (49)

By stitching an agricultural metaphor into the description of the beloved's hair – 'the ripening / crop on your head' – Heaney inserts his own 'bog poems' as an intertext. The 'ripening / crop,' with its harsh enjambment and equation of the beloved with the earth, is a variation on the 'shaved head / like a stubble of black corn' of the bog body in 'Punishment',[18] the 'wet nest of ... hair' in 'The Bog Queen' (188) and the 'wet fern of ... hair' in 'Strange Fruit' (194). Heaney has signed the translation by including one of his best-known, and oft-critiqued, metaphorical patterns. By allusively emphasising the beloved's gender and by comparing the beloved's body to the earth and its seasons, Heaney stiffens the malleable and oblique gender identifications of Ní Dhomhnaill's original poem, and in the process short-circuits the poem's feminist critique – one of Ní Dhomhnaill's most important projects. The point is not that Heaney 'mistranslates' the poem, but that his self-allusion triggers an additional transactive register that should be marked.

Though my readings here have entered at different critical angles depending on where the patches of interference occur, I have repeatedly emphasised the need to account for both sides of the page when reading such dual-language texts and to consider these two sides as continually incurring on the other. Every translation is haunted by its original, but for a large body of contemporary Scottish Gaelic and Irish poetry this haunting takes place continually and at close range. In 'The Task of the Translator,' Benjamin suggests that 'a real translation is transparent; it does not cover the original, does not block its light, but allows the pure language, as though reinforced by its own medium, to shine upon the original all the more fully'.[19] This becomes impossible when both texts are present to the reader. The English translation is not a transparency, but rather intensifies the original's opacity, and cannot help but disrupt it. At the same time, the physical presence of the Scottish Gaelic or Irish on the page prohibits erasure. We must notice how the facing pages ghost, rewrite and revivify each other, setting the other vibrating strangely – even if that means that the reading experience is never quite settled, and left abandoned along the book's heavily travelled gutters.

NOTES

1. Key studies on translation in the Irish context include Maria Tymoczko's *Translation in a Postcolonial Context: Irish Literature in English Translation* (Manchester: St Jerome Publishing, 1999) and Michael Cronin's *Translating Ireland: Translation, Languages, Cultures* (Cork University Press, 1996).
2. See especially Venuti's *The Translator's Invisibility: A History of Translation*, 2nd edn (New York: Routledge, 2008).
3. One characteristic debate about translations of Scottish Gaelic poetry occurred between Wilson McLeod, Aonghas MacNeacail and Peter France in a 1998 issue of the Scottish literary magazine *Chapman* (Vol. 89–90). Ronald Black summarises the exchange in the introduction to his landmark anthology, *An Tuil: Anthology of 20th Century Scottish Gaelic Verse* (Edinburgh: Polygon, 1999), lxiv–lxvi.
4. On the complex publishing history of MacLean's *Dàin do Eimhir agus Dàin Eile* (Glasgow: William MacLellan, 1943), see Christopher Whyte's introduction to his crucial edition of the sequence, *Dàin do Eimhir (Poems to Eimhir)* (Edinburgh: Polygon, 2008), 1–41.
5. Walter Benjamin, 'The Task of the Translator', in *Illuminations*, trans. Harry Zohn and ed. Hannah Arendt (New York: Schocken, 1969), 69–82, 71.
6. *Ibid.*, 75.
7. Meg Bateman, *Soirbheas/Fair Wind* (Edinburgh: Polygon, 1997), 174–5.
8. My thanks to Peter Mackay for pointing out the more literal translation of this phrase.
9. Rody Gorman, *Air a' Charbad fo Thalamh/On the Underground* (Edinburgh: Polygon, 2000), 168.
10. Gearóid Mac Lochlainn, *Sruth Teangacha/Stream of Tongues* (Conamara: Cló Iar-Chonnachta, 2002), 190.
11. See, for instance, Nuala Ní Dhomhnaill, 'Why I Choose to Write in Irish, the Corpse that Sits Up and Talks Back', originally published in *The New York Times Book Review* in 1995, and included in her volume of *Selected Essays* (Dublin: New Island, 2005).
12. Her work is most readily available in five dual-language volumes, but her poetry appeared first in Irish-only editions: *An Dealg Droighin* (1981), *Féar Suaithinseach* (1984), *Feis* (1991) and *Cead Aighnis* (1998). While it seems that the publication of the Irish poems separately prior to the dual-language texts would mute the force of my argument about their transactive quality, this is only the case in a reading that disregards the texts' histories and circulatory networks.
13. Nuala Ní Dhomhnaill, *Selected Essays*, ed. Oona Frawley (Dublin: New Island, 2005), 200.

14. This move is entirely tactical. The Ní Dhomhnaill/Muldoon collaborations are the subject of an essay forthcoming in *The Oxford Handbook of Modern Irish Poetry*.
15. Cronin, *Translating Ireland*, 177.
16. Nuala Ní Dhomhnaill, *Pharaoh's Daughter* (Winston-Salem, NC: Wake Forest University Press, 1993 [1990]), 48–9.
17. Nuala Ní Dhomhnaill, *Selected Poems: Rogha Dánta*, trans. Michael Hartnett (Dublin: New Island/Raven Arts, 1986/1993), 99.
18. Seamus Heaney, *Poems, 1965–1975* (New York: Noonday, 1988), 192.
19. Benjamin, 'The Task of the Translator', 79.

CHAPTER 10

'What matters is the yeast': 'foreignising' Gaelic poetry

Christopher Whyte

Writing several years ago about the Scots-language poet Sydney Goodsir Smith, I suggested that the dynamic between what we perceive as foreign and what we perceive as native may be inherently unstable. The elements on either side of the equation – an equation whose equals sign ought, we fondly hope, to have the firmest of strokes through it – tend to replace one another with maddening frequency. Indeed, they may turn into one another unpredictably and without warning.

This instability is related to two fundamental paradoxes underlying the activity of cultural nationalists, so fundamental in Ireland in the years preceding and following the 1916 Rising and, in Scotland, in the wake of the 1978 referendum and still today. If we are to evaluate, or even simply to offer a faithful account of, this activity, then we would do well to keep these paradoxes in mind. With their assistance we may avoid reproducing certain pitfalls, or stumbling into certain dead ends which characterised both enterprises.

On the one hand, cultural nationalism was itself a foreign import. MacDiarmid, for example, contemplating the potential scope and meaning of a Scottish Renaissance movement in the early 1920s, refers again and again to what is taking place abroad, in Belgium or Norway, as well as in Ireland. 'Look what is happening out there!' he effectively says. 'Should not we be doing the same here? Why are no similar changes occurring in Scotland?' To this extent cultural nationalism may accurately be described as the importation of a model that is foreign in the strictest sense, while not necessarily being alien. If I am tempted to speak of the Scottish Renaissance movement as a 'foreignisation' of Scottish culture, a movement of dissimilation from the status quo and assimilation to what is happening abroad, beyond the boundaries of the British Empire, I do so in order to highlight the paradoxical nature of the enterprise, and of any attempt to bring a culture characterised as 'national' back to its 'genuine' values by reinstating these.

On the other hand, as the Italian poet and film-maker Pier Paolo Pasolini, one of whose first major publishing enterprises was an anthology of poetry in the various dialects of the Italian peninsula, was fond of pointing out, peasant culture is by its very nature international, rather than national. It does not respect state boundaries. In other words, those elements to which cultural nationalists in Europe have consistently had recourse, when seeking to revive a national culture they perceived as degenerate, alienated or colonised, can prove the least amenable to analysis in national terms. It is a characteristic of middle-class agency, during periods of national revival, to delegate the task of representing the nation, of embodying its values, to the rural peasantry (or, as in Lowland Scotland over the past four decades, to the urban working class). A reading of the dynamics of English- or Scots-language use within cultural activism in Scotland over the past century which kept this dynamic, and the inherent paradox, in mind, could arrive at fascinating conclusions which are, however, beyond the scope of the present chapter.

In his study 'Race Purity in Music', first published in English in 1942, the Hungarian composer and ethnomusicologist Béla Bartók had this to say:

> From the very beginning I have been amazed by the extraordinary wealth of melody types existing in the territory under investigation in Eastern Europe. As I pursued my research, this amazement increased. In view of the comparatively small size of the countries – numbering forty to fifty million people – the variety in folk music is really marvellous! . . . Comparison of the folk music of these peoples made it clear that there was a continuous give and take, a constant crossing and recrossing which had persisted through centuries.[1]

This process of crossing and recrossing was, however, subject to certain restraints, which Bartók identifies, at least in part, with the intrinsic characteristics of the languages prevalent in his chosen area. As most melodies are sung, they require adaptation to the new text with which they are associated:

> When a folk melody passes the language frontier of a people, sooner or later it will be subjected to certain changes determined by environment, and especially by the differences of language. The greater the dissimilarity between the accents, inflections, metrical conditions, syllabic structure and so on, of two languages, the greater the changes that fortunately may occur in the 'emigrated' melody.[2]

Bartók views these changes as fortunate, and a cause for celebration, because of their inherently creative nature. What we might call 'the trade in melodies' is productive of difference, and generates the new: 'I say "fortunately" because this phenomenon itself engenders a further increase in the number of types and sub-types.'³ There is no danger of the overall effect resembling that of a mechanical food mixer which, as more and more ingredients are added, will progressively reduce them to a uniform sludge as colours and textures grow indistinguishable from one another:

> Contact with foreign material not only results in an exchange of melodies, but – and this is still more important – it gives an impulse to the development of new styles ... The trend towards transformation of foreign melodies prevents the internationalization of the music of these peoples. The material of each, however heterogeneous in origin, receives its marked individuality.⁴

The Hungarian artist sums up the situation of folk music in Eastern Europe in the following manner: 'as a result of uninterrupted reciprocal influence upon the folk music of these people there are an immense variety and a wealth of melodic types. The "racial impurity" finally attained is definitely beneficial.'⁵ It seems to me that Bartók, at a stage early enough to prevent his arguments being brought under the loose and often condemnatory umbrella of postmodernism, is offering a precise account, in musical terms, of the process which I provocatively term 'foreignisation'. Writing of 'racial "impurity"' in 1941, Bartók had precise polemical targets in mind. His words can help us grasp and accept the paradox that, however deep we delve into the 'native', oftener than not we will unearth the 'foreign', and vice versa.

The image of yeast in the title of this chapter originates with another cultural commentator, also from the interwar period. In a journal entry dated 25 January 1931, the French writer André Gide gives us his reactions to reading *Gott in Frankreich* by Friedrich Sieburg, which had appeared in French translation under the title *Dieu est-il français?* the year before. The book itself, and Gide's commentaries, require to be placed within the context of an ongoing dispute about the contrasting, even oppositional, values embodied by French and German cultures, whose dramatic tones were derived from memories of military confrontation during the Franco-Prussian war of 1870–1 and the First World War. Gide comments:

> Our country has many surprises in store for Sieburg (and for herself); she is rich in unsuspected resources. However inert its dough may often seem, it takes very little yeast to make it rise.
>
> Three images are too many for the same thought, alas; but let us pursue the last one. The dough does not like the yeast. The yeast for her is the *foreign*. That yeast was often necessary (in literature of course) to bring out wonderful manifestations; Italian yeast for Ronsard, Spanish for Corneille, English for romanticism, German also; the works called forth in this way are no less French, and the blame heaped on

me today for listening to the voice of the Russians is ill-founded. Despite the reproach, so often justified, of not taking the foreign into account, no literature perhaps more than the French has managed to be impregnated by it while still maintaining its own stamp and its peculiarities.[6]

More than 30 years ago, in Rome, I conversed with a lone Englishman, encountered in the library of the British Council in the Palazzo del Drago, now sadly dispersed. He was busy retranslating Homer. Shakespeare, he told me, would have been inconceivable without the Italian Renaissance. And indeed, at the crudest level, were we to remove all the Italian names and settings from Shakespeare's plays, their character would be altered irredeemably. Should this be looked on as the operation of Gide's 'yeast'?

Alongside the notion of 'foreignisation', in what follows, I would like to set the contrasting, but not complementary notion of 'nativisation'. 'Nativisation' denotes both the aspiration to purify texts and other cultural products of regrettable foreign, imported elements and the wish to render Scottish texts in course of being produced 'more Scottish', or to 're-Gaelicise' Gaelic verse. While I would hesitate to speak, in too simple a fashion, of 'foreignisation' as positive and desirable, while 'nativisation' would be negative, undesirable and backward-looking, it does seem to me that 'foreignisation' can help us describe what actually takes place, whereas attempts at 'nativisation' are all too often doomed to failure from the start. If 'nativisation' is a feature of designs 'on' texts, then 'foreignisation' can help us render visible designs 'in' texts, which are intrinsic to them.

'Nativisation' is typical of cultures that perceive themselves as under threat, in danger of dilution or absorption. Such idealised recourse to the 'genuine', the 'native', is a curse inflicted on cultures in a subaltern position. The degree to which the curse is inflicted from within, rather than from outside, would require extensive discussion which there is no room for here. Being identified with the 'natural', the 'unadulterated' or the 'unreflective' typifies the 'marked', secondary position within binaries such as 'male/female', 'civilised/uncivilised', 'literate/illiterate' or 'colonising/colonised'. A phenomenon that runs parallel to the infliction of this potential curse is what I will call 'reification'. Writing in Scotland is expected to be about Scotland, as writing in the Gaelic language should be restricted to Gaelic subjects, to the social and historical experience of individuals who spoke that language. Where such expectations would leave a text like Dante's *Divine Comedy* is a question that need not occupy us now! If Scottish writing had for many years, and in many respects still has, a 'marked', 'abnormal' or subaltern status within the larger framework of British writing, that is equally the case when writing in Gaelic is viewed as a component of Scottish writing. Where the condition of subalternity is internalised, recourse to the foreign, the injection of 'yeast', 'foreignising', is viewed as a betrayal. This makes the study of its operation within such contexts all the more fruitful and satisfying if part of one's intent is to reject subaltern status.

Time for an example. This is how Irish language poet Nuala Ní Dhomhnaill opens her bilingual *Selected Poems*:

> Támaid damanta, a dheirféaracha,
> sinne a chuaigh ag snámh
> ar thránna istoíche is na réalta
> ag gáiri in aonacht linn,
> an mhéarnáil inár dtimpeall
> is sinn ag scréachaíl le haoibhneas
> is le fionnuaire na taoide,
> gan gúnaí orainn ná léinte
> ach sinn chomh naíonta le leanaí bliana,
> táimid damanta, a dheirféaracha.[7]

As this was her first book not addressed to a specifically Irish-language audience, but to the larger world out there which uses English, it may not be mistaken to attribute a certain programmatic force to the choice of opening poem. The facing translation of this stanza was done by Michael Hartnett:

> We are damned, my sisters,
> we who swam at night
> on beaches, with the stars
> laughing with us
> phosphorescence about us
> we shrieking with delight
> with the coldness of the tide
> without shifts or dresses
> as innocent as infants.
>   We are damned, my sisters.

With its exultant celebration of feminine transgression, despite the probability of ultimate punishment and retribution, this poem could be read as a feminist tract of the milder kind. But certain readers will have recalled another poem, which had appeared in print some 17 years earlier:

> We shall not escape Hell, my passionate
> sisters, we shall drink black resins –

'Foreignising' Gaelic poetry

> we who sang our praises to the Lord
> with every one of our sinews, even the finest,
>
> we did not lean over cradles or
> spinning wheels at night, and now we are
> carried off by an unsteady boat
> under the skirts of a sleeveless cloak.

The underlying resemblance between the two poems, Ní Dhomhnaill's and what we may call her model, becomes more striking as each continues. Here are the third and fourth stanzas from her model, offered in my own literal translation from the original, which is in Russian:

> Arrayed in flimsy Chinese silks
> from the start of the day,
> we took the lead in songs of paradise
> around the robbers' bonfire.
>
> Careless seamstresses
> – whatever we did, the stitch went wrong! –
> dancers and players on the flute,
> mistresses of the whole world!

The latter part of Ní Dhomhnaill's second stanza, and the opening of her third, read as follows:

> Chaitheamair oícheanta ar bhántaibh Párthais
> ag ithe úll is spíonán is róiseanna[8]
> laistiar dár gcluasa, ag rá amhrán
> timpeall tinte cnámh na ngadaithe,
> ag ól is ag rangás le mairnéalaigh agus robálaithe
> is táimid damanta, a dheirféaracha.
>
> Níor chuireamair cliath ar stoca
> níor chíoramair, níor shlámamair,
> níor thuigeamair de bhanlámhaibh
> ach an ceann atá ins na Flaithis in airde.

Michael Hartnett renders the passage into English as follows:

> We spent nights in Eden's[9] fields
> eating apples, gooseberries; roses
> behind our ears, singing songs
> around the gipsy bonfires
> drinking and romping with sailors and robbers:
> and so we're damned, my sisters.
>
> We didn't darn stockings
> we didn't comb or tease

> we knew nothing of handmaidens
> except the one in high Heaven.

Ní Dhomhnaill has recast in her own language a poem dated November 1915 by the Russian poet Marina Tsvetaeva (1892–1941), which was available to her in an English translation by Elaine Feinstein, one of a range of versions done on the basis of literals supplied to Feinstein and first published in 1971.[10] What are we dealing with here? An Irish poem? A Russian one? An Irish poem that has become a Russian one, now its origin has been revealed? Or a poem that oscillates unsteadily between the two denominations, the foreign and the native? Will the poem be native for readers who know nothing of its model, and foreign for those who do?

It is worth observing that Ní Dhomhnaill's practice here does not come under the heading of 'aftering', according to which a poet, coming upon a translation of a poem from a language he has no knowledge of, offers us his own take on it, then published as 'after Rilke' or 'after Cavafy'. The products of aftering are validated, as is no doubt the poet's intention, by citing the name attached to the illustrious original, while at the same time withholding that of the translator who made the aftering possible. Ní Dhomhnaill does not feel the need to draw on Tsvetaeva for justification or support, and in this she must command our respect. Moreover, aftering in the strictest sense would have required her to produce another poem in English, a reworking of Feinstein's translation in the same language, whereas Ní Dhomhnaill has transferred the available content, at least in part, across a further language boundary, the one separating English from Irish.

Now for two instances of 'nativisation'. A poem in five sections entitled 'Tè gheal mo rùin' appeared in the 2007 volume of the annual anthology *New Writing Scotland*, published in Glasgow by the Association for Scottish Literary Studies.[11] The title, very reminiscent of the vocabulary of traditional Gaelic song, is translated by the author, Maoilios Caimbeul, as 'My pure love', but in fact this is an elegy on the poet's mother rather than an address to a potential, or lost, love. The third section runs as follows:

> 'S ann an seo far am biodh tu a' ruith 's a' leum
> 's tu nad nighinn bhig
> tha cuimhne mar sgàile fo uachdar na tìre.
> Seo far an robh a' bhàthach
> 's far am biodh sibh a' bleoghan na bà
> 's far an robh an sabhal 's stàball
> 's far an robh an seada an tacsa an taighe
> leis na lìn is uidheam iasgaich
> 's far am biodh an t-iasg a' tiormachadh ris a' bhalla.

The author's English version here reads:

> And here where you would run and jump
> when a little girl
> memory is a shadow under the land.
> Here is where the byre was
> and where you would milk the cows
> and where the barn and stable were
> and the stance of the lean-to shed
> with the nets and fishing equipment
> and where the fish would dry against the wall.

Though Campbell uses it in the English title of his poem, the word 'pure' does not appear in the Gaelic, where we find 'geal', meaning 'white' or 'fair'. But the poem as a whole is a retreat, or a glance backwards, into a 'pure' Gaelic world, as evidenced in the scenery of the third section, a world the poem embodies through its imagery and its diction. (An Anglicism such as 'seada' for 'shed' could be typical for native speaker usage, and there is no indication of its use being ironical or intentionally dissonant here). In the fifth section, Campbell's mother is represented metonymically by the knitted stockings which remained after her death, 'an tiùrr / stocainnean air an sgeilp' ('the heap / of stockings on the shelf'). His mother epitomised not only a life form which has vanished, but the selfless activity of the Christianity which was that life form's inspiration, 'am Bìoball agus Crìosda / mar stocainn air do chridhe' ('the Bible and Christ / a stocking on your heart').

A poem by Meg Bateman entitled 'A' Chrannghail' appeared in the Summer 2007 issue of the now sadly defunct Gaelic quarterly *Gath*.[12] It was written as part of an AHRC-funded project researching visual culture in the islands, and is a homage to a sculpture by Will MacLean, a photograph of which is featured on the page immediately following the poem. The sculpture is effectively the skeleton of a galley, set on an elliptical, shining base in view of the sea, so the homage is offered to a ship that was never completed and never sailed, to the idea or the relict of a ship. Bateman emphasises this fact in the opening stanza of her poem. She has gained a deserved reputation as a translator into English of Gaelic poetry from the medieval and early modern period. Echoes from that time are evident in this poem, particularly in stanzas 6 and 7:

> 'S i long Dhòmhnaill Ghuirm is crith air sgòdaibh,
> cop mu sròin a' leum ri daraich,

> stiùirbheirt sheòlta theann ga seòladh
> gu talla nam pìos far an òlar fion le faram.
>
> Cò i an long ud ach long mo leanaibh,
> long mo rìgh-sa, long nan Eilean;
> tha stiùir òir oirre, 's dà chrann airgid,
> is tobar fiona shìos na deiridh.¹³

Making plentiful use of internal rhyme, Bateman evokes the tone and imagery of her models, which range from bardic poetry through popular song and a masterpiece of eighteenth-century poet Alexander MacDonald to a celebrated boat poem by George Campbell Hay (1915–84), at times by means of blatant archaisms (as in the dative 'sgòdaibh', or the phraseology of the fourth line of the first quoted stanza). Certain lines have a crammed quality producing a metrical awkwardness very far from the carefully chiselled lyrics that helped Bateman make a name for herself in the late 1980s.

The two poems reveal the paradox intrinsic to 'nativisation', which unfailingly pushes the tradition further away in the very act of attempting to reproduce it, rendering any recovered 'genuineness' impossible. With Campbell, this happens both because vocabulary reminiscent of love-song is recycled with reference to the poet's mother, and because the very aim of producing a tribute to one's own, individual mother is alien to traditional modes. When items in the song tradition focus on family relations, this tends to happen only if these have gone grievously wrong. Moreover, the fact that the poem is a homage to a woman irrevocably lost implicitly sets both its imagery and its modes of expression under a similar interdict. In the last analysis, 'Tè gheal mo rùin' risks falling into the trap of sentimentalisation, depending for its effectiveness on what can be blocked out, what it refuses to see, what gets excluded from the picture. With Bateman, the self-conscious archaisms produce serious discomfort in the poet, who comes close to disavowing her own undertaking towards the poem's close.

In so far as both examples hint at a nostalgia for a seamless, Gaelic completeness, for a lost purity, one might be justified in terming them reactionary. What matters most, however, is that the 'nativisation' to which they give such eloquent testimony appears doomed to failure from the very outset.

Bartók's implicit model for what we might term 'co-creation' between differing 'national cultures' supports the view that 'foreignisation' and 'nativisation' are not parallel, or complementary, phenomena. Cultural nationalists of the more reactionary variety fondly imagine that a reserve of, for example, genuine 'Scottishness' exists somewhere, which can be tapped, had recourse to, in order to 'up' the quantity of Scottishness specific cultural products (and individuals?) possess. Their narratives of national cultural history distinguish phases of dilution and adulteration after which a 'recharging' of the national character, and of the literature, became necessary.

As one who has managed to escape (so far, successfully, but who can tell what the future holds) from an academic setting, I may be permitted to look back, if not with regret, then with puzzlement on an intellectual environment where concepts such as 'healthy indigenous Scottishness' were promulgated without any detectable hint of irony or scepticism. My puzzlement was chastened by an awareness of the human tragedies which inevitably follow on any attempt to translate such a concept into political practice. The traps such an approach involves are obvious. Once 'Scottishness' is established as a desirable quality, texts will be ranked according to the degree of Scottishness which they are perceived as possessing. I was once asked by a journalist from *The Independent*, planning a piece about a living Scottish poet, which of the figures he had named was 'the most Scottish'. Naturally I refused to offer any enlightenment. An eighteenth-century author such as James Thomson, or a twentieth-century novelist like Candia MacWilliam, would be classified as 'Anglo-Scots', as if there were a test they had demonstrably failed to pass. In the case of Thomson, the assumption that to write in Scots was desirable, whereas to write in English represented a betrayal, compounded by the author's physical displacement to the metropolis, London, was unmistakable. The distortions an attitude like this can bring to our readings of a bilingual (and bicultural) author like Burns do not need to be emphasised. Another feature of this intellectual environment which puzzled and irritated me was the attempt to define Scottishness. I had in fact been born within 20 minutes', and reared within 5 minutes' walk of the building where the department I taught in was situated, and was the only member of staff with such close links to the city where we worked. Yet again and again I found definitions of Scottishness being put forward which excluded me, either because of the Irish component in my family, or because I had received a Catholic and Jesuit education, or because of my sexuality.

'Foreignisation' is related to translation, but not identifiable with it. Both can serve as valuable strategies for the introduction of forbidden, or hitherto absent content into a literary tradition, whether that be identified with a language or a nation. A text translated from Cavafy, for example, offers an effective means for bodying forth homosexual content in a new language.

The translated text takes its place within the tradition, yet possesses the quality of having been 'always already there' in the form of its original. After it has been translated, it is present twice, not once, augmenting its influence and the power it can exert. In a translated text, or even in an imitation, the translator or imitator takes no responsibility for the subject matter. That is a 'given', a fact which makes this kind of 'foreignisation' a splendid expedient for 'smuggling' controversial material into territories where its diffusion has so far been problematic.

Had Ní Dhomhnaill wished to use the Tsvetaeva poem in order to clear ground for lesbian content in Irish-language poetry, she would have been making an excellent choice, though at the present stage of studies, we have no basis for attributing such an intention to her. 'We will end up in Hell, passionate sisters' is one of a significant group of poems from Tsvetaeva's earlier output inspired by her love affair with the poetess Sofia Parnok. In January 1912, aged 19, against her father's wishes, she married Sergei Efron, who came from a culturally significant Jewish family. Their daughter Ariadna was born that September. In late 1914, however, Tsvetaeva embarked on a passionate liaison with Parnok, several years her senior, which continued until early 1916, and gained eloquent expression in a cycle of seventeen poems entitled 'Подруга' ('Podruga', something like 'Woman Friend' in English).[14] David Bethea has written that Tsvetaeva's sexual orientation was 'nothing if not defiantly bisexual',[15] and Joseph Brodsky, faced with a claim from Solomon Volkov that 'Tsvetaeva's poetry, which is so passionate and stormy, [is] so rarely erotic', had this to say: 'My friend, reread Tsvetaeva's poems to Sofia Parnok! When it comes to erotica, she outdoes everyone there ... "I learn love through the pain all down my body." What more do you need?'[16] The 'passionate sisters', then, if they cannot be identified solely with Tsvetaeva and Parnok, definitely included them.

The reflection on Ní Dhomhnaill and Tsvetaeva is relevant because of the case of the Alexandrine, Greek language poet Constantine Cavafy and Irish poet Cathal Ó Searcaigh. What can be termed Ó Searcaigh's 'coming out' collection, *Na Buachaillí Bána* (1996), is claimed to have 'received more media coverage than any other volume of verse published in the Irish language in recent years'.[17] Notwithstanding the shadows cast on Ó Searcaigh's reputation, and the questions raised about his individual conduct, by Neasa Ní Chianáin's recent film *Fairytale in Kathmandu*, it is worth considering the use he makes of Cavafy's work as a particularly illuminating instance of 'foreignisation'. Two poems in the third section of Ó Searcaigh's 1997 collected volume, *Out In The Open*, which brings together items of an explicitly homoerotic nature, make their debt to Cavafy explicit (though the English 'after' may not be the best rendering of Irish 'i gcead', which carries the notion of 'by the leave of', 'offering due respect to', almost as if Cavafy were on hand to be asked!) The Alexandrine poet is, however, well-nigh omnipresent, for example in 'Ag na Pioctúirí ar na Croisbhealaí' ('At the Pictures on the Crossroads'), which skilfully recasts one of Cavafy's remembered encounters in terms of a surreptitious, fumbling yet ecstatic encounter in the back rows of a rural cinema.

An association of homosexuality with the foreign, as a means of disowning and rejecting, has characterised homophobic discourse at least since the Industrial Age, as well as Stalinist ideology and the discourse of state Marxism in the twentieth century. Rather than importing the phenomenon, Ó Searcaigh imports, thanks to Cavafy, the possibility of talking about it. And in importing, he transforms. If Cavafy enables the writing of certain poems, he also enables us, as readers, to draw distinctions between his own world and that of Ó Searcaigh. The debt Ó Searcaigh acknowledges serves to highlight his distance from his chosen model.

The uneven quality of Frank Sewell's facing English translations should induce caution in readers who have no access to Ó Searcaigh's Irish. If Sewell's readiness utterly to transform the formal arrangement of the originals comes over as unnecessarily cavalier, it is hard to conceive of any translator devising a workable English equivalent for Ó Searcaigh's dogged redeployment in erotic terms ('Laoi Chumainn' ['Serenade']) of the traditional vocabulary of male heroism. 'An Ghualainn Ghortaithe' ('The Injured Shoulder') takes as its point of departure a poem by Cavafy[18] whose fascination with the loved one's blood will recall Mademoiselle Bistouri to readers familiar with Baudelaire's *Petits poèmes en prose*.

Ó Searcaigh introduces elements which render the incident believable, familiar within his own surroundings. Cavafy merely says he does not believe the young man's claim to have hurt himself falling or bumping into the wall. The Irish version surmises that

> Nuair a thigeadh mearadh ar an athair chnagthaí eisean
> dá mbíodh sé i láthair agus ruaighthí an mháthair as baile.

[When his da lost the head, he'd beat him / if he was there, and throw the ma out of the house.]

Cavafy's young man dislodges the dressing by reaching for some photographs. The speaker in Ó Searcaigh's poem tells us he had a fondness for local history, and was stretching to take down a book about Gweedore. In the Irish poem the speaker not only takes his time putting on a new bandage, but rubs the wound with ointment. Ó Searcaigh omits the explicit declaration at the end of Cavafy's third section ('It was a thing of my love, that blood' in Keeley and Sherrard's translation, 'του ερωτὸς μου τὸ αἷμα εκείνο ἤταν', and the word translated 'love' is significant). But he places one stray line at the close of the Irish poem in which the bloodied rag reddens the lips the speaker presses it to ('ag deargadh', rendered by Sewell as 'darkening'), whereas Keeley and Sherrard follow the original Greek in having no visual reference. The extraordinary power of this lyric is hard to account for, and may derive in part from its provocative, unsettling recasting, in male to male terms, of the 'wise wound' of menstruation. The power is evident in both realisations, the Irish and the Greek.

These intertextualities, and the telling differences between the two poets involved, demand extended study, and here I can do no more than offer a stop-gap summing-up. Cavafy's eroticism is consistently retrospective, whereas Ó Searcaigh mixes poems that deal with the present and others that look to the past. There can be no doubting the utter quality of the erotic fulfilment Cavafy's speaker enjoyed when young, whereas Ó Searcaigh's poems have a breathless, even cloying quality that speaks of repression, of a fulfilment barely or intermittently obtained. Thirdly, while Cavafy records observing more than one pair of young men in the aftermath of an illicit erotic encounter, Ó Searcaigh's poems concentrate on the experience of a first-person speaker. Cavafy is aware of the need for duplicity, for secrecy, but the option of speaking out, in his poems, is never imperilled or questioned. They are an arena of oneiric, fiercely individual freedom. Part of the considerable attraction these poems exert derives from the reader's sense of privilege at being allowed to participate in this arena, at being a chosen witness to the exercise of such freedom. Ó Searcaigh's 'Rúnsearc' ('Secret Love'), by contrast, opens 'Agus fiú mura dtig liom trácht ar an té atá le mo mhian . . . / mura dtig liom a chuid áilleachtaí a chanadh os ard'.[19]

In conclusion, I would like to draw attention to the fact that, throughout this chapter, I have placed the word 'foreignisation' within quotation marks, like a scientist working in a laboratory who will lift a particular item for inspection only using tweezers, either because it is so fragile and flimsy, or because he wants to keep it at a distance, due to a possible risk of contamination or infection. The concept of 'foreignisation' has to be treated with such caution so as to stress yet again how difficult, and unwise, it can be to make any hard and fast distinction between the 'foreign' and the 'native'. As I suggested at the chapter's beginning, the two constantly engage in a process of osmosis, transformation and mutual exchange. Literature itself may be one aspect of this process. Had we been students of literature as little as a century ago, we would unthinkingly have drawn on a background in philology, in literature using one or both of the Classical languages, Latin and Greek. The Catholic Church was not alone in perceiving, and putting to good use, the inherent supranational potential of the Latin language. Classical literature has rarely been viewed through a prism of national belonging. Now that it has faded into the background, we are left struggling willy-nilly with the more problematic assumptions of nineteenth-century Romantic nationalism and its successor ideologies. Not content with snuggling comfortably down inside the pens where the assumptions of more dominant cultures have sought to confine them, the more reactionary among cultural nationalists are prone to compound their predicament by constructing new, ever smaller and more cramped pens to inhabit. Fences have to be demolished if we are to escape from the restrictions they impose. Boundaries, however, can be displaced and redrawn. We cross and recross them at varying tangents. The concept of 'foreignisation' offers a means of talking about such crossings and about the crucial part they play in the development of all literatures – national, or otherwise.

NOTES

1. Béla Bartók, 'Race Purity in Music', *Essays*, selected and ed. Benjamin Suchoff (London: Faber, 1976), 29–31, 29. A version of this article was published in 1942 in *Modern Music* 19, 3–4.
2. Bartók, 'Race Purity in Music', 30.
3. *Ibid.*
4. *Ibid.*
5. *Ibid.*, 30–1.
6. André Gide, *Journals 1889–1949*, translated, selected and edited by Justin O'Brien (London: Penguin, 1967), 498.
7. See Nuala Ní Dhomhnaill, *Selected Poems/Rogha Dánta*, trans. Michael Hartnett (Dublin: Raven Arts, 1988), 14–17.
8. A further indication that this poem may have had a special significance for Ní Dhomhnaill is that she chose *Spíonáin is Róiseanna* as the title for a cassette recording of her work (Indreabhán, Conamara: Cló Iar-Chonnachta, 1993).
9. Where Hartnett has 'Eden's fields'. Feinstein's translation reads 'paradisal songs', and the Irish has 'bhántaibh *Párthais*' (my italics).
10. Marina Tsvetayeva, *Selected Poems*, trans. and introduced by Elaine Feinstein with literal versions provided by Daisy Cockburn *et al.* (Manchester: Carcanet, 1999 [1971]), 6. For the Russian original see Marina Tsvetaeva, Стихотворения и поэмы в пяти томах, Vol. 1 (New York: Russica, 1980), 255.

11. Maoilios Caimbeul [Myles Campbell], 'Tè gheal mo rùin'/'My Pure Love', in Liz Niven and Brian Whittingehame (eds.), with Michel Byrne (Gaelic adviser), *The Dynamics of Balsa: New Writing Scotland* 25 (Glasgow: Association for Scottish Literary Studies, 2007), 31–4.
12. Meg Bateman, 'A' Chrannghail: do Will MacLean', *Gath* 8 (Summer 2007), 23–5.
13. A rough translation of these lines might run as follows: 'She is Donald Gorm's galley with her ropes a-tremble, / spray about her prow leaping against the oak, / a skilful, tight steering mechanism guiding her / to the hall of cups where wine is drunk with clamour. // What galley can she be but my lover's galley, / the galley of my king, galley of the Islands? / She has a helm of gold and two silver masts, / and a well of wine descending at her stern'.
14. For further information see Simon Karlinsky, *Marina Tsvetaeva: The Woman, her World, her Poetry* (Cambridge University Press, 1985).
15. David M. Bethea, *Joseph Brodsky and the Creation of Exile* (Princeton University Press, 1994), 287.
16. Solomon Volkov, *Conversations with Joseph Brodsky: A Poet's Journey through the Twentieth Century*, translated by Marian Schwartz (New York: Free Press, 1998), 43.
17. Cathal Ó Searcaigh, *Out in the Open*, translations by Frank Sewell (Indreabhán, Conamara: Cló Iar-Chonnachta, 1997), 5.
18. This item was not published during the poet's lifetime, first appearing in print in 1968. See now K. P. Kavafi, Ανέκδοτα Ποιήματα ['Unpublished Poems'], ed. F. G. Feksi (Athens: Pantazi Foukiri 1982), 152. English translation, 'The Bandaged Shoulder', in C. P. Cavafy, *Collected Poems*, trans. Edmund Keeley and Philip Sherrard, ed. George Savidis (London: Hogarth, 1984), 151.
19. 'And even if it's forbidden to refer to the one I'm after ... / even if I'm not allowed to sing his praises in the open air'.

CHAPTER 11

Outside English: Irish and Scottish poets in the East

Justin Quinn

THE IGNORANT IMAGINATION

Czechs have a saying: 'Kolik řečí umíš, tolikrát jsi člověkem' ('You are as many times a person as the languages you know'). Certainly for the Czechs, it has always been necessary for cultural and physical survival to know more than their own language. For many centuries it was German, then Russian last century, and now English is the most popular second language in the country.[1] Of course no one will tell you that it is a *good* thing to know only one language. Perhaps the main advantage of acquiring fluency in only one other language is that one begins to realise that not everything can be expressed in your mother tongue; not everything can even be translated into it. In the case of speakers of minority languages like, say, Czech or, closer to home, Irish, they are constantly and painfully reminded of this fact. Some monoglot Czechs are acutely aware that whole worlds of ideas and knowledge are closed off from them by their ignorance of English. But people whose mother tongue is English are in a different position. There is a kind of linguistic arrogance which presumes that if something cannot be translated well into English, then its existence remains at best vague and shadowy, with lip-service paid in such cases – English-speakers will politely fantasise about how it must sound in the original, Czech, Estonian, Chinese or Irish.

There is also a difference between Czechs' acquisition of German and Russian in the past, and English now. The first two were necessary: German-speakers were their neighbours, not only across the border, but – before the Sudetens were expelled – in the next village and the next house; and Russia, in the guise of the USSR, invaded the country stealthily in 1948, and militarily in 1968. However, now English is necessary as a global lingua franca, for both commercial and cultural exchange. The language is not connected with any circumstance that is particular to the Czech lands, such as geographical proximity with Germany over a millennium, and historical incursion by Russia.

In this essay, I will examine various moments when poets come up against the limits of the English language. By this I mean a kind of linguistic sublime when the poet narrates an episode in which he encounters a language he cannot understand, and yet knows that communication is going on. Traditionally the sublime is all about thresholds, and also about ineffability: the poet has such an intense and revelatory experience on, say, a mountaintop that language fails him when he attempts to write a poem about it. Such a moment is frequent in Romantic poetry and prose. I want to begin, then, with neither an Irish nor a Scottish poet, but an English one, William Wordsworth, when he encounters a Scottish girl singing in a language he cannot understand:

> Behold her, single in the field,
> Yon solitary Highland lass!
> Reaping and singing by herself;
> Stop here, or gently pass!
> Alone she cuts and binds the grain,
> And sings a melancholy strain;
> O listen! for the vale profound
> Is overflowing with the sound.
> [...]
> Will no one tell me what she sings?
> Perhaps the plaintive numbers flow
> For old, unhappy far-off things,
> And battles long ago:
> Or is it some more humble lay,
> Familiar matter of to-day?
> Some natural sorrow, loss, or pain,
> That has been, and may be again!
>
> Whate'er the theme, the maiden sang
> As if her song could have no ending;
> I saw her singing at her work,
> And o'er the sickle bending;
> I listen'd till I had my fill;
> And, as I mounted up the hill,
> The music in my heart I bore
> Long after it was heard no more.[2]

The first verse here is merely the *ecce*, but she is also identified as Scottish, and towards the end of the verse there is a subtle identification of the song with the landscape; or at least one is said to cover the other. Here is the natural acoustic of this particular valley, as though the valley sings through the girl. But of course Wordsworth does not know what she is singing about, and here begins the main imaginative work of the poem: he has to conjecture the ballad's content. The first line of the second verse quoted here is the typical gesture of the English monoglot, almost like calling for a punkah-wallah when one is too hot. It is a distinctly imperial instinct, and this comes through, above all, in the tone of the question. Is it possible that a reasonable subject of the king, such as myself, cannot have this song, which after all affects me so strangely, translated?

In another poem, Wordsworth again considers the border of the English language:

> With no restraint, but such as springs
> From quick and eager visitings
> Of thoughts that lie beyond the reach
> Of thy few words of English speech:
> A bondage sweetly brook'd, a strife
> That gives thy gestures grace and life!
> So have I, not unmoved in mind,
> Seen birds of tempest-loving kind,
> Thus beating up against the wind.[3]

Here the speech of the girl from Inversnaid, fluent in Scottish Gaelic, is figured as an heroic struggle with the elements. Wordsworth fantasises settling down with her, or at least in her neighbourhood. It is interesting that he flounders on the issue of his precise relationship to her: 'Thy elder brother I would be, / Thy father, anything to thee' (229). This last 'anything' suggests a more distant familial bond, or the closer relationship of a lover. His lack of linguistic competence brings uncertainty to the social relations between them, and, necessarily, on the distant horizon, the fraught national relations between England and Scotland. But eventually he is happy to 'bear away [his] recompense' (229). This ultimately renders him something of a tourist-poet, having been refreshed by the energy of the 'wave / Of the wild sea', which is how he elsewhere describes the girl (229).

It is much better for us as readers that Wordsworth can have neither the song translated nor a proper conversation with the girl, as these obstacles force his imagination to work harder. The accuracy of his surmises about the content of the other language is neither here nor there. Wordsworth in any case keeps things fairly generic: there is no sharp detailing whatsoever. Rather the poignancy arises from his very *un*knowledge: this is what pierces him to the heart. She is saying something that he cannot know, and thus cannot express. He generates his own poem out of his inability to say what is happening; which is exactly what he did to such great effect in 'Tintern Abbey', and in the 'spots of time' in *The Prelude*. It is the same strategy he used in the sublime, but employed here to characterise the relations between languages. Moreover, these languages delimit certain geographical domains, zones of landscape: Wordsworth does not have the same access to Inversnaid as he does to the Lake District. He is not a linguistic native there.

I have argued elsewhere that W. B. Yeats's ignorance of the Irish language played a fundamental role in his poetic career, as it forced him to kinds of work that profited his imagination greatly.[4] In this he resembled Wordsworth in the two encounters above. But the story is complicated by the fact that Yeats was the foremost poet of emerging Irish cultural nationalism. (Wordsworth's ignorance is in line with the national divide of England and Scotland that is played out between himself and the girls in both poems.) Yeats, then, has no connection with that origin which would guarantee his nationalist credentials. His cultural authority is compromised. He may dream and write about that origin, but he cannot possess it as a native.

In one of his late works, Jacques Derrida talks about his background as an Algerian Jew and its consequences for his own relationship to the French language. On the one hand, French – not Hebrew, Arabic or Berber – is his mother tongue, but that is a language which for him is not originary; that is, 'French was a language supposed to be maternal, but one whose source, norms, rules, and law were situated elsewhere.'[5] A life spent in such a linguistic situation leads to

> a desire to reconstruct, to restore, but it is really a desire to invent a *first language* that would be, rather, a *prior-to-the-first* language destined to translate that memory. But to translate the memory of what, precisely, did not take place, of what, having been (the) forbidden, ought, nevertheless, to have left a trace, a specter, the phantomatic body, the phantom-member – palpable, painful, but hardly legible – of traces, marks, and scars.[6]

This returns us to a long-familiar postcolonial manoeuvre: excluded from the originary language, or at least from imaginative creation in that language, one desires to transform the target language, which belongs to the coloniser. Not to do it violence or distort it (as some postcolonial critics would have it), but to assert partial ownership of it. Thus postcolonial writers create new literary idioms within the English language, to replicate the difference between the originary and target languages, within the target language itself. Through readings of poems by W. N. Herbert, and more briefly Ciaran Carson, I will explore the ways in which these poets of Scottish and Irish backgrounds move away from this postcolonial framework into what might be loosely described as a globalised context. By this latter term I mean that social and cultural encounters of the type experienced by Wordsworth and Yeats above no longer occur within richly textured national relationships (England/Scotland, England/Ireland). Rather, they are haphazard collisions with distant cultures, where the level of ignorance (and polite curiosity) is much higher. For instance, Carson has hardly any historical or cultural context with which to understand Polish, and this very absence becomes the motivation for his poem 'Tak, Tak'. W. N. Herbert, like most of us, seems to know little of Russia beyond its literary classics and guide-book facts, and once again that ignorance becomes the motivation for a sequence of poems about the country. As Georges Bataille put it, 'Every time we give up the will to know, we have the possibility of touching the world with a much greater intensity.'[7]

GAELIC IMPERIALIST

Now the languages in Wordsworth's encounters are English and Scottish Gaelic, and like some other linguistic pairs in Europe – such as Irish and English, French and German, Finnish and Swedish, Czech and German – they are fraught with much history. The languages themselves, in their loan words, borrowed constructions, their songs that have been traded back and forth, are, in their oblique way, records of wars, unions, negotiations, revolutions, executions, suppressions and collaborations. In short, these languages are engaged in intense commerce with one another. In the case of English, the trade deficit is mostly with the other language, purely because of the imperial force of Britain. Much has been written, and will rightly continue to be written, about the linguistic and cultural relations between English and the other adjacent languages in the Isles. It is arguably the most important work for literary critics of English and Gaelic literatures.

But I would like to side-step many of these issues in what follows, by looking at several moments when Scottish and Irish poets encounter a linguistic Other which far exceeds that of the Isles – that is, when they encounter Central and Eastern Europe. They themselves are used to being the Other, or Incomprehensible. As, for instance, when English ears cannot attune themselves to, say, Scots dialect and do not know what Hugh MacDiarmid is talking about in *A Drunk Man Looks at the Thistle*, or when Irish poets draw on certain registers or use Irish words. Often this can make the poetry more alluring and exotic for an English audience – Yeats was the supreme master in this business, helpfully drawing an English audience along, even while introducing material that was very foreign to them. To varying degrees, they have been the Highland lass singing in the valley, which the polite, sensitive Englishman simply cannot understand. As the last two centuries have demonstrated, there are many advantages to being that Highland lass. But in the following poems, Herbert and Carson are in the position of the polite, sensitive Englishman who is not sure what is being said, and who has to do some legwork to find out. That legwork, that effort, then becomes the imaginative work of the poem.

Before turning to these instances, I wish to sketch some background. Fascination with Eastern Europe is different in Irish and Scottish poetry. For MacDiarmid, in *A Drunk Man*, the work of Aleksandr Blok gives the poem a kind of cosmological resonance, but more generally Russia and its poets present the ideal of an engaged poetry. Here, for MacDiarmid, are poets who do not retreat into mere aestheticism when confronted with the violent political reality of their days. (Nowhere is this clearer than in his poem *Three Hymns to Lenin*.) Edwin Muir spent several years in Prague – in the early 1920s, but mainly after the war – working for the British Council. Only a few scattered poems register those experiences, and in any case it is a disservice to MacDiarmid to suggest any kind of parity between their engagement with the East, or indeed, simply, their poetry. Neither does Edwin Morgan approach MacDiarmid's importance, but he has translated poets such as Pasternak, Yevtushenko, Voznesensky. It must be noted that these are all poets who never stepped so far beyond the party line, although they went very close. You do not see the names of White Russian poets here, or in MacDiarmid's versions, and it seems that there is a strong political bias to these choices. Names like Vladislav Khodasevich, Georgiy Adamovich and Zinaida Gippius do not appear, as indeed they do not appear in the Anglophone canon of Russian poetry more generally.

In Ireland, the poet who has attended most closely to Eastern European poetry is Seamus Heaney, and his choices have had a strong political bias also: in his case he has been more sympathetic to poets out of favour with their various regimes, such as Mandelstam and Miłosz. But Heaney's engagement is for the most part at second- or third-hand. Unlike Edwin Morgan, he could not read the work in the original, and it is most likely that his choices were governed by friends such as Joseph Brodsky and Miłosz himself. But in recent years, especially after the fall of Communism in the East, Heaney's engagement with Eastern European poets has become less political and more aesthetic – to the benefit of his criticism, I would note.[8] Eastern Europe, if not Eastern European poetry, has played an important role in Michael Longley's poetry of the early 1990s, in *Gorse Fires* (1991) and especially poems like 'Ghetto' and 'Terezín'. It is fascinating to see the way that these stories of Eastern Europe are woven into his preoccupations with both world wars, and his community's connection with these. Paul Durcan published the provocatively titled *Going Home to Russia* in 1987, and while many of the poems are set in that country, in truth he has little interest in either its culture or its history: Russia merely becomes a way of discussing Ireland, and Durcan's own family relations. There is something disturbing about his silence on the subject of Stalin's crimes, and more generally the elision of the troubled history of the country. Durcan, as the poet of moral outrage and satire, seems to have been happy only with much more manageable targets such as Irish archbishops, gombeen politicians and the inhabitants of Dublin 4.

SCOTS RUSSIAN

But when W. N. Herbert arrives in Russia in the late 1990s, the historical moment and the circumstances of the visit are signally different. When Durcan boards the plane bound for Moscow on its way from Havana in the mid-1980s, the only official help he receives from the Irish state is as follows:

> I am the solitary passenger joining the flight at Shannon;
> The Irish immigration officer eyes me mournfully;
> 'Good luck,' he mutters as if to say 'you will need it' . . .[9]

Herbert, however, as he makes clear in his acknowledgements and in the poems themselves, has the cultural agents of the British government working for him – picking him up at the airport, negotiating difficult social encounters, etc. When Herbert asks the modern version of 'Will no one tell me what she sings?' there is usually a helpful British Council employee on hand to translate; but although words are given their lexical equivalents, this usually only serves to increase the bemusement of the visitor (one example that the puzzled Herbert returns to is that the word 'biscuit' seems to be a verb in Russian).

The British Council invested a lot of money in Eastern and Central Europe in the 1990s with the stated purposes of building 'mutually beneficial relationships between people in the UK and other countries and . . . [increasing] appreciation of the UK's creative ideas and achievements'.[10] As a visiting poet, it is obvious that Herbert must have been presented as an example of British diversity, both cultural and linguistic. What increases the allure of such visitors is that they are clearly not trained ambassadors of their culture and are very likely to satirise the very terms of the whole cultural engagement, as Herbert himself does quite wittily in 'Petrovich's Handy Phrases for the Visiting Writer' ('Thank you for greeting me my brother/sister. / You are a great poet. I have never / heard of you before this moment.' 'Thank you for your introduction, which / focussed almost exclusively on your own work. / It is indeed a pity you are not reading tonight').[11] But this is clearly an effect which both the British Council and their American counterparts in the US Information Service have already taken into account. Such spontaneous behaviour is performed within a particular steely ideological framework: we are democratic enough to fly out such unorthodox figures to make public addresses and readings. The visiting poet, then, whose bill is being paid by his or her government, is in a strange position. Not exactly a tourist, but not an alien resident either.

But first you have to get into the country, and Herbert's first poem in the Russia sequence, entitled 'Instantinople', has him approaching passport control, bemused by the Cyrillic lettering. The girl behind the counter takes his passport and leaves for a moment, which makes him feel like Harry Palmer, when Herbert feels he is 'mistranscribed, / my visa is that of a spy'.[12] Herbert suggestively ends the poem with the word 'spy', because of course he is, in his way, a cultural spy who will bring back dispatches from Russia, rhymed and lineated. It is also amusing to think of this encounter as another version of Wordsworth's with the Highland lass. The poet here has just passed the border of the English language and is at a loss, and perhaps a little anxious.

There are many funny episodes with misunderstandings in the other poems, not least of which is the visit to the Irish bar in Moscow, where Herbert looks around and remarks: 'The prints here feel they've summed up / Irishness with their views of Glamorgan.'[13] Then there is a visit to Pasternak's house in Peredelkino in the suburbs outside Moscow (somewhere Durcan also writes about). In the poem, Herbert becomes deliberately confused about the location, and the old women in the historical house blend with his grandmothers.[14] It is as though the 'journalists, guides, *babushkiy*, friends, / all talking now in distant rooms as though / they're in your other country.'[15] At the end of the poem, he sits down with an old Russian woman:

> After, I sit beside her in the sun
> of the verandah room. The samovar
> is yielding heat. I'm passing her soft cheese
> to spread upon her *glagol* biscuit, which
> means 'verb'. I'm happy not to understand.[16]

Herbert notes how official guides to culture can get it all wrong (he has listened to one of them 'booming' throughout the poem), and he relies rather on the happy silence that he shares with the old woman on the verandah. Poems written on the occasion of visiting writers' graves or houses are often predictable in their trajectory: the poet – the live one – is invariably *sad* that the other poet is dead; and so it is nice to see Herbert *happy* here. He does not try to imagine what the woman could have said, but his very lack of knowledge or supposition leaves him with a kind of freedom, and this feeling of happy freedom – as the Russian material rhymes lightly with the 'Thistle's land' (MacDiarmid's designation of Scotland), and Herbert's own grandmother's – is the subject of the poem.

It is also of note that this poem is in Standard English, as are all of the others that recount his Russian experiences, with one exception, which is the last one, entitled 'Farewell to Moscow'. Herbert goes back and forth between Scots and English in his normal work, so it is interesting that he held back for so long in his poems on Russia. Perhaps it was connected in some way to the effort of being a good and polite guest: during his time there, he could not, one presumes, have spoken Scots if he had wanted to be fully understood by either his British Council hosts or the Russians themselves.

It is important to note how much Herbert's work differs from that of his Scottish predecessors. Russia essentially is reduced to the exotic, a place, a language, a set of customs that are wildly different from those he is accustomed to. This difference made his poems 'roar', as the end of 'Farewell to Moscow' has it:[17] it is a source of short-term inspiration, and lacks any long-term imaginative or intellectual engagement with the other country. However outrageous MacDiarmid's politics were, his interest in the USSR and its poetry was generated out of profound and sustained curiosity about the ways in which the Soviets arranged the relations between poetry and society. It does not devalue Herbert's work to say that, while entertaining, it is also a British-Council-sponsored tourist's impressions. He approaches Russia and its people as irreducibly alien, and that quality makes him meditate on his own linguistic resources and background. He does not imagine possible meanings, as Wordsworth did, but stays as faithful to the surfaces and sounds as is possible.

It also makes him withhold his Scots dialect, only eventually to explode with it in the last poem of the sequence, as though finally to assert his particular purchase on the English language. Herbert places emphasis on different Englishes within the monolingualism of his poetry. His asserts difference *within* English, but not *beyond* it, say, in Gaelic. Faced with the grand incomprehensibility of Russian, he introduces small amounts of incomprehensibility into his English. This is a way of saying both that 'this language does not fully belong to me, but neither does it fully belong to some notional speaker of pure English'. We are accustomed to such arguments within the postcolonial framework, but here arguably we move beyond this, as the poet asserts his localised purchase on a globalised language, by rehearsing the linguistic scar of colonisation, presenting the phantom of Scots within English.

CARSON AND THE LANGUAGE OF THE OTHER

One of the most curious Irish engagements with Eastern European poetry and poets takes place in the work of Medbh McGuckian. Her use of biographies and memoirs of Russian and German poets has been well documented by Shane Alcobia-Murphy, especially in his *Sympathetic Ink* (2006). It would seem that McGuckian created centos from these texts *because* they were so obscure (hence her annoyance when Murphy began unearthing the sources).[18] Whereas Heaney will invoke Mandelstam as clear moral and aesthetic exemplar, a sophisticated argument to authority, McGuckian, at least in her earlier work, it would seem, wished to create a kind of foreign idiom in Irish poetry, as if these far-flung sources would make her voice sing in a different key, and thus not be constrained in the established paradigms of poetry and politics in Northern Ireland. This appears to be an issue on which people have differing opinions, thus I should state that I think McGuckian's use of these sources is felicitous. Murphy's uncoverings do not call into question the originality of the poems; if anything, they confirm a quite radical originality.

McGuckian's exoticisation of her poetic language is also connected with her stated disdain for the English language.[19] It is as though she wishes to make it a foreign language, and in some respects to Gaelicise it – sometimes violently, sometimes seductively. With such a desire, it would perhaps be more efficient to stop speaking English and only speak Irish, but it is not clear exactly how much Irish McGuckian has. More generally, however, McGuckian's aim is similar to the 'desire to invent a *first language*', discussed above at the end of the first section. Ignorance, or *un*knowledge, can be a formidable, if not greater, imaginative force than knowledge.

One of the central concerns of Ciaran Carson's collection *First Language* (1993) is translation and the ways that it configures our world. He will often describe the phonetic textures of words in different languages, describing the way they affect him and the way they work in the world. The figure of Jerome pops up now and again, the patron saint of, among others, translators. His translation of the Bible into Vulgate Latin was a crucial event in the spread of Christianity in the recently converted Roman Empire in the fourth century. The connection between empires and translation is also very much on Carson's mind, and this becomes a way for him to describe the urban environment of Belfast.

There is next to no engagement with Eastern Europe, except for two small words: 'tak, tak'. Carson tells how he heard the word on a 'crackly line from Sulejówek', the home of the Polish poet Piotr Sommer, to whom the poem is dedicated. Carson attends to the words' phonetic likenesses (they 'made me think' of this or that). He also drifts towards the memory of Babel:

> Or *verbatim*, Vulgate-black like the inside of an unopened Bible –
> *Cessaverunt aedificare civitatem. Et idcirco vocatum est [nomen] ejus Babel.*[20]

The Polish word repeated reminds Carson of the linguistic diversity of the planet. It is an especially engaging position to reach towards the end of *First Language*, which begins autobiographically, on two levels. As the child grows up, he acquires English after Irish, and this acquisition reveals a whole new world. The prospect of all the other possible languages in the world is somewhat dizzying then. This is also an example of the 'globalised' encounter that I mentioned above. If Carson had heard a refined English accent on the line, he would perhaps have been led back into the post-colonial labyrinth. But here, and indeed throughout *First Language*, he searches for ways to escape this. In 'Tak, Tak', this is provided by the general context of Babylon, which was destroyed in order to separate people. He seems to be eavesdropping, as he is reminded of a phone-tap by the sound of the Polish word, but although he can hear the phonemes, he cannot get at their sense, just as Wordsworth could not.

I do not wish to argue that Central and Eastern Europe is anything more than of marginal interest when reading the work of these poets, but such episodes when poets come up against the edge of English, the language they write in, can help us to see the importance of the borders between languages for cultural work. It also presents an understanding of language and culture that moves beyond a postcolonial to a globalised framework. Herbert asserts his ownership of English through the use of Scots dialect, which is also an assertion of locality with a seemingly borderless Anglophone global environment. Carson does not need to invent a 'first language', since he can simply write in Irish, as he does quite beautifully in the first poem of the collection. *First Language* as a whole dreams of the universal structures of language, how they enable and block translation, and the consequences of this for human relations, and indeed the larger patterns of history. Herbert and

McGuckian dwell on the spectre or phantom of the originary language, which leaves its traces in their English poetic idiom; but Carson reaches for a more general context. Returning to Derrida and his meditation on his displacement as an Algerian Jew, we are helped by his formulation of exactly such a 'general context':

> In spite of appearances, this exceptional situation is, at the same time, certainly exemplary of a universal structure; it represents or reflects a type of originary 'alienation' that institutes every language as a language of the other; the impossible property of a language.[21]

In the way that Carson has arranged *First Language*, Irish becomes such an originary language, and to write in English is to be thrown into translation and 'alienation', exactly in the sense above. But he does this not to assert, or describe, the postcolonial scar, but rather to explore imaginatively the more universal structures of language use. This work is no longer preoccupied with the Irish/English binary, but rather how we all speak and write the language of the other.

NOTES

1. According to information from one Czech daily, English is over three times more popular than any other language at primary schools in the Czech Republic. 'Školy to přehanejí s jazyky' (zpravy.idnes.cz: 3 March 2009).
2. William Wordsworth, *Poetical Works*, ed. Thomas Hutchinson (Oxford University Press, 1978), 230.
3. Wordsworth, 'To a Highland Girl', *ibid.*, 229.
4. Justin Quinn, *Cambridge Introduction to Modern Irish Poetry: 1800–2000* (Cambridge University Press, 2008), 59–79.
5. Jacques Derrida, *Monolingualism of the Other; or, The Prosthesis of Origin*, trans. Patrick Mensah (Stanford University Press, 1998), 41.
6. *Ibid.*, 61.
7. Georges Bataille, *The Unfinished System of Nonknowledge*, trans. Michelle and Stuart Kendall (Minneapolis: University of Minnesota Press, 2001), 115.
8. I argue this more fully in 'Heaney and Eastern Europe' in Bernard O' Donoghue (ed.), *Cambridge Companion to Seamus Heaney* (Cambridge University Press, 2008), 92–105.
9. Paul Durcan, *Going Home to Russia* (Belfast: Blackstaff, 1987), 65.
10. www.britishcouncil.org/home-about-us-purpose-and-values.htm.
11. W. N. Herbert, *The Big Bumper Book of Troy* (Tarset: Bloodaxe, 2002), 87.
12. *Ibid.*, 68.
13. *Ibid.*, 73.

14. 'The reference in Peredelkino is a personal one – several of the poems in that book are about the death of my grandmother and, with it, the withdrawal of access to the cultural period she represents. This is dealt with most directly in "My Grandmother is Turning into Furniture", but is alluded to in Peredelkino and again at the end of "To Schnittke", and also lies behind the "Fall of the House of Broon".

    I suppose the question is: can we separate our perception of any cultural artefact (from the Iliad to a dacha) from our apperception of encountering it? I'm interested in the way the mind perceives the foreign, exotic or "high" culture artefact through the lens of the local, the domestic, the "low". If the other is lived with as part of the intimate, whatever problems this creates, how does that affect either term?' (Email from Herbert, 12 November 2007).
15. Herbert, *The Big Bumper Book of Troy*, 93.
16. *Ibid.*, 93–4.
17. *Ibid.*, 96.
18. 'In the course of preparing this book, I published a couple of articles on McGuckian's poetry which prompted a flurry of correspondence from her. She was unhappy with the fact that I was looking for, and uncovering, the sources behind her work.' Shane Alcobia-Murphy, *Sympathetic Ink: Intertextual Relations in Northern Irish Poetry* (Liverpool University Press, 2006), 83.
19. Medbh McGuckian and Nuala Ní Dhomhnaill, 'Comhrá, with a Foreword and Afterword by Laura O'Connor', *Southern Review* 31:3 (Summer 1995), 606–7.
20. Ciaran Carson, *First Language* (Loughcrew: Gallery, 1993), 64.
21. *Ibid.*, 63.

CHAPTER 12

Names for nameless things: the poetics of place names

Alan Gillis

'Ignorance is one of the sources of poetry', claimed Wallace Stevens: 'One's ignorance is one's chief asset.'[1] Hugh MacDiarmid agreed: 'Comprehensibility is error: Art is beyond understanding.'[2] Such assertions might be borne in mind when Seamus Heaney, regarding the eponymous place name of his poem 'Broagh', brings attention to 'that last / *gh* the strangers found / difficult to manage'.[3] Heaney may appear to be saying 'hands off' to non-native speakers of his vernacular. Yet most of his readers, one assumes, are ignorant of his vernacular. As such, rather than saying 'hands off', it might be argued that Heaney is, in fact, inducting his readers into one of the chief sources of poetry.

Irish and Scottish poets often make place names perform two basic functions. First and foremost, they can create an effect of verisimilitude, rooting a poem in the actual and making it concrete. Second, the use of regional place names can be a means of asserting the cultural and artistic validity of erstwhile marginalised places and traditions. However, Irish and Scottish critics have arguably exaggerated this tribal or identitarian element; and place names in poetry can do a lot more.

Vernacular writing infects readers' ears with irregular sound, a form of otherness or inlaid ignorance within standard language, enriching it with what MacDiarmid called an 'inexhaustible quarry of subtle and significant sound'.[4] In this way, speech-forms that have been repressed, rejected, adapted, annexed, metamorphosed and mutilated by English continually rise to be heard within the auditorium of Irish and Scottish verse. In the Anglophonic poetry of these nations, we get a sense that English has been superimposed upon other tongues. Strange sounds offset and sometimes upset the English stream, sticking in the ear and mind. These can be related to sediments of culture and history submerged under the imperial dominion of English, but they also ensure that the English language remains a weird, elastic, changeable and improbably expansive medium in itself. And this is where Irish–English and Scottish–English begin to hear themselves more truly and more strange. Of course, idiomatic poetry depends upon rhythm, syntax, intonation and inflection. But lexis is also crucial, and place names provide an immensely rich treasure trove of vernacular diction.

When MacDiarmid wrote of the vernacular, he obviously meant Scots. In what follows, by contrast, attention will mostly focus on poems that use place names to create distinctive effects within the context of an otherwise 'straight' Anglophonic diction. Indeed, Robert Crawford has argued that place names are often 'deployed to function in lieu of dialect, anchoring the voice to a particular community'.[5] Concerning such techniques, W. B. Yeats was a great innovator and enabler. His early poem 'The Ballad of Father O'Hart', for example, name-drops Coloony, Knocknarea, Knocknashee, Tiraragh, Ballinafad and Inishmurray.[6] Terence Brown stresses the political nature of this: 'Yeats's use of Irish place-names suggested that in certain corners of the Empire the imperial language was beholden to other tongues.' Brown argues that, in such poems, the English language's 'imperial elasticity was stretched to the limit in the hybrid condition of Hiberno-English naming'.[7] This sounds liberating, but Cairns Craig claims that such emancipation created a troubling estrangement. He argues: 'The poem has a double existence ... its English is always interrupted by its Irish names, its Irish intent conducted through the medium of a language which can never be "at home" with the place-names of the landscape in which it has to operate.'[8] Nevertheless, despite this element of alienation, Irish and Scottish poets have continually used place names as a means of energising their English.

In his aphorism about ignorance, Wallace Stevens reminds us that sound is as important as sense in poetry. In a similar vein, invoking a language that rings with 'names for nameless things', MacDiarmid's 'Gairmscoile' proclaims: 'It's soon', no' sense, that faddoms the herts o' men.'[9] This truism is pivotal to the art of poetry, and yet, how sound actually works, in relation to sense, remains mysterious. *The New Princeton Encyclopedia of Poetry and Poetics* informs us:

Poetry, which is coded into sonal patterns which are both lexical-semantic as well as prosodic, is processed by both hemi-spheres of the brain simultaneously, the former sounds being interpreted by one side of the brain as linguistic and the latter sounds by the other as aesthetic ... As verse is heard, sense is extracted (or created) by the left brain, and aesthetic pattern by the right brain. Both sides of the brain are listening to poetry simultaneously but differently.[10]

The aesthetic attributes of poetic sound are thus bound up with emotion or affect. And place names in poetry are most certainly a phenomenon of sound and emotion as much as of sense.

In *Scottish Place-Names*, W. F. H. Nicolaisen discusses the example of Hawick, a town in the Scottish Borders. Nicolaisen explains that the name originally given to the farm from which this modern town descends was *haga wic*, which is Old English for 'hedge farm', and which, he argues, 'must have been descriptive of the place to which it applied'. But now, he claims, Hawick is a relatively large town that looks nothing like a hedge farm. As such, the name 'no longer has a lexical slot, no longer has "word meaning" but has taken on a new "name meaning" or "onomastic quality"'. He continues:

> It is indeed its existence as a *name* which has given it a 'power of survival' which ordinary words do not have. Meaningless words die because the economy of language does not allow them to be carried as ballast when they no longer serve a meaningful function. Names, on the other hand, survive because they can be meaningful as *names* even if they have become meaningless as words.[11]

Through this 'onomastic quality', place names become almost pure sound emptied of meaning, but not quite. In reading a poem, a place name can create a gravitational pull towards a sublimated ideal of belonging or, at least, of concrete situatedness. Yet this sense of belonging or placement is deferred and never actualised, and so what we get is just that strange gravitational pull: a kind of connotative energy.

Many place names will have specific historical significance, while some may provoke forms of subjective associative significance, depending on the experience of the reader. As such, the relativity of each reader's ignorance will play a huge part in the effect of the place name in the poem. But generally, the reader's ignorance is likely to reign supreme, since a broad-based readership is unlikely to have detailed knowledge of local history, or to have associations with every village, mountain and farmland in Ireland and Scotland. Such ignorance therefore suggests that the place name's connotative energy will be central to the poem.

Explaining how place names set off historical depth-charges, critics often stress the importance of etymology. Certainly, the etymologies of place names can seem like archaeological digs, revealing layers of settlement, struggle and transformation. But unless, after reading a poem, we actively engage in onomastic scholarship, the historical provenance of a place name will be mostly suggestive. As such, it might be more accurate to note that the sensualised sound-space of a place name creates an atmosphere of history and place, transposed into an aesthetic realm uprooted from fact and actuality, transferred from the left side to the right side of the brain.

Any sense of home, belonging or identity that may be generated through a poem will always be bound up with this aesthetic realm. But rather than diminishing the power of place names in verse, this in fact enhances their affect. Benedict Anderson tells us a nation is always an imagined community, always at least partially fictive.[12] Yeats, meanwhile, once wrote: 'Thought seems more true, emotion more deep, spoken by someone ... who seems to claim me of his kindred, who seems to make me a part of some national mythology.' But he immediately followed this by claiming: 'nor is mythology mere ostentation, mere vanity if it draws me onward to the unknown'.[13] The more fervently a poem creates a sense of belonging, the more that intensity of self-realisation will be a pull into the beautiful and necessary, but problematic, phantasmagoria of emotion.

This is not to ignore the actuality of violent history, cultural oppression or the importance of etymological knowledge as a crucial tool towards historical awareness. But in poetry, these matters become transmogrified into art, which is as interested in playing upon our susceptibility as instructing us towards erudition. The crucial point is that poets can then manipulate these gaps and paradoxes through differing uses of place names in their poems. Ultimately, there is no single aesthetic of place names in poetry.

It should go without saying, of course, that 'the poetics of place names' stretches beyond Irish and Scottish poetry. The naming of things, including places, has been a primal concern of poets through the ages, throughout the world. Particularly, it should be stressed that many English and Welsh poets have been drawn to the richly stratified and elastic vernacular of place names, and that these have been influential on modern Irish and Scottish poetry. Thomas Hardy's haunted rootedness in Wessex comes immediately to mind, while Edward Thomas's 'Adlestrop' remains one of the best-known and beguiling place-name poems in modern British verse. Thomas, inspirational to most, if not all, of the poets discussed hereafter, once wrote:

If only those poems which are place-names could be translated at last, the pretty, the odd, the romantic, the racy names of copse and field and lane and house. What a flavour there is about the Bassetts, the Boughtons, the Worthys, the Tarrants, Winterbournes, Deverills, Manningfords, the Suttons: what goodly names of the South Country – Woodmansterne, Hollingborne, Horsmonden, Wolstanbury, Brockenhurst, Caburn, Lydiard Tregoze, Lydiard Millicent, Clevancy, Amesbury, Amberly ...'[14]

Edna Longley argues that place names are central to Thomas's 'thinking about "word" and "thing"', and adds that, for Thomas, 'the fact that place names often defy "translation" . . . gives them a quasi-autonomous status'.[15] The denotative slipperiness of words, such as place names, is 'perhaps the founding impulse of poetry', Longley writes, and such words retain rich 'associations with the phenomenal world', even if (now quoting Thomas): 'the things are forgotten, and it is an aspect of them, a recreation of them, a finer development of them, which endures in written words'.[16]

Seamus Heaney and Ciaran Carson have been doyens of these matters in recent times. In his essay 'The Sense of Place', Heaney discusses what he sees as two fundamental modes of place-name use in modern verse, by contrasting the work of John Montague and Patrick Kavanagh. Montague's place names, Heaney argues, are 'sounding lines, rods to plumb the depths of a shared and diminished culture . . . redolent not just of his personal life but of the history of his people, disinherited and dispossessed'. By contrast, 'Kavanagh's place names are there to stake out a personal landscape, they declare one man's experience, they are denuded of tribal or etymological implications.'[17]

This greatly illuminates Heaney's own poetry, which attempts to incorporate both senses of place. However, he may be misleading with regard to Kavanagh. In 'Stony Grey Soil', Kavanagh voices an emphatic bitterness against his home in Monaghan, and against his own naïvely Romantic aspirations. The poem ends:

> Mullahinsha, Drummeril, Black Shanco –
> Wherever I turn I see
> In the stony grey soil of Monaghan
> Dead loves that were born for me.[18]

Dead love is born and woven into the sonic fabric of those place names, and emanates back again from their un-English strangeness with haunting power. They are specific to Monaghan, a poetic nowhere, yet they are everywhere. Heaney writes: 'Kavanagh's place names are used . . . as posts to fence out a personal landscape.'[19] But this poem's poignant surge draws the reader into its realm of affect, and must also, therefore, have a communal element. This stony grey soil may be Kavanagh's, but it is also Ireland's. Indeed, it belongs to any reader. The sanctity afforded the place names creates a gravitational pull, a connotation of belongingness. The poem doesn't lay claim to a communal identity, but it opens up the possibility of there being one. The poem drags one into the onomastic quality, the phonaesthetic distinctiveness of 'Mullahinsha, Drummeril, Black Shanco'.

And this effect is all the more powerful because based on negation, the self-torture of a permanently thwarted desire. The ritualistic, rhythmic naming of these places makes them presenced and palpable, even while they are void: the undead sounds of loves that never were. The place names create a kind of placeless hell.

Meanwhile, the etymological aspect of Heaney's own poetic of place names has been overstressed by critics. 'Broagh' and other poems from *Wintering Out*, in particular, are indeed etymologically ingenious.[20] But once the code has been interpreted, the poetry's musicality can be reduced by blunt readers into a kind of shorthand for an identitarian history: the imagination of place is circumscribed, and the poem becomes static. Yet Heaney has brought much attention to the sensualised sound-space of his own place-name poems. His sense of them is closely bound up with his interpretation of T. S. Eliot's 'auditory imagination'. Heaney writes:

> One of the most precise and suggestive of T. S. Eliot's critical formulations was his notion of what he called 'the auditory imagination', 'the feeling for syllable and rhythm, penetrating far below the conscious levels of thought and feeling, invigorating every word; sinking to the most primitive and forgotten, returning to the origin and bringing something back', fusing 'the most ancient and the most civilized mentality'. I presume Eliot was thinking here about the cultural depth-charges latent in certain words and rhythms, that binding secret between words in poetry that delights not just the ear but the whole backward and abysm of mind and body; thinking of the energies beating in and between words that the poet brings into half-deliberate play; thinking of the relationship between the word as pure vocable, as articulate noise, and the word as etymological occurrence, as symptom of human history, memory and attachments.[21]

Elsewhere, Heaney has argued:

> The idea that each vocable, each phonetic signal, contains a transmission from some Ur-speech and at the same time is wafted to us across centuries of speaking and writing, that the auditory imagination unites the most ancient and most civilized mentalities, this has been one of the most influential refinements of poetic theory during the last century.[22]

The nature of the transmission is by no means clear, here, yet Heaney's critics have stressed the consolidatory aspect of his technique. The idea is that the relationship of 'etymological occurrence' and 'pure vocable' implicitly unites mind and body, history and spirit.

As such, Heaney is routinely held to offer an 'old school' example, against which Ciaran Carson is frequently contrasted. Carson repeatedly brings attention to the non-Irishness of many Belfast street names. Balaclava Street, Milan Street and Milton Street, as named in Carson's poem

'Army', may well be arbitrarily denominated, but all acts of naming are at least partially arbitrary, and these are Irish place names as much as Heaney's Anahorish or Broagh.[23] In 'Belfast Confetti', we read: 'I know this labyrinth so well – Balaclava, Raglan, Inkerman, Odessa Street – / Why can't I escape?' The poem ends: 'What is / My name? Where am I coming from? Where am I going? A fusillade of question marks.'[24] The sense is that Belfast's troubles are inextricably linked with, and embedded within, a labyrinthine and violent history of European troubles. The place names bespeak a kind of cultural expansiveness, which turns on its head to become a form of imprisonment. But Carson's use of place names also involves a sense that their transportability, their partial detachment from actuality, means that history and geography can be remixed and re-formed in the imagination, the virtual space of literature. Commenting on a Belfast Street directory in *The Star Factory*, he writes:

streets named after places form exotic junctures not to be found on the map of the Empire: Balkan and Ballarat, Cambrai and Cambridge, Carlisle and Carlow, Lisbon and Lisburn, and so on, through Madras and Madrid, till we eventually arrive, by way of Yukon, at the isles of Zetland, whereupon we fall off the margins of the city.[25]

Meanwhile, Carson's use of place names also brings attention to the slipperiness of etymology. In 'Farset' we read:

Belfast is a corruption of the Irish *Béal Feirste*. *Béal* is easy. It means a mouth, or the mouth of a river; an opening; an approach . . . But it is this *feirste* in which meaning founders, this genitive of *fearsad* . . . The Rev. Dineen glosses it as a shaft; a spindle; the ulna of the arm; a club; the spindle of an axle; a bar or bank of sand at low water; a deep narrow channel on a strand at low tide; a pit or pool of water; a verse, a poem.[26]

Commenting on this, David Wheatley writes: 'there is a tone of straight-faced jiggery-pokery behind these fanciful etymologies'. He continues: 'Where a return to etymological roots in . . . Heaney offers the chance of digging down to solid and authenticated ground, in Carson's hands it has become akin to opening a never-ending series of trapdoors.'[27]

This is accurate to an extent, yet it exaggerates the degree to which Heaney's place names offer 'solid and authenticated ground'. The purely vocable element – what Heaney called the 'erotic mouth-music' – of his place-name poems ensures they provide a place to get lost in, as much as a solid bedrock of cultural identity.[28] Their 'transmission from some Ur-speech' may be powerful, but it is also untranslatable, unstable: solid air. Moreover, Heaney's 'Toome' shows that his ear is as cocked for the pun in the place name as Carson's.²⁹ As such, Heaney is less essentialist than many critics make out. At the same time, it is clear that Carson is enrapt by the aura of place names. As he obsessively returns to them, ponders them, plays with them and intones them, they become crucial to his own 'auditory imagination', which may be differently calibrated than Heaney's, but is not a million miles away either. Carson does not reify the sound of Irish names, but he nevertheless writes of all place names as magic words or amulets. Discussing Belfast street names in *The Star Factory*, he begins: 'Pondering the tome of the Street Directory, I am reminded of the cabalistic or magical implications of the alphabet', and he initially muses on the words 'abraxas' and 'abracadabra'.³⁰ As such, both Heaney and Carson mix, through their use of place names, the actuality of benighted history with the haze of song and dream.

This potent fusion of reality and imagination through the portal of the place name is equally at large in Scottish poetry. Any discussion of place names in modern Scottish verse must twist its tongue over the Babel of 'Canedolia' by Edwin Morgan, a poem which uses a bizarre kind of catechistical, Q&A structure.³¹ Responding to the question 'who saw?', somebody, somewhere answers:

> rhu saw rum. garve saw smoo. nigg saw tain. lairg saw lagg.
> rigg saw eigg. largs saw haggs. tongue saw luss. mull saw yell.
> stoer saw strone. drem saw muck. gask saw noss. unst saw cults.
> echt saw banff. weem saw wick. trool saw twatt.

The question 'how far?' is answered:

> from largo to lunga from joppa to skibo from ratho to shona from ulva to minto from tinto to tolsta from soutra to marsco from braco to barra from alva to stobo from fogo to fada from gigha to gogo from kelso to stroma from hirta to spango.

On being asked 'what do you do?', we are told:

> we foindle and fungle, we bonkle and meigle and maxpoffle. we scotstarvit, armit, wormit, and even whifflet. we play at crossstobs, leuchars, gorbals and finfan. we scavaig, and there's aye a bit of tilquhilly. if it's wet, treshnish and mishnish.

The question 'but who was there?' prompts the response:

> petermoidart and craigenkenneth and cambusputtock and ecclemuchty and corriehulish and balladolly and altnacanny and clauchanvrechan and stronachlochan and auchenlachar and tighnacrankie and tilliebruaich and killieharra and invervannach

and achnatudlem and machrishellach and inchtamurchan and
auchterfechan and kinlochculter and ardnawhallie and invershuggle.

Regarding the title 'Canedolia', it would seem the switching of two letters has created not just a brand new word, but a brand new world: an altered image that is an altered state. One of the key effects of the poem comes from delayed shock when we realise these are real Scottish place names (right up to the penultimate stanza of 'petermoidart and craigenkenneth', and so on). Scotland immediately becomes stranger, crazier, and more of it than we think.

Christopher Whyte claims that Morgan used Francis Hindes Groome's *Ordnance Gazetteer of Scotland*, whose six volumes were published between 1882 and 1885. This work can now be found online, and it does account for just about all of the names (excluding that penultimate stanza). As Whyte points out, most of the names are Gaelic ('they come unequivocally from beyond, from outside "ordinary language"') and, through the sheer strangeness and even improbability of these sounds to an Anglophonic ear, especially when modulated like this, Scotland itself becomes weird, unknowable and uncontainable.[32]

Morgan wrenches the words free from the gravitational pull towards the sense of belonging normally inherent in place names. His names are reborn in a surreal realm in which they freely morph into verbs and adjectives, or even (possibly) people. It's unclear what might be involved in having a foindle or a fungle or a bonkle, but it sounds like fun. Clearly, there's a touch of the Joycean in Morgan's poem. An overabundance of creativity prevails. The meanings may be inaccessible, but the names are promiscuous and self-perpetuating. What's more, we are invited to project our imaginations into this soundscape, to try to intuit haphazard micro-narratives here and there, wherever we can; but these are never sustainable for more than seven or eight words at a time. As Joyce puts it in *Finnegans Wake*, 'the unfacts, did we possess them, are too imprecisely few to warrant our certitude'.[33]

The aesthetic of 'Canedolia' may well be a startling reminder of the strange otherness of all language, and of all approximations of place and history; as well as a refreshing assertion of the imaginative potential and elastic adaptiveness of our sense of place and belonging in language. And yet, linguistic play is always more free the further it is from the vicissitudes of verisimilitude. In such an aesthetic, to draw on Fredric Jameson, the reality of history and place is 'gradually bracketed, and then effaced altogether, leaving us with nothing but texts'.[34] This doesn't negate the incredible nature of

Morgan's performance. But it does imply that we should refrain from too smugly celebrating the liberating effects of this aesthetic.

In many ways, Morgan's fantasia is nightmarish. His humour offsets the anxiety that arises from alienation. In the chattering Babel of 'Canedolia', we don't know what the words mean, we are cut off from history, we can't grasp reality, we don't know ourselves, we become aliens. As the place names proliferate and self-generate, we surely receive a reflection of the remorseless spread of new suburban sprawls: endless estates and culs-de-sac demanding new names, names increasingly disenfranchised from any meaningful attachment. Place names become brand names. We desire and hope they have content, but increasingly we find ourselves lost in a Canedolian fun house, unable to return to the Caledonian Real.

A different and subtly ambivalent use of place names is at work in Paul Muldoon's 'Hard Drive':

> With my back to the wall
> and a foot in the door
> and my shoulder to the wheel
> I would drive through Seskinore.
>
> With an ear to the ground
> and my neck on the block
> I would tend to my wound
> in Belleek and Bellanaleck.
>
> With a toe in the water
> and a nose for trouble
> and an eye to the future
> I would drive through Derryfubble
>
> and Dunnamanagh and Ballynascreen,
> keeping that wound green.[35]

The place names here refer to villages and parishes within the gravitational pull of Muldoon's home town, and the idea of driving through them is feasible in terms of likely continuity. However, such matters seem quite secondary. The place names' relative oddity as words contrasts with the plain diction of the poem's English, and they seem to be at least partially summoned to fit the sonnet's rhyme scheme. 'Bellanaleck' seems to have been conjured out of 'Belleek', in a manner that reflects Muldoon's delight in words that cross-fertilise into one another, or self-generate out of one another; and this casts a suspicion that the drive from 'Derryfubble' to 'Dunnamanagh' has been prosodic rather than literal. Indeed, the move from 'Dunnamanagh' to 'Ballynascreen' is an alliterative return to the 'b' sounds of 'Belleek' and 'Bellanaleck', creating a sonic circularity that is central to the sonnet.

Reference to the 'sense' of these names reveals that the move from 'Belleek' to 'Bellanaleck' is a move from 'the mouth of the flat rock' to the 'pass of the flat rock'; but otherwise, etymology doesn't really help.[36] Rather, it's the proximity of Irish sound and English sense that seems crucial. While the insistence on 'keeping that wound green' may refer to other things, it cannot help but suggest a kind of intransigent Republican sentiment. Yet this is offset by the connotative energy of the place names. The sound of 'Derryfubble', in particular, seems to lightly undermine the poem's seriousness. The English of the poem keeps a straight face regarding its own clichéd nature, but this is undermined by the phonetic rise of the Irish place names. 'Derryfubble' creates a kind of acoustic bubble reminiscent of Muldoon's fondness for childlike nonce words such as, to quote from 'Horse Latitudes': 'thingammybobs', or 'bouncey' (when rhymed with 'rouncey'), or 'scaldy' (when rhymed with 'Garibaldi'), or the 'yawl that all of a sudden yaws' (when rhymed with 'heehaw'); or, to quote from 'The Old Country': words like 'hobbledehoy', 'hobbledehobbyhorse', 'hobblehob', and 'hobbledehobbledehoy'.[37]

'Hard Drive' echoes other Muldoon poems in which overfamiliarity with the terrain leads to a foregrounding of the banal, heard-it-all-before quality of the rhetoric, which then enters into a strange relationship with a simultaneous lexical extravagance, a word-hunger for phonic texture, working in tandem with the stammering rhythms and off-key music of his lines and rhymes. At the dead centre of 'Incantata's' voicing of grief and pain, for example, is an attempt to 'make sense of the "*quaquaqua*" / of [a] potato-mouth', a 'mouth as prim / and proper as it's full of self-opprobrium, / with its "*quaquaqua*", with its "Quoiquoiquoiquoiquoiquoiquoiq"'.[38] Meanwhile, the maddening '*pink and a pink and a pinkie-pick*'-style refrains of 'The Loaf' seem to manifest some sense of historical pain that can't otherwise be articulated, with the poem's 'spots of green grass where thousands of Irish have lain'.[39] In such examples, the non-sense of the English carries the weight of that which is beyond expression; but this also becomes a parody of expression.

If 'Hard Drive' partakes of such an aesthetic, then the poem's Irish place names are somehow undermining the putative Republicanism that the poem seems to flirt with, which becomes lightened by pastiche. Muldoon seems to be exploring Republicanism's fate as it loses its bite and potential terror in a context of peace, entering instead a world of irony which creates its own problems and imprisonments. Certainly, Muldoon is often at his best when his touch is slightest, and the gentle mockery heard in 'Hard Drive' is one of his most easeful trampolinings upon the death-full but buoyant palimpsests and foundations of history. But Muldoon's slippery tone is not pleased with itself. Rather, the voice seems stuck, with no other place to go. In a sense, the place names sound rich and homely, but this is offset by the rest of the poem. From another perspective, the tired intransigence of the rest of the poem ensures the place names are somewhat cast adrift within this hard drive. Local history is losing its engine (the Troubles), even though the poem insists on driving on. The poem's familiarity is left forever bouncing off a sonic otherness which teases and taunts, rather than offering relief.

Disaffected irony can also be heard in Robert Crawford's 'Deincarnation', in which 'Digitized, blue, massive Roshven / Loses its substance, granite and grass // Deincarnated and weightless'. The poem ends:

> Each loch beyond itself is cleared of itself,
> Gaelic names, flora, rainfall
>
> So close, the tangible spirited away,
> Cybered in a world of light.[40]

Cyberspace simultaneously preserves and de-actualises Scottish reality, and thus acts in a similar manner to place names and poetry. In Crawford's 'Liglag' we read:

> Nemms o places haud thir secrets,
> Leochel-Cushnie, Lochnagar,
>
> Luvely even untranslatit,
> Cast-byes unnerneath the haar
>
> Dreepin doon tae Inverbervie
> When the haert's as grit's a peat.
>
> Youtlin souns blaw frae the glebe.
> Pour a dram an tak it neat,
>
> Neat as Cattens, Tibberchindy,
> Tomintoul or Aiberdeen.[41]

Lovely even when untranslated, this poem tells us, the names of places hold their secrets, as potent as whiskey. They must be intoned (as whiskey must be imbibed) to cast their spell. Yet an emptiness pervades, and this poem is a lament in which the acoustic promise and seductive solidity of the place names almost collapses into a void of total negation: 'Peterculter, Maryculter. / Tine heart, tine a'. Tine heart, tine a'.' (Crawford provides his own gloss: 'Peterculter, Maryculter. If you let sorrow overcome you, you lose everything. If you let sorrow overcome you, you lose everything.')[42]

This soundscape finds an echo in Don Paterson's poem '14:50: Rosekinghall'.[43] Like 'Canedolia', this is almost entirely made up of place names, listing a series of stops for a putative train journey. The list begins:

> Fairygreen – Templelands – Stars of Forthneth – Silverwells –
> Honeyhole – Bee Cott – Pleasance – Sunnyblink –
> Butterglen – Heatheryhaugh – St Bride's Ring – Diltie Moss –
> Silvie – Leyshade – Bourtreebush – Little Fithie

and it proceeds, through some sixty-four place names, to end:

> Baldragon – Thorn – Wreaths – Spurn Hill –
> Drowndubs – The Bloody Inches – Halfway – Groan,
> where the train will divide

Anna Crowe has claimed that the poem's place names can all be found in Angus county or nearby, but that 'only a quarter of them are actually on or near a railway, dismantled or in operation'.[44] Already, then, we can see that Paterson's rail journey is very much a phantom journey of the mind, but one with a vital overlap with an actual terrain.

A linked prose-poem, '12:00 Dronley', tells us: 'when I say *Dronley*, I mean more specifically 351/366 on *OS Pathfinder* map 338'.[45] So, this is a poet who is pernickety about the specificity of his place names. Yet it is possibly more accurate to say that he is pernickety about appearing to be particular. Despite Anna Crowe's claim, Paterson is surely playing a subtle game based upon the fluid line that separates reality and memory, fact and fantasia. Generally, Paterson's characteristic tone of exactitude is frequently and ironically geared towards creating a sense of ambivalence. And so, in this poem, 'Formal' is followed by 'Letter', 'Packhorse' by 'Carrot', 'Jericho' by 'Horn'.

The poem is subtitled 'Beeching Memorial Railway, Forfarshire Division', referring to Richard Beeching, chairman of the British Railways Board in the early 1960s, and his notorious Beeching Plan, which aimed to make the railway network more cost effective by closing down many of its smaller railway lines, leaving the countryside littered with abandoned stations and grassed-over tracks. As such, the poem is about the dereliction of rural Scotland, as both the poem's traverse through Scotland's geography, and its traverse through the mind, take on the irreversible momentum of entropy. Meanwhile, 'Forfarshire Division' has obvious military connotations, and the sense of a community laid to waste by war adds to the poem's atmosphere of phantasmal dislocation and dereliction.

As with Morgan's poem, we are basically invited to project our own imagination into the names; and also we're invited to look out for possible micro-narratives. Paterson certainly creates a game of coding, decoding and recoding for the reader. But it is impossible to sustain 'sense' for long; and, ultimately, any attempt to create a cohesive narrative, or to grasp a tone of at-homeness among the place names, will be subverted by the poem's forlorn sense of transience and spectral inscrutability. As such, the poem is exemplary of what another poem calls 'the sensitive, paranoid, derelict romance' of Paterson's aesthetic more generally.[46]

In key Paterson poems, the historical sense is elliptical: there is an awareness that something is missing, or is being hidden, something potentially unspeakable, which tempers the present with a pervasive unease. The mystery and aura surrounding the place names of '14:50: Rosekinghall' transposes that historical sense onto geography. The place names create a kind of vibrating but entropic energy that seems to conjure up some form of tantalisingly palpable but unknowable reality. In one of his most striking aphorisms, Paterson writes: 'The better part of etymologies lie forever buried from sight. Words are locked tombs in which the corpses still lie breathing.'[47] The furtive music of Paterson's place names creates an implicit longing for some form of historical and homely plenitude; but the place names are isolated, abandoned to a diminishing narrative, and they deliver the reader instead into a kind of otherworld, a poignant and uncanny twilit soundscape which ghosts both place and mind.

Yet not all contemporary place-name poems have been dolorous. Kathleen Jamie's 'Bairnsang' (part of a sequence called 'Ultrasound') is a kind of devotional folk-song or prayer to a baby boy, and is a stunning poem of fragility and conviction:

> My ain tottie bairn
> > sternie an lift
> gin ye could daunce, yer daunce
> wad be that o life itsel,
> but ye cannae yet daunce
> sae maun courie in my erms
> and sleep, saftly sleep, Unst and Yell.[48]

The place names in the poem, like Unst and Yell here, seem almost arbitrarily interruptive, and come at the end of each stanza. But through them, the poem lifts beyond the interdependence of mother and son, establishing a further bond with place. The son is blessed with the spirit of Scotland, and Scotland is blessed with the gift of the child, while the soft assurance of the mother strengthens the bond between all three. Yet what is striking is the lack of territorial presumption. Certainly, the place names are Scottish (Gretna Green, Macrahanish Sand, 'Ainster an Crail'), but the grace, fragility and benevolent assurance of the naming, and the poem, suggest an absence of tribal or nationalistic concern. Rather, maternal love, alertness, vulnerability and responsibility are channelled into a deep-surged blessing.

In this, Jamie's poem shares much with the verse of Michael Longley, whose *Collected Poems*, as it proceeds, becomes increasingly rich with place names from West Mayo: Killadoon, Kinnadoohy, Thallabaun, Templedoomore, Cloonaghmanagh, Dooaghtry, Tonakeera, Lackakeely, Inishdeigil and, above all, Carrigskeewaun. In these poems, all tribal assertion, etymological mastery and territorial presumption are dissolved in the poetry's ringing, Edenic fascination with the sound of the names. Discussing Longley's use of names in his poem 'The Ice-cream Man', which commemorates a murder, and a daughter's despair at the murder, through intoning a list of ice-cream flavours and then flowers, Fran Brearton has argued that the poem 'encapsulates perfectly ... how language is both meaningful and, in another sense, meaningless'.[49] Noting the poem's balancing act between incantation and hesitancy, she argues: 'it reverberates beyond its own limits in the space outside. The flowers do not so much "mean" anything as they memorialise an absence of available meaning. The killing, rather than being contained in and by the flower and flavour lists, falls in the gap between them.'[50]

The grace and agile assurance of Longley's achievement in 'The Ice-cream Man' is carried over to his place-name poems. In these, the tenuousness of the words' meaning, and the beauty of their sounds, together allegorise our relationship with the world. Carrigskeewaun becomes a minutely detailed and specific ecosphere, but also a universalised and ritualistically dream-like everywhere. As modulated through the delicately sure textures and lithe jazz-like rhythms of his verse, Longley's place names function as repositories of beguiling sound into which we fall: meaningful yet beyond meaning, foreign yet familiar, strange yet homely. The relative absence of meaning in the names is counteracted by their texture on the tongue, just as existential doubt is counteracted by the palpability of existence. What is striking is the mix of honed craftsmanship and humility, as the place names become sonic encapsulations of Longley's captivatingly pitched exploration of being and dwelling.

In such a fashion, Longley offers a far-reaching and enabling poetic model for the twenty-first century, during which the political context of vernacular poetry will surely mutate to become more ecological than tribal or nationalistic. Nevertheless, when discussing the vernacular poetry of our devolving archipelago, both Robert Crawford and Cairns Craig situate contemporary Scottish and Irish poetry within a globalised context, in which Anglophonic poetry has been enriched by American, Australian, Caribbean voices, and so on.[51] This magnificent unleashing of vernacular life and energy in verse, they imply, is one of the great literary fruits of the break-up of Empire, and of disruptive modernity. Taking such a view, it's easy to surmise that the deregulation of Standard English by vernacular forces might be taken to reflect a liberating disruption of imperialism's uniform oppression.

No doubt this is valid to an extent. But imperialism has now fully mutated into globalisation: an endlessly hybridising, deregulated and fluid complex of capitalism and power. The Empire of our present day respects no national boundaries or sovereignty. Capital couldn't care a fig what language or dialect is spoken. Writers such as Michael Hardt and Antonio Negri claim that the more heterogeneous and deregulated cultural authority becomes, the more our new Empire thrives on the perpetual deterritorialisation and reterritorialisation that results.[52] In this context, we can no longer assume that vernacularisation is liberating, for there is no 'standard' left from which it might free us.

The sense of promise that Irish and Scottish place names hint at seems to be swiftly disappearing over the horizon. However, their inner Eden has been disappearing over the horizon for many an age, and their romance has proved durable. Whatever dispensation history throws up, the purely aesthetic pleasure of embedded poetic sound persists, almost impervious to social-economic actuality. Place names are portals of contentless, connotational energy: a repository of sounds, capable of evoking ghosted communal emotions and associations. They are nothing if not versatile. As the poets I have discussed exemplify, in their different ways, place names create an aesthetic texture, in poems, which enables self-assertion through searching expression and rooted engagement with ourselves and our place, reality and dream, desire and loss, the known and unknown.

NOTES

1. Wallace Stevens, 'from Adagia', *Collected Poetry and Prose* (New York: Library of America, 1997), 911, 914.
2. Hugh MacDiarmid, *Selected Essays* (London: Jonathan Cape, 1969), 44.
3. Seamus Heaney, *Opened Ground: Poems 1966–1996* (London: Faber, 1998), 54.

4. Hugh MacDiarmid, 'From A Theory of Scots Letters', in W. N. Herbert and Matthew Hollis (eds.), *Strong Words: Modern Poets on Modern Poetry* (Tarset: Bloodaxe, 2000), pp. 74–9, 77.
5. Robert Crawford, *Devolving English Literature*, 2nd edn (Edinburgh University Press, 2000), 296–7.
6. W. B. Yeats, *Yeats's Poems*, 3rd edn (Basingstoke: Palgrave Macmillan, 1996), 56–7.
7. Terence Brown, *The Life of W. B. Yeats: A Critical Biography* (Dublin: Gill & Macmillan, 1999), 82.
8. Cairns Craig, *Out of History: Narrative Paradigms in Scottish and English Culture* (Edinburgh: Polygon, 1996), 185.
9. Hugh MacDiarmid, *Complete Poems*, Vol. 1 (Manchester: Carcanet, 1993), 74.
10. T. V. F. Brogan, 'Sound', in Alex Preminger and T. V. F. Brogan (eds.), *The New Princeton Encyclopedia of Poetry and Poetics*, 3rd edn (Princeton University Press, 1993), 1172–80, 1174.
11. W. F. H. Nicolaisen, *Scottish Place-Names: Their Study and Significance*, new edn (London: B. T. Batsford, 1986), 4.
12. Benedict Anderson, *Imagined Communities: Reflections on the Origin and Spread of Nationalism*, new edn (London: Verso, 2006).
13. W. B. Yeats, *Explorations* (New York: Macmillan, 1962), 345.
14. Edward Thomas, *The Annotated Collected Poems*, ed. Edna Longley (Northumberland: Bloodaxe, 2008), 285–6.
15. *Ibid.*, 286.
16. *Ibid.*, 151.
17. Seamus Heaney, *Preoccupations: Selected Prose, 1968–1978* (New York: Farrar, Strauss and Giroux, 1980), 140–1.
18. Patrick Kavanagh, *Collected Poems* (London: Penguin, 2005), 39.
19. Heaney, *Preoccupations*, 141.
20. See Neil Corcoran, *The Poetry of Seamus Heaney: A Critical Study*, 2nd edn (London: Faber, 1998), 37–49.
21. Heaney, *Preoccupations*, 150.
22. Seamus Heaney, 'Place, Pastness, Poems: A Triptych', *Salmagundi* 68/9 (Fall 1985/Winter 1986), 35.
23. Ciaran Carson, *The Irish for No* (Oldcastle: Gallery, 1987), 38.
24. *Ibid.*, 31.
25. Ciaran Carson, *The Star Factory* (London: Granta, 1997), 8.
26. Ciaran Carson, *Belfast Confetti* (Oldcastle: Gallery, 1989), 48.
27. David Wheatley, '"That Blank Mouth": Secrecy, Shibboleths, and Silence in Northern Irish Poetry', *Journal of Modern Literature* XXV, 1 (Fall 2001), 1–16, 13.
28. Seamus Heaney, 'Unhappy and at Home', Interview by Seamus Deane, *Crane Bag* 1:1 (Spring 1977), 70.
29. Heaney, 'Toome', *Opened Ground*, 53.
30. Carson, *The Star Factory*, 7.
31. Edwin Morgan, *New Selected Poems* (Manchester: Carcanet, 2000), 23–4.

32. Christopher Whyte, *Modern Scottish Poetry* (Edinburgh University Press, 2004), 142.
33. James Joyce, *Finnegans Wake* (London: Penguin, 1992), 57, lines 16–17.
34. Fredric Jameson, 'Postmodernism, or The Cultural Logic of Late Capitalism', in M. Hardt and K. Weeks (eds.), *The Jameson Reader* (Oxford: Blackwell, 2000), 188–233, 203.
35. Paul Muldoon, *Moy Sand and Gravel* (London: Faber, 2002), 3.
36. Seskinore, Ir. *Seisceann Odhar*: 'brownish bog'; Belleek, Ir. *Béal Leice*: '(ford-)mouth of the flat rock'; Bellanaleck, Ir. *Bealach na Leice*: '(way/pass of the (flag)stone/flat rock'; Derryfubble, Ir. *Doire an Phobail*: 'oak-wood of the field'; Dunnamanagh, Ir. *Dún na Manach*: 'fort of the monks'; Ballynascreen, Ir. *Baile na Scríne*: 'territory of the shrine'. Peter McKay, *A Dictionary of Irish Place-Names* (Belfast: QUB Institute of Irish Studies, 1999).
37. Paul Muldoon, *Horse Latitudes* (London: Faber, 2006), 3–21, 38–46.
38. Paul Muldoon, *The Annals of Chile* (London: Faber, 1994), 20.
39. Muldoon, *Moy Sand and Gravel*, 47–8.
40. Robert Crawford, *Selected Poems* (London: Jonathan Cape, 2005), 87.
41. *Ibid.*, 85.
42. *Ibid.*, 86.
43. Don Paterson, *God's Gift to Women* (London: Faber, 1997), 54.
44. Anna Crowe, 'Ghostly Battalions: Angus Place-Names in a Poem by Don Paterson' (www.st-andrews.ac.uk/institutes/sassi/spns/perthconf.htm).
45. Paterson, *God's Gift to Women*, 41.
46. Paterson, 'The Alexandrian Library Part II: The Return of the Book', *God's Gift to Women*, 47.
47. Don Paterson, *The Book of Shadows* (London: Picador, 2005), 154.
48. Kathleen Jamie, *Jizzen* (London: Picador, 1999), 15–16.
49. Fran Brearton, *Reading Michael Longley* (Tarset: Bloodaxe, 2006), 182.
50. *Ibid.*, 183.
51. See Crawford's *Devolving English*, and Craig's *Out of History*, respectively.
52. Michael Hardt and Antonio Negri, *Empire* (Harvard University Press, 2000).

CHAPTER 13

Desire lines: mapping the city in contemporary Belfast and Glasgow poetry

Aaron Kelly

In his classic nineteenth-century expression of national sentiment, 'The Library of Ireland', Thomas Davis grounded his own sense of nationality in the elemental, organic and stable:

This country of ours is no sandbank, thrown up by some recent caprice of earth. It is an ancient land, honoured in the archives of civilisation, traceable into antiquity by its piety, its valour and its sufferings. Every great European race has sent its stream to the river of the Irish mind.[1]

The Irish nation, Davis insists, is no mere sandbank but the ancestral site of an unyielding, natural continuity. Therein land and history organically suture one another. This kind of binding of place to identity and history in acts of natural union has tended to predominate all the way through to the present in Irish poetry, when the land is claimed via pastoral modes as the foundational realm of the national self. Seamus Heaney's landscape poetry is a canonical example of these processes, especially through *Wintering Out* and into *North*, given his effort to 'politicize the terrain' of his earlier collections.[2] Hence, poems such as 'Gifts of Rain', 'Anahorish' and 'Broagh' open up the familial belonging of the parish in his earlier work to a wider communal territorial claim in which language, self and place cohere in establishing an identity that not only founds itself but also excludes those deemed outsiders or others. In 'Gifts of Rain' language and landscape entwine in natural identity: 'The tawny guttural water / spells itself: Moyola.'[3] Similarly, in 'Anahorish' place becomes naturally and tautologically expressive of the communal proprietorship which claims the former: 'soft gradient of consonant, vowel-meadow'.[4] And 'Broagh', of course, concludes with 'that last / *gh* the strangers found / difficult to manage'.[5] So the self – and its more communal and national attachments – authenticates its belonging through the consonance of language and place.

Moreover, that belonging is established on a terrain which gathers a community in opposition to its strangers. Hence, even a poem such as 'The Other Side', which clearly reaches out to otherness, does so in a manner whereby alterity is still intimately familiar and ultimately secures the knowable self and place. So, under these representational conditions, the other is the guarantor of the self. By being able to reduce the other to the knowable, that other also helps ground the self.

In Scottish poetry, Iain Crichton Smith offers a comparable dynamic. A poem such as 'Shall Gaelic Die?' is justly and anxiously resistant to the obliteration of Gaelic culture. It avers that to lose your language is to lose your world. But, as with Heaney's landscape and place-name poems, Crichton Smith embeds the Gaelic language and the community assembled within it in an organic relation with the land: 'Words rise out of the country. They are around us. In / every month in the year we are surrounded by words.'[6] The identarian logic is similar to Heaney's in that 'we' and 'us' – the collective identity bound up in place – emanate from the locale while simultaneously naturalising ownership over the latter. Though this poem fears the erasure of Gaelic as both a language and a way of life it is still certain about one thing: this is a culture that has known and owned itself fully. The stark pessimism of Crichton Smith's 'The White Air of March' helps elaborate further how the organic bind between the knowable self and the knowable place demarcates identity in expressive opposition to its other:

> It is bitter
> to be an exile in one's own land.
> It is bitter
> to walk among strangers
> when the strangers are in one's own land.[7]

One of the fundamental ironies in the poem's overriding theme of self-estrangement is that the known community has become a stranger in its own land. But while the biting irony of the white air is that effectively 'we' have become strangers – that the internal exile of displacement has decayed the knowable community and place into antithesis – this mode of thinking about identity is produced under a rubric in which there is the known and the strange, there are those whose familiarity establishes their attachment to place and those who are outside that criterion. The poem concedes that 'the strangers', the outsiders, have trespassed on a land that belongs to the knowable community, and indeed that this knowable community has itself become an aggregation of strangers; but the judgement underwriting these demarcations of the familiar and unfamiliar is only possible through a sense of propriety in which we *should* belong to our land and the strangers to theirs. In other words, the poem relies upon a logic of the proper wherein displacement results from the disruption of a naturalised relation between the knowable self and place. Here, place mediates the construction of us and of them.

In both Heaney's and Crichton Smith's poems the other is always encountered in terms of the known self and on the ground of the known place, a place which is owned by the familiar and intruded upon by the unknown. My aim is neither to deny people a belonging nor to make a virtue of displacement; it is rather to highlight the kinds of identities and belongings which are constructed by these processes of establishing self and other. The local construction of identity and place in Heaney's and Crichton Smith's poetry coincides with, and indeed helps assemble, more national imperatives about belonging. For nationalism tends to construe a customary, already inherited propriety over territory that extrapolates from the localised mediation between self and other found in Heaney and Crichton Smith a much wider principle of kinship. Therein place helps establish 'us' – those who know ourselves and our land – against the encroachment of the strangers or outsiders who will never possess our customary and intimate affinity. The other, under such terms, will only ever disturb the seamless linguistic and cultural community gathered under the sign of place by identity. The city as a space, however, disrupts this logic and this is one reason why the urban never features when nationalism imagines itself spatially (where pastoral modes predominate). Incidentally, this is not to argue that anyone who writes pastoral poetry is some arch reactionary; it is more to draw attention to the ideological uses to which some forms of pastoral are put by the spaces of nationalism. The city complicates the spatialisations of nationalism in specific ways. As Roland Barthes puts it: 'the city, essentially and semantically, is the place of our meeting with the *other*'.[8] Or, as Richard Sennett would have it, the city is 'a milieu in which strangers are likely to meet'.[9] But here the situation is fundamentally different to the one discussed in relation to Heaney's and Crichton Smith's places: most people in cities are strangers to one another. The stranger is not just an outsider or alien somehow intimately trespassing in a fully known, self-affirmative place but rather a stranger as an unknown within a properly constituted public space, in which identities are perpetually renegotiated and reaffiliated according to historical contingency. There is no originary or customary starting-point by which the fully known self and place deems others to be strangers or outsiders. The city is a space that requires something more than familial intimacy to be known.

We will never have a direct, organic or immediate relation to most other people in a city. In addition, the city requires us to acknowledge our own otherness in a space where we are just as much a stranger as anyone else. Our continual encounter with our own strangeness prevents us from reducing our others to the terms of the self. This is not to laud estrangement but to propose that urban space requires a fundamentally different form of mapping than is allowed under spatial imaginations of nationalism. As Sennett observes: 'behaviour is at a distance from everyone's personal circumstances, and so does not force people to attempt to define to each other who they are. When this occurs, a public geography is on the way to being born.'[10] The city offers the means by which to construct a cartography at odds with tribal intimacy; one that is more fully public and political than the possession or dispossession of kinship.

Once you turn to the etymology of the name Belfast, as Ciaran Carson brilliantly does in *Belfast Confetti*, the certainties of naming, identity and location which structure Heaney's place-name poems start to unravel. Indeed, where Thomas Davis had insisted his fixed, elemental nationality was no sandbank, Belfast, as Carson shows, according to its ambiguous etymology, could have been a sandbank amongst many other things. There is no fixed Irish language point of stable origin from which the anglicised word 'Belfast' derives. Does Belfast, as Carson traces, come from *Béal*, the mouth or mouth of a river, in this case the Farset or *Feirste*; or from *Fearsaid*, a sandbar or sandbank at the crossing point or ford of two rivers, the Farset and the Lagan? In many ways, the city can be all these things: a crossing point, a fluid place of transgression, the mouth of a river flowing with innumerable voices. Carson's 'Schoolboys and Idlers of Pompeii' immerses itself in the city's shifting significations, the contingencies of a perpetual naming and renaming:

At times it seems that every inch of Belfast has been written-on, erased, and written-on again: messages, curses, political imperatives, but mostly names, or nicknames – Robbo, Mackers, Scoot, Fra – sometimes litanized obsessively on every brick of a gable wall, as high as the hand will reach, and sometimes higher, these snakes and ladders cancelling each other out in their bid to be remembered. *Remember 1690. Remember 1916.* Most of all, *Remember me. I was here.*[11]

However, much as the city remains non-identical to the tribal places and selves out of which nationalism extrapolates its wider organic belonging, there is another paradigm which any urban cartography must confront: namely, class. My purpose is not to oppose the city to the nation in the hope of making urban space merely the repository of some bland pluralism. Class shifts our register from diversity to inequality. As such, by tracing class cartographies in urban poetry, we follow lines that are not only non-identical to the logic of self and place within nationalism but also antagonistic to any straightforward use of the city to express a positive notion of social diversity which could be equated with post-nationalist paradigms. Hence, Carson's urban aesthetic foregrounds issues of power and socio-economic disadvantage in the city, as in 'The Ballad of HMS Belfast' where the imaginative voyage begun on April Fools' Day is sundered by the carceral realities of power and hegemony. Carson's labyrinthine geographies are not facilitated by some hybrid free-play of urban movement but are rather produced by socially conditioned and socially coded situations:

> I lay bound in chains, alone, my *aisling* gone, my sentence passed
> Grey Belfast dawn illuminated me, on board the prison ship *Belfast*.[12]

Across his work Carson's deployment of Walter Benjamin's *flâneur*, the peripatetic viewer, makes plain that the freedom of urban movement and subjectivity promised by *flânerie* is not available to everyone equally and that power (in sectarian, state and economic terms) demarcates rigidly the access of specific constituencies to civic, public or democratic spaces.

Hence, class cartographies in urban poetry offer a challenge to both nationalist constructions of place and the post-nationalist or pluralist paradigms which construe themselves as the alternative to the former. Firstly, with regard to nationalist paradigms in Irish and Scottish literary criticism, John Wilson Foster typifies a particular kind of Irish critical model which opposes an encompassing, rural national dispensation to an occluded urban aesthetic: 'only with reservation, then, could we claim that in reality or in fiction Ireland has developed a particularly urban consciousness ... [Ireland] exhibits paradoxically a nationwide provincialism.'[13] And even though Foster's intent is to bemoan the forestalling of this urban consciousness, he makes the rural and the nation one and the same while rendering the urban anomalous and peculiar. In Scottish criticism, a comparable reduction of the rural to the national and the urban to the strange or foreign can be found in Christopher Whyte's work. He makes the following point about Glasgow:

The city's relation to the rest of Scotland is problematical ... it came into being at a time when Scotland had for more than a century ceased to be an autonomous political or cultural unit. This means that Glasgow has never experienced an independent or organically functioning Scotland. It is the child, not of nation, but of empire, which alone can explain the savagery of its expansion and decline. This makes Scotland an inappropriate context for understanding Glasgow, and the distrust is often mutual ... Nor does Glasgow establish with the countryside the kind of fruitful relation so movingly described by Nan Shepherd in the process of an Aberdeen University graduation ceremony. A sizeable proportion of its inhabitants are drawn from Gaelic-speaking Scotland and north-west Ireland, a despoiled hinterland to which there is no return.[14]

It is as though there is something un-Scottish about Glasgow and the city more broadly. But it is less that, as Whyte would have it, Scotland is 'an inappropriate context for understanding Glasgow', and more that it is precisely this kind of construction of Scottishness and the nation which is unable to explain the city. Glasgow's disruptive resistance to some organic and self-identical set of relations between a nation, its people and history in fact enables an interrogation of these paradigms of belonging and identity. Whyte's inability to reconcile city and nation reworks a longstanding paradigm. This displacement of Glasgow as an alien city which troubles settled political and national narratives has long been evident in accounts from both mainstream Right and Left perspectives, cautionary protectors of the status quo or would-be reformists. From the Right, William Bolitho's 1924 effort to document the slums of Glasgow, *Cancer of Empire*, typifies a fear of the perceived malign intractability of Glasgow's social problems that has little or nothing to do with a compassion for the suffering of the working class and much more to do with assuaging the economic order responsible for social divisions in the first place. Bolitho's depiction of Glasgow is spurred by his quickening sense of its revolutionary potential, particularly amongst the agitation on Clydeside in the period. Bolitho frets:

The Red Clyde, the smouldering danger of revolution in Glasgow, owing to the swift development of political affairs in Britain, has ceased to be a local anxiety, and become an interest and an alarm to the whole civilised world. The complacent days of trust in things as they are have gone since the world war and the Russian upheaval, and no State, however geographically remote, however seemingly secure in possession of an unshakeable constitutional system, can any longer be certain of immunity from violent, bloody change in the body politic ... Revolution has grown violently infectious, and any threatened outbreak in the very heart of the universal British Empire is as much a concern to citizens in other States as an outbreak of cholera in a central seaport.[15]

In the fevered reaction of Bolitho's conservatism Glasgow is, paradoxically, at one and the same time both a local or remote anomaly and a central threat to a universal order. On the Left, Edwin Muir, in *A Scottish Journey*, is torn between acknowledging Glasgow as the most populous city in Scotland

and a simultaneous desire to deny the city the status of a typical Scottishness:

> Glasgow is in every way the most important city in modern Scotland, since it is an epitome of the virtues and the vices of the industrial regions, which comprise the majority of the population. A description of Scotland which did not put Glasgow in the centre of the picture would not be a description of Scotland at all ... Yet at the same time Glasgow is not a typically Scottish town; the worst of the many evils with which it festers were not born of the soil on which it stands or of the people who live in it – a mixed population of Lowlanders, Highlanders, and Irish – but of Industrialism; and in writing about it I shall be writing about a particular area of modern civilization which is independent of national boundaries, and can be found in England, Germany, Poland, Czecho-Slovakia and most other countries as well as on the banks of the Clyde. This No Man's Land of civilization comprises in Scotland an area which, though not very large in extent, is very densely populated. In one way it may be said that this area *is* modern Scotland, since it is the most active and vital part of Scotland as well as the most populous: the proof of its vitality being that it influences rural Scotland in all sorts of ways, while rural Scotland has no effective influence on it. But from another point of view one may say that it is not Scotland at all, or not Scotland in particular, since it is merely one of the expressions of Industrialism, and Industrialism operates by laws which do not recognise nationality.[16]

This is a strange No Man's Land in that it is 'very densely populated'. And, oddly, Glasgow is offered as modern Scotland yet also the effacement of Scottishness. It is a space which is precluded any belonging or cartographic reality because it exists in an empty terrain beyond the 'soil' of a supposedly normative national set of boundaries and alignments. Furthermore, through this interpretative lens, Glasgow is not only irreconcilable to the nation but also antithetical to art. Muir writes:

> the strongest impression of Glasgow I received was one of silence. In the centre of the city people are still busy, or seem to be so; but when one goes down the Clyde, to what used to be the busy shipbuilding quarter, there is hardly anything but this silence, which one would take to be the silence of a dead town if it were not for the numberless empty-looking groups of unemployed men standing about the pavements ... Perhaps at some time the mirage of work glimmered at the extreme horizon of their minds; but one could see by looking at them that they were no longer deceived by such false pictures.[17]

Although Muir very valiantly strives to highlight the poverty and deprivation endured by the working class, his analysis tends to make people identical with their own degradation. That is, the 'silence' allows only for the words of this intellectual who maintains a hierarchy over the very people with whom he so clearly sympathises. It is Muir who thinks, feels and expresses himself while workers merge with the incapacity of their surroundings. Objects in Muir's social commentary, these people are subjects only in so far as they are the subject of abjection. No thought, no expression, no art, no discourse seem to emerge from them. So while Muir may register this squalor, its victims are denied a register.

There is a correlation, therefore, between the apparent inappropriateness of Glasgow in a national context (or its silence therein) and the voicelessness of the Glaswegian working class who seem beyond articulation. These tensions are both continued but also challenged in Edwin Morgan's poetry. After the high(-rise) hopes of *The Second Life* (1968), Morgan's *Glasgow Sonnets* are a more measured appraisal of urban life in terms of its possibilities and limitations. Indeed, the very naming of *Glasgow Sonnets* seems to provocatively pre-empt any reader who would construe this title as an oxymoron. Morgan insists upon the worthiness of the city for art even as this insistence understands the urban as both heaven and hell, as a dialectical place of both transformation and deprivation. In many ways, the *Glasgow Sonnets* continue Morgan's capacity to recover the potential of the urban as encapsulated by his poem 'In Glasgow':

> Mercy for the rainy
> tyres and the violet
> thunder that bring you
> shambling and shy
> from chains of Easterhouse
> plains of lights
> make your delight
> in my nest my spell
> my arms and my shell
> my barn my bell.[18]

In *Glasgow Sonnets* itself Morgan is, of course, intent upon castigating poverty and inequality. There are the references to a 'mean wind', 'an air too poor to rob' and the tower blocks ironically 'condemned' to stand rather than be demolished.[19] Moreover, in Sonnet 4 Morgan alludes to Hugh MacDiarmid's 'Glasgow 1960', a poem which dryly anticipated some future Glasgow where its citizens might care about art rather than football or religion. Yet the tone of the MacDiarmid poem seems to betray any optimism by collapsing hope into cynicism, so that the anticipation of some future culture becomes the parodic and ironic condemnation of a present philistinism. Morgan, however, manages to avoid this embittered disdain which began as encouragement. Rather than make art – and its apparent inappropriateness to working-class Glaswegian life – the judge of people's lives, Morgan turns the tables and asks questions of art in the social context which has produced it: 'the feast / of reason and the flow of the soul has ceased / to matter to the long unfinished plot of heating frozen hands'.[20] And unlike the sentiment of Muir's or MacDiarmid's perspectives where the sympathy of the intellectual reserves art for the artist and keeps the working class unintentionally in their place by making them the object of both the pity and approbation of the former, Morgan finds art in nominally inappropriate places. Sonnet 10 encounters a boy in a tower block reading Shakespeare's *King Lear*:

> A multi is a sonnet stretched to ode
> and some say that's no joke. The gentle load
> of souls in clouds, vertiginously stayed
> above the windy courts, is probed and weighed.
> Each monolith stands patient, ah'd and oh'd.
> And stalled lifts generating high-rise blues
> can be set loose. But stalled lives never budge.
> They linger in the single-ends that use
> their spirit to the bone, and when they trudge
> from closemouth to laundrette their steady shoes
> carry a world that weighs us like a judge.[21]

Here, the judgement is on art and not on people; it is on the inequalities which arrogate the right to art for some and deny it to others. In particular, this sonnet, through its allusions to 'choughs' and 'samphires' (83), refers us directly to Scene IV, Act VI, of *King Lear*, to a moment where Edgar, who is disguised as a pauper, is required to invent a landscape whose description is intended to forestall his blinded father Gloucester's suicide. This allusion in turn impels the consideration of how the boy in the multistorey Red Road Flats can invent or imagine the landscape of a city from whose civic heart he is excluded, to which he is blinded. In other words, in mapping a city, how do you assemble a cartography which accounts for your local displacement within the wider totality of urban space? This also, of course, raises issues of the power of imagination in situations of despair, of art as the touchstone of endurance. But in terms of Glasgow, unlike the intimate spaces of Heaney's or Crichton Smith's locales which are personally knowable, the city demands a very different form of mapping. Here, the unknown is not simply about what is other in the sense of difference. What is other is also what is excluded from the purview of a boy in a marginalised housing scheme. The unknown in this context is the bearer not of cultural pluralism but social inequality. The other or stranger is encountered in the landscapes of Heaney or Crichton Smith within a criterion of customary and intimately familiar placements owned by the organic parish or ground of the tribe. No one in a city – whether as friend or foe – will ever know every other urban dweller, will ever be able to view the city in its entirety in a direct or unmediated way. This is especially true of a boy from a peripheral housing scheme. Another kind of act of imaginative cartography is required if a sense of the city as a place is to be established beyond the immediately known and familiar. Morgan's strategy not only reconnects art to working-class life but also reintegrates a sense of Glasgow as a totality of differing, unequal relations and forces. It both indicts and repairs a sense not only of the other but of the self being othered or excluded. In surmounting this alienation, this exclusion from an intimate knowledge of Glasgow as a totality place, Morgan's aesthetic in *Glasgow Sonnets* finds affinity with Fredric Jameson's concept of 'cognitive mapping'. Therein the symbolic geography of the individual's attempt to reconcile his/her urban displacement with a sense of the city as total network is extrapolated to our contemplation of the social structure itself:

the dialectic between the here and now of immediate perception and the imaginative or imaginary sense of the city as an absent totality ... presents something like a spatial analogue of Althusser's great formulation of ideology itself ... [T]his positive conception of ideology as a necessary function in any form of social life has the great merit of stressing the gap between the local positioning of the individual subject and the totality of class structures in which he or she is situated.[22]

So just as the allusion to *King Lear* provides a compass by which to instigate the imaginative recovery of a terrain which will never be known directly, *Glasgow Sonnets* coalesces political and urban cartographies, so that cognitive mapping acts as the methodology of class consciousness itself. These poems extract from the locale a more consummate knowledge of the class system which has caused the fragmentation of its constitutive parts. Where place in the national paradigm would find organically via synecdoche the logic of the overarching unity of belonging in the local parish or terrain of the tribe, a class cartography must reconvene the systemic from the disjunctive.

Urban planners use the term 'desire lines', or 'lines of desire', to describe how people will always resist what has been planned for them by architecture and design. Although urban planners construct walkways and pathways in housing schemes, shopping precincts, parks or thoroughfares, people disorder these designs by finding their own routes. Desire lines, then, are the contestation of what has been laid down, the active renegotiation of space. In many ways Morgan's cognitive mappings in *Glasgow Sonnets* enact these desire lines; his poems attest to despair yet also weave a circuitry which returns that despair to the urban totality which is its cause. Through poetry, therefore, Morgan allows his working-class personae to go where they were not intended to go, both to enter the protectorate of art and to grasp the city as a totality. The exclusion of working-class life from both poetry and the civic heart of Glasgow is challenged in these sonnets. It is not only that a boy in the Red Road Flats is capable of thought and aesthetic contemplation (where Muir could find only silence or MacDiarmid philistinism) but also that the poems transcend alienation by returning to the isolation of the boy the society which is its cause. The aesthetic core of Morgan's urban poetic is crystallised in another poem, 'The Starlings in George Square'. The starlings embody the capacity of poetry as *desire lines* to disorder the official routes and allocations of place in the city:

> At the General Post Office
> the clerks write Three Pounds Starling in the savings-books.
> Each telephone-booth is like an aviary.
> I tried to send a parcel to County Kerry but –
> The cables to Cairo got fankled, sir.
> What's that?
> I said the cables to Cairo got fankled ...
>
> I wonder if we really deserve starlings?
> There is something to be said for these joyous messengers
> that we repel in our indignant orderliness.
> They lift up the eyes, they light the heart,
> and some day we'll decipher that sweet frenzied whistling
> as they wheel and settle along our hard roofs
> and take those grey buttresses for home.
> One thing we know they say, after their fashion.
> They like the warm cliffs of man.[23]

Like his starlings, Morgan uncovers ways by which to remap the city in abeyance of what has been determined by power. In doing so, he disputes power's capacity to exclude, to deny the right to be heard or counted.

To return to Belfast, these disordering starlings also appear in Alan Gillis's poetry. In particular, 'Lagan Weir' signals both a resigned fatalism about the city's stasis and an energised resistance which perpetually disorientates established certainties:

> any way I look the writing's
> on the wall. I watch the hurly-burlyed,
> humdrummed traffic belch to a stop,
> fugging, clacking, charring the clotted air,

>   making it clear things are going to get
>   a whole lot worse before they get better . . .
>
>   That hue and cry, those hurricanes
>   of starlings swoosh and swirl their fractals
>   over towers, hotels, hospitals, flyovers,
>   catamarans, city-dwellers, passers-through,
>   who might as well take a leap and try following
>   after that scatter-wheeling circus of shadows
>   as slowly turn and make their dark way
>   homeward, never slowing, not knowing
>   the way things are going.[24]

Gillis's poetry perfectly encapsulates the spirit of desire lines, of going where you not are supposed to, or not staying where you are supposed to, of flouting the logic of what is proper and appropriate. Instead of conceding that writing about the city requires free verse or some reworked modernism, Gillis stretches the lyric to new places. The way in which his peripatetic lines adapt form beyond its usual template serves as an analogue of his broader renegotiation of the city. The twists and turns of these elaborate, imaginative pathways disorder the preordained plan. Most specifically his work challenges the idea that lyric is somehow inappropriate to the city. 'Laganside' is another good example which, as with Morgan's revision of the silence which is all Muir finds in Glasgow, contests the pessimism of Derek Mahon's 'Ovid in Tomis' in order to find an urban aesthetic that offers more than just a blank page. The 'crash and build'[25] of the poem dialectically embraces simultaneously the possibilities and containments of the city, its inequalities and yet its capacity to disorder and renew identity and belonging:

>   No wonder I'm astray, a little bit this way
>   and that way, for the dockyards and ghettoes
>   look like a grey-quiffed and tattooed uncle
>   intensely line dancing on a hot night-
>   club floor, thinking he might yet score,
>   like I've been caught with my guard down
>   by this dizzy glint and easy rapture
>   of polar and clover, wire-fence and river
>   flooding towards the basin's broken jaws
>   as if hit-and-running from a crime scene,
>   though flushed and peach-blushed with pleasure
>   at the prospect of coming to a head,
>
>   having it out once and forever
>   as the missing months and years dredge

> past the massage of washed-out slogans,
> sleek towers, ghosted union buildings,
> the river overrunning its own ledge
> to find itself played out in a final flush
> into open seas, under drizzled rain,
> while the sky arrests an outbound plane,
> and my better half lags behind to savour
> the shifting terrain, leaving me to find
> our way back to the streets, knowing
> I'll never leave here, or come back again. (76–7)

Gillis's ability to use lyric in a context in which it supposedly does not belong – the city – correlates with a wider sense of inappropriateness in which people and social experiences nominally incommensurate with art are suddenly and radically heard. Gillis's inappropriate aesthetic tallies with Jacques Rancière's work in its effort to confound the rubric by which certain literary forms are deemed to appropriately correspond with certain kinds of social experience.[26] Rancière traces his argument all the way back to Ancient Greece and the attempt to delimit the possibilities of literature in Plato's ideal republic. As Rancière explains, Plato felt art was permissible only to the extent that it would support the *ethos* of the citizenry, that it had a moral purpose. There were permissible forms of art on this basis and permissible recipients of this ethical education. This model excludes not just inappropriate artistic forms but also people deemed too vulgar to count as citizens. Concomitantly, the Aristotelian model accepts this ethical regime of prescribing literary forms but takes things further by deciding that where art is morally sanctioned it should also obey certain formal rules and laws in terms of its own structure, so that its own formal order best encapsulates the moral order of the public sphere (and here we have the basis of today's notion of genre, a set of formal appropriateness built upon an ethical code of delimitations). But Rancière argues there is much more to literature than this. He notes that one of the reasons Plato so mistrusted literature or the written word and privileged speech was that in the case of the latter, Plato could be sure of who was speaking and who was receiving the message. This is because the philosophers and citizens who met to debate had a monopoly on the public sphere, while slaves and workers were banished from the *polis* – they did not count, they had no voice there, they could not hear and misinterpret the message. So Plato felt sure that speech could be policed, in terms of its proper subject, message, receivers and context. No word could go astray, those privileged enough to be citizens could be sure what the message was and who was appropriately receiving it. Plato trusts speech to help order his *polis*: you can be sure of who is saying what, to whom, in what context, and how the recipient responds, if the *logos* is possessed by philosophers and citizens and denied to lower beings who are silenced by the ordering of public life.

By contrast, Plato fears writing because it cannot be regulated in this manner. Where speech demarcates the hierarchy between the philosophers or thinking subjects and the mute workers, writing is potentially accessible and available to everyone. It can be produced, read, disseminated or interpreted in ways and contexts that are not sanctioned by the public ordering of the *polis*. In writing, Plato cannot be sure who is the designated subject or receiver, the ethical purpose of the text and so on. In other words, even those who are not entitled to the *logos*, according to Plato, those who he would relegate to non-speaking status, have access to writing since it is capable of going to places that it should not, into the hands of those whom Plato would make mute manual workers and nothing else. Rancière uses the term 'literarity' (*littérarité*) to describe the disordering effect of literature and writing. For Rancière, democracy – in the truest sense – is a certain sharing of the perceptible, a more equitable redistribution of its sites. And, in an affirmation of the relations between the aesthetic and the political, literature is part of this redistribution, this recasting of who can perceive and speak, of what is possible and of what can be registered and acknowledged by a society. Of necessity, this process of democratisation must sunder the criteria of appropriateness that polices not only which people are deemed suitable producers or readers of literature but also the regulation of forms and genres within literature. In this sense, a static notion of poetry is the very antithesis of literature, which should not be about foreclosed labels or orders but rather a continual, rebellious recasting of what can be thought, said, registered by a society; particularly by people excluded from what prevailing logic deems appropriate, by those who wish to disagree.

Moving back to Glasgow, Tom Leonard's poetry also flouts these criteria by which access to literature may be delimited. His phonetic vernacular obviously flouts rubrics of appropriateness in terms of literary language more evidently than the other poets covered. Workers are thinkers, vernacular is the language of poetry:

> right inuff
> ma language is disgraceful
>
> ma maw tellt mi
> ma teacher tellt mi

> thi doactir tellt mi
> thi priest tellt mi
>
> ma boss tellt mi
> ma landlady in carrington street tellt mi
> thi lassie ah tried tay get aff way in 1969 tellt mi
> sum wee smout thit thoat ah hudny read chomsky tellt mi
> a calvinistic communist thit thoat ah wuz revisionist tellt mi
>
> po-faced literati grimly kerryin thi burden a thi past tellt mi
> po-faced literati grimly kerryin thi burden a thi future tellt mi
> ma wife tellt mi jist-tay-get-inty-this-poem tellt mi
> jist aboot ivry book ah oapnd tellt mi
> even thi introduction tay thi Scottish National Dictionary tellt mi
>
> ach well
> all livin language is sacred
> fuck thi lohta thim.[27]

With reference to Carson's and Gillis's Belfast, or Morgan's and Leonard's Glasgow, poetry retains the right to disagree rather than agree not only its own terms and forms but also its subjects and places. The city facilitates a challenge to our place as preordained or already agreed by both intimately known nationalist landscapes and post-nationalist terrains of diversity. The desire lines of these poets take us to places we are not meant to go, they allow those who are not accounted for to transgress into an art which conventionally would reduce them to silence. The unknown, the excluded, the unfamiliar retain their right to unsettle the consensual, settled and appropriate.

NOTES

1. Thomas Davis, *Essays Literary and Historical by Thomas Davis* (Dundalk: Dungalan, 1914), 134.
2. Quoted in J. Randall, 'An Interview with Seamus Heaney', *Ploughshares* 5:3 (1979), 17.
3. Seamus Heaney, *Wintering Out* (London: Faber, 1972), 15.
4. *Ibid.*, 6.
5. *Ibid.*, 17.
6. Iain Crichton Smith, *Collected Poems* (Manchester: Carcanet, 1992), 102.
7. *Ibid.*, 159.
8. Roland Barthes, 'Semiology and the Urban', in M. Gottdiener and A. Lagopoulos (eds.), *The City and the Sign* (New York: Columbia University Press, 1986), 87–98, 96.
9. Richard Sennett, *The Fall of Public Man* (Cambridge University Press, 1977), 48.

10. *Ibid.*, 49.
11. Ciaran Carson, *Belfast Confetti* (Newcastle: Bloodaxe, 1989), 52.
12. Ciaran Carson, *The Ballad of HMS Belfast: A Compendium of Belfast Poems* (London: Picador, 1999), 116.
13. John Wilson Foster, *Colonial Consequences: Essays in Irish Literature and Culture* (Dublin: Lilliput, 1991), 37–8.
14. Christopher Whyte, 'Imagining the City: The Glasgow Novel', in Joachim Schwend and Horst W. Drescher (eds.), *Studies in Scottish Fiction: Twentieth Century* (Frankfurt: Peter Lang, 1990), 318.
15. William Bolitho, *Cancer of Empire* (London: G. P. Putnam's Sons, 1924), 13.
16. Edwin Muir, *A Scottish Journey* (Edinburgh: Mainstream, 1979 [1935]), 102.
17. *Ibid.*, 138–9.
18. Edwin Morgan, *Selected Poems* (Manchester: Carcanet, 1985), 59.
19. *Ibid.*, 78.
20. *Ibid.*, 79.
21. *Ibid.*, 82.
22. Fredric Jameson, 'Cognitive Mapping', in Cary Nelson and Lawrence Greenberg (eds.), *Marxism and the Interpretation of Culture* (Chicago: University of Illinois Press, 1988), 347–60, 353.
23. Morgan, *Selected Poems*, 28–9.
24. Alan Gillis, *Hawks and Doves* (Oldcastle: Gallery, 2007), 60–1.
25. *Ibid.*, 76.
26. Cf. Jacques Rancière, *The Politics of Aesthetics: The Distribution of the Sensible*, trans. Gabriel Rockhill (London: Continuum, 2004).
27. Tom Leonard, *Intimate Voices: Selected Work, 1965–1983* (Devon: Etruscan, 2003), 56.

CHAPTER 14

'The ugly burds without wings'?: reactions to tradition since the 1960s

Eleanor Bell

In 'The Beatnik and the Kailyaird', first published in 1962, Edwin Morgan highlights the need to challenge the 'prevailing mood of indifferentism and conservativism' pervading Scottish literary criticism, 'a desperate unwillingness to move out into the world' and connect with the present both within Scotland and beyond. '"Scotland's heritage" is hung around our necks like a taxonomical placard. Conform or depart!' he writes, drawing attention to the neglect of experimental writers at the expense of the more dominant stronghold of the Scottish Literary Renaissance movement and its followers.[1] Morgan was one of the few writers and critics both to respect Scottish literary tradition and to interrogate its function. While denouncing often restrictive concepts of Scottish tradition, engagements with Scottishness nonetheless permeate his work, and in this way he adopts an interstitial position between the literary canon and its critique. Acknowledging that the '"Literary culture of Scotland" is a desperately plastic phrase for what people actually feel, write, speak, sing, and act', that 'obviously the literature of any place will remain to some extent as unamenable to encouragement as to polemic or apathy', he admits that 'the bristly, defensive dismissiveness of so much Scottish culture, however wellrooted it has been in real differences and real difficulties, has had a long innings and not always a very productive one, and we might as well give its opposite a chance'.[2] Since the 1960s Morgan repeatedly provided refreshing alternatives to this perceived apathy and introversion in Scottish literary studies. While he is known mostly for his diverse forms of poetry, in his critical writing he frequently stated the need to give the 'opposite a chance', whether explicitly or implicitly, and while this work has yet to receive significant critical attention, it nonetheless helps contextualise the period in significant ways. This chapter will examine his push for experimentation, the need to give the 'opposite a chance', in the context of Morgan's early work on concrete poetry and some of the fierce debates taking place in Scotland in the early 1960s. In doing so, it will also focus on

Morgan's connections with Ian Hamilton Finlay from a Scottish literary point of view, before going on to consider the work of Paul Durcan and parallels in Irish literary studies; I also want to broaden out some of the contemporary implications of these ideas for both disciplines.

While Morgan's critique of the dominance of the Scottish Literary Renaissance over Scottish literary studies has usually been measured and largely sympathetic, Finlay's position on the contrary has often been regarded as hostile and difficult; this is perhaps one of the main reasons why his work is still largely marginalised and excluded from literary discussions and anthologies. That situation, of course, was not helped by his famous disagreements with Hugh MacDiarmid, resulting in the latter refusing to be published in the *Oxford Book of Scottish Verse* if works by Finlay appeared alongside his own: Finlay's work, he wrote, 'has nothing in common with what down the centuries, despite all changes, has been termed "poetry"'.[3] It is telling that Finlay's work to this day is still omitted from the anthology. Despite MacDiarmid's being best man at Finlay's first wedding in 1948, strong temperaments and divergence of aesthetic interests led to seemingly irreconcilable differences. In the 1960s, in the period just after publishing *The Sea-Bed and Other Stories* (1958) and prior to moving to Stonypath, the garden now known as Little Sparta, in 1966, Finlay was well known for his antagonistic stance. He set himself in opposition to much of the Scottish literary scene and what he regarded as its introverted concerns. Working against this dominance in his experimentations with form, he advertised his magazine *Poor.Old.Tired.Horse* (1962–7) with a quotation from Hugh MacDiarmid, claiming that it was 'Utterly vicious and deplorable'. Following the publication of Finlay's *Glasgow Beasts, an a Burd, Haw, an Inseks, an, Aw, a Fush* (1961), a collection of eleven poems written in Glasgow dialect, MacDiarmid responded in fury with a pamphlet, *The Ugly Birds without Wings*, in which he paints Finlay and his collaborator Jessie McGuffie as 'juvenile delinquents', associating them with the 'uneducated', or 'undereducated beatniks' of the day.[4] The response was certainly lively. Finlay started a rumour that the he was to stage an anti-MacDiarmid protest march in Edinburgh during the 1962 Edinburgh International Writers' Conference from the Mound to McEwan Hall, which the magistrates, in a state of panic, created a special law to ban. There were also rumours that the next stage of their revenge would be to bombard the Edinburgh Festival with a zeppelin – an incident that, needless to say, never occurred.[5]

One of the main tensions between Scottish writers at this time, therefore, largely focused on defence of, and reaction to, tradition: a tension between MacDiarmid's Renaissance project and a growing impatience with this amongst younger writers. In 1962 MacDiarmid sent an open letter to Edwin Morgan via *New Saltire* magazine, which read:

'Question to Edwin Morgan'

Sir,

Is there even ane o' thae Beatnik poets
Wi' which the place is sae raji rife
Da'en mair than just feelin' a lassie's bloomers
And thinkin' he's seein' Life?

Yours, etc.,
HUGH MACDIARMID
Brownsbank, Candymill, Biggar[6]

In a review of *The Scots Literary Tradition* by John Speirs in the same edition of the magazine, Hamilton Finlay commented: 'I suppose I'm an angry 36-year-old man. For anger, as well as good poetry, is what has been left to some of my generation by Hugh MacDiarmid and the Scottish Renaissance. The anger, of course, is *at* the Renaissance.'[7] Many critics, however, were wholly sympathetic to MacDiarmid's reaction to these new forms of experimentalism. In his article, again in the same edition, for example, Maurice Lindsay published his response to Finlay, 'The Anti-Renaissance Burd, Inseks and Haw'. He begins by noting that 'One of the strangest manifestations of our time is the cult of the anti. We have now become familiar with the anti-novel, and with that remarkable surrender to formlessness, anti-art. Up in the van, from Scotland, comes the anti-Renaissance.'[8] Finlay and McGuffie are dismissed as young upstarts, too influenced by international, experimental literary developments to be taken seriously as Scottish writers of merit.

This need to openly critique forms of national insularity characterises much of the early 1960s Scottish literary context. One of the most significant literary events in Scotland during this period was the Edinburgh International Writers' Conference mentioned above, organised by the publisher John Calder. As one of the leading publishers of experimental writing in the 1960s, publishing Beckett, Ionesco, French writers such as Alain Robbe-Grillet, Margarite Duras, Nathalie Sarraute; American writers such as Henry Miller, William Burroughs; and Scottish writers including Alexander Trocchi and Elspeth Davie, Calder was ideally placed to organise the event. The conference, part of the Edinburgh Festival of that year, arguably laid the foundations for the Edinburgh International Book Festival as it is now known. With his extensive connections in writing and publishing, Calder brought together an unlikely combination of approximately eighty writers and thinkers, including James Baldwin, William Burroughs, Truman Capote, William Golding, Aldous Huxley, Norman Mailer, Henry Miller, Bertrand Russell, Muriel Spark and Stephen Spender. Thus the conference marked what is now generally recognised as a significant moment in literary history. According to William Burroughs, for example, it was attending the conference in Edinburgh that firmly established his literary career: 'as regards the Writers's Conference I shared with Mary McCarthy a feeling that something incredible was going on beyond the fact of people paying to listen – I could not but feel that it was indeed the Last Writers's Conference'[9]. The fact that writers such as Mary McCarthy and Norman Mailer publicly supported *Naked Lunch* strengthened the case for the text in the obscenity trial that was to result the following year.

The conference itself lasted for 5 days and covered a range of topics including 'difference of approach', 'Scottish writing today', 'commitment', 'censorship' and 'the future of the novel'. The Scottish writing day was well attended by many of the international writers and was characterised by some sensational debates surrounding the context of national identity in literature – in particular some very angry reactions to the perceived introversion and parochialism of Scottish literary studies prompted by Alexander Trocchi. The Scottish panel, chaired by David Daiches, comprised Hugh MacDiarmid, Alexander Trocchi, Douglas Young, Robin Jenkins, Alexander Reid, Walter Keir, Sidney Goodsir Smith, Edwin Morgan and Naomi Mitchison. This second day generated a huge amount of controversy at the time in newspapers, magazines and radio. Explaining his objectives for the Scottish event in the conference programme, Calder wrote:

Those Scottish writers whose reputation is principally local, may find themselves so stimulated by direct contact with some of the most brilliant minds from abroad as to spark off the long-promised renaissance in Scottish letters, and discover a major writer to conquer the world as Sir Walter Scott and Robert Louis Stevenson once did.[10]

It was at this Scottish event that Hugh MacDiarmid, in an off-stage remark, famously labelled Alexander Trocchi, William Burroughs and Ian Hamilton Finlay 'cosmopolitan scum' and where Trocchi claimed that MacDiarmid's work was akin to 'stale porridge'.[11] Trocchi asserted his view that 'the whole atmosphere [of Scottish literature] seems to me turgid, petty provincial', provocatively suggesting that his own literary works were the only developments of note in the discipline in the previous 20 years. MacDiarmid defended himself stating that actually 'he wanted no uniformity', to which Trocchi mockingly responded 'neither do I ... not even a kilt', in his bid to humiliate the tartan-clad MacDiarmid.[12]

Although the scenes from Calder's conference were particularly spectacular, there were many sensational outbursts and reactions to the seeming grip that MacDiarmid's Renaissance still had on Scottish culture at this time. Another important debate surrounded the fierce reaction to Norman MacCaig's publication of *Honour'd Shade: An Anthology of New Scottish Poetry to Mark the Bicentenary of the Birth of Robert Burns*, published in 1959, which became known as 'Dishonour'd Shade' amongst younger writers who felt that the former book was too elitist and conservative in nature, too focused on the work of Hugh MacDiarmid and the aims and objectives of the Renaissance movement, or the 'Lallans boys' as Tom Wright referred to them in 1962.[13] Alan Jackson's poem 'A Scotch Poet Speaks', for example, from 1962, self-consciously mocks what he regarded as the sentimentalism of Scottish poetry, its humour expressing an underlying bitterness towards what he perceived as the fundamental restrictiveness of the discipline at the time:

> Och I wish you hadn't come right now;
> you've put me off my balance.
> I was just translating my last wee poem
> into the dear auld Lallans[14]

In 'The Knitted Claymore', a long essay written for *Lines Review* in 1971 (also discussed here by Edna Longley), Jackson was clearly still resentful towards this dominant cultural nationalist strain in Scottish studies, commenting in *The Scotsman* of that year: 'I wrote it because I was disturbed by the publications and statements of a small number of Scottish writers over the last few years. They claim to be the proud and lonely bearers of a fine tradition but seem to me increasingly to display narrowness, reaction, loss of integrity and corruption of values.'[15] With the exception of Morgan, the work of experimental writers such as Finlay, Trocchi and Jackson has largely been neglected in Scottish studies, and until very recently their work has often been left to the interests of international art circles and the avant-garde.

Contemporaneous with 'Dishonour'd Shade', Ian Hamilton Finlay published 25 issues of *Poor. Old. Tired. Horse* from 1961 to 1967. The magazine published poetry and was very much internationally focused, the title being inspired by Robert Creeley's poem 'Please':

> This is a poem about a horse that got tired.
> Poor. Old. Tired. Horse.
> I want to go home.
> I want you to go home.

> This is a poem which tells the story,
> which is the story,
> I don't know. I get lost.[16]

It published a wide variety of national as well as international writers (Mayakovsky, József, Günter Grass, Neruda as well as concrete poets from Brazil and Cuba). This was the period immediately prior to Morgan co-editing *Scottish International* magazine (1968–74), which was also attuned to international literary developments and their impact on Scottish literature and culture, and he was also becoming increasingly interested in concrete poetry at this time. Both Morgan and Finlay were drawn towards engagements with geometric form and the embrace of technology espoused by Constructivism and Futurism. Despite their shared interests in concrete poetry there was also a divergence in their aesthetic interests: Morgan favouring self-conscious experimentation with language and cognitive ideas, such as his emergent and news poems, and Finlay focusing more intently on visual objects – the sea, fishing boats, rocks and natural settings. While Morgan often commented on his debt to Russian Futurists, such as Mayakovsky, he was clearly also influenced by the Beat and Black Mountain writers and later the LANGUAGE poets. Finlay was less interested in the work of the Beat writers, but nonetheless shared Morgan's interest in Russian Futurism and its growing influence on writers at an international level in the 1960s.

In 'Into the Constellation: Some Thoughts on the Origin and Nature of Concrete Poetry', Morgan refers to Eugen Gomringer's article 'From Line to Constellation', in which he writes that 'The aim of the new poetry is to give poetry an organic function in society again, and in doing so restate the position of poet in society ... The constellation is an invitation.'[17] For Morgan, therefore, by encouraging new forms of semantic experience the concrete poem as constellation promoted new interrelationships between time and space, complicating boundaries between reading and viewing (for example, the poem as visual object which often adopts kinetic properties where the eye can take nothing for granted). Both Morgan and Finlay were drawn to this constructivist aspect offered by concrete poetry – the focus on the poem as form in itself, with an emphasis on particular words, images and concepts. In Finlay's work we can see this focus on constellation quite literally in a poem such as 'Star/Steer', whereby, typographically, the stars in the constellation appear to be reflected in the moonlit water. Only the word 'steer' provides a sense of navigation and agency against the power of these natural forces. There is also a sense of the boat in movement, being guided by the stars in the moonlit water.

In defence of this poetry, Morgan argued: 'The concrete movement considered merely as a phenomenon has forced a whole new series of creative confrontations on the use of language, sign, metaphor, typography, and space, and in this there is no going back.'[18] Also commenting on the timeliness of concrete poetry in a letter to Pierre Garnier in 1963, Finlay asserted: '"Concrete" by its very limitations offers a tangible image of goodness and sanity; it is very far from the now fashionable poetry of anguish and self [. . .] It is a model of order, even if set in a space filled with doubt.'[19] For both writers, therefore, concrete poetry provided an outlet for conceptualising the relationship between ideas and the visual in quite liberating ways, simultaneously encouraging a heightened sense of mutability and destabilisation of meaning for the viewer.

During this period Morgan was also actively involved in translating the work of concrete poets into English (such as the well-known example of Pignatari's 'beba coca cola'). Reflecting on the concept of translation in an article in 1976, Morgan observed:

Here is another paradox; at times when states are anxious to establish their national identity and to prove the virtues of their language, they have very often in history indulged in widespread translation from other cultures; yet in the process of doing this they subtly alter their own language, joining it in many unforeseen ways to a greater confinement of almost undefined and non-specific human expression.[20]

Arguably it is this focus on the importance of 'non-specific human expression', a sense of going beyond what can be written and read in more conventional forms of poetry, that draws Morgan to the translation of concrete poetry. For Morgan, therefore, this impulse to translate concrete poets could be read as part of his own process of resisting definition, part of his own search for new possibilities for literary expression in both a Scottish context and beyond. In his attraction to the generation and translation of concrete poetry, Morgan therefore differed very markedly from MacDiarmid, who commented: 'these spatial arrangements of isolated letters and geometrically placed phrases, etc. have nothing whatever to do with poetry – any more than mud pies can be called architecture'.[21] While Morgan was always sceptical of tradition, and went as far as labelling himself an 'anti-traditionalist', he nonetheless frequently returns to issues of Scottishness and belonging in his work. Despite his resistance to MacDiarmid in 1962, perhaps surprisingly in his later work he remained ultimately sympathetic to the legacy of MacDiarmid's Scottish Renaissance project, an open-mindedness that also seems to extend to much of the Scottish literary tradition (as a nationalist with a small 'n' he carefully balanced his interests in experimentation with a measured respect for national literary tradition). On the other hand, after his initial reaction against the Scottish Renaissance movement in the 1960s, Ian Hamilton Finlay moved away from such concerns. Despite his art being literally rooted to Scotland, in the form of Little Sparta, an 'avant-gardener' as he has humorously termed himself, he remained by choice apart from the Scottish literary scene.

In 'In the Light of Things as They Are: Paul Durcan's Ireland', Fintan O'Toole observes:

One of the peculiarities of modern Irish culture is that there has been no real division between the mainstream and the avant-garde. Some writers have been more conservative about form than others, but on the whole Irish writing has been remarkable for the extent to which it is impossible to divide it into a mainstream that tries to reflect social reality on the one had and an avant-garde that is concerned to explore the limits of form and language on the other. The reason is not hard to find: Irish reality has been, in a period of crisis and change, itself so angular and odd, so full of unlikely junctions and broken narratives, that a good realist has had to be also a surrealist.[22]

For O'Toole, Paul Durcan's poetry similarly encapsulates many contradictory impulses of contemporary Irish culture, reflecting a sense of the surreal in the real, the oddness of the everyday. He comments: 'Before Samuel Beckett shocked European culture with theatrical images of things that were not happening, there were people in Ireland who had images in their heads of a theatre like his, not as an exercise in the avant-garde, but as a description of reality.'[23] As a result, Irish culture has developed a hybrid form, where traditional conceptions of mainstream and experimental poetries have necessarily become fused in attempts to record the limits of lived experience. While this lack of clear distinction between mainstream and avant-garde may initially seem at odds with the experimental concerns of the Scottish literary scene already discussed, it could be suggested that, in its attempt to map the changing nature of place, Durcan's work shares many similarities with that of Morgan.

In 1969 Paul Durcan began editing *Two Rivers* with Martin Green, a poetry journal that was to run from 1969 to 1971. The remit of the journal, as set out in the first edition, was to 'contribute to a climate more sympathetic to the writer', to provide an outlet for writers who might otherwise have difficulty in being published in an age of 'giant groups' of publishers.[24] *Two Rivers* sought to provide an alternative space for poets, therefore avoiding 'the deliberations of a group of some tycoon's hatchet-men as to whether or not the tycoon could increase his wealth out of the writer's work'.[25] Yet, central to this oppositional, DIY aesthetic was also an inherent reverence for literary tradition. In the editorial we are told: 'it is more important than ever to foster what little hope we have for a culture and language that have produced not only Shakespeare and Blake, or Yeats and Joyce, but those who we are lucky enough to still have with us; Auden, Ezra Pound, George Barker and MacDiarmid (the latter two being represented in this issue). Let us acknowledge the legislators.'[26] Whereas *Scottish International* and *New Saltire* involved a strong sense of polemic, in Durcan's publication the 'critical' was viewed as interference on an otherwise protected literary space. While antagonisms such as those found in the Scottish literary scene are absent, in this independent magazine culture there is a similar urge to resist the encroaching world of mass publishing while retaining openness to developments in experimental form.

In *Teresa's Bar*, published in 1976, this fluid space between mainstream and experiment is readily apparent. Short, condensed poems such as 'Bugs Bunny' ('There is a schoolteacher in my town and he looks like Bugs Bunny; / He is a mass murderer and I am not being funny') or 'Cahirciveen Labour Exchange' ('We all do not live in a yellow submarine – / Scream the unemployed of Cahirciveen'), while seemingly flippant, erring on the side of the zany, also simultaneously demonstrate an inherent seriousness.[27] This duality and need to flit between odd extremes is something that Edna Longley has commented on: 'Surrealism is also Durcan's most powerful weapon, crystallising incongruities between the ideal and the actual.'[28] Such playfulness with the actual is also evident in Durcan's news poems in which the sensational again inverts expectations ('Wife Who Smashed Television Gets Jail', 'Minister Opens New Home for Battered Husbands'), and in this sense he shares with Edwin Morgan an urge to defamiliarise the reader with shocking, often bizarre images: '"She came home, my Lord, and smashed-in the television; / Me and the kids were peaceably watching Kojak . . ."'[29] In *Nothing Not Giving Messages*, Morgan suggests that in his own news poems he sought to make a collage of sorts between the 'found poem' and contemporary advertising in order to experiment with perception, the ways in which perception is actually closely associated and intertwined with misperception. He writes: 'Everyone will have had some such experience as misreading a headline or placard, taking from it an entirely different meaning from the one intended. The misread meanings may be quite as meaningful as the correct one.'[30] As with Morgan, Durcan playfully inverts expectations often in order to embrace the absurdities of the experience of contemporary consumer culture, leading O'Toole to label him 'the national bard of the Republic of Elsewhere'.[31] Unlike

Finlay's concern with drawing attention to awareness and perception in more obviously abstract and avant-garde ways (for example, in his one-line poems, such as 'mower is less'), in both Durcan's and Morgan's work there is a shared interest in the 'hybrid' form described earlier: a seamless vacillation between known and unknown worlds, often in quite irreverent ways.

Durcan published *Endsville* with Bryan Lynch in 1967. Shortly afterwards he became a regular contributor to *The Lace Curtain*, a magazine edited by Michael Smith and Trevor Joyce that ran for six issues from 1969 to 1978. Whereas *Two Rivers* distanced itself from polemical engagement, *The Lace Curtain* was more akin to *New Saltire* and *Scottish International* in its openness to wider literary and cultural critical debates, its sense of tapping into the literary *zeitgeist* of the times, its oppositional stance. The second issue states:

The awarding of the Nobel Prize to Samuel Beckett affords the Irish literary establishment another occasion for pushing the lie that Ireland is an incorrigibly literary country and that Dublin is an internationally important centre of literary activity ... Dublin as a literary centre is a myth, the work of Bórd Fáilte admen, an indigenous multitude of tenth-rate non-poets and bombastic shamrock-nationalists (mostly, thank God, in exile).[32]

At the heart of *Lace Curtain* was a felt need to challenge 'national' poetry and 'native soil' modes of thinking. Influenced by Patrick Kavanagh, it controversially promoted a rejection of such common assumptions in order to challenge 'nationalism and its concomitant bogus traditionalism'[33] at all costs, suggesting that 'a whole generation of Irish poets, whose work is positively unaccommodating to lovers of Anglo-Irishism in literature, has been completely ignored as if it didn't exist'.[34] *The Lace Curtain*, in its suspicion of the remit of a 'national' poetry, shared with its Scottish counterparts a need to critique what Smith and Joyce refer to as the 'Irish literary *thing*', the 'bad habits' that held Irish literature in a cultural nationalist stranglehold. In both Scottish and Irish quarters, therefore, there was a shared impulse to resist dominant concerns surrounding heritage and perpetuation of national tradition, in order to give 'the opposite a chance', in the knowledge that to do so was to risk being further alienated from an already dominant centre.

While Scottish and Irish magazines of the 1960s and 1970s both notably contained this impulse to resist the centripetal forces of nationalist literary culture, to position themselves often in stark opposition to it, arguably in more recent decades the role of the avant-garde has become more incorporated into the mainstream and aligned with the remit of academic study.

There are, however, some notable exceptions. Building on the work of *The Lace Curtain* and the thirtieth anniversary of the New Writers' Press, The Cork International Poetry Festival, SoundEye, was established in 1997 in order to promote, and generate space for, experimental writing both within Ireland and beyond, its remit being to challenge 'simplistic notions of mainstream and margin by juxtaposing the familiar with the strange, thereby augmenting the power of each'.[35]

Writing about the role of the avant-garde in a 1992 edition of the journal *Gairfish*, dedicated to the 'McAvant-garde', and perhaps echoing the work of Tom Nairn in its usage of the term, Robert Crawford comments on the sense of 'belatedness' that surrounds the role of the avant-garde in Scotland. For Crawford, the experimentation of writers such as Morgan has still to be fully addressed from a Scottish context, and he suggests that there has subsequently been an inherent resistance to come to terms with the potential of experimental forms, such as concrete poetry.[36] In this article he also draws attention to the irony that despite his international gaze, MacDiarmid strongly critiques the work of Ian Hamilton Finlay precisely at the point where he is at the forefront of a new international movement of poetry. This resistance to avant-garde experimentation continues to inform the discipline, he asserts, partly due to the strong influence that MacDiarmid still holds over Scottish literary studies and partly due to the drive for 'a genuinely popular and accessible democratic poetry' that can be more easily incorporated into a national paradigm.[37] Following on from Crawford's points it could perhaps be argued that more recent critical engagements with concrete poetry and avant-garde aesthetics in Scottish studies have been overly imbued with the need to assert connections with Scottish literary tradition, as a way of 'making safe'.

Reaching towards a conclusion, it is also worth drawing attention to the publications of Alec Finlay, son of Ian Hamilton Finlay, in particular his recent Pocketbook series. Whilst working in an interdisciplinary way, engaging with the visual arts, literature and other media, often veering towards the avant-garde, this series has also played an important role in opening out a contemporary sense of belonging in Scotland whilst at the same time challenging its very construction. One of the most popular, *Without Day: Proposals for a New Scottish Parliament* (co-edited with John Burnside), dealt with the subject in an experimental way, drawing attention to a multiplicity of aspirations for the political potential symbolised by the new building, the accompanying CD providing recordings of public opinion from around Scotland. Yet perhaps the most apposite Pocketbook to mention here is *The Order of Things: An Anthology of Scottish Sound, Pattern and Concrete Poems* that Finlay edited with Ken Cockburn in 2001. In their introduction they comment:

> The Concrete Poetry movement is a late episode in Modernism which, when presented alongside its precursors, suggests alternative routes through the landscape of Scottish poetry as a whole. Arranging the contents of the anthology according to form rather than chronology offers surprising and often illuminating points of contact between poems, writers and eras. The anthology demonstrates the vital creative energy that comes from the interplay of tradition and experiment – a defining feature of Scottish culture.[38]

While recent concerns with the avant-garde have challenged boundaries of representation through experimentation and form, it might be suggested that there is also an openness to tradition, albeit in reconfigured ways, that differs markedly from the more adversarial kinds of experimentation taking place in the 1960s.

NOTES

1. Edwin Morgan, *Essays* (Cheadle: Carcanet, 1974), 175.
2. *Ibid.*, 158.
3. Hugh MacDiarmid, *The Letters of Hugh MacDiarmid*, ed. Alan Bold (London: Hamish Hamilton, 1984), 703.
4. See Hugh MacDiarmid, *The Ugly Birds without Wings* (Edinburgh: Allan Donaldson, 1962).
5. See Yves Abrioux, *Ian Hamilton Finlay: A Visual Primer* (Edinburgh: Reaktion, 1985).
6. Hugh MacDiarmid, letter, *New Saltire* 4 (Summer 1962), 50.
7. *Ibid.*, 79.
8. Maurice Lindsay, 'The Anti-Renaissance Burd, Inseks and Haw', *ibid.*, 61–7, 61.
9. realitystudio.org/texts/burroughs-statements-at-the-1962-international-writers-conference.
10. *Edinburgh International Festival, 1962: 'The Novel Today': International Writers' Conference: 20th–24th August, McEwan Hall, Edinburgh: Programme and Notes* (Edinburgh International Festival, 1962), 52.
11. Andrew Murray Scott, *Alexander Trocchi: The Making of the Monster* (Edinburgh: Polygon, 1991), 108.
12. John Calder, *Pursuit: The Uncensored Memoirs of John Calder* (London: Calder, 2001), 204.
13. See Duncan Glen, *Selected Scottish and Other Essays* (Kirkcaldy: Akros, 1999), 102.
14. *New Saltire: Festival Issue* 5 (August 1962), 71.
15. Alan Jackson, 'The Knitted Claymore', *Lines Review* 38 (1971), 3–38, 2.
16. Robert Creeley, *For Love: Poems, 1950–1960* (New York: Scribner, 1962), 60.
17. Morgan, *Essays*, 25.

18. *Ibid.*, 24.
19. See Ian Hamilton Finlay, *The Dancers Inherit the Party: Early Stories, Plays and Poems*, ed. Ken Cockburn (Edinburgh: Polygon, 2004), xxiv.
20. Edwin Morgan, *Nothing Not Giving Messages: Reflections on Work and Life* (Edinburgh: Polygon, 1990), 243.
21. MacDiarmid, *Letters of Hugh MacDiarmid*, 703.
22. Fintan O'Toole, 'In the Light of Things as They Are: Paul Durcan's Ireland', in Colm Tóibín (ed.), *The Kilfenora Teaboy: A Study of Paul Durcan* (Dublin: New Island, 1996), 26–41, 26.
23. *Ibid.*, 27.
24. Editorial, *Two Rivers* 1:1 (Winter 1969), 5.
25. *Ibid.*, 5.
26. *Ibid.*, 6.
27. Paul Durcan, *Teresa's Bar* (Dublin: Gallery, 1976).
28. Edna Longley (ed.), *The Selected Paul Durcan* (Belfast: Blackstaff, 1982), xii.
29. Paul Durcan, *A Snail in my Prime: New and Selected Poems* (London: Harvill, 1993), 22.
30. Morgan, *Nothing Not Giving Messages*, 261.
31. O'Toole, 'In the Light of Things as They Are', 40.
32. Editorial, *The Lace Curtain* 2 (1970), 3–10, 2.
33. *Ibid.*, 6.
34. Editorial, *The Lace Curtain* 4 (1971), 3–4, 3.
35. www.soundeye.org/a-festival-of-the-arts-of-the-word.
36. Robert Crawford, 'Thoughts about a Scottish Literary Avant-Garde', in W. N. Herbert and Richard Price (eds.), *The McAvant-garde* (Dundee: Gairfish, 1992), 26–31, 26.
37. *Ibid.*, 30.
38. Ken Cockburn and Alec Finlay (eds.), *The Order of Things: An Anthology of Scottish Sound, Pattern and Concrete Poems* (Edinburgh: Morning Star Publications, 2001), 13.

CHAPTER 15

'And cannot say / and cannot say': Richard Price, Randolph Healy and the dialogue of the deaf

David Wheatley

Contemporary poetry has reserved a special welcome for the extraterrestrial perspective since Craig Raine's *A Martian Sends a Postcard Home* (1979), and a passing Martian who turned up at a Six Nations rugby game, if such a thing can be imagined, might find itself puzzled by the use among commentators of the phrase 'Celtic nations'. The presence of France and Italy complicates things slightly, but what does the label mean, the Martian might reasonably ask, apart from 'not England'?[1] The two poets I wish to consider, Randolph Healy and Richard Price, occupy a territory somewhere between 'the Celtic nations' and 'not England', without my being able to locate where exactly they do belong; and this is both a classificatory problem and a symptom of what makes their work as distinctive and absorbing as it is. It is almost a century since T. S. Eliot wondered 'Was There a Scottish Literature?', before gingerly deciding that no, there were only British writers who happened to live north of the border.[2] It might be almost as heretical as Eliot appears to us, now, to wonder if there is such a thing as a non-Irish or non-Scottish writer anymore, one who originates in Ireland or Scotland but whose writing defiantly has nothing to do with those countries and the discourse of the nation that still surrounds so much academic writing on poetry.

Looking at Scottish and Irish poetry today, it is not difficult to find writers whose horizons are still governed in significant ways by the theme and discourse of the nation: Thomas Kinsella, Eavan Boland, Tom Paulin and Robert Crawford. At the other end of the scale it is also easy to think of writers who fail to lend themselves to this critical discourse, and whose academic reputations may have suffered as a result: Peter Sirr or Frank Kuppner, for instance. Where poetry and the nation are concerned, however, it is one of the ironies of decentralisation in these islands that, in odd ways, poetic pluralism can shore borders up as well as pulling them down. In the case of Irish-language poetry, the work of Nuala Ní Dhomhnaill has conjured an audience hugely in excess of anything it has enjoyed in recent decades. Yet this audience, I would hazard, is reading her work almost exclusively in dual-language editions, while the books she publishes in Irish alone continue to reach the same audiences as the work of Biddy Jenkinson or Liam Ó Muirthile: tiny, in other words, but tiny in a way that her very fame in translation may be serving to mask.

On the Scottish side, a similar distortion can be found in the format, often used for poems in Scots by W. N. Herbert and Robert Crawford, of Scots followed by an English glossary. A historical precedent might be the glossary used in the old Penguin *Selected MacDiarmid*, which explained his Scots words without feeling the need to extend the same treatment to the Latinate jaw-breakers of 'On a Raised Beach'. The difference here is less the choice of words for translation than the fact, in Herbert and Crawford's case, that the authors have supplied their own glosses, internalising the Penguin editors' assumption that literary Scots cannot be properly understood except through a gloss darkly.[3] The poem is effectively reverse-engineered, from glossary to text. This is not an argument against writing in Scots, but a statement of honest confusion as to whether it is a poet's responsibility to provide the reader with a user's manual for the text. To give another example of the tectonic plates of poetry and the nation colliding: it has become a political cliché to hear complaints about the absence of a devolved English assembly to go with the assemblies in Cardiff and Belfast and the parliament in Holyrood; yet in their anthology *New British Poetry*, Don Paterson and Charles Simic achieved a small measure of revanchism by deselecting Northern Ireland from the union in their efforts to break the US market for contemporary British poetry, with a Union Jack splashed on the cover, too, in what they may have envisaged as the poetry equivalent of Ginger Spice's flag dress.[4] The result, coupled with a full-tilt Paterson flyting of postmodernism (no fan of Randolph Healy or Richard Price he), is a strikingly defensive and parochial piece of anthologising, made all the more unfortunate by its designs on an unsuspecting American public.[5]

Wrong-headed and excessive though I believe Paterson's preface to be, it does at least summarise some of the most frequently held complaints against 'postmodern' poetry, or Paterson's bogeyman version thereof. To Philip Larkin, in the notorious introduction to *All What Jazz*, modernism (never mind its postmodernist bastard offspring) represented a severance of the traditional bond between artist and audience, leaving the isolated artist to 'bus[y] himself with the two principal themes of modernism, mystification and outrage'.[6] Paterson repeats the charge, retreading Roland Barthes's 'Death of the Author' to emphasise the experimental writer's contempt for the reader: 'The work of the Postmoderns *delegates* the production of meaning to the reader, their poetry being largely derelict in its responsibility to aid it. The reader is alone.'[7] While T. S. Eliot thought the modern poets 'must be *difficult*',[8] Paterson no longer sees any umbilical cord to 'literal sense':

> Difficulty and figure, in the traditional lyric poems, are where the differences of interpretation will lie. These very ambiguities often grant the reader the freedom to have that part of the poem *they have grounded in literal sense* find some emotional resonance within their individual life-experience. 'Literal sense' playing little part in the Postmodern game, the freedoms their poets grant to the reader are almost infinite, and therefore, by any commonsense standard, worthless.[9]

This is, finally, an art of radical solipsism, devoted to snuffing out communication and rejecting all aesthetics but its own ('the first literary movement to have conceived the masterstroke of eliminating the reader entirely').[10] Although I disagree profoundly with Paterson's critique, his confession in passing that 'Amongst the UK postmoderns are a handful of attractive voices',[11] coupled with the fact that he cannot bring himself to anthologise any of them, suggests that this is an ideological argument that only tangentially involves the reading of actual poems. It is, rather, a reminder of the fractious relations between critical models based on the nation and on linguistic innovation or, more accurately, that follow from using one of these models to freeze the other out. MacDiarmid's heady mix of nationalism and hyper-modernism offers an epic mandate for those who see things differently, though many Scottish writers – notably Douglas Dunn – have taken a very different path from MacDiarmid-inspired obligatory Scots modernism.

Where Ireland is concerned, much ink has been spilled in pursuit of its avant-garde, even if only to say it does not and should not exist. Edna Longley, for instance, the most consistently intelligent and articulate reader of contemporary Irish lyric poetry, has displayed a lifelong aversion to the avant-garde.[12] Much of this debate might be flippantly assigned to the category of what the American comedian Stephen Colbert calls 'truthiness', things that are not quite true but which the speaker intuitively knows to be a fact none the less. One of the tenets of avant-garde truthiness is that talk of the nation is the eternal alibi of writing which refuses to turn its attention instead to the revolution of the word.[13] Conversely, sceptics of any deviation from strict lyricism can equate experiment with a dereliction of the poet's national(ist) birthright. Describing a period of creative disillusionment in a *Poetry Ireland Review* interview, Thomas McCarthy formulates his aesthetic options in just such stark terms:

I ended up believing in the mirage of an Irish modernism to counteract the meanness of 1980s Ireland. I threw away Kavanagh and Heaney and read Brian Coffey and Denis Devlin ... A poetry that's based only on ideas of poetry is a very thin creature, a lifeless thing. I'm a pro-life poet rather than a pro-ideas poet ...[14]

Why should the opposite of Kavanagh and Heaney be Coffey and Devlin rather than René Char or Paul Celan? Patrick Kavanagh is a minor poet on the world stage, one of whose achievements was to lead to the considerably more major Seamus Heaney, but if Coffey and Devlin are minor figures, too, their minor status becomes unanswerable (non-'pro-life') proof of the irrelevance to Irish writing of all things modernist. The opposite of Irish parochialism, it should be said against this, is not Irish modernism but the world.

Here again, though, my two chosen writers complicate any premature binary between the nation and rootless cosmopolitanism. I may be denouncing binaries, but as a pair Healy and Price have a lot in common. Both have a background in small-press publishing, Price with his Vennel Press, Healy with Wild Honey Press; both have written well on science, while Price also coined the term 'informationism' for the loose group of Scottish poets that included David Kinloch and W. N. Herbert as well as himself; both use lineation and page-layout in adventurous ways; and both, despite the innovative tendencies I am describing, are anything but detached from questions of politics and the nation.[15] Healy's work is far from well known even among academic critics of Irish poetry: one further overlap between Healy and Price is the fact that, despite the proverbially symbiotic (or parasitic) relationship between the contemporary avant-garde and the academy, neither has worked in a university English department (Price works at the British Library). These are emphatically not academic poets. It was not until the publication of Healy's *Green 532: Selected Poems* in 2002 that his poems were available to a commercial audience, and his critical reception has suffered accordingly. He is discussed in Robert Archambeau's pamphlet *Another Ireland*,[16] and to John Goodby his work 'emphasises the mind's inability to make sense of a world far too vast for "the suburbia of the psyche" to grasp it and order it', with an 'implied critique of a poetry which assumes mastery of contingent flux'.[17] To Justin Quinn, Healy is notable for a 'mordantly satirical' engagement with Irish Nationalism and tradition, though '*Arbor Vitae*' is judged a failure ('ultimately ... just a collection of essayistic fragments').[18] This satirical engagement takes the form of Oulipian or Mylesian squibs such as 'The Republic of Ireland' and 'Anthem', with their anagrammatic play and rewriting of the Irish-language national anthem in English ('Sheen a fin with oil'), while 'Out-Takes' shows his more serious side, in a thinly veiled riposte to the bog poems of Heaney's *North*,[19] and the long poem I wish to consider (and defend against Quinn's negative judgement), '*Arbor Vitae*', is a meditation on cultural politics which evolves into a full-scale statement of poetics.

The back-story to the poem is Healy's discovery that his daughter is deaf and his subsequent studies in sign language. This leads him to revisit the intense debates in deaf culture between advocates of sign language and the opposing method of Oralism; Healy is particularly scathing on the effects of oral-fixated campaigns against sign language, and the evils of self-defeatingly closed intellectual systems. Under Oralism adherents of signing were 'silenced', reduced to a second speechlessness.[20] For Healy, though, obstacles to communication become the occasion and the medium for continued communication, in and through apparent silence. Beyond debates on sign language, I read the poem as part of a larger plea for radical linguistic pluralism in the face of suffocating orthodoxy. To complete the comparison, communication difficulties also feature prominently in the sequence 'Hand Held', from Price's 2005 collection, *Lucky Day*. Its poems focus on Price's daughter, who suffers from Angelman syndrome, whose sufferers exhibit 'severe learning difficulties, problems walking and sleeping, epilepsy and no speech'.[21] Price writes about the condition with sensitivity, but also with an underlying idea of expanding the possibilities of the short lyric poem to accommodate forms of speech far removed from the assumed transparent, communicative function of language.

To look at Healy's '*Arbor Vitae*' first: there is the immediate problem of how to categorise its genre. Healy is a fine lyric poet when the mood takes him, but '*Arbor Vitae*' is something more akin to a poetic essay, and in fact ends with an essay-length prose footnote. Any suspicion that this might be a poetic watering-down should be resisted; the essayistic poem-prose hybrid demands to be seen as a genre unto itself, which writers as diverse as Susan Howe, Peter Riley and Wendell Berry have tried, not to mention Bashō ('haibun' is the Japanese term for a composition that mixes poetry and prose), while Thomas Kinsella's *A Dublin Documentary* was a resourceful example (adding images to the mix too).[22] As such a rare genre, it lends itself well to another point of comparison between Healy and Kinsella: Healy's meditation on forms of attention and process, as in this example of a spider and its web:

> Start with radial strands, then go
> alternately anticlockwise up and clockwise down
> for four circumspins

> then anticlockwise all the way to the centre
> and home, sixty thousand individual movements later.
> Ocsha, sacoh.
> If moved before the end
> will continue the web where it left off
> however useless either result.²³

The Oulipo writings of Raymond Queneau and Georges Perec are an important part of modern avant-garde writing in French, but, despite the work of American Oulipo writer Harry Mathews, it has always been an open question as to how well these techniques translate into English. Healy uses one Oulipo stand-by, the anagram, throughout '*Arbor Vitae*', with a series of variants on the five letters of the word 'chaos': hence the 'ocsha' and 'sacoh' in that last extract, which a reader might otherwise be forgiven for thinking were herbs or Native American tribes. Opponents of signing associate it with unhealthy secondariness, just as experimental writing is often seen as turning its back on the sacred primacy of the spoken word for a Babylonian, written dialect: '*Why learn a sign when they might learn a word*'; while among the 'central doctrines' of Oralism is the belief 'that one form of language excludes another' (10). Exclusion returns in the claim that 'deep signing is never used in front of hearing people', with its overtones of travellers' cant, designed to keep the outsider at bay; but society returns the exclusion in kind, as 'the unemployment rate among deaf people is 91%' (12, 13).

Section 2 of the poem invokes evolution, Saint Augustine, Neolithic ideograms and electronic switches in the brain activated during the language acquisition process. Healy's fascination with DNA encoding extends to acrostic inscriptions down the left-hand margin, reminiscent of the scribal marginalia of Old Irish manuscripts and other pre-Gutenberg texts, not to mention how interesting these proved to the Joyce of *Finnegans Wake*, and John Cage in his 'mesostics' too. The concern with patternings that might escape our usual readerly attention leads to forms of expression that prefer a covert to a visible show of control; as a note comments, a flock of birds is an example of a complex structure without a centre or leader: 'you never see one of them fall off, yet no one is in charge' (29). If the deaf community described by Healy appears closed, it is so in a self-sufficient and sustainable way, thriving without outside interference, as in the examples produced in section 3 of the deaf communities in eighteenth-century Martha's Vineyard, Massachusetts.

The interest in alphabets and characters straddles Poundian ideograms and Robert Graves's writings on the druidic tree alphabet in *The White*

Goddess. Graves liked to joke that the Chinese symbols in Pound had been copied 'from the nearest tea-chest',[24] but if Pound's influence is at work here it has been humanised and shamanised at once. Here is the opening of section 3, with its semiotic creation myth:

> The hieroglyph representing a hand,
> became *daleth*, a door,
> later *delta*,
> now *d*, a voiced alveolar stop.
>
> *But what they don't know*
> *is what what they do does.*
>
> *Guth*,
>
> where voice becomes God,
> as the suffixed zero-grade of the same root. (21)

Healy's treatment of etymology makes for an interesting comparison with Heaney's. Where *North* relishes its echo chamber of Norse rumblings, and its Anglo-Irish stand-off of Saxon versus Gaelic roots, coding difference and conflict into linguistic history, for Healy the prospect of tribal differentiation leads only to confusion and downfall. A note describes the sectarian legacy of Oralism in Ireland, where sign language fragmented into different dialects for men, women, Protestants and Catholics. The belief in the centrality of the voice, otherwise phonocentrism, evokes a political echo from the Troubles, when the voices of Sinn Féin members would be dubbed on television, lest the literal oxygen of publicity incubate the seed of terror in the watching public in a way that mere actors' voices could not. This has, of course, been written about by an Irish poet with many affinities to Healy's work, Ciaran Carson, most semiotic of writers, and someone who has written about Esperanto, too, a language much beloved of his father. Unlike Heaney's dark etymologies and historical taproots, Healy's signing is presented as a language with all its generative grammar on open display, as in the schemes of one Abbé de l'Epée to provide signs with 'verb endings, articles, prepositions and auxiliaries' (21).

The idea of a conflict-free lingua franca is given extra licence by Healy's account of signing being adopted by the hearing in Martha's Vineyard, and his belief that everyone should learn to sign. This would help overcome the identification of deafness with deficit, and the chauvinism towards other language models that Healy finds everywhere among non-signers. I have invoked Joyce, and Healy shares with *Finnegans Wake* not just a compulsion to riff on the origins of language and an interest in made-up lingua francas

(Volapük features a lot in the *Wake*) but also a fascination with frogs: on the second page of the *Wake* Joyce parodies Aristophanes' frogs, and in his poem 'Frogs' Healy pays tribute to a species that is, he tells us, 'ten thousand times older than humanity' (59). The nineteenth-century French philosopher, or pataphysician rather, Jean-Pierre Brisset (1837–1923), developed a theory that human language developed from frogs, which Jean-Jacques Lecercle has described in *The Violence of Language*.[25] His theories are frankly insane, but while recruiting them to a reading of Seamus Heaney's childhood encounters with frogs would be an absurdist step too far, they chime perfectly well with the do-it-yourself philosophising of '*Arbor Vitae*'. The fact that crackpot etymologising and frogs both abound in Joyce's *Finnegans Wake* reminds us, by way of Brisset, of the Joycean textures of Healy's work. With his interest in obscure theology and saints, not to mention his joyous carnality, another point of comparison for Healy's work here would be Aidan Mathews, a similarly neglected and Joycean Irish poet. Such connections are more than a little arbitrary, and need not be overly belaboured, but serve to suggest the larger poetical vistas, both within Irish poetry and beyond, that Healy's work enables.

Lest I fall into the nets of monocular nationalism I have been denouncing, however, I must also attend to the Scottish half of my comparison, Richard Price. As mentioned, the child in 'Hand Held' suffers from Angelman's syndrome, and from the outset the opacity of language features heavily. As in Les Murray's poem about his autistic son, 'It Allows a Portrait in Line Scan at 15', there is a dramatic tension between the poet's language and the desire to do justice to, and even in some way internalise, the neurological condition it is describing. Language difficulty becomes both theme and trope. Angelman's is caused by a chromosome deficiency, and the child's confusion in 'Speech Absent' ('Can't speak any. // Doctor Dad didn't know: "What's a bad chromosome?"') recalls another moment in Murray, when the 'simple man' in 'Twelve Poems' says '*Mum, what sex are we?*', with its characteristic Murray concern for the excluded.[26] In Murray we have a 'simple man', and in Price the child puzzlingly refers to herself with a male pronoun as 'Dopey': 'Dopey's dopey – / the drugs he's on'.[27]

Communication between child and parents requires ingenuity: these are language games lacking the rules to make them games for more than one, as in the poem 'Thanks':

> Fractures, but mending
> slowly, needs care,
>
> and nothing forensic –

> 'dad', 'mum',
> no crime tonight,
>
> can't make the sign
> of the remote
>
> (so the sign
> that's a hand on a shoulder,
> the sign
> of the eyes, of the mouth –
> your eyes, your
>
> mouth).
>
> *That's plenty,*
> *plenty thanks.* (76)

There is something Creeleyesque in the knotted ambiguities here, especially when combined with the more cross-grained line-breaks: 'fractures' is a verb, not a noun, it would seem, but where is the subject, and the subject, too, of 'no crime tonight'? The 'remote' is a television remote control, but the girl is one of the socially 'remote' whose trouble with making signs has consigned her to that status. It is not only the child who is having difficulty 'mak(ing) the sign' here, many readers will feel by now, though the poem still manages to end by signalling that all is well: '*That's plenty, / plenty thanks.*' Marjorie Perloff has recently made a bid to redeem the term 'constructivist',[28] and as a label it is especially apt in describing poetry like this that bares the device, in the Russian formalist phrase, and shows us the process of its self-assembly. Another poem, 'So the palm faces', echoes Healy's work in talking us through the actions required to sign the words 'affection' and 'love', while 'See, touch on the baby gym' reads like Sylvia Plath's 'You're' in reverse, a kind of 'I'm', based on the child's own perceptions. If these poems are sudden snapshots, Price resists the temptation to tidy up or wipe any mess away, and in 'Little Bear', which allows the child to speak in her own voice, he refuses to fast-forward to what she is 'trying' to say, repeating the sound 'mah' thirteen times and pointing out that this is in fact her word for bear, not mother.

Charles Olson may have become a poet more invoked than read outside innovative circles, but the language and layout of Price's work show how much he has learned from the author of 'Projective Verse'. Michael Donaghy referred to Olson as a 'virtuoso typist' whose theories of one perception leading directly to another, he thought, were less about radical poetics than 'a recipe for staying awake',[29] but Price's measured tread through the short lines of 'the frame' (not from the 'Hand Held' sequence), and sense of pauses and breathing spaces, place him in the company of Niedecker and Oppen as a poet able to think intelligently outside the frame of iambic verse:

> a seine net
> casting the hill
>
> *
>
> (this overlaps to frame, includes)
> the sky overlaps to frame, includes
>
> *
>
> triangulated
> by the peak
>
> we are
> our bearings
>
> at home
> in our surroundings   (14)

We make, not merely find, our bearings and surroundings. In 'Fob', the poet's daughter does her own exploring of the signifying field, licking a television screen. Don Paterson, that foe of postmodernists, has a Rab C. Nesbittesque poem called 'Postmodern' which also involves a television screen, but what the girl and Paterson's character have in common is a problem working out where signification stops and reality begins.[30] The girl changes channels (she thinks) with the on/off button, and her lick-mark becomes a football that scores a goal and wins the World Cup for Scotland. In 'The World is Busy, Katie', Price records his daughter's hyperactivity winding down: the world is busy, 'but *you're* the world' (90). An older, now pejorative term for Angelman's is Happy Puppet syndrome, which allows for the sufferer's happiness on condition that she be a kind of human toy. But the poem is not a baby-sitter putting the girl down for the night while it talks over her head in adult language: Price repeatedly allows his language to follow his daughter instead to states of aporia and speechlessness: she solicits a fatherly laugh and 'laughs beyond thinking, /and cannot say /and cannot say' (80). He drains the potential for tweeness out of these moments with frank confessions of his powerlessness to help. After one of his daughter's fits, 'I'm worse / than a bead of nothing. / Subtract // everything you could hope for. / Keep subtracting' (82). Some poems seem to subtract themselves from the page in front of our eyes, as in 'Surely the certainties', whose search for 'words for / sounds of / sounds – / of sounds' (96), turns up a pair of empty parentheses, like a frozen, speechless grimace, while in '121' it is the poet's daughter who unsuccessfully tries to coax speech from her father:

> Dad!
>
> Speak!
>
> Speak, Dad.
>
> I can do a twenty-piece puzzle.
>
> Dad!
>
> Dad? (100)

One final comparison I might add to the mix is to the work of George Oppen. In the 1970s, Oppen began to suffer from Alzheimer's disease, and as his condition began to rob him of speech, he posted notes to himself on his study wall, some of which were first published in Robert Creeley's *Best American Poetry, 2002*. 'Music, that marvel / trying to exist / out of this forest to come forth', reads one.[31] Last-gasp utterances, they seek out the point at which poetry disconnects from speech, meaning and poetry itself, yet, movingly, somehow conspire to put this dilemma to work. There is something grisly about this example, but as Thomas Mann said, 'A writer is a man to whom writing comes harder than to anyone else',[32] and both the Oppen and Price examples remind us how difficulty, in poetry of this kind, can answer to human and artistic needs very far removed from neo-modernist affectation or obscurantism, enabling the representation of conditions at the extreme end of human experience and suffering, such as Alzheimer's or Angelman's. What the poems I have considered by Price and Healy have in common is a concern with the resistant, opaque dimension to language, the naïveté of our assumptions of its naturalness, and a fear of the coercion lurking under the belief in a single linguistic practice, to the exclusion of others: the tyranny of 'speaking for'. No writer can ever truly speak 'for' the silenced other, and Price and Healy do not flatter themselves that they can.

I have no interest in rehashing familiar debates about the mainstream and the avant-garde, and believe it would be a disappointing reading of Healy and Price that found nothing better than that to discuss in their work. Nevertheless, each poet leaves the reader with a sense of expanded possibilities: in their subject matter, their form, their diction, their conception of the poem as a field of composition, whether in the short lyric poem, the sequence, the poem-prose hybrid or the conceptual poem. They stretch and renew the Irish and the Scottish poem, if one wants to read them against that backdrop, and if neither writer exactly demands to be read in such a manner, they do not rule the exercise out either. Nevertheless, the idea that the 'Irish' or 'Scottish' in the 'Irish poetry' or 'Scottish poetry' should receive equal billing with the word 'poetry' would, I think, not be a constructive way of reading this work. Ireland, Scotland, these nations we live in, are so much material, and these poets take or leave them as such. In this they chime with the work of other interesting younger Scottish and Irish poets such as David Kinloch, W. N. Herbert, Justin Quinn and Caitríona O'Reilly, none of whom writes exclusively under a lyric or innovative flag, or indeed under any flag at all. And for this reminder, too, as for their other reproofs to our lazier assumptions in approaching the contemporary Irish and Scottish poem, Healy and Price deserve our thanks.

NOTES

1. The literature on Celtic identity and Celticism is vast, but for a contemporary overview see Murray Pittock, *Celtic Identity and the British Image* (Manchester University Press, 1999).
2. T. S. Eliot, 'Was There a Scottish Literature?', *The Athenaeum* (1 August 1919), 680–1. For a Scottish perspective on Eliot, see Robert Crawford, *The Savage and the City in the Works of T. S. Eliot* (Oxford: Clarendon, 1987).
3. An Irish response to the same condition of linguistic in-betweenness can be found in Eiléan Ní Chuilleanáin's 'Gloss/Clós/Glas', in *The Girl Who Married the Reindeer* (Oldcastle: Gallery, 2001), 46. *Glas* (pronounced 'gloss') means both 'lock' and 'green' in Irish, suggesting nationalist as well as linguistic cryptologies at work in the traffic between English and Irish.
4. In strict constitutional fact and contrary to both Ulster Unionism's self-image and Seamus Heaney's assertion that 'Ulster was British, but with no rights on / the English lyric' (Heaney, *North* [London: Faber, 1975], 65), Northern Ireland is a part of the United Kingdom but not British.
5. An important context for a full understanding of *New British Poetry*'s anti-postmodern diatribes is its hostility to Keith Tuma's (American-edited and postmodern-friendly) *Anthology of Twentieth-Century British and Irish Poetry* (Oxford University Press, 2001).
6. Philip Larkin, 'Introduction', *All What Jazz* (London: Faber, 1970), 23.
7. Don Paterson, 'Preface', in Don Paterson and Charles Simic (eds.), *New British Poetry* (Saint Paul: Graywolf, 2004), xxix.
8. T. S. Eliot, 'The Metaphysical Poets', in *Selected Prose*, ed. John Hayward (London: Penguin, 1953), 118.
9. Paterson and Simic (eds.), *New British Poetry*, xxx–xxxi.
10. *Ibid.*, xxxiii.
11. *Ibid.*, xxix.
12. Longley's account of Irish poetry since Yeats omits any reference to the avant-garde, whether in its present or 1930s incarnation, nor do any writers of that

description feature in her *Bloodaxe Book of Twentieth-Century Poetry*, with its preference for Louis MacNeice and the generations of Northern Irish poets who follow his example. Her hostility to the avant-garde, however, should not blur possible linkages between these otherwise non-communicating traditions, such as Derek Mahon's championing of Beckett's poetry and his rating of Thomas MacGreevy and Denis Devlin 'higher than any "Movement" poet' (Derek Mahon, letter to *The Irish Times*, 10 July 1982).

13. For a sympathetic account of Irish innovative writing, but one that places it in a state of near-apartheid from the rest of Irish poetry, see J. C. C. Mays, 'Flourishing and Foul: Six Poets and the Irish Building Industry', in *Irish Review* 8 (Spring 1990), 6–11. Mays's article elicits a withering rejoinder from Edna Longley in the same issue ('The Irish Poem', 55–7). The most comprehensive effort to date to supply contemporary Irish poetry with a 1930s modernist pedigree can be found in Patricia Coughlan and Alex Davis (eds.), *Modernism and Ireland: The Poetry of the 1930s* (Cork University Press, 1995).

14. 'An Interview with Thomas McCarthy: Catherine Phil MacCarthy in Conversation with Thomas McCarthy', *Poetry Ireland Review* 95 (October 2008), 60.

15. Both Wild Honey Press and Vennel Press have internet presences, at www.wildhoneypress.com and www.hydrohotel.net. The term 'informationist' was coined by Price in the journal *Interferences* and popularised in Price and W. N. Herbert's anthology *Contraflow on the Information SuperHighway* (Staines: Southfield, 1994).

16. Robert Archambeau, *Another Ireland* (Bray: Wild Honey Press, 1988).

17. John Goodby, *Irish Poetry since 1950: from Stillness into History* (Manchester University Press, 2000), 302–3.

18. Justin Quinn, *The Cambridge Introduction to Irish Poetry, 1800–2000* (Cambridge University Press, 2008), 109–10.

19. Randolph Healy, 'Out-Takes', in *Rattling the Bars* (Old Hunstanton: Oystercatcher, 2009), 5.

20. For a history of sign language and the debates surrounding it, see Douglas C. Baynton, *Forbidden Signs: American Culture and the Campaign Against Sign Language* (Chicago University Press, 1996).

21. Richard Price, *Lucky Day* (Manchester: Carcanet, 2005), 69. All further quotations from Price's work will be from this volume, with page references in-text.

22. Thomas Kinsella, *A Dublin Documentary* (Dublin: O'Brien, 2006).

23. Randolph Healy, 'Arbor Vitae', in *Green 532: Selected Poems 1983–2000* (Cambridge: Salt, 2002), 10. All further quotations from Healy's work will be from this volume, with page references in-text.

24. Robert Graves, *The Crowning Privilege: The Clark Lectures, 1954–1955* (London: Cassell, 1955), 123.

25. Jean-Jacques Lecercle, *The Violence of Language* (London: Routledge, 1990).

26. Les Murray, 'It Allows a Portrait in Line Scan at 15', in *Collected Poems* (Manchester: Carcanet, 1998, 430–1); 'Twelve Poems', in *The Biplane Houses* (Manchester: Carcanet, 18).

27. Price, *Lucky Day*, 76.
28. See Marjorie Perloff, *Twenty-First-Century Modernism: The 'New' Poetics* (Oxford: Blackwell Publishing, 2002).
29. Conor O'Callaghan, 'Interview with Michael Donaghy', *Metre* 4 (Spring/Summer 1998), 75–84, 81. For Charles Olson's theory of poetics see 'Projective Verse', in Ralph Maud (ed.), *A Charles Olson Reader* (Manchester: Carcanet, 2005), 39–49.
30. Don Paterson, 'Postmodern', in *God's Gift to Women* (London: Faber, 1997), 51.
31. George Oppen, 'Twenty-Six Fragments', in Robert Creeley (ed.), *The Best American Poetry, 2002* (New York: Scribner, 2002), 131–5, 131.
32. Thomas Mann, *Death in Venice, Tonio Kröger, and Other Writings*, trans. David Luke and Helen Tracey Lowe-Porter (New York: Continuum, 1999), 84.

CHAPTER 16

On 'The Friendship of Young Poets': Douglas Dunn, Michael Longley and Derek Mahon

Fran Brearton

Douglas Dunn's sonnet 'The Friendship of Young Poets', from his second collection, *The Happier Life* (1972), celebrates what its speaker also claims to have missed out on in his youth. 'My youth', he writes, 'was as private / As the bank at midnight, and in its safety / No talking behind backs, no one alike enough / To be pretentious with and quote lines at'.[1] If there is a certain security and solidity to this kind of isolation, there is also by implication an acknowledgement that allied with the youthful pretension of young poet-friends is a competitive and critical dialogue that helps bring the mature poetic voice into being. Significantly, the poem is also, in its way, a love poem, evocative of Morgan's 'The Unspoken', with its 'talking in whispers in crowded bars / Suspicious enough to be taken for love'. The love of literature, talking about poetry in public, is as potentially subversive as the homosexual love that dare not speak its name in Morgan's poem.[2] There may be a 1890s homoeroticism and decadence to the 'Two young men, one rowing, one reading aloud. / Their shirt sleeves fill with wind...'; but the closing image – 'from the oars / Drop scales of perfect river like melting glass' – is about capturing in poetry an ideal, and therefore in true decadent sense a transient beauty, a passing moment symbolic also of the aesthetic potential inherent in the friendship. The rowing, the 'reading aloud', the billowing sleeves, are about rhythmical momentum, about the ebb and flow of dialogue and ideas.

'[A] boat on the river' is a phrase Michael Longley takes from Dunn's poem as the title of his introduction to a selection of Irish poems from the 1960s, a decade in which friendships and connections were established between a generation of Irish poets – Mahon, Longley, Heaney, Boland, Kennelly, Simmons and others. He comes close to arguing that the decade for him resembled the 'ideal scene' at the close of Dunn's poem.[3] Resistant to the emphasis given to Philip Hobsbaum's 'Group' in critical accounts of Northern Irish poetry since the 1960s, Longley points out that 'Friendship was the important thing'. If, as he avers, 'Creative spirits seldom occur singly', it is not ultimately creative writing workshops, or such organised activities, that bring about talent and originality, even if they might provide a forum in which such talents flourish.[4] Rather, Longley is drawn to Dunn's poem because it epitomises his own undergraduate experience of literary friendships in Trinity College Dublin – most notably that with Derek Mahon. Being pretentious with Mahon, quoting lines at each other was, as Longley suggests, a vital part of his poetic development: 'In my forty years of writing', he says, 'nothing (apart from my marriage) has been more important than that first friendship with Mahon.'[5] The penultimate poem of Longley's first collection, *No Continuing City*, 'To Derek Mahon' (later retitled 'Birthmarks: for D.M.') posits Mahon as his co-conspirator, a fellow subversive who whispers in bars about poetry: 'You alone read every birthmark, / Only for you the tale it tells . . .' Mahon and Longley are the friends who see each other's failed poems – 'the poems we cannot write'.[6] The drafts that ended up in the fireplace of their Merrion Square flat ended up there in part because their stringently critical friendship encouraged a more ruthless self-editing than might otherwise have been the case. Mahon reciprocally dedicates his first collection, *Night-Crossing*, 'For Michael and Edna Longley'; when his first selected poems appears, *Poems 1962–1978*, 'The Spring Vacation', one of the poems from *Night-Crossing* (originally titled 'In Belfast'), appears with a dedication 'for Michael Longley' (the poem had originally been dedicated to Longley in the 1965 pamphlet *Twelve Poems*); when his next *Selected Poems* appears in 1991 and the 'The Spring Vacation' is omitted, a new dedication to both Longleys is added, appropriately enough, to 'An Unborn Child', also, like Longley's early 'Birthmarks', a poem about the process of creativity, about bringing the poem-child into the light.

The complex dedicatory network is accompanied, particularly through the late 1960s and early 1970s, by an exchange of letters between Michael Longley and Mahon (and also between Edna Longley and Mahon) which constitute a sustained critical commentary on each other's writings. The years immediately following their undergraduate friendship mark a continuation, by post (as Mahon travelled first in the States, then settled in London, while Longley returned to Belfast) of the practice established in Dublin of showing each other all new poems, and commenting on them; in diluted form, the exchange of poems, although not the critical commentary, continues for many years after this – certainly into the late 1970s. As Mahon's letters from the 1960s make evident, the criticisms offered were more astute than diplomatic. In a letter to Edna Longley (*c.* January 1967) he begins:

Am in receipt of your rare and priceless missive which has joined Virginia Woolf, James Joyce, a CBC stage-frieze, the Proclamation of the Irish Republic and the Ulster Covenant on the wall behind the bar, the toast of Toronto. Your casual and quite terrifying vivisection (didn't feel a thing) of the Mahoon [sic] canon has left me stunned . . . I will refute you with laboured nonchalance in my next letter. For the present I will merely record the fact that the poem 'Charles River (Charles who?) in January' does not exist. Does not exist, do you hear me? On this issue, however I may have wavered on 'Night-Train Journey', I am prepared to fight, if need be, on the beaches and in the streets, which would be a spectacle worth seeing in itself.[7]

Edna Longley seems here to have begun an early campaign (which failed) to prevent Mahon's habitual revision of a 'finished' poem and the editing of poems out of his *oeuvre*. In turn, Mahon's critical insights into Michael Longley's early poems possibly help to facilitate Longley's emergence from writer's block in the late 1960s, as Longley's comments on Mahon's work lead to a process of self-reflection about his own development. The correspondence also shows the (male) combativeness of the friendship. Referring to a poem ('What would you say if I were to tell you darling') which he later, and this time justifiably, discarded, Mahon writes: 'when you describe it as "chopped prose" I cannot be silent. Do you really think it's that bad? Or are you not just so prejudiced in favour of the regular pentameter that you are blind to a modest experiment with form and rhythm?' Going on to respond to Longley's 6 months without writing, he asks: 'Could it be that you are working in an exhausted vein in terms of form? If the words don't just fall into place any more in accordance with your preconceived notion of what a really good, genuine, solid-gold, floodlit and revolving Poem should be like, why not loosen up a bit [. . .] really go slack – write humorous verse, pastiche ee cummings, a new Dingleberry Song, a Hobsbaumiad, riddles.'[8]

If Dunn, who matriculated at the University of Hull in 1966 after several years working as a librarian, missed out on the 'friendship of young poets' in its decadent teenage undergraduate phase, and missed out, at least initially, on this kind of intense yet supportive rivalry, he is nevertheless a part of this network of relations, tangibly so from the early 1970s onwards. (Longley and Mahon are his near contemporaries, Longley born in 1939, Mahon in 1941, Dunn in 1942). '[M]y devotion to poetry', he observes, 'was one I could not declare even to myself with a round, warm, full-blooded conviction until my late twenties.'[9] Nevertheless, before Dunn came out as a poetry-lover, he was an early closet reader of contemporary poetry. As he notes in his chapter for this book, he first came across Mahon's work in an early 1960s copy of *Arena*, recognising Mahon immediately as a writer with whom he had an 'affinity'. (The poem in question is the uncollected 'Lovers wake to difference', which appeared in *Arena* in the Spring of 1963.)[10] They share, among other things, a fascination with lives, afterlives, vanishing empires, changing civilisations, lost utopias; they share at times what Mahon describes in 1971 as the 'metaphysical unease in which all poetry of lasting value has its source'.[11] That Mahon's *Lives* and Dunn's *The Happier Life*, their second collections, both appeared in 1972 is a happy coincidence, since the poems – and poets – were already in dialogue with each other. Dunn and Mahon met, probably in 1971, when both were (unsuccessfully) interviewed in London for a post at East Anglia University, and they corresponded – and exchanged poems – for many years following.[12] In 'The Hunched', from *The Happier Life*, Dunn writes: 'They will not leave me, the lives of other people ... Mysterious people ... Whose lives I guess about, whose dangers tease.'[13] Here and elsewhere in the collection his fascination with lives, epitomised by, and in, a sometimes bizarre selection of objects, finds an echo in Mahon's own 'Lives'; his vision of 'the rubble fields where once houses were' ('Under the Stone') and the sometimes bleak metaphysic of poems such as 'The Philologists' or 'The Hour', allied with a will to transcendence and a yearning for immanence, also reverberates with Mahon's early 1970s aesthetic as epitomised in poems such as 'Beyond Howth Head' or 'An Image from Beckett'.

To some extent, of course, the sensed affinity with Mahon comes not just from their being of the same generation; it is also to do with their respective Scottish and Northern Irish backgrounds. The friendships with other poets begin a little later for Dunn, but it is worth noting that his self-educating through the 1960s takes him in some similar directions to Longley and Mahon too – through Donald Hall's *Penguin Book of Contemporary American Poetry*, for instance, and, like Mahon, to America itself from 1964 in what he suggests was a 'flight' from the provincialism of Scotland. Returning to Scotland in January 1966 to avoid being drafted for Vietnam, Dunn subsequently allowed his call-up notices to accumulate inside the pages of a book significant for Mahon, Heaney and Longley too – Robert Lowell's *Selected Poems*.[14] In the poem 'Realisms: to Derek Mahon', from his third collection, *Love or Nothing* (1974), Dunn writes 'You have the same concern', trying to find out and write the 'real stuff'. In the process of 'Whittling down / An algebra of "sympathies" ... To a sudden Nothing', Dunn's 'glimpse of housing estates' is wonderfully evocative of Mahon's 'Houses along the shore' and 'Washing hung to dry' in 'An Image from Beckett' as is the poem's downwards trajectory to 'the moist limits / Of Zero, where worlds turn / Vegetable or wiry // And politics dissolve,

/ Gunfire is silent'.[15] Also shared with Mahon is the pressure of being 'elsewhere', living in England: there are, he writes, 'friends who stayed // To admonish our absences' (21). (Mahon responds to, and implicitly repudiates, such an admonishment from James Simmons in 'Afterlives' from his third collection, *The Snow Party* [1975].) Partly explaining the affinity with Lowell, too, is an inevitable fascination with, allied with a complex rejection of, forms of religious and political evangelism that nevertheless prove at some level inescapable:

> We puff our alphabets
> Back to the oratorical soup
>
> Of Ireland, Scotland,
> To a thousand stabs in the back,
> The inhabitants of opposition.
>
> Our cities of shipyards,
> Belfast, Glasgow, fervent closures
> Of protestantism dispensed with –
>
> We never escape them ...   (20)

'Realisms' explicitly connects Dunn with Mahon both in terms of the inevitable pull of origins, an awareness of the possible futility of poetry, and yet in the retention of a 'dream' of 'The existential clarity / Of love and nothing, the peace / Poets in patched trousers deserve' (21). That his closing line redefines his title – from *Love or Nothing* to 'love and nothing' – is significant, too, a look back perhaps to Wallace Stevens (with his 'listener, who ... nothing himself, beholds / Nothing that is not there and the nothing that is'),[16] but also Mahonian in its vision of a kind of terminal fulfilment. Hugh Haughton notes that Stevens's observation – 'it is one of the peculiarities of the imagination that it is always at the end of an era' – is 'particularly true of Mahon'.[17] In Mahon's 'Going Home: for Douglas Dunn', published a year later in *The Snow Party*, the Hull shift workers 'vanish for ever / With whisper of soles / Under a cindery sky'.[18] 'Going Home' is Mahon's reciprocal gesture, a response to 'Realisms' (the poems mimic each other's forms) which draws on a visit to Dunn when he was working, with Larkin, in the university library at Hull ('the dreary capital of cod', as Dunn calls it).[19] The poem preserves poetry as the 'end of the rainbow', but whether the poem is then the crock of gold, or what value it possesses, is open to question. Mahon revisits the 'limits / Of Zero' with a metaphysical bleakness, a Larkinesque deflation, and a residual Beckettian humour, even as he resists (with a typical 'As if') a definitive statement:

> A sunken barge rots
> In the mud beach
> As if finally to discredit
>
> A residual poetry of
> Leavetaking and homecoming,
> Of work and sentiment;
>
> For this is the last
> Homecoming, the end
> Of the rainbow –
>
> And the pubs are shut.
> There are no
> Buses till morning.　　　　　　　　　　　　　　(6–7)

As the silent gunfire in 'Realisms' suggests, Dunn's encounters with Irish writing and writers in the early 1970s, and his visits to Belfast in the same period, served to hone his awareness of critical issues and (political) pressures faced by the poet, since these were, as he acknowledges, experienced in a particularly acute form by Northern Irish poets in the early years of the Troubles. It was, he observes, 'an experience against which poetic technique (let alone imagination) had to contend in ways which to most of us are hardly imaginable'.[20] Invited to read in Belfast in 1971 (a time when the Troubles were so bad others refused such invitations), Dunn met Heaney and Longley for the first time, and was also introduced to Muldoon, then an undergraduate at Queen's. He sustained, in the years that followed, a correspondence with Michael Longley (as well as with Mahon) that continued some of the practices established by the two Irish poets in the 1960s – the exchange of poems and ideas about poetry, the critical insights into the other's work. As with the Mahon–Longley correspondence, many of the observations are, from the outset, deliberately testing, and in time the analyses become both more searching and more revealing of the letter-writer's own aesthetic. In April 1973 Dunn writes to Longley:

I've read your poems, and like them. In the Double-Barrel sequence [he is referring to a draft of the sequence 'Riddles' which appears in *Man Lying on a Wall* (1976)], I think you've made a few lapses of style. The poetic behind such dense poems is, I feel, of a sort that forbids easy tricks like similes ... Longer poems can stand or benefit from similes. They make short poems into flashes of insight, here now, gone in a minute. Similes, I feel, are the journalism of poetry, and I am myself hoping to rub my own gifts in that direction out, and keep only those which have mystery. Mallarmé or someone said that if you write a poem too clearly, or plainly, you do something unforgiveable to the mystery of life which all poems celebrate in some arcane way. The way of writing ought to be as mysterious as the life it celebrates. Dr Dunn's tutorial is now over for the day ... Derek starts a job in advertising next week. We can expect all sorts of soapy and cosmetic similes in his poems in the future.[21]

Equally characteristic of such exchanges is a liberating irreverence towards other writers ('Glyn Hughes even looks like Shakespeare, but writes about sex as if he'd just discovered it yesterday'; 'Had lunch with Dennis Enright [...] A great man, Dennis, and his new book, out early in May, is extremely good, quite different from his others')[22] the effect of which is to generate, if not a shared agenda, at least some sense of aesthetic affinity with the letter's recipient.

Criticism of the other here is also exploration of the self. The point is made more explicitly in a letter from 1975, where Dunn writes to Longley:

I begin to feel about your poems in general that you might be hemming your imagination in by too rigorous an application of your idea of craft in verse. Having met you just a few times, I'd chance my assessment and say your imagination to be shaggier of mind and wilder of restraint than your poems let on ... The poems are good, some really catching. Yet there does seem like an absence of flame where fire is being suggested. Oh dear, I think I'm talking about myself.[23]

Dunn is astute here in his response to an inward-looking period in Longley's writing life, later to be countered in the more public mode and the expansiveness, formal and thematic, of *The Echo Gate* (1979) and *Gorse Fires* (1991). His own move from *Love or Nothing* to the more public concerns and outspokenness of *Barbarians* (1979) is implied here too. That Dunn has been one of the more astute critics of Irish poetry, particularly that of his contemporaries, owes something to this level of informal critical exchange in the early years of friendship; that he is unusually sensitive to the problems faced by the Northern Irish writers informs his own practice too. It may be significant that of two poems written by Dunn in 1972 directly about his experience of visiting Belfast, the more obviously Troubles-related poem – 'Spring: No Spring' – is the one he is unable to finish. (Both poems were sent to Michael Longley in June 1972; 'Spring: No Spring', he explains, 'isn't really finished yet', and appears to have been subsequently abandoned.) An attempt to respond to images of 'Stray citizens ... carried dead across the screen' and the brutalities of 'the province of mad opposites', its overt anger ('Death makes them true democrats, / Victims for a song with sentimental jaw') mars its effectiveness, and the uneasy final lines point up the difficulty of finding a mode of response to Northern Ireland's violence:

> Quaking boy with the bomb, girl with a gun,
> Spring has no history, but is flowers and light;
> In the hushed bombardment of the night
> Your prim and barbarous dreams attack the sun,
> And little leaves are weak as flies or hair
> To put out politics from the Irish fire.[24]

More successful, however, is the (also unpublished) poem 'Landing at Belfast', sent at the same time and written, Dunn tells Longley, 'in your mother-in-law's house, inside a fag packet, and on the back of a receipt':[25]

> LANDING AT BELFAST
>
> I could never get used to forever sunlight
> Above the clouds, a nowhere of summer,
> Or Antrim's grey Lough tilted like a roof.
> Some transport goes underground,
> Earthbound on silver rails, momentous power
> Each second of each universal hour,
> Stronger than the energies of human love.
>
> Upwards a spreading stain of small birds;
> A rabbit leaps on turf the Spring will touch
> Beneath jet-stream diagonals, our fighters
> Flexing their bravado for the eyes of murderers.
> My first glimpse of armed men makes me wave to you
> Four hundred miles away, across a sea,
> A mountain chain; but I've no machine to speak with.
> Our hearts that imitate the dot and dit
> Of radio, signal stupidly and don't transmit.
>   Douglas Dunn, 15, vi.72, Tursac[26]

The poet, who cannot live (metaphorically) in the 'clouds', is grounded in place, implicated in the earthbound, even as he is also cautiously aware of his own unfamiliarity with this terrain, his outsider status epitomised by his slightly panicked and emotional reaction to that 'glimpse of armed men'. The poem is sensitive to the fragility of 'human love' in the face of other forms of 'power', which, being 'momentous', can seem to take on a life of their own. Yet in its acknowledgement of a failure to communicate across time and space, the poem in another sense does have the 'right' machine to speak with; it does 'transmit' in the way the fighter planes, for all their signals and codes, cannot; it builds its own momentum and energy to counter an unfamiliar and violent world.

In 1975, Dunn edited *Two Decades of Irish Writing: A Critical Survey*. One of the earliest books to respond, not just to the literary 'renaissance' in the North of Ireland, but to the felt need for a critical reassessment of Irish literature and history more generally over the previous 30 years, it contains essays which have become essential reading for those working on modern Irish poetry – Seamus Deane's 'Irish Poetry and Irish Nationalism', Seamus Heaney's 'The Poetry of Patrick Kavanagh: From Monaghan to the Grand Canal', Michael Longley's 'The Neolithic Night: A Note on the Irishness of Louis MacNeice'. It is perhaps neither irrelevant nor coincidental that the book is edited by a Scottish poet living (at the time) in England. If Dunn's connection to contemporary Northern Irish writers was one of the factors which brought about the project, his own displacement and his complex sense of identity may be pertinent too. Outlining briefly in the introduction the complex and contradictory positions taken by some of his contributors in relation to place and history, nationalism and provincialism, Dunn draws the following broad conclusion about Irish writing:

What appears to be different in contemporary Irish writing, from, say, English writing, is that Irish writers are forced to make practical *decisions* about their perspectives on history, politics and literature. As a catalyst to talent, the thinking demanded of an Irish writer in that situation ought not to be discounted. There is a searching turbulence about John Montague's poems, for instance, or John McGahern's novels, an absence of comfortable mannerisms and relaxations, which indicates not only seriousness of purpose but a scrupulousness of forethought rare in contemporary English letters.

Having been consistently developed, history and locality are unavoidable themes (or a reaction against them is unavoidable for some). They are themes not merely inherited, but real. 'Searching the darkness', a phrase from Thomas Kinsella ... indicates that if the subject of history can be unattractively sombre, it has the inevitability of night.[27]

What is at work here is not what sometimes appears as envy of Northern Irish writers, whose war on the doorstep was, as Edna Longley points out, seen by some (in England) to provide them with a 'raw material' that could only be to their aesthetic advantage, if they would so use it.[28] Rather, it is a recognition of the difficulty posed by a traumatic history, and about the need to respond to that difficulty through 'scrupulousness of forethought'. In this, Dunn echoes the scruples and scrupulousness of poets such as Heaney, Longley and Mahon, whose perpetual questioning of self and history eschews knee-jerk and over-simplified reactions to the Troubles, even as they acknowledge the need, as Michael Longley puts it, 'to respond to tragic events in [their] own community, and ... to endorse that response imaginatively'.[29] There may also be here an implied comment that Scottish writers are more likely to do that kind of thinking too, and that English writers really need to start it.

Two Decades acknowledges the inevitability of history as subject-matter; but the point of the book is also to reread contemporary writers away from the burden of their literary past: 'Yeats, Joyce, and Beckett', he notes, have received a level of attention that has contributed towards 'the emergence of "Irish literature" as a subject'. But while this has its benefits for the younger writers, it is also 'less than helpful to Irish writers ... that they stand to be forever discussed in relation to what Yeats said on the same subject, or ... the extent to which a novelist might echo patterns found in Joyce'.[30] Elsewhere in this book, Dunn discusses ways in which his generation responded to, and differentiated themselves from, older poets and groups such as the Movement. Friendship, he makes clear, is not about belonging to a particular 'school' of poetry; rather, what those friends have in common is a scepticism about schools and movements per se. In an early editorial for the Trinity undergraduate magazine *Icarus*, Michael Longley makes the same point: 'At the moment there are in College several lyric poets, but it is being too optimistic to read into this happy coincidence a movement, and dangerously presumptuous to grace it with a capital "M".'[31] Friendship is, however, about a process of poetic education, and if there is no 'group' affiliation as such there may yet be the sense of a common endeavour: 'Young poets', Heaney observes, 'thrive on a mixture of affection and disaffection ... they get involved in a kind of vying that's not quite rivalry, more an aspiration to outdo, pure and simple.'[32] Yet at the same time, and in the pressure wrought by the political situation in the 1970s, he acknowledges some commonality of purpose: 'All of us, Protestant poets, Catholic poets [...] probably had some notion that a good poem was "a paradigm of good politics" [...] And without being explicit about it, either to ourselves or to one another, we probably felt that if we as poets couldn't do something transformative or creative with all that we were a part of, then it was a poor lookout for everybody.'[33]

Part of that common endeavour is also an absorption of, and differentiation of oneself from, one's predecessors – 'appraising our roots', as Longley puts it, 'and at the same time scanning the horizon'.[34] One instinctive tendency, as Dunn suggests in *Two Decades*, is to link writers back to the earlier dominant figures in their particular national tradition (reading Mahon in the light of Yeats, or Dunn in the light of MacDiarmid, for instance). Another is to follow the trails left by writers themselves at particular times – so the 1960s obsession with American poetry, with its exciting new horizons, its seeming 'escape' from provincialism, accounts in part for the pervasive influence of Lowell, Stevens, Frost, Wilbur and others, on contemporary Irish and Scottish poets of this generation. But 'appraising ... roots' is more complex than that, and for the three poets under discussion here, one of the more obvious precursors (and for Dunn a friend too) is the poet – Philip Larkin – whose association, however misleadingly, with a quintessential 'Englishness' seems to make him a slightly uncomfortable presence in the telling of Irish or Scottish literary history.

In so far as Larkin has been associated with Irish poetry, he tends to take his place in a line that runs Yeats–Larkin–Heaney, in which Heaney reacts against Larkin's own reaction against Yeats, thereby ensconcing Larkin as the English filling in an Irish sandwich. Larkin left Queen's University Belfast (where he worked as librarian from 1950 to 1955) before Seamus Heaney came to it. But Philip Hobsbaum, who began the Belfast 'Group' in 1963, was so profoundly (and, as far as his own poems are concerned, unfortunately) influenced by Larkin that Belfast in the mid-1960s is where Larkin's significance is seen to come into play. Heaney, in writing critically on Larkin too, has also co-opted him into his pantheon of precursors. Yet Hill, Larkin and Hughes had also been powerful presences for Mahon and Longley in their undergraduate days in Dublin. In an unpublished prose piece from the 1970s, Longley writes, revealingly, that 'The Irish psyche is being redefined in Ulster, and the poems are born ... out of a lively tension between the Irish and the English traditions ... Books of the undeniable stature of Larkin's *The Whitsun Weddings* ... encourage a fruitful schizophrenia in someone trying to write poetry in Ireland.'[35] Larkin's influence in particular is traceable in their first books as it is also in Dunn's *Terry Street*. Longley's 'Graffiti', for instance, is, consciously or unconsciously, in dialogue with Larkin's 'Sunny Prestatyn'. Mahon's 'First Principles' revisits the anxieties of Larkin's 'If My Darling', where the female invades and occupies the poet's (disturbed) psyche. Similarly, Mahon's metaphysical sweep is not as tonally remote from Larkin as it might seem (the close of 'Day Trip to Donegal' bears comparison with the tonal shift at the end of 'Next, Please'); Longley also obliquely echoes a Larkinesque tone, diction and idiom (as in 'Home is So Sad' or 'An Arundel Tomb') in 'A Headstone'.

If such intertexualities are under-explored (not least in the ways they both absorb and, more importantly, revise Larkin), the association between Dunn and Larkin has tended to receive more attention because the two became friends in the late 1960s while Dunn worked at Hull University Library. (Dunn also later introduced Larkin to Tom Paulin, whose first collection also shows an indebtedness to the older poet.) Larkin advised on Dunn's early poems, and helped him to get his first collection, *Terry Street*, published with Faber in 1969.[36] Living and working in close proximity as they were, the Dunn–Larkin relation is one of direct friendship and mentoring. But the fact that Larkin was such a significant figure for Irish poets later to become close to Dunn is revealing too. One rather too easy perception of Dunn's work is that his early poems, whose overt subject-matter is the working-class area of Hull in which he was living at the time, and which are seemingly written under the influence of Larkin, are somehow less 'Scottish' than his later ones. He expresses frustration with this kind of attitude more generally in a letter to Edna Longley in 1973: 'Some Scotsmen don't think I'm Scots enough, which infuriates me, as a), I don't see any need to be anything, and b) I'm as much Scots as they are.'[37] Longley's attribution of Larkin's importance in terms of a 'fruitful schizophrenia' for the Northern Irish poet perhaps helps to explain Larkin's influence on, and interest for, Dunn in a different way too, the Scottish writer living and working in England, assessing in his own first collection the importance of elsewhere. And in a reverse scenario, when Larkin's influence on Longley and Mahon is perfunctorily noted, it is sometimes seen as compromising their status as 'Irish' poets,[38] despite the corrective offered by Mahon in 1971: 'there is a group of poets whose ambiguous ethnic and cultural situation extenuates in their work the Anglocentricity Devlin dislikes. These are the Northern poets – Protestant products of an English education system, with ... an inherited duality of cultural reference. They are a group apart, but need not be considered in isolation, for their very difference assimilates them to the complexity of the continuing Irish past ... Whatever we mean by "the Irish situation", the shipyards of Belfast are no less a part of it than a country town in the Gaeltacht.'[39]

Studies of Scottish or Irish poetry tend, understandably, to look first for Scottish or Irish influences respectively, the critical coherence of the narrative established through a national line of descent. Yet however persuasive and necessary those patterns might be (not least in their marketability), the tendency to tell literary history along national lines obscures some poetic relations. It sometimes obscures lines of friendship that step outside national bounds, such as the 'friendship of young poets' seen in Dunn, Mahon and Longley: Dunn is largely unmentioned in the major studies of Irish poetry to have appeared in the past decade, despite his pervasive presence in the lives and writing of the North's leading poets during the 1970s. 'National' literary histories may also obscure lines of influence that cross national borders, perhaps particularly so when the influence is English and thereby politically (colonially) suspect: yet the extent to which, as suggested here, Larkin's influence works productively, and in different ways (even through modes of resistance to it), for writers outside an English tradition can serve also to revise any complacency or insularity found in English as well as Irish or Scottish criticism.

Since the concern of these poet-friends is with poetic not national identities, then in that context at least, the friendship of poets can cut across large-scale solidarities to become emblematic of future possibility. To say so is to risk sentimentality, as if the friendship of young poets were a cure for political ills. Heaney perhaps takes the argument as far as it is possible to go when he says of his friendships with other Northern poets: 'In the end, I believe what was envisaged and almost set up by the Good Friday Agreement was prefigured in what I called our subtleties and tolerances – allowances for different traditions and affiliations, in culture, religion and politics.'[40] In the 1970s, Michael Longley may have been too optimistic about what friendship could accomplish: his verse letters to Simmons, Mahon and Heaney in *An Exploded View* (1973) implicitly call for a form of unified poetic resistance to political violence.[41] Yet that his addressees reacted tetchily rather than rallying to the call is, of course, part of the point and, ironically enough, a measure of how much the relationships are to be trusted: friendship is the sound basis for productive argument as against ideological deadlock. Longley implicitly acknowledges in 'A Boat on the River' that this might all be the stuff of nostalgic dreams: 'As I think back to the friendships of the 60s, I find myself believing again in a sodality of the imagination.' Nevertheless, as he goes on to suggest, the real importance of the friendships lies in the affirmation of the individual poetic voice, whose effect may then be incalculable: 'as Eugene Montale puts it: "only the isolated communicate. The others – the men of mass communication – repeat, echo, vulgarise the words of the poet".'[42] Perhaps Longley's only 'mistake' in the verse letters of the 1970s was in attempting to render explicit something that must inevitably function under the surface, as impossible to pin down as Dunn's 'scales ... of melting glass'.

NOTES

1. Douglas Dunn, 'The Friendship of Young Poets', *The Happier Life* (London: Faber, 1972), 14.
2. Edwin Morgan, 'The Unspoken', *New Selected Poems* (Manchester: Carcanet, 2000), 36.
3. Michael Longley, 'A Boat on the River: 1960–1969', *Watching the River Flow: A Century in Irish Poetry*, ed. Noel Duffy and Theo Dorgan (Dublin: Poetry Ireland, 1999), 141.
4. Michael Longley, letter to Heather Clark, n.d. *c.* 2002. Private collection.

5. Michael Longley, interview by John Brown, *In the Chair: Interviews with Poets from the North of Ireland* (Cliffs of Moher: Salmon, 2002), 89.
6. Michael Longley, 'To Derek Mahon', *No Continuing City* (London: Macmillan, 1969), 55.
7. Derek Mahon to Edna Longley, n.d. (*c*. January 1967). Longley Papers, collection 744, Robert W. Woodruff Library Special Collections, Emory University, Atlanta.
8. Mahon to Michael Longley, n.d. (*c*. December 1966). Longley Papers, collection 744.
9. Quoted in Robert Crawford and David Kinloch (eds.), *Reading Douglas Dunn* (Edinburgh University Press, 1992), 5.
10. This is the only poem by Mahon to appear in *Arena* in this period. See Jody Allen-Randolph, 'Derek Mahon: Bibliography', *Irish University Review* 24:1 (Spring/Summer 1994), 132.
11. Derek Mahon, 'Introduction', *The Sphere Book of Modern Irish Poetry* (London: Sphere, 1972), 12.
12. Douglas Dunn, conversation with the author, 12 January 2010.
13. Dunn, *The Happier Life*, 38.
14. See Jane Stabler, 'Biography', *Reading Douglas Dunn*, 7–8. Dunn's immigrant status on his visa – he was working in the States – rendered him eligible for the draft.
15. Douglas Dunn, *Love or Nothing* (London: Faber, 1974), 19–21.
16. Wallace Stevens, 'The Snowman', *Collected Poems* (London: Faber, 1955), 10.
17. Hugh Haughton, *The Poetry of Derek Mahon* (Oxford University Press, 2007), 93.
18. Derek Mahon, 'Going Home', *The Snow Party* (London: Oxford University Press, 1975), 6. The poem was also published as 'Going Home' in *Poems 1962–1978*. It was then dropped from his next *Selected Poems* (1991) and has not subsequently been reprinted by Mahon. The title 'Going Home' was given in the *Selected Poems* and subsequent *Collected Poems* (1999) to a poem which in *Poems, 1962–1978* had been called 'The Return: for John Hewitt'. Incidentally, 'The Return', which was one of the new poems of *Poems, 1962–1978* also invites comparison with Dunn's poem of that title, which is the final poem in Dunn's 1979 collection, *Barbarians*.
19. Dunn to Michael Longley, 15 June 1972. Longley Papers, collection 744.
20. Douglas Dunn, 'The Poetry of the Troubles', review of Michael Longley, *Selected Poems, 1963–1980*, in *Times Literary Supplement* (31 July 1981), 886.
21. Douglas Dunn to Michael Longley, 27 April 1973. Longley Papers, collection 744. (The letter is signed 'Gerard de Nerval'.)
22. *Ibid.*
23. Dunn to Longley, 6 April 1975.
24. Dunn to Longley, 15 June 1972.
25. *Ibid.*
26. The poem was sent to Longley in a letter of 15 June 1972 and a typescript is held with the Longley papers, collection 744, Emory University. I am grateful to Douglas Dunn for permission to reproduce the poem in its entirety here.

27. Douglas Dunn (ed.), 'Introduction', *Two Decades of Irish Writing: A Critical Survey* (Cheadle: Carcanet, 1975), 2–3.
28. See Edna Longley, *Poetry in the Wars* (Newcastle: Bloodaxe, 1986), 94. She quotes a review by Peter Porter from the early 1980s in which he observes: '[The Ulster poets] have more urgent matter to write about than most, but they commonly opt for style rather than message.'
29. Michael Longley, letter to *The Irish Times*, 18 June 1974.
30. Dunn, 'Introduction', *Two Decades*, 1.
31. Michael Longley, Editorial, *Icarus* 34 (June 1961), 1.
32. Dennis O'Driscoll, *Stepping Stones: Interviews with Seamus Heaney* (London: Faber, 2008), 76.
33. *Ibid.*, 123.
34. Longley, 'A Boat on the River', 141.
35. Untitled and undated prose piece. Longley Papers, box 37, folder 21, collection 744. A reference to the burgeoning younger generation of Muldoon and Peskett places this around the mid-1970s.
36. See Jane Stabler, 'Biography', *Reading Douglas Dunn*, 8–10.
37. Dunn to Edna Longley, 18 April 1973.
38. See, for instance, Declan Kiberd's 'Contemporary Irish Poetry', in Seamus Deane (ed.), *The Field Day Anthology of Irish Writing*, Vol. 3 (Derry: Field Day, 1991), 1364, in which he argues that Longley has 'more in common with the semi-detached suburban muse of Philip Larkin and post-war England than with Heaney or Montague', that he is aligned with 'British post-modernism' rather than Irish writing. One suspects a certain sectarianism may inform such critical perspectives, since Heaney's indebtedness to Ted Hughes in his first collection, *Death of a Naturalist*, appears not to have prompted suggestions he is more English country town than Co. Derry farmland.
39. Mahon, 'Introduction', *The Sphere Book of Modern Irish Poetry*, 13–14.
40. O'Driscoll, *Stepping Stones*, 123.
41. The issue is discussed at length in Fran Brearton, *Reading Michael Longley* (Tarset: Bloodaxe, 2006), ch. 2. See also Douglas Dunn's discussion of the 'Letters' sequence in 'Longley's Metric', *The Poetry of Michael Longley*, ed. Alan J. Peacock and Kathleen Devine (Gerrards Cross: Colin Smythe, 2000), 21–4.
42. Longley, 'A Boat on the River', 141.

CHAPTER 17

'No misprints in this work': the poetic 'translations' of Medbh McGuckian and Frank Kuppner

Leontia Flynn

Little would seem to unite Medbh McGuckian's dislocated lyricism with the mock epigrams and poetic parodies of Frank Kuppner. Yet, as well as being close contemporaries, both poets have occupied, in their respective Northern Ireland and Scotland, positions on the outer rim of the established poets of their generation; both combine formalism with avant-garde or experimental sensibilities, and both have perhaps experienced a falling-off of their readership in recent years. This, in turn, may be related to a certain *unco-operative* quality which the poets also share. Questions were raised about their audiences' patience long before either really put it to the test. James Simmons famously went so far as to suggest that McGuckian's poems were 'a salutary joke by one who hates the excesses of reviewers or literary critics or bad poetry and knows she can elicit rave reviews by writing an alluring sort of nonsense';[1] Robert Crawford foresaw diminishing returns to Kuppner's tricks and repetitions, and suggested: 'For some readers, Kuppner's work proves too obsessively repetitive, tries too hard to show off.'[2] In addition to examining these traits, this chapter will argue that Frank Kuppner and Medbh McGuckian also repeatedly present poetry as a kind of translation. I will sketch the different ways in which their 'translations' work, and suggest briefly what this insistence on literary mediation might be intended to keep at bay.

While Frank Kuppner's attraction to cultural otherness was announced with his first collection, *A Bad Day for the Sung Dynasty*, and Robert Crawford has commented on the poet's relishing of 'translatorese',[3] the element of translation in Medbh McGuckian's work is perhaps less well known. At the beginning of her career, the difficulty of McGuckian's work was often felt to be the result of deliberate veiling of meaning. McGuckian once characterised her poetry as 'A whirlpool around me to protect the inner inwardness ... There must always be this inner inviolability to it. The language is just spinning around all the time, and it's never going to be "This is what happened"',[4] and some feminist commentators have speculated that within the whirlpool of the poem were 'female erotic truths, to which the canon offers limited hospitality'.[5] Yet if McGuckian's poems frequently refer, self-consciously, to their withholding of their 'secret', some of them also describe their obscurity as the result of the poetry's status as *translation*. This is perhaps particularly so with the work of her mid-career (although, like Kuppner, McGuckian's prolific output quickly renders designations such as this outdated). 'Visiting Rainer Maria', from *Marconi's Cottage*, concludes triumphantly: 'Because / the *it* of his translation may mean silence, / But the *she* of mine means Aphrodite',[6] while in 'Clotho', from the same collection, McGuckian seems to begin by addressing her muse, 'Music is my heroine', before finishing with the lines:

> I am possessed of such strength
> That I knock down my servant,
> My house god, my all-powerful
> Mistress of tone, and her moan
> Comes clear-cut from another world,
> As if translating.[7]

In interviews, the poet has also commented on her attraction to this 'other world' and its voices, for whom she is a medium: 'I feel that actually every poem I write is a resurrection of some individual', she has said, 'it's a biography, a conversation, a reworking of someone's life. My words are just to rekindle some of their life that is spoken through me.'[8] Precisely *how* the language of her poetry brings about this 'resurrection', however, has been suggested only recently.

For while McGuckian may hint that she is channelling poetic predecessors in a mystical act of inspiration, research by Shane Alcobia-Murphy has suggested that the 'other world' from which her words issue is a solidly textual one – in other words, more prosaically, it's a library. Alcobia-Murphy, who has investigated the poet's method of composition, has found that the poems are collage-like structures, or works of bricolage.[9] Therefore, although the intertextual nature of *some* McGuckian poems, such as 'The Dream Language of Fergus' (which is entirely made out of words and phrases from a translation of Osip Mandelstam's collected essays),[10] has been known for some time, now it seems possible that *all* of McGuckian's poems have been written this way. Within *Marconi's Cottage*, certainly, Alcobia-Murphy's findings point to a large number of poems with such intertextual sources. To name only four, 'Visiting Rainer Maria' is drawn piecemeal from a study of Osip Mandelstam by Clarence Brown, and the last lines are an inversion of Brown's remark about the difficulty of translating Mandelstam's 'Silentium'.

In their original context, the words refer to Brown's comment on Richard McKane's version of the poem: 'The "it" of my translation means silence; the "she" of his meant "Aphrodite".'[11] The poem 'Gigot Sleeves', with its mysterious female figure and striking imagery of dress, also borrows its phrases, this time from Winifred Gérin's study *Emily Brontë*;[12] 'A Small Piece of Wood' is drawn from a translation of Tatyana Tolstoy's memoir of her father, *Tolstoy Remembered*;[13] and 'Road 32, Roof 13–23, Grass 23' is taken from Susan Chitty's study of Gwen John, *Gwen John: 1876–1939*.[14] The title of the last poem, obliquely explicated in a footnote, refers to Gwen John's adoption of 'tonal modelling': 'she made notes like the following on the backs of drawings: "Road 32, roof 13–23, grass 23, black coats 33"',[15] and, in fact, Chitty's book suggests that John was an expert in tone. If 'mistress' is the feminine version of 'master', in the sense of 'Old Master' (although with very different connotations), it may also be Chitty's text in translation – 'my all powerful mistress of tone ...' – that we hear at the end of 'Clotho'.

Alcobia-Murphy's discovery certainly sheds light on McGuckian's poetic effects, and on the 'erotic fluency' which Alan Jenkins observed in her earliest work, relating it to the 'endlessly proliferating phrases' and 'syntactical surprises' of John Ashbery's poetry.[16] However, the contention that the poet regards her acts of bricolage as *translation* needs further explanation. What kind of translations are these? Leaving aside for now the oddity of the materials McGuckian chooses to rework (academic studies – and often, in *Marconi's Cottage*, studies of women), they are, most notably, *unacknowledged* translations. Moreover, the text books from which she borrows tend to reflect on this very process. Thus, Clair Wills has noted the significance of a remark by Russian poet Marina Tsvetaeva in a series of letters between Marina Tsvetaeva, Boris Pasternak and Rainer Maria Rilke, from which the title 'Visiting Rainer Maria' likely derives. Tsvetaeva describes poetic composition thus:

Today I would like Rilke to speak – through me. In everyday language this is called translation. How much better the Germans put it – *nachdichten*! Following in the poet's footsteps to lay again the path he has already laid. Let *nach* mean follow, but *dichten* always has a new meaning. *Nachdichten*, laying a new path all traces of which are grown over instantaneously. But 'translate' has another meaning: to translate not into (into Russian, for example) but also to (to the opposite bank of the river). I will translate Rilke into Russian and he, in time, will translate me to the other world.[17]

McGuckian's 'Visiting Rainer Maria', in turn, lays a new path 'all traces of which are grown over instantaneously', making an entirely new poem out of existing words and phrases. Its vocabulary is drawn from Brown's text more substantially and transformed more completely than is some of McGuckian's other appropriated work. For example, lines at the end of the poem suggesting romantic struggle – 'For four more virgin months I have been / *Not* his, *not* his, *not* his, *his*' – entirely transform Tsvetaeva's account, quoted in Brown, of waving Mandelstam's train off as he departs from the Crimea: 'The cars go past: not his, not his, not his ... His.'[18] The essay by Osip Mandelstam on which McGuckian relies most heavily in 'The Dream Language of Fergus' likewise contains sentiments which also seem to approve McGuckian's poetic process. As well as describing poetic material, in a way which seems to look forward to theories of intertextuality, as 'a carpet fabric containing a plethora of textile warps differing from one another only in the process of coloration ...'[19] Mandelstam claims that *Dante's* poetic mode was essentially translation:

The secret of Dante's capacity resides in the fact that he introduced not a single word of his own fabrication. Everything sets him going except fabrication, except invention ... He writes to dictation, he is a copyist, he is a translator ... He is completely bent over in the posture of a scribe casting a frightened sidelong glance at the illuminated original he borrowed from the prior's library.[20]

If McGuckian has been found to introduce 'not a single word of [her] own fabrication', the unoriginal materials Alcobia-Murphy has uncovered behind (or beneath – or *within*) McGuckian's work now point to a convergence of ideas about appropriation and translation, recycled as the very building blocks of her poetry. Phrases from 'Harem Trousers' have been shown by Alcobia-Murphy to derive from Simon Karlinsky's study of Marina Tsvetaeva, *Marina Tsvetaeva: The Woman, Her World and Her Poetry*. In turn, this study, should we read it, discusses *Tsvetaeva's* tendency to appropriate sources without signalling the practice. Like McGuckian, the Russian poet proclaimed a mystical relationship to the sources and Karlinsky notes that, like McGuckian, her works baffled their readers by refusing to signal what they were 're-telling'.[21] So, too, the phrase 'I said I must find it, using the feminine form of must', from 'Visiting Rainer Maria', derives from a letter, quoted by Clarence Brown's study, from Osip Mandelstam to his wife Nadezdha. It describes how, separated from her, he imagines her speaking through him – in rather the way Tsvetaeva desires Rilke to speak through her: 'Yesterday, without meaning to, I thought to myself "I *must* find it" – using the *feminine* form of "must" – for you, that is, you said it *through* me.'[22] On a more literary level, Mandelstam also practised the appropriation of sources in a way that was 'oblique and atmospheric'.[23] Therefore McGuckian speaks through words by or about artists and writers who believed *they* themselves were vehicles for the words and lives of others. The 'sources' with which McGuckian makes her poems continuous form an apologia for poetry as *inherently* unoriginal, intertextual and dialogic – an act of simultaneous translation. Since the texts to which she refers (fleetingly and invisibly) echo back the mysterious, vatic and sibylline figure of McGuckian herself, rather than touching discursively on their subjects, there is also more than a whiff of the wild goose chase about the whole thing.

If McGuckian is making a point to her more intrepid readers about poetry's *un*originality, Frank Kuppner signals his preoccupation with 'copyism' and translation much more explicitly. In the case of his poetry, the joke (for the humour of Kuppner's enterprise is more overt too) is also repeated. From the 511 quatrains which comprise *A Bad Day for the Sung Dynasty*, Kuppner insistently presents his work as partial translations of, accompanying annotations to, or comments on, existing sources. His work may be a response to something found in books (*A Bad Day for the Sung Dynasty* was apparently prompted by a book on Chinese art by Oswald Siren; the prose work *A Very Quiet Street* (1989) is a rereading of casebooks about the a famous murder trial which took place in Glasgow in the early twentieth century); it may be the reproduction, along with lacunae, of a manuscript of bawdy 'classical epigrams' ('The Uninvited Guest'), a riff on *The Waste Land* ('West Åland or Five Tombeaux for Mr Testoil'),[24] or other arcane philosophical ponderings, but seldom is it presented as something originating with the author. Instead, the 'I' of *A Bad Day for the Sung Dynasty* is encountered in the act of interpreting or speculating on 'scenes' of Sung Dynasty life. And while this figure may seem to be, as Robert Crawford notes, Kuppner himself looking at Chinese art in the library, at other times the 'I' disappears entirely, or remains implicit (as foreign interpreter or translator) only because the mundane and slapstick vignettes recorded seem fragments of a larger, hardly comprehended whole: 'A man is standing among the trees, singing / And I have to admit, I have no idea why he is doing it.'[25] Again, Crawford has noted that this estrangement, or tone of puzzled, strained decipherment, 'robs us of the sense of the precise location of the writer's voice';[26] and that Kuppner's 'literary techniques involve both secrecy and self-protection'.[27] Rather than self-expression or personal disclosure, Kuppner's poems turn on the constructions placed on things – on the 'scholar' baffled by the ancient text, or the little man in the middle of the universe unable, imaginatively, to transcend it. In this way, they resonate with a figure at the end of one of the interwoven threads of McGuckian's text: Dante the hunched scribe in the prior's library as imagined by Mandelstam.

They may also remind us of the 'modern scriptor' heralded by Roland Barthes: 'the hand, cut off from any voice, born by a pure gesture of inscription (and not of expression)'.[28] Indeed Barthes directly invokes the notion of 'copyism' in 'The Death of the Author':

> We know now that a text is not a line of words releasing a single 'theological' meaning (the 'message' of the Author-God) but a multi-dimensional space in which a variety of writings, none of them original, blend and clash. The text is a tissue of quotations drawn from the innumerable centres of culture. Similar to Bouvard and Pécuchet, those eternal copyists ...[29]

If this sounds strikingly like McGuckian's very literal 'clash' of unoriginal words, Kuppner's third volume, *Ridiculous, Absurd, Disgusting*, actually contains a 'Lost Work' voiced by a divine being – the late 'author-God', perhaps.[30]

For it is the loss of origins or of authority which preoccupies Kuppner's scribes and translators most. On one hand, this is a result of the bathos with which Kuppner describes classical epigrammists in 'The Uninvited Guest' or the Sung Dynasty poets:

> With a yell of triumph he finishes the great work;
> He slumps back in his seat, exhausted but happy;
> Idly he fingers through it, and reads the very first lines;
> Little by little the smile disappears from his face.[31]

Yet as well as the slapstick and bawdiness at work in subjects popularly considered lofty or arcane, in Kuppner's work the matter of loss is often very literal. Scribes and poets are often figured destroying manuscripts, and a repeated motif is that of intelligibility. *A Bad Day for the Sung Dynasty* contains quatrains prefixed by '*A **Faded Inscription**'* (bold added), while some of the 'original' text is so bad as to render the meaning altogether lost. Quatrain 247 from 'Yellow River Dreaming' reads:

> Something breasts something something bosom;
> Something bust something bosom something;
> Breast something something caterpillar something;
> A look of doubt crosses the old scholar's face.[32]

'Preserving the Moment', the first poem from 'What Else is There?' (which also contains 'Four *Mistranslated* Sonnets' [italics added]), suggests another pitfall which perhaps particularly afflicts scholars of Medbh McGuckian's work: that of interpreting everything *but* the poem:

> Look! There is the poet's original manuscript.
> There are some dark marks where (perhaps) a droplet of tea was spilled.

> And there are some lighter marks, caused perhaps
> By a few stray drips when the plants were being watered.
>
> And look there! On the reverse side of the paper
> There is an invitation to a wonderful-sounding party
> Which took place fifty-odd years before the poem was written.
> The poem? Oh, yes. Yes. There was a poem there too.[33]

The issue here is with what Robert Crawford calls 'scrutability': how scrutable is this text Kuppner is dealing with, and how scrutable is the text he has produced for us? It also, as Crawford notes, 'confronts us again with a writing which is also a reading, a way of bringing into communion Kuppner and his audience in the act of investigation'.[34] If Kuppner's blurring of the boundaries between translation/interpretation and active readerly construction brings us back to Barthes's celebration of text as 'a single signifying practice' which 'asks of the reader a practical collaboration',[35] it also brings us back to the lengthy investigations apparently demanded by Medbh McGuckian's poetic technique. As the handful of her 'sources' discussed here suggests, the materials used by McGuckian are often unwieldy or overlapping (as with the Tsvetaeva/Mandelstam/Pasternak studies), are in translation in the first place (as with Tatyana Tolstoy's text, or Mandelstam's essays), or are by a number of different authors.

From the number of footnotes needed to catalogue McGuckian's borrowings, and the little they interpretively add to the poems, it is clear that readers seeking to collaborate with McGuckian on an intertextual level would have to make an active contribution. Indeed, if James Simmons believed that McGuckian's work was a 'literary joke' or 'hoax' at face value, one wonders what he would have made of her invitation to dig for her poetic language's sources, only to find, at length, an argument about the impossibility of really retrieving them. McGuckian's 'translations' refute the idea of origins by 'translating' words without regard to their meaning, and by taking them from books which point to an ever-receding line of other authors and copyists. Their status as translations, indeed, exists only in the understanding of the reader willing to read between the poet's lines. Frank Kuppner's poems, by contrast, loudly pretend to be translations, but their source texts don't really exist, or are of less importance than the scribe's act of deciphering them. McGuckian's translations transform meaning; Kuppner's are unable fully to retrieve it. For instance, although the final note to 'The Uninvited Guest' boasts 'I am proud to be able to state that there are no misprints in this work', 'A Cosmic Footnote' to *A God's Breakfast* is less optimistic about the purity of the text:

> Alas a copyist has introduced a few errors
> Into this classical text about the unity of opposites
> Making it mean something else entirely.³⁶

Kuppner's joke is not merely on 'eternal moments' or solemn philosophical truths, but is at the expense of the purity of texts, or of translations which pose as anything other than partial and provisional.

As for what both Frank Kuppner and Medbh McGuckian distance or displace themselves from by being so much in the library, there is the issue of their relationship to the national or regional literatures of which they are part. Kuppner has firmly positioned himself in his poetry in both Glasgow and Scotland as a whole, while McGuckian has also spoken out about her Northern Irishness and Catholicism. Yet the Borgesian figure conjured up by their poems suggests a preference for second-hand experience or the boundaryless-ness imaginary of the obsessive scholar/reader. Kuppner's poem 'An Old Guide Book in Prague' begins:

> 1
> It being my almost invariable habit
> To visit a second hand bookshop on a Friday afternoon,
> And wander among those rearranged heaps of the past,
> Rearranging them myself each Saturday afternoon.
>
> 2
> And surely I can afford this little book:
> This little book of photographs of a city:
> Almost any city, provided I can afford it:
> I shall go and ask the man what price he sets on it.³⁷

This figure can afford to visit 'almost any city' or rearrange 'heaps of the past' via the pages of a book – and Kuppner visits the immensity of China not merely once but twice, since *Second Best Moments from Chinese History* (1997) more or less repeats the joke of *A Bad Day for the Sung Dynasty*, which says something about how little the poet cares for originality. McGuckian, likewise, conducts her restless travelling primarily through reading, and one might say that what China is to Kuppner's poetic, Russia is to the poems of *On Ballycastle Beach* and *Marconi's Cottage*. Despite the apparently 'local' title of her third collection, McGuckian's poems insistently return to Russian vocabulary, and, intertextually, to the figures of Tsvetaeva, Pasternak, Akhmatova and Mandelstam. And while contemporaries, such as Seamus Heaney, have been drawn to the human struggle of Osip Mandelstam, for one, against an oppressive regime, McGuckian's poetry and intertextual borrowings suggest a fixation instead on the Russian poet's reflections on linguistics:

a word is not a thing. Its significance is not a translation of itself. Indeed, it never happened that anyone has christened a thing, calling it by an invented name.[38]

Indeed, so mediated is McGuckian's translated poetry (though she might prefer to emphasise her status as *medium*), that even when her work appears to refer to the poet's immediate locale, it does so by circuitous routes. Thus, as Clair Wills notes, though 'the familiar campus trees' of 'The Dream Language of Fergus' seem to be those of Queen's University, where McGuckian was writer in residence, the phrase is also borrowed from Mandelstam's essay *About the Nature of the Word*.[39] Her refusal to 'speak with roots', as she puts it in 'The Wake Sofa' from *Captain Lavender* (suggesting her difficult uprooting of words from other contexts as well as her refusal to give voice to 'a sense of place'), makes it unsurprising that she has not been celebrated as a particularly *Northern Irish* poet. Ireland/Northern Ireland is sifted through McGuckian's imaginative elsewheres. As early as *The Flower Master*, 'Ireland' is 'So like Italy Italians came to film it'.[40] Similarly, Robert Crawford notes that Frank Kuppner's 'readerly' poems 'do not conform to the ready stereotypes of "Scottishness" or "Glasgow literature" . . . [which] may also mean that his work receives less critical attention than other Scottish writers' and that it sits uneasily with those who approve an essentialist, unproblematic Scotland.[41]

However, the essentialist concept most troubled by Medbh McGuckian's poetic technique is perhaps that of female identity and 'women's poetry'. Since her debut, McGuckian's elusiveness had been attributed to gender by critics who often fudged the issue of whether her syntactical surprises were intended deliberately to disrupt 'masculine' language, or were the mystical outpouring of some innate femininity. The discovery, therefore, that her mysterious language derives from language in the *public* domain (libraries) directs us back to the 'outside world' at the point when we seem to have discovered the poet's 'inner' one, collapsing the distinction between public/ private (male/female), and insisting on the *interpreted* nature of gender identities. Another effect of McGuckian's intertextuality, I would argue, is to avoid any simplistic definitions of what women's poetry is, and where it fits within the broader poetic tradition. For while McGuckian's use of second-hand language suggests that she does not seek private testimony or self-expression, her work is, nevertheless, highly feminist. This is particularly the case with *Marconi's Cottage*, which is filled with female figures, and contains poems dedicated to writers Nuala Ní Dhomhnaill, Anne Devlin, and Joan and Kate Newman, as well as to McGuckian's own daughter. The revelation, then, that McGuckian has written these poems using texts *about* women writers suggests that the book is an investigation into female authorship, and literary foremothers.[42] Put briefly, the intertextual dimension of her poems suggests the need for an 'enabling' foremother which feminist critics have argued is necessary for women writing in a patriarchal tradition. Indeed, contrary to some perceptions of a wholesale absence of literary women, readers 'directed' to these works by McGuckian's poems may learn more about the numerousness, independence, sexual appetites and physical vulnerabilities of women artists in the nineteenth and twentieth centuries than feminist undergraduates engaged in 'gynocriticism'. However, the first thing to note is that McGuckian's 'scholarly' approach to her female subjects assumes no more intimacy with her literary ancestors than that available to *any* reader of a book – or rather text book. Her mediation, then, could be seen as a strategy which avoids 'possessing' these women by identifying with them.[43] By keeping these 'foremothers' at arm's length, and questioning any 'natural' female identity which allows her to claim solidarity with them, McGuckian does not so much 'represent' women writers politically, as literally '*re*-present' them. The second thing to note is that since McGuckian does not signal her 'resurrection' of women from the past (silencing them once again), the poems reopen the question of whether women writers suffer more at the hands of their historical reception or by being retrieved and therefore appropriated.

This, at least, is one path through the labyrinth of McGuckian's intertextual 'sources'. On the whole her political message lies not in any content, but in an implicit argument about intertextuality *as* feminist in nature. Women's histories are notionally woven throughout her poems alongside those of Rilke, Pasternak, Mandelstam and so on – which brings us back to 'Clotho', the Greek goddess who spins the thread of human life on her distaff. Likewise McGuckian's poems incorporate the *distaff*, in the sense of a female grouping or line of descent, into their very hybrid forms. McGuckian refuses to consider women's writing as a separate category, but suggests the contingency – sexually, historically and in terms of inspiration – of writers on each other. Though Frank Kuppner's work also turns on contingency (of verse units which seem part of a larger whole, and of lives in texts, photographs and tenement buildings), it might seem to be overstating matters to suggest that his intertextuality, too, has a feminist dimension. This, after all, is the poet who 'transcribes' an ancient 'Drinking Song' which goes 'Hey, little girl: show me your genitalia! / Hey, young woman: show me your genitalia! / Hey, mature matron: show me your genitalia! / Hey, ancient hag: help me down from this tree, will you!'[44] Yet, in debunking authority or originality, Kuppner's poetry, too, upsets notions of hierarchy and the 'Great Man'. Following (again) Barthes's claim that should the writer 'wish to *express himself*, he ought at least to know that the inner "thing" he thinks to "translate" is itself only a ready-formed dictionary',[45] the vision of the poet-as-translator points to a (gender) neutral activity, which has its own momentum in endlessly recycling inherited material. As such scholars/experimenters who must keep *copying*, it is notable that Frank Kuppner and Medbh McGuckian have both been called 'obsessive': Kuppner for repeating the distinctive four-line verse structures of his first 'translations', and McGuckian for going on and on without stopping to see whether anyone understands. This, though, is part of their singularity, and their book-bound, self-displacing art. More people should read them, but they probably do not care one way or the other.

NOTES

1. James Simmons, 'A Literary Legpull?', review of *Venus and the Rain*, in *The Belfast Review* (August 1984), 27.
2. Robert Crawford, *Identifying Poets: Self and Territory in Twentieth-Century Poetry* (Edinburgh University Press 1993), 132.
3. *Ibid.*, 123.
4. 'Comhrá: A Conversation with Medbh McGuckian and Nuala ní Dhomhnaill', *The Southern Review* 31:3 (1995), 608.
5. Peggy O'Brien, 'Reading Medbh McGuckian: Admiring What We Cannot Understand', *Colby Quarterly* 28:4 (1992), 239.
6. Medbh McGuckian, *Marconi's Cottage* (Oldcastle: Gallery, 1991), 10.
7. *Ibid.*, 51.
8. Frankie Sewell, 'Interview with Medbh McGuckian', *Brangle* 1 (1993), 54.
9. Shane Alcobia-Murphy's research detailing the intertextual dimension of McGuckian's work is found in *Sympathetic Ink* (Liverpool University Press, 2006) and *Governing the Tongue* (Cambridge Scholars Press, 2005), as well as in several earlier essays.
10. Clair Wills discusses how the phrases of this poem are borrowed from Osip Mandelstam's critical essays, particularly 'Conversation about Dante', in *Improprieties: Politics and Sexuality in Northern Irish Poetry* (Oxford University Press, 1993), 173; for the borrowed phrases see 'Conversation about Dante', in Osip Mandelstam, *The Complete Critical Prose and Letters*, ed. Jane Gary Harris, trans Jane Gary Harris and Constance Link (Ann Arbor, Mich.: Ardis, 1979).
11. Clarence Brown, *Mandelstam* (Cambridge University Press, 1973), 77, 78.
12. Winifred Gérin, *Emily Brontë: A Biography* (Oxford: Clarendon, 1971).
13. Tatyana Tolstoy, *Tolstoy Remembered*, trans. Derek Coltman (London: Michael Joseph, 1977).
14. Susan Chitty, *Gwen John: 1876–1939* (New York: Franklin Watts, 1987).
15. In a footnote to *Marconi's Cottage*, McGuckian gives only the information 'The title derives from the notebooks of the artist Gwen John and signifies the

graduated numbers of the spectrum of colours she used': McGuckian, *Marconi's Cottage*, 42.
16. Alan Jenkins, 'Private and Public Languages', *Encounter* 59:5 (November 1982), 59. Ironically, too, although space does not permit the discussion of it here, some of the materials out of which McGuckian assembles the phrases of her poems are essays or commentary on the meaningless musicality of poetry's first promptings, while McGuckian, in turn, uses the borrowed words themselves more for music than meaning.
17. Boris Pasternak, Marina Tsvetayeva and Rainer Maria Rilke, *Letters: Summer 1926*, trans. Margaret Wettlin and Walter Arndt (London: Cape, 1986). See Wills, *Improprieties*, 173.
18. For the individual words and phrases borrowed in 'Visiting Rainer Maria' see pages 48, 82, 89, 94, 21, 22, 242, 86, 88, 95, 79 in Clarence Brown's *Mandelstam*.
19. Mandelstam, 'Conversation about Dante', *Complete Critical Prose and Letters*, 398.
20. *Ibid.*, 436.
21. See Simon Karlinsky, *Marina Tsvetaeva: The Woman, Her World and Her Poetry* (Cambridge University Press, 1985), 181–8.
22. Brown, *Mandelstam*, 66. The quotations of Mandelstam's translation of his wife were first noted by Sarah Broom, who uses a slightly different translation of Mandelstam's letter as the 'source' of McGuckian's poem, contained in Osip Mandelstam, *The Collected Critical Prose and Letters* (London: Harvill, 1991), 484. See Sarah Broom, 'McGuckian's Conversations with Rilke in *Marconi's Cottage*', *Irish University Review: A Journal of Irish Studies* 4:28 (1998), 133–50.
23. Brown, *Mandelstam*, 173.
24. Frank Kuppner, *A God's Breakfast* (Manchester: Carcanet, 2004) contains these three books: 'The Uninvited Guest', which contains '800 fragments composed of lacunae and annotations in a manuscript of classical epigrams'; 'West Åland or Five Tombeaux for Mr Testoil'; and 'What Else is There: 120 Poems'.
25. Frank Kuppner, *What? Again? Selected Poems* (Manchester: Carcanet, 2000), 13.
26. Crawford, *Identifying Poets*, 123.
27. *Ibid.*, 132.
28. Roland Barthes, 'The Death of the Author', *Image, Music, Text*, essays selected and trans. by Stephen Heath (London: Fontana, 1977), 146.
29. *Ibid.*
30. On a similar theme, Kuppner's most recent collection, *Arioflotga* (Manchester: Carcanet, 2008), is described as 'a copy of a version of the index of first lines of the lost Great Poetic Anthology which has turned up in a Latin American restaurant in Glasgow'.
31. Kuppner, *What? Again? Selected Poems*, 11.
32. *Ibid.*, 12.
33. Frank Kuppner, *A God's Breakfast* (Manchester: Carcanet, 2004), 157.
34. Crawford, *Identifying Poets*, 136, 134.
35. Barthes, 'From Work to Text', *Image, Music, Text*, 134.

36. Kuppner, *A God's Breakfast*, 205.
37. Kuppner, *What? Again? Selected Poems*, 27.
38. Mandelstam, *Complete Critical Prose and Letters*, 129.
39. See Wills, *Improprieties*, 179.
40. McGuckian, 'The Swing', *The Flower Master* (Oxford University Press, 1982), 38.
41. Crawford, *Identifying Poets*, 121.
42. The clearest suggestion of this may be McGuckian's use of vocabulary from Gilbert and Gubar's seminal feminist text, *The Mad Woman in the Attic: The Woman Writer and the Nineteenth-Century Literary Imagination* (New Haven and London: Yale University Press, 1979), in the poem 'Journal Intime' (McGuckian, *Marconi's Cottage*, 26).
43. Indeed, the academic nature of the 'sources' used by McGuckian means that should her readers turn to these library books as a means of understanding McGuckian's poems, we tend to find her female subjects become more, rather than less, elusive. Both Susan Chitty's study of Gwen John and Winifred Gérin's biography of Emily Brontë emphasise the unknowable nature of these figures. In the foreword to the original edition of Chitty's book, we encounter John Rothenstein's remark: 'In spite of the highly illuminating character of this book – and Susan Chitty has assembled an impressive range of facts, mostly hitherto unpublished – something of a shadow Gwen John still remains . . .' (7).

    Likewise, Gérin's notes that she has had to rely on often competing accounts of Emily Brontë (these are the descriptions of the writer's appearance McGuckian uses in 'Gigot Sleeves'), and contend with her sister Charlotte's destruction of her papers and protection of her reputation. Thus, 'Emily Brontë is heard through their medium, at second hand, seldom speaking in her own voice', and like John, she continues to remain shadowy: 'When every writer who has something to say on the subject has said it, Emily Brontë will still elude us; we can hardly wish it otherwise. It is a part of her fascination to elude definition' (ix).

    To the reader of McGuckian's 'sources', then, these texts appear to overlap, once more, with McGuckian's own mysteriousness, both stylistically and as an author. McGuckian and her texts have a hall-of-mirrors quality of refraction and repetition. Gérin and Chitty emphasise the spirituality or mysticism of their subjects – and McGuckian's mystical pronouncements have not been limited to her 'resurrection' of others through poetry. Gérin considers accusations against Brontë of plagiarism at the same time as McGuckian's unacknowledged use of this material leaves the poet open to the same charge. Once again, then, McGuckian seems to seek to identify with certain shared historical literary techniques and traits (including secrecy or reclusiveness), while avoiding dealing with them discursively in her work. She both brings her own artistry into continuity with that of Emily Brontë and Gwen John (as well as Tsvetaeva, etc.), and refuses to universalise from her own historical perspective – a criticism which has been made of the feminist poems of, say, Eavan Boland. The effect is to create a provisional, textual female genealogy while at

the same time in fact disrupting the simple 'representativeness' of women poets which allows one to speak for all. For example, in his essay '"A Pen Mislaid": Some Varieties of Women's Poetry' Neil Corcoran describes McGuckian's poems as sometimes 'more or less unannounced dramatic monologues or ventriloquisings on behalf of nineteenth century women, with their needlework, embroidery, portrait painting and so on' (Neil Corcoran, *English Poetry since 1940* [Harlow, Essex: Longman, 1993], 222). This would seem to be true of 'A Small Piece of Wood', which features a 'poetess' riding out to hunt in 'a pale frock and raspberry / boots'. Yet the knowledge that these are Tatayana Tolstoy's *own words* confuses the issue of who is speaking, and for whom. Indeed, it asks whether it is ethical for McGuckian to speak 'on behalf of' nineteenth-century women (or Mandelstam 'for' his wife, as he records doing in his letter), and by implication for McGuckian's poetry to represent a thing called 'Women's Poetry', of which hers is one variety.
44. Kuppner, *What? Again? Selected Poems*, 125.
45. Barthes, *Image, Music, Text*, 146.

CHAPTER 18

Phoenix or dead crow? Irish and Scottish poetry magazines, 1945–2000

Edna Longley

In 1930 Ezra Pound called T. S. Eliot's *Criterion* 'a diet of dead crow'.[1] *Phoenix* was a 1960s poetry magazine edited by Harry Chambers, first in Liverpool, finally in Manchester, most significantly in Belfast. Literary magazines attract metaphors of birth, death and biorhythms. To quote Robin Fulton: 'Some dull magazines have survived for a long time. Some bright ones have scarcely survived infancy.' Launching *The Lace Curtain*,[2] Michael Smith wrote: 'Poetry magazines . . . have, like butterflies, an all too short life; and in our mean Irish climate this brief span is even more curtailed.'[3] Ian Hamilton concludes:

> ten years is the ideal life-span for a little magazine . . . There are the opening years of jaunty, assertive indecision, then a middle period of genuine identity, and after that . . . identity becomes more and more wan and mechanical . . . It is in the nature of the little magazine that it should believe that no one else could do what it is doing. This belief is almost always tied to the requirements of a particular period, to a particular set of literary rights or wrongs . . . Each magazine needs a new decade, and each decade needs a new magazine.[4]

Magazines can be reborn under new editors, as when Fulton took over *Lines Review* (for a decade) in 1967. In 1969 Frank Ormsby and Michael Foley gave James Simmons's *Honest Ulsterman*, '60s-styled 'handbook for a revolution', a more strictly *literary* dynamic. There are Phoenix-like editors: Duncan Glen, best known for *Akros*, edited *Zed 2 O* in his later years, although idolatry of Hugh MacDiarmid remained a constant. But Hamilton's rule holds. And since poets need magazines more than do other writers, poetry's own flickering pulse is also at stake ('dead crow' implicates Eliot's post *Waste Land* poems), as is a poet-editor's poetic ego. Cairns Craig says of an extreme case: 'MacDiarmid the poet is regularly published by MacDiarmid the editor.'[5] In 1952 Patrick Kavanagh edited *Kavanagh's Weekly*.

Internet pick'n'mix has led pundits to prophesy the death of the little magazine itself, along with its life-support system for poetry and poetry criticism. Certainly, magazines have lost (or do not even seek) 'authority' now that Vanity Press, both on and off line, has become poetry's main publisher. As for their academic afterlife: apart from those rare ventures attached to a new literary movement, 'little' magazines have been less researched than the weighty 'journal' or 'periodical'. Wolfgang Gortschacher's encyclopaedic *Little Magazine Profiles* (1993) remained an exceptional study until the *Oxford Critical and Cultural History of Modernist Magazines* got underway.[6] Yet Irish and Scottish circumstances ensure that, more than elsewhere, periodical and magazine overlap. This can be gauged from Yug Mohit Chaudhry's *Yeats, the Irish Literary Revival and the Politics of Print* (2001), Tom Clyde's *Irish Literary Magazines: An Outline History and Descriptive Biography* (2003), Frank Shovlin's *The Irish Literary Periodical, 1923–1958* (2003) and Malcolm Ballin's *Irish Periodical Culture, 1937–1972: Genre in Ireland, Wales, and Scotland* (2008); also from Cairns Craig's 'Modernist Journals in Scotland' and Margery Palmer McCulloch's discussions of Scottish 'Inter-War Criticism' and 'The Importance of Little Magazines in the Interwar Movement for Scottish Renewal'.[7] A material cause of the overlap is the need to maximise resources (financial and human) in a small country: Derick Thomson's Scottish Gaelic magazine *Gairm* (1952–2002) also catered for the extra-literary concerns of a linguistic community. An ideological cause – which generates conceptual tension as well as holistic possibility – is the founding role of literary nationalism, and poetry's founding role in that. Poetry magazines belong to a history of speaking for Ireland or Scotland. Chaudhry analyses Yeats's complex symbiosis with nationalist journals like *United Ireland*. In the early 1920s MacDiarmid's frenetic editorial enterprises ranged from *Scottish Chapbook* (which theorised 'Scots Letters', sought to bring 'Scots Vernacular into the mainstream of European letters' and printed his own Scots lyrics) to the scope implied by *Scottish Nation*.[8]

Like Yeats in the 1890s, MacDiarmid bemoaned London's hegemony over literary journalism, although both colluded in it, and saw indigenous criticism as aborted by a lack of literary journals. These deficits, and an associated decline in Irish and Scottish publishing, would persist. The 1950s magazine conceived itself as a strike against provincial paralysis. During the '50s and '60s (still censorship years) Ireland's 'overall publishing production ... was among the lowest in the developed world'.[9] In 1961 Edwin Morgan attacked Scottish publishers for failing to publish Scottish poetry: a frugality that did not save them from metropolitan takeovers.

Alisdair Skinner quotes Morgan when he claims in the first issue of *Scottish International*: 'in this world of more books, more readers, more writers, the writers and readers of Scottish books are in a worse position than they ever were'. A negative version of the magazine–periodical overlap is that 'too few magazines [are] expected to do too many things at once'. Vivian Mercier noted that the Irish *Bell* had to be 'a sort of *Horizon, New Statesman and Nation, John O'London's Weekly* and *World Review* all rolled into one'.[10] Multitasking across the arts and politics may have hastened the death of poet-led *Scottish International*, as it did of an Irish counterpart, *Envoy* (1949–51). *Cencrastus* (1979–92) had more stamina as a cultural review. '[B]orn in the dark days of post-referendum Scotland', it tapped new commitment to 'the underlying principles of a Scottish Literary Renaissance'.[11] But here poetry was less central.

Malcolm Ballin thinks that the periodical/magazine has been undertheorised in Irish literary studies, if more discussed than in Scottish literary studies. Dividing the field into 'reviews', 'miscellanies' and 'little magazines', he argues for a 'generic' approach to how these perceive themselves and their audiences at a particular historical moment. He also pioneers a comparative approach within the archipelago. As regards Irish–Scottish comparisons, however, Ballin applies a predetermined template. Diagnosing 'chronic generic instability' in the 'periodicals of the Scottish Renaissance', he connects this with MacDiarmid's 'artificial' Scots; his unviable pan-Celticism; Scottish postwar 'cultural insecurity'; and the questionable basis of Scottish Nationalism: 'fabricated or synthesised from elements of the experience of other countries, rather than ... founded on a strong material base'. Ballin's view of MacDiarmid and post-Union Scotland ('grasping at available commercial and imperial opportunities') leads him to overstate the periodical's stability in 'post-revolutionary' Ireland. If Irish periodicals more often kept 'their original forms', this may reflect counter-revolutionary urgency.[12] Hubert Butler wrote in 1954: 'An Irish journal is like a sortie from a besieged city.'[13]

Before the Second World War, neither Ireland nor Scotland had a real equivalent of Geoffrey Grigson's London-edited *New Verse*. Then a few magazines began to specialise in poetry: Maurice Lindsay's *Poetry Scotland* (1943), David Marcus's *Poetry Ireland* (1948), Roy McFadden's and Barbara Hunter's *Rann* (1951) and Alan Riddell's *Lines Review* (1952). Frank Shovlin questions the belief that any magazine can ever be purely 'literary': thus he detects covert unionism behind the professed 'regionalism' of the Northern Irish *Rann*.[14] Similarly, a link between poetry in Scots and Scottish Nationalism may lurk in the editorial unconscious even where it does not rise to the textual surface. Yet a magazine's socio-political contexts are finally significant for how they condition its aesthetic horizons – which includes the tendency to mistake one for the other. The rest of this chapter will focus on the poetic milieu invoked/created by certain (English-language) magazines: the traditions to which they appeal; their critical principles and practices; the flashpoint controversies. Milieux differ within, as well as between, Ireland and Scotland. The fulcrum of attention will be around 1970 since, alongside new waves of poets, a magazine boom (sometimes bust) occurred during the 1960s – in Scotland: *POOR. OLD. TIRED. HORSE.* (1962–7), *Akros* (1965–83), *Scottish International* (1968–74), *Chapman* (1970 to today); in Ireland: a new *Dublin Magazine* (initially *The Dubliner*, 1961 [1965–74]), a new *Poetry Ireland* (1962–8), *Arena* (1963–5), *The Holy Door* (1965–6), *The Honest Ulsterman* (1968–2001), *The Lace Curtain* (1969–78).

By 1970, too, an older economy of the poetry magazine was giving way to the era of Arts Council subsidy. If this '[did] not magically solve all financial problems', British and Irish magazines no longer wholly depended on subscriptions, advertisements, patrons like *Lines* benefactor Callum Macdonald, and shaky sales. John Jordan, editor of *Poetry Ireland*, complained in 1964: 'The Irish do not buy literary magazines if they can possibly beg them, borrow them, steal them, or riffle through them in bookshops.'[15] We may miss the ads for Youghal Carpets or feel that subsidy artificially prolongs a magazine's lifespan or believe that, by definition, poetry magazine editors are self-starting obsessives who do it for love. There is something a bit politburo about the fact that the state body Poetry Ireland now appoints rotating editors of what has become *Poetry Ireland Review*. But, back in the 1950s, David Marcus could not sustain the original *Poetry Ireland*; Hubert Butler could not finance a mooted cross-border magazine, *The Bridge*; and a British Board of Trade ban limited sales of *Envoy* and *Poetry Ireland*, thus preventing other kinds of circulation.

In the 1960s the sociology of editors also began to change: Jordan was a university lecturer, if an erratic one; his predecessor, Marcus, was a lawyer, then a publisher and literary journalist. Alan Riddell worked as a journalist. Although still mainly young male poets 'in a hurry', editors would soon be writing doctorates as well as poems. Here, *Verse* (founded 1984) and *Metre* (1996) are Scottish-Irish counterparts; as they are in flagging their 'international' scope and 'glocalised' address: *Verse*, then based in Oxford, styles its editors 'two Glaswegians and a New Englander'. *Metre* left Dublin for Prague/Hull. As poet-editors, Robert Crawford and David Kinloch, Justin Quinn and David Wheatley, brought the poetry magazine closer to the mobile academy. *Verse* 'consciously tried to straddle [the] divide' between 'poets and academics' (Jerome McGann on 'Postmodern Poetries' may have been a step too far).[16] *Metre*'s characteristic emphasis was on evaluation, standards, precise reading. Wheatley writes: 'Moving between academic publishing and writing for a magazine such as ours is an excellent way of testing your work against utterly different sets of expectations ... The small magazine represents ... a third way between the rough and tumble of newspaper reviews ... and the straggling attentions of the academic reviews.' *Metre*'s critical stringency, however, provoked some 'hostile reaction'.[17]

Or perhaps the academy had caught up with the magazine: mid-twentieth-century magazines attack the neglect of Irish and Scottish literary studies. In 1940 Austin Clarke wrote: 'It is quite possible to pass through [the Irish universities] with merely a dim feeling that there has been some kind of literary activity in this country during the last fifty years'; in 1945 John Hewitt accused Queen's University Belfast of being a region-blind 'foreign oasis'.[18] In 1955 James Kinsley, editor of *Scottish Poetry: A Critical Survey*, sparked off a debate in *Lines* by arguing: 'Our assessment of modern poetry – and all its cultural implications – is conditioned by our understanding of the traditions which our contemporaries have inherited and enriched.' The debate touched on relations with 'English' and 'Anglo-Scottish' literature; the case for separate university departments; the academic critic versus the non-academic. David Craig made a Leavisite plea for 'good criticism', rather than scholarship, as 'a power for live thinking about our culture'. Edwin Morgan's reply to Craig would prove self-defining: 'criticism, creative writing, and scholarship must *all* gather up their forces in Scotland'.[19]

To compare Irish and Scottish poetry magazines is to find differences and unrealised parallels; rarely, conversation. Space and contingency are factors here: the parallels include duty to 'native' poets, verse-stuffed postbags, unmet deadlines, editorial living from hand-to-mouth. Duncan Glen apologises for all the books that *Akros* has failed to review. Yet magazines develop a characteristic ethos, even if editors protest their eclecticism or Irish and Scottish poets shamelessly publish in every available outlet. To quote Robin Fulton: 'An effective identity is not necessarily of the kind which is immediately apparent, through polemically hardened outlines or declarations of intent ... [It] is a much more complex, tentative and dialectical affair, evolving over the years as a mesh of responses between editors, contributors and readers.'[20] The danger is coterie. W. Price Turner writes in *Chapman*: 'Edinburgh makars drift together / like sheep farts in wet heather.'

Magazines that draw on the same local pool may lose distinctiveness (not that bland globalism is the answer). Turner continues: 'And Och, the originality in the magazines! / Contents as varied as a tin of beans'. An *Akros* contributor proposes 'a law agin poets or wad-be poets actin as reviewers and creetics and editors' to end 'the self-advertisement and "ye scart my back and I'll scart yours" outlooks that are sic a curse on Scots letters'.[21] But magazines do get caught in literary crossfire, as between Kavanagh and Clarke (*Envoy*); or between MacDiarmid and 'Quisling attackers of the Lallans Movement', MacDiarmid and Ian Hamilton Finlay, MacDiarmid and the editors of *Scottish International*.[22] The magazine is the first rough draft of literary history and criticism – more so in the 1950s and 1960s, when it was harder to publish a collection of poems. Editors anxiously kept the national tally, while Irish and Scottish anthologies from London publishers were an intensely debated event. Magazines and their pamphlet outreach carried much of the art's freight.

If Irish and Scottish magazines appear mutually unaware, this may also reveal little about poets' or editors' individual consciousness: poets read poems; editors prefer to showcase more 'foreign poets'. But that fails to explain absence from aesthetic horizons: the recurrent impression of parallel universes. Scottish poetry magazines have more Irish features than vice versa, but almost invariably edited by Hayden Murphy, an Irish resident of Edinburgh. *Chapman*'s Murphy-edited Irish issue (1999) has a lurid cover emblazoned 'Flames of History'. Editors assume a need for native/national gatekeepers – as informants or boosters rather than critics. Reviewing John Montague's *The Rough Field* in *Lines*'s Irish issue of 1975, D. M. Black says, 'it feels like an impertinence for a non-Irishman to attempt to assess it', and finds the poem's ethos of 'violence and grievance' alien to Scotland. In fact, he praises recent Northern Irish poetry for 'present[ing] the detail of actuality without the tedium of excessive circumstance', and for attaining Ezra Pound's objective of 'a "more or less good" average style'. In 1979 there was an equally rare moment of critique when Edwin Morgan complained that English critics favoured Irish poetry – partly owing to 'subconscious' historical guilt, partly because it is 'very accessible and manageable' – over Scottish poetry, which 'seems more various and adventurous, more willing to take risks'. W. N. Herbert writes similarly in *Gairfish*: 'the traditional prosody of a great deal of modern Irish writing permits the English to domesticate it without too much violence to their own post-Movement definition of verse'. Accusing English critics of literary 'divide and rule', Herbert calls the Yeats tradition 'assimilated' unlike MacDiarmid's 'awkward' squad. There can be a sense that

Scotland's poetic (if not political) separatism is more advanced than Ireland's: in a review of Irish anthologies, Derick Thomson finds some nineteenth- and twentieth-century Irish Anglophone poets to be 'lost in a limbo that is neither Irish nor English, and their poetry is none the better for it'.[23] All this brings aesthetic (and cultural) differences into focus, if hardly into critical argument. *Verse* and *Metre* involve Irish/Scottish poets in their 'international' remit, but here again latent archipelagic issues may slip between the cracks. Kevin Higgins, writing on Kathleen Jamie and devolution, does use comparison critically when he notes the 'pitfalls ... for poets lauded for speaking on behalf of the "Nation" or this or that fashionable cause ... In Ireland, Eavan Boland (for her feminism) and Paul Durcan ... were both once similarly lauded, but have lately come to be rather tame laureates for things as they are.'[24]

Now: a brief history of Scottish poetry in Irish magazines. Cork-based David Marcus was generous to 'Ulster' poets: a transregional solidarity that implicated Scotland. John Hewitt's poem 'Overture for Ulster Regionalism' appears in *Poetry Ireland*'s first issue: 'The Welsh have started well ... / Scotland going a long time now with M'Diarmid, / has room for Drinan's salty lilt and Young's / polyglot gallimaufries on the pipes.' Later, Hewitt reviewed Maurice Lindsay's *The Scottish Renaissance* and his collection *Hurleygush*:

so far in Ireland, North or South, little interest has been shown in what should be for us a most fascinating experiment, the assertion by a culture of its independence of the dictatorship of London, the enthusiastic effort of a group of writers to recover their native tradition. For Ulster especially, this should be deeply significant ... because much of our own tradition has the same roots.

In an 'Ulster Issue' Hewitt plays the Scots card against the 'Irish Mode' (Thomas MacDonagh's term), defined as an attempt to reproduce Gaelic assonance in English: 'for most of the Ulster poets Irish has never been the folk-tongue'.[25] The next landmark is Douglas Sealy's advocacy of MacDiarmid in the *Dubliner* (1964). Sealy stresses MacDiarmid's (southern) Irish connections, and ends: '[His] faults are patent ... But amid the careless rhymes, the slack inversions, the formlessness, the sometimes inaccurate information and the transcription of others' writings, the true spirit of poetry emerges.' As the magazine's leading critic, Sealy also notices other Scottish poetry, and discusses Edwin Muir's *The Estate of Poetry*. He may have written an anonymous review that commends Norman MacCaig's 'succinctness' as a model to most of the *Six Irish Poets* anthologised by Robin Skelton in 1962.[26]

Mutuality may require either a widely curious poetry critic or a cultural agenda like Hewitt's: Ireland looms larger in Scottish magazines as the temperature of Scottish Nationalism rises. The first poem in the first issue of *Verse* is by Seamus Heaney, and an article on his politics follows. More intricate contact partly depends on historical or structural ties. *Phoenix* and *The Honest Ulsterman*, which publish and review Scottish and English poets, contextualise Douglas Dunn's sense of generational affinity with poets from Northern Ireland (see his chapter here). 'British' poetic regionalism, though not in Hewitt's sense, was rife around 1970. Dunn says of 1969, when he published *Terry Street*: 'Something was in the air' – 'something' that he derives from the 1944 Education Act.[27] Poets and magazines resisted metropolitan Edinburgh and Dublin as well as London, while northern England (e.g., Jon Silkin's *Stand*) resisted London too. This northerly axis, to which redbrick universities were important, aligns the 1960s generation of Scottish and Northern Irish poets with postwar intellectual democratisation and devolution, rather than with national or regional cultural politics.[28]

Scottish poetry is absent from the Dublin magazines *The Holy Door*, *Arena* and *The Lace Curtain*, although Sorley MacLean figures in *Cyphers* (founded 1975). A fascinating case is the short-lived *Two Rivers* (1969), edited by Paul Durcan and Martin Green in London. While the rivers in question must be Liffey and Thames, the first poem in the first issue is MacDiarmid's 'The Point of Honour (On watching the Dumfriesshire river Esk again)'. The magazine also prints MacDiarmid's 'The Poet's Task'. New magazines set the coordinates of tradition by invoking elder or dead poets. MacDiarmid is also godfather to *Lines*, *Akros*, *Cencrastus*, *Verse*, *Gairfish*, and *Zed 2 O*: an *Akros* MacDiarmid issue contains over forty photographs of him. Unsurprisingly, Yeats is never trusted with an Irish baby, but MacNeice's image appears on the cover of the first *Honest Ulsterman*, while the Republic's magazines of the 1960s and '70s usually genuflect to Kavanagh or his shade: the first *Two Rivers* carries a bad elegy for him. The London-Irish bearings of this magazine, at a time of southern Irish migration to England, inscribe Irish–British poetic horizons that differ from the northerly axis.

John Hewitt refers to London's 'dictatorship'. If Irish and Scottish magazines silently ignore one another, they ignore England loudly. In this *Lines* collage, Philip Larkin and the Movement represent English poetry: 'flat, characterless verse'; '[t]he hard, dry, tough, intermittently witty Davie-Wain-Gunn grid system'; 'Betjemaniacs, philistines, rotten reactionaries... a sly sort of I'm-all-right-Jack, lower-middle class look'. Meanwhile, the 'Scottish accent', and hence Scottish poetry, has 'a more definite taste, a stronger savour: the past is alive and kicking in it ... the voice of a recognisable and rooted people'.[29] Such tropes resemble Daniel Corkery's images of the effete Anglo-Irish as against native vigour (variants are employed by those English poetic dissidents who identify with American poetry). For Duncan Glen, dutifully 'Anglophobic', English poetry, poetry in English, is always 'polite'. Robin Fulton writes more tolerantly: 'although reviewers in the south may still give the impression of looking northwards through the wrong end of a telescope ... a metropolitan/provincial scheme is clearly obsolete'.[30]

In *Cyphers* Eiléan ní Chuilleanáin applies anti-English tropes to some 'poetry produced in the North in the last fifteen years'. She says, 'the political packaging is evident ... [D]epending on the market they could be filed under British Regional or Irish Provincial', before attacking poetry that reflects the 'recognisable surfaces of the world', the 'eleven-plus poem' and a lack of 'thought about what a poem is'. While this connects with some points made above, it mistakes conditions for structures, and the British–Irish dichotomy does not allow for archipelagic cross-currents. Ní Chuilleanáin implicitly folds Larkin and Heaney into some inferior, superficial and alien aesthetic (1960s Dublin had been unsure whether to call Heaney's poetry 'Irish'). There are odd class-tones, too, as if Ní Chuilleanáin were speaking for ancient Ireland rather than a Dublin coterie: Belfast's 'artisan culture' has 'imposed itself ... on peasant and scholar'. In 1992 she still finds the very name *Honest Ulsterman*, with its 'promise of a no-nonsense, anti-rhetorical compact between writer and reader', 'suspect to southern readers'.[31] *Cyphers* may have been named to point a contrast (an own goal?). In *Chapman* J. M. Hendry takes a similarly lofty line with Glasgow upstarts, Tom Leonard *et al.*: 'What they have in common is, if anything, immaturity.'[32]

Differences between *Cyphers* and the *Honest Ulsterman* in the 1970s have more to do with literary politics than the national question. Yet a deeper argument about the coordinates of tradition – the national poetic question – was subtextually underway. Later, in an outraged review of Paul Muldoon's *Faber Book of Contemporary Irish Poetry* (1986), Eamon Grennan complained that 'Muldoon's critical compass seems fixed at poetic North'.[33] Grennan does not ask whether divergent compass settings have anything to say about the aesthetic ground (rather than literal regions or provinces) of Irish poetry. My quotations from Scottish magazines and from *Cyphers* suggest how political paradigms and cultural stereotypes can pre-empt analysis. Neither Douglas Dunn's nor Derek Mahon's reading of Larkin, say, is accommodated.

The unconscious nationalism or unionism of some Irish poetry criticism came closer to the surface after 1969. Yet even then, despite culture war, identity politics and revisionist tendencies in criticism as well as history, nothing quite matched the stone thrown into the Scottish pond in 1971 by the issue of *Lines* devoted to Alan Jackson's 'The Knitted Claymore: An Essay on Culture and Nationalism'. Jackson touches on 'the unspeakable and schizophrenic politics of Hugh MacDiarmid', the 'paranoia and neurosis' induced by 'the present position of Scots as a literary language', and the 'need to separate the issue of Scots from nationalist politics'. He regrets that, owing to recent SNP success at the polls, 'men I thought had slunk away to prickly sulks on couches of thistle ... came breengin' hurriedly back, reknitting their half unravelled claymores and pulling behind them pramfuls of young poets waving tartan rattles'. Ireland figures in Jackson's critique '[s]ince [Yeats] and the Irish are constantly quoted parallels for the Scottish Renaissance and its works'. He cites MacNeice on Yeats's latterday admission that 'nationalism can sidetrack the poet into narrowness, aridity, even hypocrisy'. The row made the newspapers, and *Lines* printed further responses, the most nuanced being D. M. Black's distinction between 'bad nationalism' (a 'womb-substitute') and the possible baby 'in all that tartan bath-water'.[34] Jackson's recourse to Ireland contrasts with an issue of *Gairfish* 20 years later, where Richard Price resurrects Neil Gunn's essay 'The Hidden Heart', much indebted to Daniel Corkery's *Hidden Ireland*. For Price, Gunn's 'look at the vexed historiography of Ireland seem[s] to be in the spirit of Scottish internationalism'. Earlier, *Scottish International* itself would not have assumed that two nationalisms made a right. For its editors (Robert Tait, Robert Garioch and Edwin Morgan), poetry's 'ironies, ambiguities, subtle contemplativeness and ... "shock of the new"' were 'integral' to their 'policy of stimulation and renewal of thinking'.[35] The second issue contains Morgan's satirical poem 'The Flowers of Scotland'.

Before 1969 the link between poetry and the Easter Rising sometimes brought Irish poetry magazines into a political frame. Marcus's *Poetry Ireland*, open to the North and awash with pallid Twilight poems, suddenly has a fiery Rising commemorative issue ('After Easter Week the poets sang as spontaneously and passionately as the birds in springtime'), and then resumes the even tenor of its way. A more focused *Dublin Magazine* Easter Rising edition (1966) features Monk Gibbon's account of Captain Bowen-Colthurst murdering Francis Sheehy Skeffington, but examines, rather than sanctifies, the poetry of Padraic Pearse, Thomas MacDonagh and Joseph Mary Plunkett. A neo-Yeatsian editorial reflects bitterly 'on what forty-five years of autonomy have done for Irish culture', on Ireland's 'sheer philistinism' compared with other 'European nations' (some Scottish magazines ascribe philistinism to lack of autonomy).[36] After 1969 Irish poetry was less often left to its own devices. Hence its somewhat instrumental function in Richard Kearney's *Crane Bag* (1977–85), dedicated to a utopian 'fifth province', and the brief *engagé* career of *Atlantis* (edited by Seamus Deane and others) in the early 1970s. John Wilson Foster's occasional 'Critical Forum' in the 1980s *Honest Ulsterman* debates issues such as 'Must the War Continue?' Like the *Dublin Magazine*, the first *Atlantis* editorial attacks Irish philistinism, but in a different tone. Aiming 'to see Ireland in an international perspective, to lift its drowsy eyelid', the writer says: 'Adorno died last August. Who cares? We have a depopulated West and a rancid North.' Calling 'Dublin's latest literary magazine' a 'polished coffin', the *Honest Ulsterman* squashed these pretensions: 'Ah so poor old Adorno has gone to meet the Great Critic. God, how few are left from the old days in Paris.'[37]

Tension between the poetry magazine and the intellectual outcrop of the Troubles is epitomised by a 1975 *Honest Ulsterman*, in which a skit by Frank Ormsby, featuring a Troubles poet called 'Tragic Anguish', conflicts with Seamus Deane's slightly anguished essay 'An Irish Intelligentsia: Reflections on its Desirability'. Michael Foley had put 'a sense of the absurd' at the head of his editorial priorities, and the magazine uses jokes to shield poetry from the political scrimmage – literary scrimmaging being another matter. Even Seamus Heaney was provoked into writing a verse-letter of complaint: 'I write to say I am fed up / finding myself too much in gossip columns. / Show proper respect, you editorial dope. / You're dealing with a prefect from St Columb's' (the Derry school attended by Heaney and Foley).[38] Similarly, in Ian Hamilton Finlay's *POOR. OLD. TIRED. HORSE.*, wit protects 'creators of beauty' and 'the warm voice of poetry' against MacDiarmid and other offenders: 'AYE to panache / AYE to humour / AYE to Rangers AND Celtic / AYE TO THE RHUBARB AS IT GROWS TO HEAVEN THROUGH A RAGGED HOLE IN A RUSTY PAIL.'[39] In the *Honest Ulsterman* the Troubles figure most intricately in actual poems (the 'Tragic Anguish' issue contains Paul Muldoon's 'Mules') or in reviews like Ciaran Carson's well-known response to Heaney's *North*.[40]

Back in 1950 an *Envoy* editorial argued: 'Far too much has been made of ["Irishness"] recently to the exclusion of the normal values of a work of art.' Yet this was partly an attack on Revival principles; other kinds of Irishness were due for a long run yet; and *Envoy* itself felt, rather than filled, the critical void: 'Of thoughtful and exact criticism we have had lamentably little since the beginning of the century.' In both Ireland and Scotland, pleas for better criticism (usually from poets) recur. Even in 1985, as he assumed the editorship of *Poetry Ireland Review*, Terence Brown wrote: 'The problem of criticism in Ireland remains to be solved.'[41] Shovlin argues that literary criticism had to wait: 'while British editors such as Eliot and Middleton Murry were wrangling over the merits of Classicism and Romanticism, their Irish counterparts were trying to heal the trauma of revolution and to define the culture of a new nation'.[42] Yet a dose of neo-Classicism may have been just what Ireland needed, and Yeats hardly gave up on the poetic trade, or on criticism, after 1921. Part of the 'problem', as in Scotland, was that a small country's critical impulse may lapse into alternations of 'backscarting' and backstabbing. In 1955 Donald Davie thought that Irish people had the 'idea that any degree of objectivity in criticism is impossible'.[43]

For David Daiches in 1959: 'one of the greatest needs of modern Scottish culture today is a more genuinely critical attitude towards Scottish literature'. Daiches accuses Kurt Wittig's *The Scottish Tradition in Literature* (1958) of 'playing up to all the complacency, the acceptance of a lack of real standards, the facile repetition of untenable generalisations about what is Scottish and what isn't' (for MacDiarmid, however, Wittig had justified Scottish literary separatism).[44] In 1971, reviewing *The Akros Anthology of Scottish Poetry* and other anthologies, Tom Buchan finds more of the same. He berates 'the Doric besotted mish-mash in which the latterday Kailyard rail at cosmic unfairness or hand down their homilies, apothegms, heugh-aye ejaculations and waterlogged nationalist or socialist insights'; and urges: 'We must not kid ourselves about Scottish poetry.'[45] A source of friction between *Akros* and *Lines/Scottish International* is Glen's uncritical attitude to MacDiarmid and to all poetry in Scots. Like idolatry of MacDiarmid, denial of Yeats bears on critical belatedness. In 1986 Sean Lysaght provocatively argued that most southern Irish poets had espoused 'the poetry of character and idiosyncratic privacy', because '[t]he language of aesthetics has been alien to [them] since the foundation of the Republic ... [A] nationalism politically hostile to the authority of colonialism could not allow, in aesthetics, a similar authority to influence its literature.'[46]

Theoretically, the poems that an editor selects might suffice to promote 'a genuinely critical attitude' (Daiches). But it does not shine through those magazines where the editor writes most of the reviews (David Marcus); which contain no reviews (the second *Poetry Ireland*); or which, like *Arena*, refuse to admit 'critics of any kind': *Arena* prints a poem by Leland Bardwell that begins: 'Twinkle twinkle mad star of the poets / That mocks the shivering critics / Jostling for places at Cowards Gate'.[47] In some Irish and Scottish poetic quarters, during the 1960s, nobody can have been reading Ian Hamilton's rigorous if metropolitan *Review*. Before the 1980s, the magazines with the most sustained critical content, including criticism of criticism, were *Lines*, the *Dublin Magazine*, *Scottish International* and the *Honest Ulsterman*. The partly magazine-based argument about 'concrete poetry' (discussed here by Eleanor Bell) was, indirectly, about standards, since it implicated MacDiarmid's critical authority and the value of his later poems.

Beyond critical flashpoints, poetry magazines define their milieux through the patient work of sifting new collections. Irish and Scottish magazines are also more likely than English magazines to conduct a live debate about tradition. Thus Thomas Crawford says of John MacQueens' and Tom Scott's *Oxford Book of Scottish Verse*: 'Only on a narrow interpretation of what constitutes a "Scottish" poem . . . is it possible to represent Sir Robert Aytoun and William Drummond by one poem each.'[48] Young poets, discovering elders or ancestors, mediate tradition most significantly. John Hewitt's 'Ancestral Voices' slot in *Rann* includes Ulster poets who wrote in Scots. In the *Dublin Magazine* poets engage with MacNeice, Kavanagh and (see below) Yeats. 'Poets of the Sixties', an alert series in Riddell's *Lines*, mixes up the generations. Here Edwin Morgan writes of Iain Crichton Smith: 'for all the poet's expressed fondness for "precision", these poems are sometimes vague and muffled in the too constant play of images and wit'; Stewart Conn of George Mackay Brown: 'he must beware of over-shuffling a pack which not withstanding the radiance of its colours could become frayed'.[49]

Timothy Brownlow, who co-edited the *Dublin Magazine* with Rivers Carew (1964–9), speaks of being 'blissfully unaware of how deeply political literary matters are in Ireland'.[50] Lingering innocence may explain why this is the only magazine of its day that really accepts Yeats as the begetter of modern Irish poetry. It does so by reviewing studies of his poetry, by producing a Yeats centenary edition, and (crucially) by manifesting a collective sense of Irish poetry. Not that everyone else was a Yeats begrudger. *Arena* and *The Holy Door* also paid centenary tribute, although the latter oddly announces: 'We make George Moore patron of this issue, partly as a sop for Protestant Yeats's centenary.' Anthony Cronin is torn in *Arena*: finding Yeats 'the most exciting poet of this century', the poet with 'the best ear', yet saying that he 'knew nothing' of 'the people to whom most of us belong'.[51]

Arena and *Holy Door* contain many poems of 'character and idiosyncratic privacy' (Lysaght). *Arena* editor James Liddy, author of sentimentally egocentric verse and prose ('I, the poet, muse-mad'), 'believes in the coming of the bards'; while Kavanagh as presiding genius legitimates the anti-critical bias. But, like *Two Rivers*, these magazines also belong to a wider neo-Romanticism: a quasi-Bohemian libertarian ethos to which the English Apocalyptics, the Beats and Bob Dylan contribute. A *Holy Door* editorial calls most English poetry 'the poetry of the mere sad intelligence' (Larkin again), and hopes to make intelligence 'passionate'. Another attacks 'academic joylessness'.[52] More constructively: the second issue stars John Montague's joyful poem 'At the Fleadh Cheoil, Mullingar' ('Puritan Ireland's dead and gone'); Michael Hartnett was an associate editor; and Paul Durcan somehow makes aesthetic sense out of this variously permissive milieu, which in turn throws light on his Irish–London poetic origins. The contrast with the neo-Yeatsian *Dublin Magazine* also reflects cultural distances between (mainly Catholic) University College and (mainly Protestant) Trinity College. So does the first issue of *Lace Curtain*, where James Hogan writes that *Dublin Magazine* poetry 'has retreated into the select restaurant', and shows 'an uncommon regard for form and a common disregard for content . . . [it] reveals contemporary Irish poetry [as] not only dead but stuffed' – class and biorhythms once again.[53] Hogan is spot-on about some feeble poems. Yet, apart from Trinity's *Icarus*, this had been the principal southern Irish magazine to introduce the new poetic generation from the North – Seamus Heaney, as well as ex-Trinity Derek Mahon and Michael Longley: poets who were conscious of Yeats, but whose 'regard for form' amounted to more than Yeatsian pastiche.

In effect, *Lace Curtain* was declaring a poetry war, although Peter Barry's *Poetry Wars* (2006) reminds us that such wars can be wars of three or more kingdoms. The magazine appeared erratically, but consistently pleaded the cause of Irish 'modernism' and 'urban internationalism': most notably, through an influential issue which reprinted 1930s testaments and retrospects by Samuel Beckett and others; and which praised 'work [that] is positively unaccommodating to lovers of Anglo-Irishness in literature'. Here 'Anglo-Irishness' may not be a strictly literary-critical term. *Lace Curtain*'s godfather was Brian Coffey, 'considered by many to be the greatest living Irish poet'.[54] One problem with *Lace Curtain*'s agenda is a variation on Lysaght's analysis. The editorial 'language of aesthetics' lacks a basis in new poems that have received an identifiable stimulus from Coffey or other 'modernist' precursors (theory and practice at least connect in the *Dublin Magazine*). As in *Holy Door* and *Arena*, the technique with greatest claim to be called 'modernist' is freeish verse. Herein lies the retrospective contrast with *POOR. OLD. TIRED. HORSE.*: experimental in its very format, owing to Finlay's cross-overs with the visual arts. The contrast explains why *Gairfish* can plausibly celebrate 'The McAvant-garde', even while printing a Burns parody by Edwin Morgan, 'Scotia Nova', that subverts his own enrolment in that category: 'O wha my maglev-buits will buy, / O wha will prent my jaggy cry; / Wha will kick me when I lie, / The avant-gaird the daddie o't'.[55] *The Lace Curtain* does little more than invoke a generic cosmopolitan modernism (Eliot's 'central line') in binary opposition to 'an obviously national poetry'.[56] This is not a modernism based on evolving practices or critical ideas to which Irish poets – Beckett is a special case – have made innovative rather than imitative contributions. And, besides parking Yeats, Smith's 'Thirties Generation' excludes MacNeice, who complicates issues of form and 'urban internationalism'. Circa 1970 Irish and Scottish magazines increasingly affirm, but do not always conceptualise, their international horizons. Finlay and Morgan are rare in their ability to mesh home and abroad.

Then (as now) arguments about aesthetics and form struggled to disentangle themselves from literary nationalism, literary anti-nationalism, and confused blends of the two. Because of Yeats, Irish controversies usually pivot on form; because of MacDiarmid, Scottish controversies usually pivot on language. In each case, form and language often drift away from their anchor in, or as, a poem. Thus Duncan Glen has little to say about form, except to remark briskly: 'The poetic mainstream of our age ... is the open form of Whitman, Pound, William Carlos Williams, the early Eliot, and the later MacDiarmid.'[57] Hence the contrary force of Finlay's aestheticism; hence the Irish surprise of the linguistic (if simultaneously formal) turn initiated by Paul Muldoon.

The intellectual regrouping after the 1979 devolution referendum, or after MacDiarmid's death, allowed *Verse* to broker a Scottish poetic peace process, if not a critical resolution. Robert Crawford associates the magazine with 'recognition that the multicultural, multilinguistic nature of Scotland is a source of complex invigoration'. MacDiarmid now becomes an 'international modernist' alongside Morgan and Finlay; comparison with Pound validates his 'later' manner; and the national and international merge: Thomas Docherty praises Morgan's *Sonnets from Scotland* as '[a]t once aggressively Scottish and unyieldingly international'. The ambiguous ground between the titular terms of *Scottish International* has closed up. In a *Verse* interview, however, the McAvantgardist Frank Kuppner resists pressure to profess debts to MacDiarmid: 'Actually, I am conscious of major differences.' MacDiarmid's 'habitual rhythm' reminds Kuppner 'of someone walking up and down an old sprung mattress'.[58] Crawford himself qualifies the construction of 'a Scottish Literary Avant-Garde' when he says: 'Even today the work of Edwin Morgan ... draws a good deal of its formal "modernity" from the Russian poetry of sixty or more years ago [and] the reaction which still greets some of his ... "experimental" work is surely a function of Scottish belatedness.'[59]

Yet the twists and turns of magazine-history suggest that it may be as problematic to align 'the language of aesthetics' (Lysaght) with historical progress, as to think that it includes the terms 'national' or 'international'. Like magazines, poetic idioms become 'dead crow'. But that applies to failed or derivative avant-gardism as well as to twilight, kailyard or petrified formalism. The most damaging 'belatedness' has usually been critical belatedness: Kuppner notes that MacDiarmid came 'to view criticism as a sort of betrayal'.[60] The formality that appeared dead or dated to *Lace Curtain* had more shots in its locker, and helped to engender Muldoon's innovations: a 'phoenix', perhaps. Similarly, poetry in Scots continues to be reinvented, and the multifarious 'experiments' of Morgan, Finlay and Leonard remain alive because they never depended on narrowly applied theory. Finlay's cry 'BEAUTY TRADITION EXPERIMENT' is a comprehensive manifesto for any magazine.[61]

CODA: NAMING (IRISH/SCOTTISH) MAGAZINES

Greek ideals:	*Akros, Krino*
Roman combat:	*Arena*
Myth-kitty:	*Phoenix, Icarus, Atlantis, Eildon Tree, Crane Bag, Cencrastus, Gorgon*
Mission:	*Envoy, Innti, Chapman*
Menagerie:	*Rhinoceros, Mongrel Fox, POOR. OLD. TIRED. HORSE., Dark Horse, Blind Serpent, Cencrastus* again, *Salmon, Gairfish, Chanticleer, Gairm*'s cockerel
Globalisation:	*Haiku Scotland, Scottish International*
National aim:	*Scotia, Voice of Scotland, Scottish Review, Irish Review, Poetry Scotland, Poetry Ireland, Poetry Ireland, Poetry Ireland*
Metropolitan claim:	*Edinburgh Review, Dublin Magazine, Dublin Magazine* again
Regional revolt:	*Kilkenny Magazine, Cork Review, Belfast Review, Northern Review, Northman, Northern Lights, Southlight, Fife Lines, Drumlin, Uladh, Honest Ulsterman, Lagan*

Echo of *Blast*:	*Force 10, Klaxon*
Ego trip:	*Kavanagh's Weekly*, MacDiarmid as Scotland's *Voice*
Humility trip:	*Acorn, Windfall, Red Wheelbarrow, Cyphers*
Catholic self-stereotype:	*Holy Door, Lace Curtain*
Protestant self-flattery:	*Honest Ulsterman*
Multiculti:	the unbuilt *Bridge, Two Rivers, Archipelago*
Pseudo-science:	*Graph, Matrix, Catalyst, Zed 2 O*
Orality:	*An Guth*
Writing:	*Ulster Quill, Yellow Nib, Scrievins*
Language:	*Words, Ullans, Lallans*
Form:	*Rann, Verse, Metre, Lines*

NOTES

1. Quoted by Jason Harding, *The Criterion* (Oxford University Press, 2002), 19.
2. The following abbreviations for magazine titles will be used throughout this chapter: *AK*: *Akros*; *AR*: *Arena*; *AT*: *Atlantis*; *CH*: *Chapman*; *CY*: *Cyphers*; *D/DM*: *Dubliner/Dublin Magazine*; *E*: *Envoy*; *G*: *Gairfish*; *HD*: *The Holy Door*; *HU*: *The Honest Ulsterman*; *L*: *Lines Review*; *LC*: *The Lace Curtain*; *M*: *Metre*; *PI*: *Poetry Ireland*; *PIR*: *Poetry Ireland Review*; *POTH*: *POOR. OLD. TIRED. HORSE*; *SI*: *Scottish International*; *V*: *Verse*.
3. *L* 42/43 (September 1972 to February 1973), 5; *LC* 1 (1970), 3.
4. Ian Hamilton, *The Little Magazines: A Study of Six Editors* (London: Weidenfeld & Nicolson, 1976), 9.
5. See Cairns Craig, 'Modernist Journals in Scotland', in Peter Brooker and Andrew Thacker (eds.), *The Oxford Critical and Cultural History of Modernist Magazines, Vol. 1: Britain and Ireland, 1880–1955* (Oxford University Press, 2009), 759–84.
6. See previous note. 'Modernist', however, seems an inexact categorisation.
7. For Craig, see note 4. For McCulloch, see Cairns Craig (ed.), *The History of Scottish Literature*, Vol. 4 (Aberdeen University Press, 1987), 119–32; *Journal of Irish and Scottish Studies* 1:2 (2008), 143–55.
8. Hugh MacDiarmid, *Selected Prose*, ed. Alan Riach (Manchester: Carcanet, 1992), 22.
9. Malcolm Ballin, *Irish Periodical Culture, 1937–1972: Genre in Ireland, Wales, and Scotland* (Basingstoke: Palgrave Macmillan, 2008), 10.
10. *SI* 1 (January 1968), 10; *SI* 3 (August 1968), 5; *Bell* 10:2 (May 1945), 159.
11. Scottish Poetry Library Index, Vol. 7: *Cencrastus*, 1979–92.
12. See Ballin, *Irish Periodical Culture*, 196–9.
13. Hubert Butler, '*Envoy* and Mr Kavanagh', *Escape from the Anthill* (Mullingar: Lilliput, 1985), 154.

14. See Frank Shovlin, *The Irish Literary Periodical, 1923–1958* (Oxford: Clarendon, 2003), 5, 156–79.
15. Robin Fulton, *L* 60 (January 1977), 4; Jordan, *PI* 3 (Spring 1964), 91.
16. Scottish Poetry Library Index, Vol. 2: *Verse*, 1984–95.
17. See David Wheatley, '"Great Hatred, Little Room": The Writer, the University and the Small Magazine', in Aaron Kelly and Alan A. Gillis (eds.), *Critical Ireland* (Dublin: Four Courts, 2001), 208–15.
18. Articles reprinted in Gregory A. Schirmer (ed.), *Reviews and Essays of Austin Clarke* (Gerrards Cross: Colin Smythe, 1995), 99; Tom Clyde (ed.), *Ancestral Voices: The Selected Prose of John Hewitt* (Belfast: Blackstaff, 1987), 117.
19. *L* 10 (December 1955), 7; *L* 13 (Summer 1957), 28; *L* 14 (Spring 1958), 28.
20. *L* 42/43 (September 1972 to February 1973), 5.
21. *CH* 3 (November 1970), unnumbered; *AK* 3:9 (January 1969), 65.
22. Advertisement for *Voice of Scotland*, *L* 9 (August 1955), 4; for MacDiarmid's belief that *SI* was a plot against the national literary movement, see John Herdman, *Poets, Pubs, Polls and Pillar Boxes* (Kircaldy: Akros, 1999), 28–9.
23. *L* 52/53 (May 1975), 92–3; *Aquarius* 11 (1979), 73; *G* 5 (Spring/Summer 1992), 6–7; *L* 52/53 (May 1975), 77.
24. *M* 13 (Winter 2002/3), 47.
25. *PI* 1 (April 1948), 13; *PI* 5 (April 1949), 25; 'Poetry in Ulster: A Survey', *PI* 8 (January 1950), 7.
26. *D/DM* 3:3 (Autumn 1964), 35; *D/DM* 2:1(Spring 1963), 78–9; *D/DM* 6 (January/February 1963), 67.
27. Interview, *Scottish Review of Books* 4:1 (2008), 16.
28. See Edna Longley, 'Back in the 1960s: Belfast Poets, Liverpool Poets', in Nicholas Allen and Eve Patten (eds.), *That Island Never Found* (Dublin: Four Courts, 2007), 139–67.
29. *L* 4 (January 1954), 2; *L* 9 (August 1955), 14; *L* 20 (Summer 1963), 9–11.
30. *L* 42/43 (September 1972 to February 1973), 6.
31. See Eiléan ní Chuilleanáin, 'Drawing Lines', *CY* 10 (Spring 1979), 47–51; and 'Borderlands of Irish Poetry', in Elmer Andrews (ed.), *Contemporary Irish Poetry* (Basingstoke: Macmillan, 1992), 25–40.
32. J. M. Hendry, 'The 70's and Scottish Poetry', *CH* 3:5 (1975), 3.
33. *HU* 82 (Winter 1986), 61.
34. See *L* 37 (June 1971) and *L* 38 (September 1971), Supplement.
35. *G* 1 (Winter 1990), 11; Robert Tait, '*Scottish International*: A Brief Account', Scottish Poetry Library Index, Vol. 6.
36. *PI* 13 (April 1951), 2; *D/DM* 5:1 (Spring 1966), 5.
37. *AT* 1 (March 1970), 5; *HU* 24 (July/August 1970), 3.
38. *HU* 46/47 (November 1974 to February 1975); *HU* 20 (December 1969), 3; *HU* 31 (November/December 1971), 7.
39. 'Hate for Hate', *POTH* 3 (June 1962), Insert.
40. 'Escaped from the Massacre?', *HU* 50 (Winter 1975), 183–6.
41. *E* 1:2 (January 1950), 7–8; *PIR* 14 (Autumn 1985), 6.
42. Shovlin, *Irish Literary Periodicals*, 11–12.

43. Donald Davie, 'Reflections of an English Writer in Ireland', *Studies* 44 (1955), 141.
44. *L* 15 (Summer 1959), 4; Hugh MacDiarmid, *The Letters of Hugh MacDiarmid*, ed. Alan Bold (London: Hamish Hamilton, 1984), 819.
45. *L* 36 (March 1971), 38.
46. *PIR* 17 (Autumn 1986), 12.
47. *AR* 2 (Autumn 1963), 1; *AR* 4 (Spring 1965), 1.
48. *L* 24 (Summer 1967), 19.
49. *L* 21 (Summer 1965), 15; *L* 22 (Winter 1966), 17.
50. David Quin, 'How now Brownlow?', *PIR* 90 (2007), 90.
51. *HD* 2 (Winter 1965), unnumbered; *AR* 4 (Spring 1965), 43.
52. *AR* 1 (Spring 1963), 18; *AR* 2 (Autumn 1963), 1; *HD* 1 (Summer 1965), 2; *HD* 3 (Spring 1966), unnumbered.
53. *LC* 1 (March 1970), 36–8.
54. *LC* 4 (1971), reprinted as *Irish Poetry: The Thirties Generation*, ed. Michael Smith (Dublin: Raven Arts, 1983); *LC* 6 (Autumn 1978), 60.
55. *G* 5 (Spring/Summer 1994), 4.
56. *LC* 6 (Autumn 1978), 56; *LC* 3 (Summer 1970), 6.
57. *AK* 3:7 (March 1968), 5.
58. *V* 4:2 (June 1987), 45; *V* 2 (1985), 47; *V* 6:2 (1989), 48.
59. *G* 5 (Spring/Summer 1992), 27.
60. *V* 6:2 (1989), 48.
61. 'Hate for Hate', *POTH* 3 (June 1962), Insert.

CHAPTER 19

Outwith the Pale: Irish–Scottish studies as an act of translation

Michael Brown

> Do the stones, the sea, seem different in Irish?
> Do we walk in language, in a garment pure
> as water? Or as earth just as impure?[1]

This chapter takes as its prompt two propositions. The first of these is from Edna Longley's ambition enunciated in a programmatic statement of intent in the *Journal of Irish and Scottish Studies*. There, she asserted that the aim of that volume was to provide 'alternative narratives' in which Irish and Scottish comparisons might complicate the traditional rubric of literary analysis.[2] She made plain that 'comparison is about difference, about distinctiveness as well as identity'.[3] 'Has Scottish or Irish exceptionalism been the enemy of Scottish or Irish particularism,' she enquired, positing the possibility that 'perhaps latterday identity politics and multiculturalism have actually re-inscribed habits of national segregation'.[4] This opened up one anxiety about the capacity to conduct Irish–Scottish studies at all.

The second prompt came from Peter Mackay's article in the next issue of the same journal in which he traversed the contentious contours of the border between cultures.[5] His exploration of the vexatious and controversial nature of literary translation provided a valuable metaphor for precisely the challenge that Longley had laid down. If Irish–Scottish studies is to be of value it must be capable of translating the experience of one culture into that of another and overcoming the national segregation against which Longley rails. Certainly, as other essays in this volume bear testimony, translation is not without its difficulties and idiosyncrasies, its cultural baggage and political overtones. Yet, in the spirit of experimentation which Irish–Scottish studies fosters, I offer up one possible reading of Irish–Scottish studies since its inception in the 1970s through the metaphor of translation. In doing so, I provide an assessment of its achievement, some indication of the array of alternative narratives it has already essayed, and thoughts about further exploration of the landscapes and languages, the prose and, indeed, the poetry of these countries.

TRANSLATION AS TRANSITION AND TRANSGRESSION

In T. M. Devine's *The Scottish Nation* (1999) Scottish modernisation is documented across the three centuries since union consigned the book's subject to the political shadows. Yet the real shade haunting the pages is the insurgent Irish nation whose counter-narrative underpins Devine's claim to Scottish success. Famine is avoided, civil strife repeatedly quelled, ethnic nationalism does not gain credence amongst the class-conscious masses that populate the pages, who dutifully work for the union and vote for Labour. Although brought up to the point of devolution – 'this truly was the "settled will" of the Scottish people' – the culmination of the narrative is really the rejection of nationalism concocted in the 'debacle of the 1979 referendum' that ends the penultimate chapter and opens the last, a coda entitled 'A nation reborn?'.[6]

Although superficially similar to R. F. Foster's revisionist rendering of the national tale, *Modern Ireland* (1989), in its ambitious temporal scope and austere formal style, the meta-text with which Devine is concerned is really L. M. Cullen's earlier and more meditative account, *The Emergence of Modern Ireland* (1981), which in turn shadows Scotland. Cullen, for instance, concludes his ruminations on the unique quality of Irish attitudes to history – which frame his considerations on economy and politics – with the observation that 'the contrast between Maria Edgeworth and [Walter] Scott epitomises the Irish lack of self-confidence. Maria Edgeworth looked at her own country with some condescension, whereas Scott exalted Scottish history, culture and even food, marking the crest of a great wave of Scottish self confidence.'[7] Cultural cringe was here construed as an Irish, not a Scottish, trait; one forged by the failure of the country to engage adequately in the project of modernisation.

Ultimately both historians are impelled by anxiety about an older meta-narrative of modernisation, the Ur-text of Max Weber, *The Protestant Ethic and the Spirit of Capitalism* (1904–5). For both Cullen and Devine the challenge is to overcome Weber's identification of modernisation with the Calvinist ethos. For Cullen, the fear of Catholic economic inferiority is exorcised by a sophisticated multi-causal explanation which foregrounds the unique and foundational experience of the Famine and the 1798 Rebellion. As he asserts in the conclusion to *The Emergence*: 'two events in modern

Irish history are exceptional: the Great Famine and the 1798 Rebellion, and they mirror much of the character of Ireland and of Irish history'.[8] In the case of the first, it was primarily the result of a subtle division in the dietary habits of the upper and lower ranks, leaving the western peasantry desperately exposed to dearth, while the east coast could sustain themselves on corn; the second was similarly the consequence of local relations to the land, with the displacement of Catholics from Armagh across the country placing pressure on regions that were already experiencing competition over land use. To Cullen, paradoxically, 'the key counties in these troubles [the term is telling] were the most prosperous in Ireland' but they were also, fatally, 'evenly divided in religion', translating the economic tension into sectarian conflict.[9] Crucially 'the situation made Catholic and Protestant alike aggressive', the counties sliding into a vicious tit-for-tat cycle of neighbourly contempt that prompted the wider conflagration.[10] The parallels with Northern Ireland's crisis of resources (jobs and housing), its history of regional displacement and the rise of sectarian hatred are plain, and subliminally suggested.

In Devine's case, his concern with the Weber thesis drew him to the issue of regionalism and the centrality of Glasgow. Having made a name for himself with a study of the city's tobacco lords – those doyens of imperial enterprise – his real concern for the city lies in the way it confounds any simple application of the Weber thesis.[11] Devine could easily show that the Protestant/Catholic divide did not equate to levels of capitalistic activity, for Glasgow was to become a Catholic heartland (albeit pumped by out-migration from Ireland) and an industrial heartland (albeit manned by Irish labourers). As with Cullen, this is coupled by a concern for sectarian conflict – the ethical axis in Weber's thesis – and a desire to explore the Scottish response to Catholic migration. Thus, in *Scotland's Shame* Devine compiles responses to composer James MacMillan's charge that Scottish Catholics experience 'sleepwalking bigotry' emanating from a 'visceral anti-Catholicism' that permeates the national life, albeit a picture that Devine in his commentary thinks might serve as a 'more accurate vision of the Catholic experience in the 1950s and 1960s', while simultaneously contending that 'the historic identification of Scot with Presbyterian will no longer suffice'.[12]

In both cases, then, what appears to be a national competition – a race to industrial modernity won handsomely by the Scots – can also be read as a shared defence of Catholic confessional identity. This is achieved by articulating the social group's economic vibrancy in Scotland and explaining away the troubling economic lethargy of Ireland while simultaneously recovering the Catholic ethic by parsing the blame for sectarian conflict evenly across the Reformation divide. That the politics of Scottish Catholicism was shaped by union, and that of the Irish equivalent led to independence, is sublimated in the Irish–Scottish concern for a wider discourse of the ethical cultures of economic activity.

But Devine's and Cullen's modernisation thesis is discommoded by cultural under-lays. Note how Devine's Glasgow is transfigured into a Catholic citadel, one built by and for Irish migrants fleeing a famine housed in a British colony. Cullen's economic schema is similarly infiltrated by sectarian identities, a demographic schism which originated in Scottish intrusions into Ireland. So migration confuses, causes slippage and anxiety in the meta-narratives of nations. Hence Cullen's work on the Irish in Europe – a close focus on the brandy trade of France opening out to a consideration of Franco-Irish connections and, indeed, to the shape and structure of the Diaspora as a systemic phenomenon – and Devine's rendition of a *Scottish Empire* (2004) found in America, India and New Zealand.

This agenda speaks to a wider theme, one permeated by a concern for globalisation and the fate of the nation-state. Therein national narratives are not merely disrupted by such intrusions; they fear being overwhelmed by them. Might modernity remove the subject of the study – the nation – and replace it with a universal, if disembodied, modular man? Indeed, the interface and interplay of Scottish and Irish peoples through migratory encounters has been a constant conceit of Irish–Scottish studies, whether in the towns and villages of the homelands, the streets and alleys of London or on the American edges of the imperial world.

As this suggests, the translation of Scottish experience onto Irish soil – and vice versa – is not without a kind of mental dissonance. Rather, this kind of translation of peoples from one location to another has repeatedly created frontier fights and demarcation disputes. This simple fact confronts us with the ways in which Irish–Scottish relations are rarely without mutual suspicion, antagonism and recrimination. And at the heart of this interpretive line is the Rising of 1641, the nuclear meltdown of Irish–Scottish relations. Ulster here becomes not a utopian melting pot of assimilation but a dystopian charnel house of atrocity: an eerie and uncanny foreshadowing of the traumas of the Troubles.[13]

Indeed the shadow of the Troubles hangs over the migration literature as much as it underpins the modernisation literature, although confessional identity gives way here to ethnic concerns. So the recent resurgence in interest in 1641 has been associated with a strengthening awareness of the Scottish content of the plantation, and a rehearsal of the events in a New

British History garb that at times belies a concern for more parochial and patriotic interests. In a wider perspective the revisionist language of political groupings – Old English, New English, Ulster Scot, and Irish – has been co-opted to establish the verities of ethnic conflict. Micheál Ó Siochrú, for instance, inflects his treatment of the Confederate government in Kilkenny with a concern for their claim for all-Ireland governance, and their multi-sided resistance to Scottish and English incursion. Here is his opening paragraph:

> On 22 October 1641 the native Irish of Ulster, led by Sir Phelim O'Neill, captured a number of key towns and fortifications in that province. Within weeks they had forged an alliance with the old English of the Pale, and controlled a large swathe of territory as the revolt spread throughout the country. After an initial period of confusion and chaos, the insurgents began to organise themselves, united by an oath pledging loyalty to God, king and country. This was the beginning of confederate Ireland, a period from 1642 to 1649 when the Irish [note the elision of the old English] governed a unitary state, covering most of the island [akin to the Republic], and engaged in a bitter conflict with royalists [despite their earlier pledge to the king], parliamentarians, and Scots covenanters. Despite the pressures of war, the confederates developed a highly sophisticated system of representative government [positioned against monarchical rule], from which emerged the genesis of modern Irish nationalism.[14]

In the hands of historians, then, Irish–Scottish studies becomes an act of translation. Either translation is transitional – translating the past into the present, configuring the narrative of history as a transition into wider economic industrial commercial modernity – or it sees the translation of peoples across borders as an act of transgression. This turns Irish–Scottish studies into an interrogation of mass dislocation, the conundrums of empire and nation, and the transfer of cultures. The first approach sets Ireland and Scotland in relation to their silent sibling, for in imagining the possibility of modernity the mind turns to England and the furnaces of the smelt works and the dark shafts of the coal mines. The second places Ireland and Scotland in a relationship with the British Empire, and poses problems related to imperial outreach and withdrawal. Irish–Scottish studies finds many echoes in the decolonisation processes and the populations beached by the tidal retreat of European power.

TRANSLATION AS ENTITLEMENT AND ESTRANGEMENT

This contest over empire may take the form of an either/or zero sum conflict between communities, as in 1641, or a mutually damaging spiral of spite as in the Troubles. But it can also be contained within an intra-communal contest, which recalls Cairns Craig's inscription of the nation as a 'suspended civil war', in which the varied interests of communities beneath the state fight to a standstill and submit to the reasoned and shared symbols of national unity in an attempt to pre-empt further slaughter.[15] Historically he contends,

> almost every nation is born out of civil war and continues as the unended but suspended confrontation of the parties to that war. The temporary unity of any actually existing nation, the projected unity of any desired nation, has to be balanced by the reality of its civil conflicts, conflicts that project alternative bases for the unity of the nation.[16]

This is to recognise the hybridity embedded in all nations – as Craig states, utilising a coinage of Alasdair Macintyre, 'the nation ... is an embodied argument'.[17] In that, the country is held together, not by a shared culture or a history of struggle, but by the peace treaty, and the state signifiers that articulate that settlement.

So, too, as Craig notes about Scotland's failure 'to develop an "organic" nationalism in the nineteenth century', problems over entitlement can germinate when 'the space of the nation extended tentacularly around the world, and like the ships launched on the Clyde to carry much of the world's trade around the globe, took the ground of Scotland only as its launching pad'.[18] The place, purpose and power of the diasporic communities surrounding both Ireland and Scotland are here put under scrutiny. In Scotland's case he suggests that 'there can be no coherent narrative of the nation, not because the nation lacks narrative development but for precisely the opposite reason: its narrative spills out over many territories'. Scotland is, Craig provocatively asserts, 'a boundless nation'.[19] The extent to which the Irish Diaspora produces a similarly boundless nation remains a troublesome question for national essentialists torn between founding the nation in land and forging it in blood.

A similar interest in locating 'the whereabouts of literature' asserts itself in the criticism of Edna Longley, who shares Craig's deep concern for overcoming intra-communal conflict and his trust in the possibilities of the state – in both cases these potentialities have not yet been actualised.[20] While for Craig this failure is implicit in the nature of national imagining as the nation is always a possible future, intended but not realised, for Longley the tortuous recent past provides a polemical charge that complicates any easy rendering of cultural symbolism into political identification. Thus, in her meditation on the legacy of Patrick Kavanagh, 'Poetic Forms and Social Malformations', Longley recognises how partition has kept the channels between Northern Irish poetry and the English canon more vital than those open in the south. So, 'Northern poets, from Catholic and Protestant backgrounds alike, have been motivated (as Yeats was) by a desire to show English poets that they can make better use of that lyric inheritance.'[21] In contrast Brendan Kennelly, a southern voice, practises 'iconoclastic methods to get "the English tradition" off his back'.[22]

Yet, elsewhere Longley expresses some anxiety that 'the scant tradition of ecumenism between nationalist and unionist ideology means that the 1998 Good Friday agreement lacks cultural roots'.[23] The use of the adjective is here freighted with meaning, for Longley is no ethnic nationalist. Rather, the roots she seeks are to be found at the symbolic level, vectors of shared meaning in the creation of which poets can play a crucial imaginative role. With regard to Kavanagh, therefore, she situates a southern response in a shared, often presumed, spiritualism – writing of how 'there is, of course, a lot of spilt Catholicism in this', even though 'Durcan and Kennelly wear differently the priestly vestments inherited from Kavanagh. Durcan prays to God in the sight of the congregation. His incantatory voice sounds from the altar [. . .] Kennelly, within whose sensibility the spirit, world, flesh and the devil still conduct their quarrels, speaks in a secular voice from the pulpit.' Yet this high strain seems intimately linked to the success of the Republic in producing shared signifiers: 'Thus their methods not only draw on the ritual formulae of the Church, but imitate press-reports, television commentary, anecdote, advertising, ballads (not only Irish), blues, pop-songs, documentary programmes, revue monologues, pub-talk.'[24] The parenthesis is significant: the presumption until otherwise noted is that the context is Irish, and in particular the success of the Republic in generating normalised, and normalising, habits of social discourse that eventually, after the brackets close, open out into internationally recognisable norms of conduct and conversation.

In the North, Kavanagh's inheritance is bound up not with spiritual signifiers but with a paradoxical need to at once escape the parochial context – MacNeice moves to London, not Dublin, but the impetus is the same – and accommodate its requirements: Heaney digs in, rather than digs out. The problem of location thus becomes central to Longley's reading of Ulster. At once open to England and Scotland, it is closed in by the narrow ground of sectarian dispute, by imagined and real frontiers. The poets respond accordingly, trying to translate parochial experience into something more generalised and fashioning a vocabulary – Longley here cites Ciaran Carson's *Belfast Confetti* – which traces the labyrinth of 'a shifting battleground where survival and syntax have become arbitrary'.[25]

Far, then, from being an advocate for 'partitionism', Longley's work speaks with precision of geographic and political location, troubled as she is by the failure of Northern Ireland to posit a shared set of cultural signifiers that might transcend the conflict.[26] She asserts in her essay 'Multi-Culturalism and Northern Ireland' that 'the symbolic domain, revealingly matters most', although I suspect the revelation here is to do with her own positioning. 'Hence the row', she proceeds, 'when Sinn Féin ministers objected to union jacks flying on the buildings that house their departments. Hence, too, the extraordinary conflict over the title and badge rather than the actuality of the police.' This failure to produce agreement over symbols is intrinsic to the legitimacy crisis that bedevils the Northern Irish state, and the dispute over 'parity of esteem' which 'to Northern Irish Catholics [...] means long-overdue recognition for their modes and emblems of communal self-expression. To Unionists, however, the UK's state is imperilled if its ceremonial is diluted, its emblems relativised, because they contribute to an unequal environment.'[27]

Crucially, in this rendition Irish–Scottish studies is intimately connected to a discourse of civic nationality – a self-conscious project of nation building through the symbols and signifiers of an emergent state. In stating the problem this way, the shade haunting the imagination is once again the civil strife and ethnic conflagration of Ulster. There is a silent anxiety that Scottish civic nationalism is in danger of subsiding into the kind of ethnic nationalism that is associated with the Irish condition – and the wider conflagrations of European nation building. This is the queasiness that prompted Tom Nairn to offer medicinal advice 'On Not Hating England'.[28] The underlying presumption is that civic nationalism is inherently more civil, less volatile; less violent as it is not fuelled by ethnic estrangement but fraternal fellow feeling. Any ethnos can pronounce loyalty to the neutral, civic symbols of the state.

But as Ernst Gellner once provocatively asked, 'Do nations have navels?'[29] By this he was enquiring of the origins of the nation: can any symbol be raised to the status of national icon? Can any of the multiple languages and dialects spoken inside the boundaries of the state be chosen as the *langue d'état*? Is it as simple as adopting a national anthem – as Ireland did in 1926, with a song written in 1907 – or must the state relay more antique and traditional expressions of community? In configuring the Republic of Ireland, Northern Ireland and Scotland commentators are confronted with a nation-state, a nation-less state, and a state-less nation. Questions – what state; whose nation; which symbol – overhang any attempt to create meaningful comparisons and contrasts.

The programme of research produced by such conundrums only underlines the complexity of these queries. John Kerrigan's *Archipelagic English* (2008) reveals the vibrancy of regional expression in the early modern period, before the standardisation of accent, vocabulary and structure took full effect. Set alongside the residual Latinate culture of the period and the existence of rich Celtic-language literatures, the matrix of cultural expression is shown to be rich, variegated and polyphonic.[30] There is no easy reduction to the structures of state power – as the declension in the reach of Irish in the nineteenth century and its failure to re-establish itself in the twentieth highlight, the motor for change is often found within the wider culture and not in the engine rooms of policy making.

Indeed the process of centralisation and conformity in linguistic matters has the intriguing effect of estranging the very tongue you speak. Standard English is rendered artificial; a consequence of state patriotism and civic nationalism: its home is the school room not the school yard. Language is seemingly rendered impersonal – to speak is to replicate and reproduce the symbolic power of the state. The poetry of dissidence is translated into the prose of orthodoxy.

This concern for symbolism makes Irish–Scottish studies into a venue for disputes over state formation and nation creation. It places Ireland and Scotland in a vexed relationship with that rebel from the British cause, the United States, where civic nationalism and state creation enable a multi-ethnic, multilinguistic society to flourish despite a hinterland of slavery and the bitterness of a civil war. But the anxiety about estrangement and the imposition of state-sponsored systems onto the cultural life of the communities places Irish–Scottish studies into a relationship with the European nightmare: absolutism and totalitarianism; systems under which culture is politicised and circumscribed.

TRANSLATION AS TOLERANCE?

The challenge set is to recuperate language. In that task Jürgen Habermas's construction of a concept of communicative action, against which he sets the 'mute violence of terrorists' and the 'fatally speechless clash of worlds', may be of use.[31] If the modes of translation I have explored are all haunted by the silence of brutality and death, might Habermas's defence of speech be of any value? Might his conception of a personal ethical imperative towards speech, a historically vital public sphere of transparent debate, and a democratic procedural state that legitimises disagreement help us to reconfigure Irish–Scottish studies?

In 2007 I published an article which calls for a perspective on Irish studies informed by my experience of Irish–Scottish studies, and one which could easily be extended to its peculiar comparative demands. There I wrote of how 'we need to rethink ourselves out from under the theoretical umbrellas of the nation-state and empire', proposing that we re-explore the potentialities of civil society. 'At its simplest', I argued, 'civil society is where unrelated humans congregate for common purposes. Thus it accommodates and displays difference, inscribes and revises itself in reflexive observation, and propounds a philosophy of politeness that precludes the intensities of uncivil war.'[32]

One advantage of this approach is that it has no referent beyond Ireland or Scotland to which it conforms or contrasts. Rather, in focusing attention on associational life of the communities of these countries we are writing within a genre that has Irish–Scottish origins in the Enlightenment. Indeed Habermas's Kantian vocabulary occludes, but does not obliterate, his (and Kant's) debt to the Irish and Scottish progenitors of the concept of communicative action – Burke, Ferguson, Hume, Hutcheson and Smith. And as recent scholarship has begun to recover, the multi-layered analysis offered by civil society emanates from, and informs, numerous Irish and Scottish writers.[33] Indeed, Northern Ireland's complex balance of powers within the Assembly offers us a practical example of the kind of procedural construction necessary to accommodate polarised differences within the kind of state Habermas would envisage as a capstone to a fully communicative democratic state. In other words, to posit one answer to Edna Longley's fertile question concerning 'the whereabouts of literature' it might indeed be located beyond Scotland; or beyond Ireland for that matter. It is not fashioned by the nation-state. Nor is it located in a kind of mythic no-place. Rather, Irish–Scottish studies provides a distinctive place from which to conduct comparative analysis: the thick, intricate weave of social networks and associational institutions which make up a civil society first theorised by Adam Ferguson, celebrated by Edmund Burke and repeatedly given ethical expression through the history of Ireland and Scotland.

In this scheme – in which ethical guidance for the individual is provided by social networks, where fraternal fellowship is supplied by clubs and societies, and where the politics of recognition is provided by a democratic state – language is fundamental. As Peter Burke has observed of the term 'community', it recognises 'that collective solidarities and identities are . . . a part of everyday life. To make the point in a linguistic way, whenever we say "we" we are expressing a sense of solidarity with some others, a sense of belonging to a community, whether it is small or large, temporary or permanent, harmonious or discordant.' He argues that in confronting how such communities are shaped, 'we have to examine the role of languages not only as expressions or reflections of a sense of community cohesion, but also as one of the means by which communities are constructed or reconstructed'.[34]

One central benefit of this approach is underlined by Burke when he notes how 'individuals can and usually do belong to a number of different communities: local and national, religious, occupational and so on. Some of these communities are in competition', as in Northern Ireland's religious and political cross-mapping, 'or even in conflict' as with the Democratic Unionist Party's regionalised opposition to the British government, 'for the loyalty of individual speakers – region versus nation for instance': Scotland and Britain perhaps. 'As sociolinguists have often pointed out,' he proceeds, 'people use different forms or varieties of language, whether consciously or unconsciously, to express their solidarity with those different communities. This is a major reason for what is sometimes termed "code-switching", the practice of shifting between languages or varieties of languages.'[35] In other words, we are all, in the socio-linguistic sense, multilingual and involved in 'code-switching', translating one set of social practices into the language of another as we work our way through our daily lives – translating our speech acts in our occupation to those in informal leisure time, to those in the domestic sphere. This is how we make ourselves coherent to ourselves and to others.

Yet, all this has problems of its own, including what Jürgen Habermas (nicely, given our conceit here) terms a-symmetrical translation. While at the heart of his understanding of communicative action is an understanding of how faith groups, for instance, convert their 'worldview' to the norms demanded of secular proceduralism – he writes of how 'the mode for non-destructive secularisation is translation' – he does accept that the cognitive burden is not equally placed on religious believers and non-believers.[36] Thus 'the translation of the notion of man's likeness to God into the notion of human dignity', while it allows the insertion of religiously grounded ethical premises to enter into the democratic debate, is little more than 'a saving translation'.[37] In a startling passage Habermas contends that if these secular translations are not adhered to 'in parliament, for example, the rules of procedure must empower the house leader to strike religious positions or contributions from the official transcript'. This is in spite of his avowed recognition that 'religious traditions have a special power to articulate moral intuitions, especially with regard to vulnerable forms of communal life'.[38] Even more substantively, in entering into the democratic process, 'religion has to give up [the] claim to interpretive monopoly and to a comprehensive organisation of life' while non-believers must only 'rationally reckon with the fact of continuing disagreement', itself surely part of the process institutionalised in the state system.[39] In other words, in this a-symmetrical relationship, 'for the expectation of an on-going lack of agreement between rational factual knowledge and religious tradition [religion] deserves the predicate "reasonable" only when religious convictions are accorded an epistemic status that is not merely irrational from the perspective of secular knowledge'.[40] In the process of translation that occurs between faith and knowledge, it seems the traffic is primarily one way.

If we take Habermas's trope of translation more literally, we can see how this kind of a-symmetry affects the wider realm of cultural exchange between the state and the society. For instance, it is surely relevant that it tends to be cultural artefacts – poems, for instance – that are translated into the wider tongue, while procedural instructions – laws, bureaucratic forms, etc. – are translated into the minority language. The rules of the game are those of the state, and it retains the right to determine the means of entry into the debate. Culture retains a valuable vantage-point, but its insight is only permissible when translated into an acceptable vocabulary of political intention.

So, too, the literature and life of any form of civil society contain hidden costs. One such is the perplexing sedative effect that can be brought on by the very ubiquity of shared symbols of power and legitimacy. As Michael Billig has recognised, the commonality of symbols of nationality – what he nicely terms 'banal nationalism' in which 'flagging of nationhood' is constant and yet therefore unobtrusive, generating a shared background of assumptions and perspectives that underpin loyalty and patriotism – can actually undermine these signifiers' purpose. Billig argues that the power of banal nationalism is partially produced by its intentional shyness: 'the sociological forgetting is not fortuitous; nor is it to be blamed on the absent-mindedness of particular scholars. Instead it fits an ideological pattern in which "our" nationalism ... is forgotten: it ceases to appear as nationalism, disappearing into the "natural" environment of "societies".'[41] Nations, then, become like the weather, as ubiquitous, unavoidable and natural as rainfall. Yet, the self-effacement involved also presumes a disengagement from the heat and emotion, the vigour and motivating force of nations. This in turn is projected outward; as he notes, 'the irrationality of nationalism is projected on to "others"'. In the civility gained, something of the moral energy is dissipated, and the power to motivate self-sacrifice diluted. If, as Billig asserts in the opening sentence of his study, 'all societies that maintain armies maintain the belief that some things are more valuable than life itself', banal nationalism can subvert that tenet.[42]

But perhaps the most fundamental cost of tolerance is the acceptance that the world of the good has been translated into the world of the right. As David Hume realised, neither superstition nor enthusiasm can now validate action to destroy perceived heresy.[43] The real cost of living in civil society – to believers and non-believers alike – is the realisation that we do not have access to a higher order of understanding: there is no metaphysics, no superhuman, no channel of the divine. We are locked in the mundane reality of mutual humility, committed to our minute philosophies and trapped on the narrow ground of empathy. It is to admit that the age of heroes has passed.

Yet despite such reservations I still think we need to explore the possibility of taking civil society, and not the nation-state, as our starting point. This would, for instance, demand a comparative, inter-subjective awareness. It would be predicated on the concept of shared communal space and, crucially, an ethics grounded in discursive practice. It would be to imagine a society where the individual lives as a translator, constantly rendering the experience of the self and the other into a shared vocabulary through which argument and agreement might be conducted. It would reignite language with the possibility of communication; it would re-enchant the world with a variegated landscape of difference. It would provide a politics of recognition and an emotional hinterland of memory.

What might just such a poetic utterance look like? The challenge is set down, I think, in the poem that I have used as an epigraph to this chapter, for, in concluding, Crichton Smith reiterates a phrase taken 'from an Irish poem / turned into English', writing:

> And I gaze at the three poets. They are me
> poised between two languages. They have chosen
> with youth's supreme confidence and decision.
>
> 'Half of my side you were, half of my seeing,
> half of my walking you were, half of my hearing'.
> Half of this world I am, half of this dancing.[44]

NOTES

1. Iain Crichton Smith, 'For Poets Writing in English over in Ireland', *Collected Poems* (Manchester: Carcanet, 1996), 238.
2. Edna Longley, 'Relations and Comparisons between Irish and Scottish Poetry: 1890 to the Present Day', *Journal of Irish and Scottish Studies* 1:1 (2007), 231–9, 231.

3. *Ibid.*, 234.
4. *Ibid.*, 234, 235.
5. Peter Mackay, 'An Guth and the Leabhar Mór: Dialogues between Scottish Gaelic and Irish Poetry', *Journal of Irish and Scottish Studies* 1:2 (2008), 175–88.
6. T. M. Devine, *The Scottish Nation* (London: Penguin, 2000), 617, 591.
7. L. M. Cullen, *The Emergence of Modern Ireland* (Dublin: Gill and MacMillan, 1983 [1981]), 255.
8. *Ibid.*, 250.
9. *Ibid.*, 252.
10. *Ibid.*, 253.
11. T. M. Devine, *The Tobacco Lords: A Study of the Tobacco Merchants of Glasgow and Their Trading Activities*, c. 1740–90 (Edinburgh University Press, 1990 [1975]).
12. T. M. Devine (ed.), *Scotland's Shame: Bigotry and Sectarianism in Modern Scotland* (Edinburgh: Mainstream, 2000), 14, 15, 263.
13. See Brian MacCuarta (ed.), *Ulster 1641: Aspects of the Rising* (Belfast: Institute of Irish Studies, 1997).
14. Micheál Ó Siochrú, *Confederate Ireland, 1642–1649: A Constitutional and Political Analysis* (Dublin: Four Courts, 1999), 11.
15. Cairns Craig, 'Scotland and Hybridity', in Gerard Carruthers, David Goldie and Alastair Renfrew (eds.), *Beyond Scotland: New Contexts for Twentieth-Century Scottish Literature* (Amsterdam: Rodopi, 2004), 229–53, 248.
16. *Ibid.*
17. *Ibid.*; see also 250.
18. Cairns Craig, *The Modern Scottish Novel: Narrative and the National Imagination* (Edinburgh University Press, 1999), 237.
19. *Ibid.*, 237.
20. Edna Longley, 'The Whereabouts of Literature', in *Beyond Scotland*, 151–66.
21. Edna Longley, 'Poetic Forms and Social Malformations', in *The Living Stream: Literature and Revisionism in Ireland* (Newcastle-Upon-Tyne: Bloodaxe, 1994), 200.
22. *Ibid.*, 199.
23. Edna Longley, 'Multi-Culturalism and Northern Ireland: Making Differences Fruitful', in Edna Longley and Declan Kiberd, *Multiculturalism: The View from the Two Irelands* (Cork University Press, 2001), 2.
24. Longley, 'Poetic Forms', 218, 218–19.
25. *Ibid.*, 211.
26. *Ibid.*, 200.
27. Longley, 'Multi-Culturalism and Northern Ireland', 6.
28. Tom Nairn, 'On Not Hating England', *After Britain: New Labour and the Return of Scotland* (London: Verso, 2000), 192–222.
29. Ernst Gellner, *Nationalism* (New York University Press, 1997), 101.
30. Peter Davidson, *The Universal Baroque* (Manchester University Press, 2007).
31. Jürgen Habermas, 'Faith and Knowledge', *The Future of Human Nature* (Cambridge: Polity, 2003), 103.

32. Michael Brown, 'Teaching Irish Studies in Ireland: After the End', in Liam Harte and Yvonne Whelan (eds.), *Ireland Beyond Boundaries: Mapping Irish Studies in the Twenty-First Century* (London: Pluto, 2007), 58–70, 64–5.
33. See, for instance, Cairns Craig, *Intending Scotland: Explorations in Scottish Culture since the Enlightenment* (Edinburgh University Press, 2009), 179–202.
34. Peter Burke, *Language and Communities in Early Modern Europe* (Cambridge University Press, 2004), 6.
35. *Ibid.*
36. Habermas, 'Faith and Knowledge', 114; Jürgen Habermas, 'On the Relations between the Secular Liberal State and Religion', in Hent de Vries and Lawrence E. Sullivan (eds.), *Political Theologies: Public Religions in a Post-Secular World* (New York: Fordham University Press, 2006), 251–60, 258.
37. Habermas, 'The Secular Liberal State and Religion', 258.
38. Jürgen Habermas, 'Religion in the Public Sphere: Cognitive Presuppositions for the "Public Use of Reason" by Religious and Secular Citizens', *Between Naturalism and Religion: Philosophical Essays* (Cambridge: Polity, 2008), 131.
39. Habermas, 'The Secular Liberal State and Religion', 259; Jürgen Habermas, 'Religious Tolerance as a Pacemaker for Cultural Rights', *Between Naturalism and Religion*, 264.
40. Habermas, 'Religious Tolerance as a Pacemaker', 264.
41. Michael Billig, *Banal Nationalism* (London: Thousand Oaks, 1995), 38.
42. *Ibid.*, 1.
43. David Hume, 'Of Superstition and Enthusiasm', in *Essays: Moral, Political, Literary*, ed. E. F. Miller (Indianapolis: Liberty Fund, 1985).
44. Crichton Smith, 'For Poets Writing in English over in Ireland', *Collected Poems*, 239–40.

Guide to further reading

Books that deal comparatively with modern Irish and Scottish literature include:

Liam McIlvanney and Ray Ryan (eds.), *Ireland and Scotland: Culture and Society, 1700–2000* (Dublin: Four Courts, 2005)

Ray Ryan, *Ireland and Scotland: Literature and Culture, State and Nation, 1966–2000* (Oxford University Press, 2002)

Fiona Stafford, *Starting Lines in Scottish, Irish and English Poetry: from Burns to Heaney* (Oxford University Press, 2000).

Books that deal comparatively with the historical, literary-historical and linguistic background include:

Frank Ferguson and Andrew R. Holmes (eds.), *Revising Robert Burns and Ulster: Literature, Religion and Politics, c. 1770–1920* (Dublin: Four Courts, 2009)

Christopher Harvie, *A Floating Commonwealth: Politics, Culture, and Technology on Britain's Atlantic Coast* (Oxford University Press, 2008)

Hugh Kearney, *The British Isles: A History of Four Nations*, 2nd edn (Cambridge University Press, 2006)

John Kerrigan, *Archipelagic English: Literature, History and Politics 1603–1707* (Oxford University Press, 2008)

John M. Kirk and Dónall P. Ó Baoill (eds.), *Language Links: the Languages of Ireland and Scotland* (Belfast: Cló Ollscoil na Banríona, 2001)

Edna Longley, Eamonn Hughes and Des O'Rawe (eds.), *Ireland (Ulster) Scotland: Concepts, Contexts, Comparisons* (Belfast: Cló Ollscoil na Banríona, 2003)

E. W. McFarland, *Ireland and Scotland in the Age of Revolution* (Edinburgh University Press, 1994)

Liam McIlvanney, *Burns the Radical: Poetry and Politics in Late Eighteenth-Century Scotland* (East Linton: Tuckwell Press, 2002)

Wilson McLeod, *Divided Gaels: Gaelic Cultural Identities in Scotland and Ireland, c. 1200–c. 1650* (Oxford University Press, 2004)

Murray G. H. Pittock, *Poetry and Jacobite Politics in Eighteenth-Century Britain and Ireland* (Cambridge University Press, 1994)

Scottish and Irish Romanticism (Oxford University Press, 2008)

Andrew Newby, *Ireland, Radicalism and the Scottish Highlands, c. 1870–1912* (Edinburgh University Press, 2007)

Graham Walker, *Intimate Strangers: Political and Cultural Interaction between Scotland and Ulster in Modern Times* (Edinburgh: John Donald, 1995).

Overviews that deal wholly or partly with modern Scottish poetry include:

Ronald Black (ed.), *An Tuil: Anthology of 20th Century Scottish Gaelic Verse* (Edinburgh: Polygon, 2000)
Ian Brown *et al.* (eds.), *The Edinburgh History of Scottish Literature*, Vol. 3 (Edinburgh University Press, 2007)
Gerard Carruthers *et al.* (eds.), *Beyond Scotland: New Contexts for Twentieth-Century Scottish Literature* (Amsterdam, New York: Rodopi, 2004)
Cairns Craig (ed.), *The History of Scottish Literature: Twentieth Century*, Vol. 4 (Aberdeen University Press, 1987–9)
Robert Crawford, *Scotland's Books: The Penguin History of Scottish Literature* (London: Penguin, 2007)
Colin Nicholson and Matt McGuire (eds.), *The Edinburgh Companion to Contemporary Scottish Poetry* (Edinburgh University Press, 2009)
Berthold Schoene (ed.), *The Edinburgh Companion to Contemporary Scottish Literature* (Edinburgh University Press, 2007).
Christopher Whyte, *Modern Scottish Poetry* (Edinburgh University Press 2004)

Overviews that deal wholly or partly with modern Irish poetry include:

Fran Brearton, *The Great War in Irish Poetry* (Oxford University Press, 2000)
Matthew Campbell (ed.), *The Cambridge Companion to Contemporary Irish Poetry* (Cambridge University Press, 2003)
Patricia Coughlan and Alex Davis (eds.), *Modernism and Ireland: The Poetry of the 1930s* (Cork University Press, 1995)
Neil Corcoran, *Poets of Modern Ireland: Text, Context, Intertext* (Cardiff: University of Wales Press, 1999)
  (ed.), *The Chosen Ground: Essays on the Contemporary Poetry of Northern Ireland* (Bridgend: Seren, 1992)
Alan Gillis, *Irish Poetry of the 1930s* (Oxford University Press, 2005)
John Goodby, *Irish Poetry since 1950: from Stillness into History* (Manchester University Press, 2000)
Margaret Kelleher and Philip O'Leary (eds.), *The Cambridge History of Irish Literature*, Vol. 2 (Cambridge University Press, 2006)
Peter McDonald, *Mistaken Identities: Poetry and Northern Ireland* (Oxford University Press, 1997)
Justin Quinn, *The Cambridge Introduction to Modern Irish Poetry, 1800–2000* (Cambridge University Press, 2008).

Anthologies that bring together Irish and Scottish poetry include:

Rody Gorman (ed.), *An Guth* 1– (Dublin: Coiscéim, 2003–)
Ian MacDonald and Michael Davitt (eds.), *Sruth na Maoile: Twentieth Century Gaelic Poetry from Ireland and Scotland* (Edinburgh: Canongate, 1993)

Jim McGonigal *et al.* (eds.), *Across the Water: Irishness in Modern Scottish Writing* (Glendaruel: Argyll Publishing, 2000)

Malcolm MacLean and Theo Dorgan (eds.), *An Leabhar Mòr: the Great Book of Gaelic* (Edinburgh: Canongate, 2002).

Online resources include the project's pages on the Seamus Heaney Centre for Poetry website – www.qub.ac.uk/schools/SeamusHeaneyCentreforPoetry/irishscottishpoetry – and the homepage of the Research Institute of Irish and Scottish Studies: www.abdn.ac.uk/riiss. The Research Institute also publishes, both online and in printed form, the *Journal of Irish and Scottish Studies* (2007–).

Index

Adcock, Fleur, 127
Adorno, Theodor, 73, 304
agency, 93, 166, 177, 212, 219, 227–9, 230–6, 243, 260, 284–5, 324–5
Aiken, Conrad, 95
Akhmatova, Anna, 287
Albright, Daniel, 24
Alcobia-Murphy, Shane, 200, 281–2, 283
Alexander, Michael, 153
Alighieri, Dante 44, 45, 283, 284
Alvarez, Al, 120, 123
Amairgin, 170
Amis, Kingsley, 151
Anderson, Benedict, 207
Archambeau, Robert, 254
Aristophanes, 133, 258
Aristotle, 234
Armitage, Simon, 132
Arnold, Matthew, 3, 30–1
Ashbery, John, 282
Auden, W. H., 23, 25, 64, 120, 135
authorship, 89, 103, 164, 171–3, 200, 280–90
avant-garde, the, 1, 238–41, 242–5, 247–9, 253, 254–62, 280, 299, 307–9
Aytoun, Sir Robert, 306

Ballin, Malcolm, 295, 296
Bardwell, Leland, 305
Barker, George, 246
Barry, Peter, 307
Barthes, Roland, 102, 224, 252, 285, 286, 289
Bartók, Béla, 177–8, 184
Bashō, 255
Bataille, Georges, 195
Bateman, Meg, 132, 165–7, 171, 183–4
Batstone, Stephanie, 90
Baudelaire, Charles, 187
Beckett, Samuel, 23, 245, 247, 274, 307, 308
Beeching, Richard, 216
Behan, Brendan, 94
Belfast Group, 14, 139, 265–6, 275

Benjamin, Walter, 164–5, 173, 226
Berry, Wendell, 255
Berryman, John, 26
Bethea, David, 186
Betjeman, John, 301
Billig, Michael, 324–5
Black, D. M., 299, 303
Blok, Aleksandr, 196
Bloom, Harold, 24, 102
Boland, Eavan, 251, 265, 300
Bolitho, William, 227
Boyd, Ernest, 23
Bradbury, Malcolm, 129
Brearton, Fran, 88, 218
Breathnach, Colm, 104
Brisset, Jean-Pierre, 258
Brodsky, Joseph, 186
Bronowski, Jacob, 129
Brontë, Emily, 282
Broom, Sarah, 291
Brown, Clarence, 281, 283
Brown, Oliver, 26
Brown, Terence, 205, 305
Browning, Robert, 127–8
Brownlow, Timothy, 306
Buchan, John, 29
Buchan, Tom, 305
Buchanan, George, 133
Burke, Edmund, 322
Burke, Peter, 322–3
Burns, Robert, 12, 30, 35, 40, 46, 48–9, 51, 53, 120, 185, 308
Burnside, John, 248
Burroughs, William, 241
Butler, Hubert, 296, 297
Byron, George Gordon, Lord, 48–53, 58–9

Cage, John, 256
Caimbeul, Aonghas Pàdraig, 104
Caimbeul, Maoilios, 182–3, 184
Calder, John, 240–2

331

Caledonian anti-syzygy, 46–7, 67
Campbell, Roy, 60
Campbell Hay, George, 91, 92, 184
canonicity, 6, 155, 196, 238, 274, 281, 302
Carew, Rivers, 306
Carlos Williams, William, 27, 308
Carson, Anne, 139
Carson, Ciaran, 131, 194, 195, 196, 200–2, 208, 209–11, 225–6, 236, 257, 304, 319
Catullus, 40, 133, 135
Cavafy, C. P., 92, 185, 186–8
Cawdor, Wilma, 90
Chambers, Harry, 294
Chaucer, Geoffrey, 148, 151
Chaudhry, Yug Mohit, 295
Chitty, Susan, 282
Clancy, Thomas Owen, 131
Clark, Heather, 139
Clarke, Aidan, 317
Clarke, Austin, 23, 298, 299
class, 2, 14, 20, 25–6, 32, 34, 68–9, 74, 122, 129–30, 134, 140–1, 144, 177, 225–6, 227–36, 276, 301, 302, 307, 314, 315
Clyde, Tom, 295
Cockburn, Ken, 249
Coffey, Brian, 254, 307
Coleridge, S. T., 31
Conn, Stewart, 127, 306
Corbett, John, 158
Corkery, Daniel, 302, 303
Craig, Cairns, 107, 143, 205, 219, 294, 295, 318
Craig, David, 298
Crawford, Robert, 3, 5, 205, 215–16, 219, 248, 251, 252, 280, 284, 286, 288, 297, 308
Crawford, Thomas, 306
Creeley, Robert, 242, 261
Crichton Smith, Iain, 1, 4, 11, 119, 144, 223–4, 230–1, 306, 325
Cronin, Anthony, 306
Cronin, Michael, 171
Crotty, Patrick, 133
Crowe, Anna, 216
Cullen, L. M., 314–16
cultural nationalism/internationalism, 3, 4–5, 6–10, 15–16, 20–3, 26, 29–30, 34, 46–50, 53, 61, 65, 67, 78–9, 91, 92–3, 94–5, 106, 107–9, 121–2, 125, 131, 132–3, 135, 136, 139, 142–3, 147–8, 151, 152, 153, 161, 176–89, 191–202, 207, 208, 222–36, 238–49, 251–5, 274, 276–7, 287–8, 295–7, 301, 303–4, 305, 307–9, 321–5
cummings, e.e., 27, 267

Daiches, David, 305
Davidson, John, 1–3, 29
Davie, Donald, 301, 305
Davie, George Elder, 14
Davis, Thomas, 222, 225
Davitt, Michael, 112–13
Dawe, Gerald, 95
Day Lewis, Cecil, 25, 87–8, 130
de Paor, Louis, 116, 165
Deane, Seamus, 273, 304
Deguy, Michel, 137
Dermody, Thomas, 12
Derrida, Jacques, 194, 202
Devine, T. M., 314–16
Devlin, Ann, 288
Devlin, Denis, 254
devolution, 7, 8, 132, 300, 301, 304
Didsbury, Peter, 129
Dodds, E. R., 134
Donaghy, Michael, 259
Donaldson, Talbot, 155
Donne, John, 39–40, 41–7, 48–9, 51, 53
Donoghue, Denis, 24
Douglas, Keith, 88, 91, 93
Drummond, William, 306
Dunbar, William, 47, 124, 150–1
Dunn, Douglas, 12, 253, 265–6, 267–77, 301, 302
Durcan, Paul, 197, 198, 239, 245–7, 300, 301, 307, 319
Dylan, Bob, 307

Eagleton, Terry, 151, 153
Edgeworth, Maria, 314
Einstein, Albert, 48
Eliot, T. S., 2, 5, 26, 28, 39, 59, 60, 74, 102, 120, 121, 143, 209, 251, 253, 284, 294, 305, 308
Ellmann, Richard, 24
English Studies, 9, 135, 151, 153, 155, 298
Enright, Dennis, 129, 271
Ewart, Gavin, 129

Falck, Colin, 125
Feinstein, Elaine, 182
Ferguson, Adam, 322
Ferguson, Frank, 15
Ferguson, Maggie, 91
Ferguson, Samuel, 14–16
Finlay, Alec, 248–9
Fisher, Roy, 134
Flynn, Tony, 129
Foley, Michael, 294, 304
Forgaill, Dalánn, 10
Foster, R. F., 314
Frost, Robert, 120, 274
Fuller, John, 125, 127, 128
Fulton, Robin, 294, 298, 302

Garioch, Robert, 25, 94, 122, 133, 303
Gellner, Ernst, 320
gender, 2, 8, 78–9, 109, 110, 111–13, 139, 145, 173, 180, 186–8, 281, 282, 283, 288–90
genre, 4, 64, 105, 143, 234, 235, 255
Gérin, Winifred, 282
Gibbon, Monk, 303
Gide, André, 178
Gillis, Alan, 232–4, 236
Girard, René, 108
Glen, Duncan, 294, 298, 302, 305, 308
Goethe, J. W., 93
Gomringer, Eugene, 243
Goodby, John, 254
Goodsir Smith, Sydney, 24, 94–5, 176, 241
Gorman, Rody, 10, 165, 167–9, 171
Gortschacher, Wolfgang, 295
Graham, Colin, 7
Graham, W. S., 25, 119
Grassic Gibbon, Lewis, 21
Graves, Robert, 88, 256
Green, Martin, 245, 301
Greene, Graham, 122
Gregory Smith, G., 5, 6, 14, 47, 67
Gregson, Ian, 148
Grennan, Eamon, 302
Grierson, Herbert, 39–53
Grieve, Christopher M. *See* MacDiarmid, Hugh
Grigson, Geoffrey, 296
Gunn, Neil M., 21, 303
Gunn, Thom, 301
Gwynn, Stephen, 14

Habermas, Jürgen, 321, 322, 323–4
Hackett, Sir John, 88
Hall, Donald, 120, 268
Hamilton, Ian, 121, 125, 127, 128, 294, 306
Hamilton Finlay, Ian, 143–4, 239–40, 241, 242–4, 245, 246, 248, 299, 304, 307, 308, 309
Hardt, Michael, 219
Hardy, Thomas, 207
Harrison, Tony, 124, 127, 135, 141
Harsent, David, 125, 127, 128
Hartnett, Michael, 171, 172, 180, 307
Haughton, Hugh, 269
Healy, Randolph, 251, 254–8, 259, 261–2
Heaney, Seamus, 1, 2, 3–4, 10, 11, 23, 89, 91, 121, 127, 128, 135, 139, 140, 141, 142–3, 145, 153–7, 172–3, 200, 204, 208–9, 210–11, 222–3, 224, 225, 230–1, 254, 255, 257, 258, 265, 268, 270, 273, 274, 277, 287, 301, 302, 304, 307, 319
Henderson, Hamish, 13, 14, 91–3
Hendry, J. M., 302
Henn, T. R., 24
Henryson, Robert, 11, 124, 143
Herbert, W. N., 144, 194, 195, 196, 197–200, 201–2, 252, 254, 262, 299
Herbert, Zbigniew, 141–2
Herron, Tom, 64
Hewitt, John, 12, 16, 87, 89, 298, 300, 301, 306
Hiberno-English, 137, 154–7
Higgins, Kevin, 300
Hill, Geoffrey, 275
Hindes Groome, Francis, 212
Hobsbaum, Philip, 13, 265
Hobsbawm, Eric, 103
Hogan, James, 307
Hoggart, Richard, 129
Hölderlin, Friedrich, 93
Holub, Miroslav, 141–2
Homer, 134, 136
Horace, 134
Housman, A. E., 136
Houston, Douglas, 125, 129
Howe, Nicholas, 159
Howe, Susan, 255
Hughes, Glyn, 271
Hughes, Ted, 129, 275
Hume, David, 325
Hunter, Barbara, 296
Hyde, Douglas, 102

Imlah, Mick, 132
international influences, 120, 141–2, 180–2, 185–9, 196–7, 199, 200, 268, 269, 281–3
Irish language poetry, 10–11, 76, 77, 95–6, 102–16, 161–5, 169–74, 180–2, 186–8, 251–2
Irish Revival, 8, 12, 15, 20–1, 22–3, 43, 51, 61, 62, 71, 102, 103, 105, 295, 304

Jackson, Alan, 242, 303
Jameson, Fredric, 212, 231
Jamie, Kathleen, 217–18, 300
Jamieson, John, 29
Jarmain, John, 91
Jenkins, Alan, 282
Jenkinson, Biddy, 111–12, 115, 165, 252
John, Gwen, 282
Jones, Chris, 150
Jones, David, 29
Jordan, John, 297
Joyce, James, 23, 29, 35, 212, 256, 257–8, 274
Joyce, Trevor, 247
Justice, Donald, 120

Kant, Immanuel, 322
Karlinsky, Simon, 283
Kavanagh, Patrick, 23, 96–7, 208–9, 247, 254, 294, 299, 301, 306, 307, 318, 319

Kearney, Richard, 304
Kennedy, X. J., 120
Kennelly, Brendan, 265, 319
Kerrigan, John, 9, 321
Keyes, Sidney, 91
Kinloch, David, 254, 262, 297
Kinsella, Thomas, 23, 251, 255, 273
Kinsley, James, 298
Kipling, Rudyard, 50
Kuppner, Frank, 251, 280, 284–7, 288, 289–90, 308, 309
Kwesi Johnson, Linton, 169

l'Epée, Abbé de, 257
Larkin, Philip, 23, 123–4, 125, 128–30, 252, 269, 274–6, 301, 302, 307
Leavis, F. R., 121
Lecercle, Jean-Jacques, 258
Leerssen, Joep, 103
Lehmann, John, 25
Leonard, Tom, 13, 235–6, 302, 309
Liddy, James, 119, 306
Lindsay, Maurice, 240, 296, 300
Linklater, Eric, 63, 67, 68
Longley, Edna, 6, 127, 208, 246, 253, 262, 263, 266, 267, 273, 276, 313, 318–20
Longley, Michael, 13, 23, 60, 127, 128, 132, 134, 136–9, 141, 196, 218–19, 265–7, 268, 270–2, 273, 274–7, 307
Lowell, Robert, 120, 129, 268, 269, 274
Lyons, F. S. L., 87
Lysaght, Sean, 305, 306, 307, 309

Mac Annaidh, Séamus, 169
Mac Craith, Mícheál, 108
Mac Lochlainn, Gearóid, 165, 171
Mac Mhaighstir Alasdair, Alasdair, 104
MacAulay, Donald, 111, 114
MacCaig, Norman, 1, 4, 25, 60, 119, 134, 139–42, 242, 300
MacDiarmid, Hugh, 2–3, 4, 6, 12, 13, 15, 20–36, 47–9, 53, 59, 60–2, 63, 64, 65–6, 67, 70, 71–2, 73, 74, 75, 77, 78, 79, 91, 119, 121–2, 131, 136–7, 143, 148, 176, 195, 196, 199, 204, 205, 229–30, 232, 239–40, 241–2, 244, 246, 248, 252, 253, 274, 294, 295, 296, 299, 300, 301, 303, 304, 305, 306, 308, 309
MacDonagh, Thomas, 303
Macdonald, Alasdair, 63–4
MacDonald, Alexander, 184
Macintyre, Alasdair, 318
MacIver, Hector, 60, 64, 72, 73
Mackay, Peter, 10–11, 313
Mackay Brown, George, 1, 2, 4, 91, 119, 122, 306

Mackenzie, Compton, 61, 63, 64, 65, 66, 67, 68–9, 70, 72, 73, 75
MacLean, Sorley, 1, 4, 21, 25, 63, 88–9, 91, 92, 93–4, 97–8, 104, 109, 111, 113, 164, 166, 301
MacLean, Will, 183
MacMillan, James, 315
MacNeacail, Angus, 107
MacNeice, Louis, 23, 25, 58–79, 90, 96, 120, 134–5, 140, 301, 303, 306, 308, 319
Macpherson, James, 10
MacQueen, John, 306
Mahon, Derek, 60, 119, 126–7, 128, 233, 265–70, 273, 274–7, 302, 307
Mailer, Norman, 241
Mallarmé, Stéphane, 270
Mandelstam, Osip, 200, 281–2, 283, 284, 287–8
Mann, Thomas, 261
Marcus, David, 296, 297, 300, 303, 305
Markus, Gilbert, 131
Mathews, Aidan, 258
Mathews, Harry, 256
Mayakovsky, Vladimir, 243
Mays, J. C. C., 263
McCarra, Kevin, 150
McCarthy, Mary, 241
McCarthy, Thomas, 253
McFadden, Roy, 296
McGahern, John, 273
McGann, Jerome, 298
McGonigal, James, 132
McGuckian, Medbh, 171, 172, 200, 201, 280–4, 285, 286, 287–90
McGuffie, Jessie, 239, 240
McIlvanney, Liam, 8, 11
McKane, Richard, 282
McLeod, Wilson, 10
Mercier, Vivian, 296
Middleton Murry, John, 305
modernism, 5, 8, 13, 26–9, 43, 44, 47, 53, 60–1, 140, 249, 252, 253–4, 295, 307, 308
Montague, John, 208, 273, 299, 307
Montale, Eugenio, 277
Moore, George, 22, 306
Moore, Henry, 138
Morgan, Edwin, 3, 119, 122, 132–3, 147–53, 156, 157, 196, 211–13, 217, 229–32, 233, 236, 238–9, 241, 243–5, 246, 247, 248, 265, 295–6, 298, 299, 303, 306, 308–9
Morris, William, 51
Muir, Edwin, 21, 59, 60–1, 64, 67, 70, 91, 119, 122, 142, 196, 227–9, 230, 232, 233, 300
Muir, Thomas, 133
Muir, Willa, 21

Index

Muldoon, Paul, 23, 60, 127, 171, 172, 213–15, 270, 302, 304, 308, 309
Murphy, Hayden, 299
Murray, Les, 136, 258

Nairn, Tom, 248, 320
Negri, Antonio, 219
Newman, Joan, 288
Newman, Kate, 288
Ní Chianáin, Neasa, 186
Ní Chuilleanáin, Eilean, 171, 262, 302
Ní Dhomhnaill, Nuala, 107, 112, 113, 114, 115, 165, 166, 170–3, 180–2, 186, 251, 288
Nicolaisen, W. F. H., 206
Niedecker, Lorine, 260
Northern Ireland Troubles, 127, 128, 136–7, 139, 210, 214–15, 218, 257, 269, 270, 271–2, 273, 274, 277, 299, 304

Ó Cadhain, Maírtín, 94
Ó Curraoin, Seán, 115
Ó Direáin, Máirtín, 109
Ó Doibhlin, Breandán, 107
Ó Muirthile, Liam, 252
Ó Rathaille, Aodhagán, 4
Ó Riada, Seán, 106
Ó Ríordáin, Seán, 109–11, 164
Ó Searcaigh, Cathal, 186–8
Ó Siochrú, Micheál, 317
Ó Tuama, Seán, 108
O'Brien, Flann, 23
O'Brien, Sean, 110–11, 129
O'Casey, Sean, 23
O'Reilly, Caitríona, 262
O'Toole, Fintan, 245, 246
Olson, Charles, 29, 259
Oppen, George, 260, 261
Ormsby, Frank, 294, 304
Orr, James, 12
Owen, Wilfred, 89, 91

Palmer McCulloch, Margery, 295
Pasolini, Pier Paulo, 177
Pasternak, Boris, 198, 282, 287
Paterson, Don, 134, 145, 216–17, 252–3, 260
Patten, Eve, 14
Paulin, Tom, 129, 144, 251, 275
Pearse, Patrick, 102, 303
Perec, Georges, 256
Perloff, Marjorie, 259
Petrarch, 44
Plath, Sylvia, 23, 259
Plato, 234–5
Plunkett, Joseph Mary, 303

Porter, Peter, 122
postmodernism, 29, 178, 252–3, 260
Pound, Ezra, 26, 27, 29, 120, 138, 143, 257, 294, 299, 308
Praeger, Rosamund, 89–90
Praxilla, 138–9
Price, Richard, 251, 254–5, 258–62, 303
Price Turner, W., 298

Queneau, Raymond, 256
Quinn, Justin, 254, 262, 297

Raine, Craig, 251
Rancières, Jacques, 234–5
regionalism, 12, 15–16, 89, 296, 300
Riach, Alan, 24
Riddell, Alan, 296, 297, 306
Riley, Peter, 255
Rilke, Rainer Maria, 282–3
Robertson, Robin, 144
Robinson, Edward Arlington, 120
Roethke, Theodore, 23
Romanticism, 5, 12, 28, 29–33, 44, 46–9, 50, 51–3, 192, 307
Ross, William, 105
rural topographies, 30, 34, 70–2, 76–7, 89–90, 128, 173, 181–3, 192, 213, 216, 218, 222–4, 226, 319
Russell, George, 3
Ryan, Ray, 8

Sappho, 40, 139
Saurat, Denis, 33
Scannell, Vernon, 91
Schleiermacher, Friedrich, 158
Scots poetry, 3, 11–13, 15, 22, 24–5, 28–9, 35, 47–8, 53, 58–9, 60, 61, 66–7, 94, 133, 137, 144, 147, 148, 149–50, 176, 199–200, 205, 215–17, 242, 252, 295, 296, 303, 305, 306
Scott, F. G., 21, 36
Scott, Margaret, 152
Scott, Tom, 306
Scott, Sir Walter, 314
Scottish Gaelic poetry, 4, 10–11, 14, 25, 63, 64, 88–9, 92, 94–100, 102–16, 144, 161–9, 173–4, 182–4, 295
Scottish Renaissance, 8, 12, 15, 20, 21, 22, 23, 29, 47–9, 59, 61–2, 63, 64, 65, 67, 70, 91, 176–7, 238, 239, 240, 242, 244–5, 303
Sealy, Douglas, 107, 300
Sennett, Richard, 224, 225
Sewell, Frank, 187–8
Shakespeare, William, 179, 230
Sharp, Nancy, 64, 69, 78

Shelley, P. B., 32, 44, 51, 128
Shepherd, Nan, 21
Shippey, Tom, 151, 159
Shovlin, Frank, 295, 296, 305
Sieburg, Friedrich, 178
Silkin, Jon, 123, 301
Simic, Charles, 252
Simmons, James, 265, 269, 277, 280, 286, 294
Siren, Oswald, 284
Sirr, Peter, 251
Skelton, Robin, 300
Skinner, Alisdair, 295
Smith, J. A., 68
Smith, Ken, 123
Smith, Michael, 247, 294, 308
Snodgrass, W. D., 120
Socrates, 140
Sommer, Piotr, 201
Soutar, William, 24, 62
Spender, Stephen, 79
St Columba, 132, 133
St Jerome, 200
Stallworthy, Jon, 134
Standard English, 12, 148, 150, 157, 199, 204–5, 214, 219, 235, 321
Steiner, George, 105
Stevens, Wallace, 30, 204, 205, 269, 274
Stobart, John Clarke, 134
Synge, J. M., 22, 41, 42, 46, 58, 61, 63

Tait, Robert, 303
Tannahill, Robert, 121
Taylor, A. E., 68
Thomas, Dylan, 120
Thomas, Edward, 207–8
Thomas, R. S., 23
Thomson, David, 76, 77
Thomson, Derick, 295, 300
Thomson, James, 185
Todorov, Tzvetan, 115
Tolstoy, Tatyana, 282
Tomalin, Ruth, 89–90
traditional forms, 2, 3, 11, 27, 30, 34, 45, 50–1, 58, 109, 132, 148, 150–1, 233, 235, 267, 270–1, 307, 308, 309, 318–19

translation, 4, 11, 13, 14, 109, 131, 132–3, 137, 147–57, 161–74, 180, 182, 183, 185–8, 191–202, 207–8, 210, 212, 213, 215, 244, 280–90, 313–14, 316, 317, 321, 323–5
Trocchi, Alexander, 241
Tsvetaeva, Marina, 180–2, 186, 282–3, 287
Tuve, Rosemond, 40

UCC Group, 171
urban topographies, 2–3, 13–14, 31–2, 209–10, 213, 224–36, 319

Vendler, Helen, 24, 26
Venuti, Lawrence, 158, 163
Vergil, 134, 142
virtual topographies, 215–16

Wain, John, 301
Watkins, Vernon, 24, 125
Watson, Roderick, 12, 29
Weber, Max, 314, 315
Westwater, R. H., 29
Wheatley, David, 210, 297, 298
Whitman, Walt, 308
Whyte, Christopher, 105, 107, 212, 226–7
Whyte, J. H., 135
Wilbur, Richard, 120, 274
Williams, Hugo, 125, 127
Wills, Clair, 95, 96, 97, 282, 288
Wilson Foster, John, 226, 304
Wittig, Kurt, 305
Wordsworth, William, 31, 192–4, 195, 198, 199, 201
World Wars I and II 21, 178
Wright, James, 120
Wright, Tom, 242

Yeats, W. B., 1–3, 4, 14, 15, 20–36, 41–6, 49–53, 61–2, 74, 120, 134, 143, 194, 195, 205, 207, 274, 275, 295, 299, 303, 305, 306, 307, 308, 319
Young, Denholm, 91
Young, Douglas, 94